THE BORN AGAIN SKEPTIC'S GUIDE TO THE BIBLE

with

THE BOOK OF RUTH

By Ruth Hurmence Green

Published by

Freedom From Religion Foundation

P.O. Box 750

Madison, Wisconsin 53701

Born Again Skeptic's Guide To The Bible © Copyright 1979
by Ruth Hurmence Green

First printing 1979
Second printing 1982
Third printing 1991
Fourth printing 1999

The Book of Ruth © Copyright 1982
by The Freedom From Religion Foundation, Inc.

ISBN 1-877733-01-6

1999 Cover design by Chris Pike
Illustrations by Alma Cuebas

Ruth Hurmence Green

Introduction
To The Fourth Edition

On the twentieth anniversary year of the first publication of Ruth Hurmence Green's enduring work, *The Born Again Skeptic's Guide to the Bible*, the Freedom From Religion Foundation, Inc., is proud to present this new edition, combining her classic book with *The Book of Ruth*—the posthumous collection of Ruth's other writings on religion.

The staff of the Freedom From Religion Foundation wishes to gratefully acknowledge the support and financial assistance of Truman Green, now living in Florida, who made publication of this combined edition possible, as well as the other members of the Freedom From Religion Foundation who contributed to this special project.

The Born Again Skeptic, the first book published by the Foundation, has remained continuously in print since 1979, and has been the Foundation's "bestseller." *The Born Again Skeptic* has proven itself to be simply invaluable to anyone engaging in debate with religionists over the merits of bible contents. I would venture to suggest the *Born Again Skeptic* is primarily responsible for the fact that the freethought community today is far more bible-literate than the religious population at large!

Fans of the *Born Again Skeptic* will be delighted to become acquainted with Ruth's later essays on religion, which remain timely and uniquely useful critiques, such as her "Christian Family or Christian Fantasy?" which skewers the idea that the bible is our source of "family values." Where the *Born Again Skeptic* offers a carefully organized and detailed dissection of the bible's contents, the essays in the *Book of Ruth* reveal the "big picture," Ruth's insightful overview of the flaws and foibles of bible lore, law and morality. Ruth's speech to a Unitarian society, "What I Found When I Searched The Scriptures," is a 13-page freethought *tour de force*.

At the turn of the twenty-first century, Americans more than ever are in need of Ruth's reasoned and rational approach to biblical edicts and claims. As she cautioned in 1979: "A nation on its knees is on its last legs."

Annie Laurie Gaylor, Editor
Freethought Today
Freedom From Religion Foundation, Inc.
January 1999

Acknowledgments

I should like to acknowledge assistance from the following persons:

My brother Howard for arousing my curiosity about the Bible.

My sister-in-law Billie for her suggestions about writing and preparing a manuscript and for encouraging me to finish it.

My husband for practical help in photocopying and for enthusiastic support.

My daughter Sheila Conner for the [original] cover design and Alma Cuebas for illustrations.

Anne Gaylor, president of the Freedom From Religion Foundation, for getting this book into print.

Ruth Hurmence Green, 1979

The Bible

(A Grim Fairy Tale)

Suppose you had never heard of Christianity, and that next Sunday morning a stranger standing in a pulpit told you about a book whose authors could not be authenticated and whose contents, written hundreds of years ago, included blood-curdling legends of slaughter and intrigue and fables about unnatural happenings such as virgin births, devils that inhabit human bodies and talk, people rising from the dead and ascending live into the clouds, and suns that stand still. Suppose he then asked you to believe that an uneducated man described in that book was a god who could get you into an eternal fantasy-place called Heaven, when you die. Would you, as an intelligent rational person, even bother to read such nonsense, let alone pattern your entire life upon it?

Contents

The Born Again Skeptic's Guide To The Bible

The Book of Ruth

NOTE

The King James Bible was used as the basis of this book. All scriptural references are taken from it. The object was to employ a version that had not been subjected to cosmetic treatment recently. Emphases and parenthetical words and phrases added to Bible quotations are the work of this author.

ABBREVIATIONS

Gen. — Genesis
Ex. — Exodus
Lev. — Leviticus
Num. — Numbers
Deut. — Deuteronomy
Josh. — Joshua
Sam. — Samuel
Chron. — Chronicles
Prov. — Proverbs
Eccles. — Ecclesiastes
Jer. — Jeremiah
Lam. — Lamentations
Ez. — Ezekiel

Dan. — Daniel
Hab. — Habakkuk
Zech. — Zechariah
Mal. — Malachi
Matt. — Matthew
Cor. — Corinthians
Gal. — Galatians
Eph. — Ephesians
Philip. — Philippians
Col. — Colossians
Thess. — Thessalonians
Tim. — Timothy
Rev. — The Revelation

Foreword

Those of us who promote separation of state and church would be quite content to leave it at that and remain silent on the subject of the shortcomings of religion, but we find, unhappily, that religionists are not willing to accept our premise that it is constitutionally proper and eminently wise to keep religion out of government.

"How can you object to prayers in the legislature?" they ask. "Why shouldn't we have tax money for our parochial schools?" and "Why don't you want the Bible used in public ceremonies?"

So the activist who works for separation of state and church in this country is also forced to talk about religion, to discuss the merits of the Bible. This presents a problem for several reasons. First, we are a country of Bible illiterates. The Bible is probably the most available, most purchased, and least read book in the world. It is the best seller that is rarely opened. Since most religionists have not read the Bible and have heard only those palatable passages their clergy wish them to hear, they are totally unprepared for any Bible criticism, and their knee-jerk reaction is to attack the critic. Second, the media in this country promote religion and try, with outstanding success, to stifle criticism of it. Manuscripts that criticize religion come bouncing back from editors, and television and radio station managers are reluctant even to sell time to state-church separation groups, much less consider their public service announcements. Third, tax-exempt religion represents power and money and those who dare to criticize must not only be personally courageous but financially uncaring, since religion's critics always risk social and economic reprisal.

To help one critic's voice be heard, the Freedom From Religion Foundation has published this book. Written by Ruth Hurmence Green, a Foundation member from Missouri, the book is a guide. It is not necessarily a book to be read straight through, but rather one that will give you, the reader, directions and help along the way as you take on that most frustrating of tasks, Bible-reading.

Ruth first read the Bible cover to cover when she was convalescing from cancer a few years ago. In her first letter to me in September, 1978, when she joined the Foundation, Ruth wrote: "My agnostic brother told me it was a waste of time to read . . . the Bible, but I plodded through it, to my increasing incredulity and horror. I was a half-hearted Methodist who had always disliked religion, but, like 97% of Christian laity, I had been taught that the

Bible was a good book and Jesus a wonderful man. I think the shock I suffered was worse than the trauma caused by my illness. The superstitious ignorance, the atrocious inhuman cruelty, the obvious derivation from mythology, and above all the depravity of Bible personalities—they all left me stunned."

Ruth, who is now 64, studied the Bible for about two years and then wrote her book. Its approach is refreshing. So much of the writing about religion, pro and con, is deadly dull, and the thread of humor throughout Ruth's book will be appreciated by those who fall asleep over the professional scholar's efforts. Then, too, Ruth brings to Bible criticism something sadly lacking over the centuries—the woman's point of view. The rampant sexism in the Bible is apt to be overlooked by the otherwise critical male eye.

Finally, the book itself is a tribute to its author, not only as a critic in a verboten area, but as a lovely and loving person who could demonstrate cheerful persistence in the face of grave and repeated illness. Despite three battles with cancer, Ruth remains cheerful, vital and concerned. *The Born Again Skeptic's Guide to the Bible* is a memorial to her courage.

Anne Nicol Gaylor
President
Freedom From Religion Foundation
July, 1979

Preface

I'm fond of saying that reading the Bible turned me into an atheist. But reflection makes me realize that the process wasn't that simple.

As a child in Sunday School I thought of the Bible legends as an extension of Grimm's and Andersen's Fairy Tales, which children of my generation devoured. There were the same imaginary persons (or so I thought) and the same unlikely happenings. Very vivid in my memory is the astonishment I felt when I began to realize that the Holy Land was an actual place and that Jesus and the other Bible personalities were supposed to be real persons. The whale really *did* swallow Jonah! Daniel really *was* thrown into the lions' den!

No less vivid, but building much more gradually, was the revulsion I felt from childhood toward the Christian religion. When I was young, Easter was a time of horror for me. During the days leading up to it, I wanted to go into hiding. I avoided magazines and church publications and any other source of pictures or stories about the crucifixion, and I still cannot bear the sight of a crucifix.

Why is it accepted practice to display a replica of a suffering man, often life-size, on a cross, where the eyes can't escape it? Few would tolerate such flaunting of a figure writhing in an electric chair or dangling from a rope, but there is no refuge from the Christian torture symbol. Borrowed from paganism, the cross decorates necks, walls, steeples, and billboards. It violates our sensitivity on every hand. The Catholic High School in a central city of Missouri features in its entrance hall a towering cross with a 10-foot aluminum Christ affixed to it. Surrounded by huge windows, it is the first thing students entering the building must gaze upon, and passersby cannot avoid the grisly execution scene.

As a Christian, I attended a Passion Play, not realizing what a Passion Play was. I ate the body of Jesus and drank his blood. I heard the screams of Dante's Inferno. I saw the head of John the Baptist on a platter. I pictured Abraham's knife at Isaac's throat and watched the Flood waters rise.

I didn't rebel then, but I am convinced now that children should not be subjected to the frightfulness of the Christian religion. It profanes their sweet innocence by introducing them to episodes of exquisite anguish and brutalizes their sensibilities with descriptions of cruelties that even the adult mind does not like to contemplate. Finally, it suggests to the impressionable consciousness of the young that violence and bloodshed are sanctioned means of making the world better, and that the pagan savagery of human sacrifice is the loveliest gesture of all time.

If the concept of a father who plots to have his own son put to death is presented to children as beautiful and as worthy of society's admiration, what types of human behavior can be presented to them as *reprehensible?* For what will society hold its members to account, if its Bible promotes human cruelty of the most depraved kind?

That depravity is upheld by the Christian God everywhere in the Holy Book. From Genesis to The Revelation, despicable patterns of conduct are not only set forth but stamped with approval.

In my eventual role as housewife and mother, I was too busy or entertained too little incentive to delve into theology, and I continued as a skeptical church attender of more or less regularity. My only sister died after a long siege of breast cancer, and in 1960 I underwent a radical mastectomy. Several years later I was treated for skin cancer, and in the summer of 1975 a biopsy revealed an invasive carcinoma of my throat.

Without waiting for help from the supernatural or even asking for it, my husband arranged for medical treatment. I had to choose between extensive surgery and radiation therapy with a permanent risk of paralysis, a decision arrived at in a rational frame of mind and free of any appeal to a god. My 37 radiation treatments combined the best equipment and professional skill available, and I was supported further by my family and friends and my own resources. (There are atheists in foxholes, and they fare very well.)

During this traumatic period of time, religion had no meaning for me in spite of years of indoctrination, and I began to examine what part, if any, it played in my life, and indeed what part it had ever played. Following a conversation with an older brother, who holds a doctorate in chemical engineering and labels himself an agnostic, I awakened to the possibility that the Bible might be somewhat different from what I had assumed it to be based upon the way it has always been represented for the benefit of those who usually prefer to read something else. Curiosity assailed me, and, faced with enforced leisure, I waded in. The shock I experienced produced this book, and the skeptic was born again as an atheist.

I had also become interested in the feminist movement and could readily now see that the Bible is a formidable barrier to woman's right to realize her potential and even control her own body. The assent which women granted to the Church to use the Bible in a way detrimental to their self-interest goals alarmed me.

Aware that not only women, but the great majority of the Christian community, are Bible illiterates, I accepted a "call" to put into writing my personal observations and considerations born of an unsophisticated examination of the scriptures. The result is the Bible as I saw it, and, since I feel that theology should require no "expert" interpreters, I believe my impression is admissible. The Bible is, after all, the product of the talents and purposes of human beings, as are all holy books. I chose to regard it in that light.

My book is not a scholarly review of the Bible extracted from what others have written about it. It is only such an essay as anyone might compose after actually reading the Good Book in its entirety and after coming to the shocked realization that it is opposed in every way to what one had perceived it to be, having heard it excerpted and "interpreted" from childhood.

Admittedly drawing upon a modest familiarity with mythology and upon information assimilated from random reading during my 64 years, I tried to formulate the *Guide* from the standpoint of rationality, as well as from an attitude of skepticism. Many of the ideas and conclusions expressed are of necessity not new and must surely have been voiced by others in their own fashion, but the criticisms are those that also occurred to me and are offered from my own point of view.

A sense of the ridiculous, which came over me at times as I persisted in plowing through the widely-owned, seldom-read veritable idol of a book called the Bible, crept into my manuscript. It helped to balance the indignation I felt at the way I had been hoodwinked by the Good Book.

The reader will find a certain amount of repetition of comment, incidents, and hypotheses, because each chapter was written to be inclusive and able to stand more or less alone. An attempt was made by the author, however, to use a variety of Bible verses to illustrate material that is similar but that seemed to belong under several headings.

Ruth Hurmence Green, 1979

"God shall send them strong delusion
that they should believe a lie."

II Thessalonians 2:11

OLD TESTAMENT LEGEND — I

Silly Putty World

"In the beginning" darkness was on the face of the deep. The story of the Creation as told in the Bible doesn't fool around. It starts right in without any preliminaries and takes care of this vast mystery in short order. Actually, in *two* short orders, for there are two stories of the Creation, in one of which the sun and moon and stars aren't set into the firmament until the fourth day, although God has ordered that light and darkness be separated on the first day: "God made two great lights; the greater light to rule the day, and the lesser light to rule the night: he made the stars also." *Gen. 1:16* Today even elementary school students know that the greater light and the lesser light are one and the same, and that night and day are the result of the earth turning on its axis.

Apparently God, for it is he, is just sitting there (or dog-paddling) in the water in the dark, when he has an impulsive urge to create a world (with all the enthusiasm displayed by someone deciding to repair a leaky roof on "an unclouded day"). Inevitably one has to wonder who or what created this god, who is assumed in Genesis to have been unimaginative enough to have spent possibly eons of time in the dark and all wet besides.

Considering its muddled time-table and naivete, the biblical Creation story might have been contrived by a child and surely must have been the product of a pen whose wielder was dismally ignorant of what the sciences of astronomy, biology, zoology, botany, and anthropology have revealed. One must actually turn to the scriptures themselves to appreciate the primitive mindlessness of this ancient Hebrew account of a firmament (heaven) on pillars, with its windows open, resting upon a body of water and supporting another body of water above. (There is not a hint of the universe as scientists have come to know it, with countless fixed stars and galaxies and planets orbiting in endless space.)

From the shapeless lower waters, God makes the dry land separate itself, and out of the same "seas" he brings forth the fish, and the beasts and fowl, which are to feed upon green herbs. Finally, a smug Creator looks around at his finished toy and declares everything about it very good. Pleasing to him are the earth's deserts and swamps and frozen wastelands; its germs, viruses, and bacteria; its beasts of prey, leeches, hornets, poisonous snakes and spiders, tsetse flies, fire ants, sting-rays, plague-carrying rats and malaria-bearing mosquitoes; its extreme climates, storms, floods, earthquakes, and volcanoes. (Genesis doesn't promise mankind a rose garden after Adam and Eve leave the original Garden of Eden.)

Ah, well, and Lo, a pale horse! How the world came about is impossible to know as of now, and surely curiosity is served by either primitive or modern cultures advancing theories about it. But to preserve a guess born of imagination and fantasy in the Holy Book of Christianity, presenting it as the revealed Word of God, all to be taken on faith, is an insult to the intelligence and reasoning ability of members of societies which might be expected to have undergone some scientific advancement over a period of several thousand years, and comprises just one of the many absurd impositions of the Bible.

Geologists must crack up when they read how all the strata were deposited in six days or even in 6,000 years. (Peter says that one of God's days may equal 1,000 earthly years, so it would seem that supernatural creatures who travelled frequently between heaven and earth in Bible days must have suffered prodigious jet lags.) There is evidence that the Archaeozoic Era of geology began almost 2 billion years ago, and volcanic activity and erosion still continue.

Incidentally, the Bible is very specific about the chronology of the world. Matthew lists 63 generations from Adam to Jesus. Add 2,000 years to that and allow 30 years for each generation. That makes the biblical world a little younger than science and geologists have found the universe to be.

Moses, at home in the New Jerusalem, must count as a large part of his eternal bliss the knowledge that Bible historians discount the validity of the tradition that he is the author of the first five books of the Bible (Genesis, Exodus, Leviticus, Numbers, Deuteronomy) and therefore cannot be held responsible for the drivel about the Creation or for the tales of carnage related with such gusto in those books of the Law.

One is driven to suspect that Moses did not write the Pentateuch when one reads in Deuteronomy a description of his death, the disposal of his body, and the length of the mourning period.

OLD TESTAMENT LEGEND — II

The First Chest Surgery

Women don't have to be feminists to resent the Old Testament story of the creation of Eve, fashioned as she was from the rib of a member of the opposite sex.

Actually, men don't have too much to crow about, either, for they were modeled from dust, according to the Bible, only when it occurred to the Creator that there was no one to till the new-born land. With this need in mind and with the Garden of Eden next on God's impulse list, fortunately Adam *was* a "man of the soil."

A careful perusal of the early verses of Genesis, however, reveals yet another tale of the creation of the two sexes, one that puts both of them on a par. "And God said, Let us make man in our image, after our likeness . . . So God created man in his own image, in the image of God created he him; male and female created he them." *Gen. 1:26,27* These verses suggest that females are also in God's image, contrary to the claim of St. Paul, whose narcissism precluded a feminine deity.

In any case, this version of the creation of man and woman appears 1o verses before the one describing the manufacture of Adam, who became alive through artificial respiration applied by God, and 24 verses before God put Adam to sleep and took one of his ribs, then "closed up the flesh." Apparently some Bible writer, whipping up his fairy tale about the Creation, felt the same about women as Paul, who later was to capture the title of "male chauvinist pig" of the first century A.D., and proceeded to insert a passage more inducive to keeping women in their place than the story a more open-minded ancient scribe had fabricated before him.

It is an exercise in stupidity to give any thought to the whole nonsensical matter, but for fundamentalists let it be observed that since the author of the book of Genesis is not known, there is no reason to place any confidence whatever in its feeble attempts to explain the so-far unexplainable, attempts which have their real origin in mythology, have no scientific bases at all, antedate all anthropological studies, and issue from the imaginations of ignorant ancients.

OLD TESTAMENT LEGEND — III

A Tale Of Two Trees

The setting is idyllic—a garden near the river Euphrates. Four streams flow from this paradise, and Adam has been created to till it and tend it, with whatever tools he can whip up from sharp rocks and stones. Already mentally exhausted from thinking of a name for every living creature, his chest hurting, and minus a rib, he nevertheless has one compensation. At his side, or in the near vicinity, and like Adam in her birthday suit, gambols Mother Eve.

Being almost alone on this newly-formed planet, she not surprisingly is eager to talk to anyone or anything however "subtil," and is not at all taken aback to find herself addressed (in a language with a preponderance of hissing sounds) by a serpent. This snake, aha, has an evil intent, although God has just looked over his new universe and declared everything in it very good.

To back-track just a little, it is necessary to know that two trees exist in the garden, besides at least one fig plant with rather large leaves. One of these two trees bears fruit which contains the god-like knowledge of good and evil, the other the fruit of everlasting life.

God has started right out laying down organized rules, getting into shape for the prodigious task-to-come of formulating the Mosaic law, and has warned Adam and Eve (apparently in the same sibilant Esperanto being used by all members of the cast) not to eat the fruit of one of these trees. But how anyone who doesn't know right from wrong could be expected to practice obedience (for disobedience is the original sin for which all persons will be branded evil-doers from birth) presents a bit of a mystery. How can the innocent sin?

Rather than sink her teeth into this ethical question, Eve, precursor of Snow White, chooses instead to bite into the apple from the tree of knowledge, at the urging of the serpentine tempter, who is beginning to show his true colors (garter-snake green). She then proceeds to compound the felony by submitting to a generous impulse and offering Adam a taste.

Now, to whom will go the eventual blame for this verboten snack? Biblical chivalry can admit of no other but Eve. "She gave me of the tree, and

I did eat." Adam thus became the world's first tattletale and finger-pointer, and Eve learns that the Lord won't tolerate unselfishness. So she puts the blame on the snake, who retires behind a familiar sign: "The Buck Stops Here."

The two culprits have barely swallowed the first bites when they notice that they are naked (me Tarzan, you Jane). Of course, they have no marriage license, so "before breakfast" they make aprons of fig leaves from a tree that is kosher.

God, just their luck, decides to take a constitutional in the garden that very evening, wearing an appropriate ensemble, one trusts. They play hide-and-seek, and God is the winner, after Adam gives himself away. Abiding by the Garden of Eden decency code, God turns tailor and fashions coats of skins for them. Since quite a time period is due to elapse before the invention of the sewing machine, or even the needle and thread, this task might have loomed rather large (especially when one considers that the skins haven't been tanned) for anyone who could not put together a universe in six days.

Now it is time for all-around reprimands, starting with the snake, who henceforth has to crawl on his belly instead of making his mischievous forays on his tail. Adam and Eve can't stay in the garden, because they haven't profited from this first fiasco and can be expected to partake of the fruit of everlasting life next. The fact that under the terms of the New Testament God *decrees* everlasting bliss or never-ending agony for everyone comprises bit-of-mystery number two.

God is a tough customer, and Eve (woman) is condemned to bear children in sorrow, and Adam (man) is sentenced to eat bread with a sweaty face and return to dust (he does hang in there for 930 years, however). And man will rule over woman, to scarcely anyone's surprise.

The two have no problem leaving the garden instantly at God's command, since they have nothing to pack and are not given five minutes to present a defense. Adam gets another first by becoming the earliest groundskeeper to be fired by his boss—those were non-union days, so he can't register a complaint. Besides, he doesn't feel like arguing with the guard, those ever-on-call cherubim with the flaming swords.

So they repair to another area where they proceed to "multiply," as the Bible delicately puts it, one of the few times the Bible is delicate. How long it takes Adam to recognize his part in this arithmetic is debatable.

It is unfortunate, but right in the spirit of the Bible, that one of their first two sons is to become the murderer of his own brother, although with provocation born of God's preference for the "sweet savor" of Abel's burnt animal offerings over Cain's "fruit of the ground." From then on, God's flawed creation (human beings) waxes naughtier and naughtier, until God decides that practice makes perfect and he can do better the second time around. But that's another unlikely story.

The unlikely story of Adam and Eve, however, cannot be passed over as nonsense. It is to have serious consequences for God, because, having branded humankind born-sinners, condemned to eternal death, he is now required, according to Christian theology, to repent of his hasty curses, come to earth as a specimen of his own creation, and cause himself to be put to a hideous death, in order to redeem humanity from the condemnation which he himself imposed upon it.

In a nutshell, here is the preamble to the Christian religion and its evolution from a myth fashioned by superstitious guesswork on the part of people whose identity and qualifications are unknown, but who, it is claimed, were infallible for all time in their portrayal of God and his dealings with the human race.

OLD TESTAMENT LEGEND – IV

The Biggest Do-It-Yourself Project

Thoroughly disgusted with the first nine generations of humankind, who have become increasingly corrupt because they now have consciences, God's short-fused temper flares, and he tells Noah to "embark upon the ark" in order to escape the divine plan to banish wickedness from the earth. (God forgot that Satan, as an angel, however "fallen," could fly and rest on clouds.)

No one of any age has found favor in God's sight at this time, except Noah, his three sons, and the four wives. (With a happy happenstance these men have managed to annex the only virtuous women in the whole world.) No warning goes out to the poor unfortunates who are to be left behind, none of whom seems to have a boat. As far as is known, the eight favored individuals had no compunction about making preparations to abandon friends and loved ones to a watery fate, but, on the other hand, they may have been too simon-pure to have had any friends.

Perhaps one can forgive Noah for his callous attitude when one contemplates the enormity of the task which has been dumped so casually into his lap by a God who could make a universe but not an ark. At a time surely before tools had been invented, Noah is commanded to build out of gopher wood a water-tight vessel 500 feet long, 85 feet wide, and 60 feet and three stories high, proportions not far from those of a latter-day ocean liner. This monstrosity was to have the magnificent total of one door and one window.

In Noah's *spare* time, he was to bring into the ark seven of every clean beast and two of every unclean beast (a wise discrimination) and seven of every fowl of both sexes, in addition to a male and female of every creeping thing. (Obviously Noah knew all about the birds and the bees.) Insects were on their own, if they couldn't creep, and fish had it made. It is hoped these were pre-dinosaur days.

The fact that certain animals inhabit only areas of the globe where they can survive didn't seem worthy of God's mention, and the sanitary conditions on this houseboat can best be left to the imagination. Few, no doubt, have the stomach for them.

But sure enough the water does cover the whole earth, drowning babies and pregnant women along with other wrong-doers, over a period of 40 days of rain. And as the waters "prevail" 30 feet, they do inundate all the mountains for 150 days. Then Noah keeps sending out one of his seven doves until it finally returns with an olive leaf in its mouth (probably for Noah's martini, as the reader discovers that Noah has a weakness for the bottle).

The process of being fruitful and multiplying starts inevitably all over again with the same mix-up of who's who, and God promises never to send another flood, thereby winning the humanitarian-of-the-year award. This has all been too much for Noah, and if anyone deserves to hang one on, it is he, and he does, succumbing to too much wine and lying around in the altogether, only to be spied upon by one of his sons. Ham can't keep a secret and lets his two brothers in on the situation. When Noah sobers up, instead of joining A.A., he curses Ham and relegates his son to the servitude of *his* brothers. (Racists today claim, trying to justify slavery, that Ham became the ancestor of the black race. In such ways has the Bible been used in the cause of oppression.)

Other religions tell of floods, and Greek mythology had a flood and a "Noah," as did Zoroastrianism, so this whole dismal tale is just another instance of the borrowing done by authors of the Bible from the myths found among those with whom they came in contact. And floods *have* been known to cover vast areas at times.

Still, the search for remnants of Noah's Ark continues to be conducted on what is believed to be Mt. Ararat, and dark hints of success lead one to believe that a few old pieces of wood found lying around or "planted" up there will some day be enshrined as the evidence that evangelists hope will prove "the many authenticities of the Bible."

Whether the succeeding groups of human earthlings were to be an improvement behaviorwise over the first is doubtful, for one finds Satan in the New Testament tempting Jesus with the promise of "all the kingdoms of the world," which must already have belonged to the generous tempter.

CHAPTER ONE

The Judeo-Christian God

God is a being of terrific character . . .
cruel, vindictive, capricious,and unjust.
                    —Thomas Jefferson

God may be male; then again God may be female: "And
God said, Let *us* make man in *our* image, after *our* likeness . . . So God created man in his own image, in the image of God created he *them, male* and
female created he *them*." *Gen. 1:26,27* Plural gods of both sexes?
Hermaphrodites? After these first befuddled verses, however, the Bible treats
of God as an anthropomorphic male, with the characteristics not only physical, but also mental and emotional, of a human (although not earthbound)
creature able to assume other shapes at will.

≡>·◇·<≡

God indulges in self-description that is at once vague, pompous, and more
than somewhat contradictory. To Moses he boasts: "I AM THAT I AM . . . say
that I AM hath sent me unto you." *Ex. 3:14* Later, again to Moses on Mt.
Sinai, he elaborates: "The Lord, the Lord God, merciful and gracious, long-
suffering . . . forgiving iniquity and transgression and sin, and that will by no
means clear the guilty; visiting the iniquity of the fathers upon the children,
and upon the children's children, unto the third and to the fourth generation." *Ex. 34:6,7*

≡>·◇·<≡

Has God been seen by earthly beings? Whether or not cannot be proved by
the Bible. Jesus says: "Not that any man hath seen the Father." *John 6:46* The
Lord himself says: "Thou canst not see my face, for there shall no man see
me and live." *Ex. 33:20* Other statements, however, make other claims: "The
Lord spake unto Moses face to face." *Ex. 33:11* And: "The sight of the glory
of the Lord was like devouring fire." *Ex. 24:17* Jesus himself claimed to be
God in the flesh.

    After his wrestling match with God, Jacob declares: "For I have seen God face to face, and my life is preserved." *Gen. 32:30* David is quoted as main-taining: "I foresaw the Lord always before my face." *Acts 2:25* When God appeared to Moses and Aaron and 70 Jewish elders: "They saw the God of Israel: and there was under his feet as it were a paved work of a sapphire stone, and as it were the body of heaven in his clearness." *Ex. 24:10* Such gar-bled phrases are characteristic of parts of the Bible that keep it from achiev-ing the clarity of God as revealed to the ancient Hebrew "sojourners."

Of course, God appears many times in visions and dreams in the pages of his Holy Book, especially to those wild-eyed prophets, who seem to spend most of their lives in a daze, and to Peter, Paul, and John in the New Testament, who spend *their* share of time in similar stupors. One could hope that Ezekiel's many visions were clearer than his description of one of them: "And upon the likeness of the throne was the likeness as the appearance of a man above upon it." *Ez. 1:26*.

From another of Ezekiel's dreams (to give him the benefit of the doubt) one's impression of God as a man is re-enforced: "And I saw as the colour of amber, as the appearance of fire round about within it, from the appearance of his loins even upwards, and from the appearance of his loins even down-ward, I saw as it were the appearance of fire, and it had brightness round about . . . This was the appearance of the likeness of the glory of the Lord." *Ez. 1:27,28* Ezekiel's syntax may be open to criticism, but his affinity for prepositions stands alone.

⇒•◇•⇐

God converses readily with people in the Bible, although his voice hasn't been heard since, not even by use of the electronic marvels of television com-mercials that allow voices to be heard, strangely disembodied, from out of the blue. "Thus saith the Lord" is enough to announce his appearance, for what may involve lengthy instructions and rules for behavior, in the scrip-tures, however.

Sometimes it is hard to tell whether he is speaking and emerging as an angel or in person. When, as one of three men, he stops over with Abraham on his way to destroy Sodom and Gomorrah and keeps revising the number of righteous persons (with un-God-like indecision) who will have to be found in those cities in order for a reprieve to be granted, it turns out to be the Lord in person in the company of two angels. (Angels are ill-defined super-natural creatures which appear on the scene often in the pages of the Holy Book to carry out the brutal orders of an implacable deity and which have become as invisible as the Tooth Fairy ever since.)

On this occasion Abraham recognizes God from a previous encounter wherein God changed Abram's name and promised to make him the progenitor of the *greatest nation on earth*, no less. *Gen. 17* (Among the conditions laid down then was that Abraham would have to be "perfect.") This covenant was the "old testament."

———◆———

God existed somehow (?) and somewhere (?) before the creation of heaven and the earth, before time began, in total darkness, and in some watery abode. *Gen. 1:1,2* He had divine companions in this nowhere, including Jesus (later scriptures claim), for he talks to them. *Gen. 1:26* and *3:22* He creates the host of heaven and earth, however, in those first six days. *Gen. 2:1*

———◆———

God definitely has a sense of humor. He enjoys a masquerade now and then and displays unexpected talents. In the Garden of Eden he plays hide-and-seek with Adam and makes outfits of animal skins for the first two nudists to wear. There is no record that God furnished a change of attire, but for the time being at least he was spared the offensive sight of the naked man and woman he had created.

He plays peek-a-boo with Moses on Mt. Sinai: "And I will take away mine hand, and thou shalt see my back parts: but my face shall not be seen." *Ex. 33:23* Capriciously, though, he changes his mind and gives Moses a frontal view several times: "And there arose not a prophet since in Israel like unto Moses, whom the Lord knew face to face." *Deut. 34:10* (Allegedly, these are Moses's very words.)

During the wandering of the Israelites in the Wilderness, decreed and engineered by God in case anyone wonders why it took the Jews 40 years to cross a desert, the Lord hovers over them as a pillar of cloud by day and a pillar of fire by night, scattering manna daily and a little extra just before the Sabbath.

He also enjoys a bit of legerdemain with blooming rods and brass snakes. Disguised as cloven fiery tongues (or a dove) he lands on people's heads (even his own) and makes them jabber. Often he plays obstetrician and helps barren women and even virgins get pregnant (once correctly predicting twins) and also assumes the role of God-father.

He keeps a variety of plagues and famines in his portfolio of punishments and pulls them out whenever he is having a rotten day because of someone's misbehavior. Misery loves company. But when he becomes his own father, there's no denying: "With God all things are possible." *Matt. 19:26*

———◆———

God has another side from the mischievous one. It could be labelled unfeeling and vengeful. It makes the attempt at whitewash—"God is love"—look pretty feeble. The scriptures are so full of references to, and definitions of, this unsavory deity that almost any chapter in both Testaments is likely to contain at least one. Does Bible study by Christians include these portrayals of God as a killer of innocents and pitiless wreaker of vengeance? To bypass them would require skillful verse-hopping indeed, for they are everywhere.

The Lord of the Old Testament is almost less despicable than the Father of the New. At least Jehovah's wrath was swift and direct. It didn't await some indeterminate date, in preparation for which the Christian God stokes the coals of hell, anticipating the pleasure of inflicting "deserved" punishment. No human parent could be so depraved as this "marker of the sparrow's fall."

The biblical Almighty is as barbaric as any gods of the Gentiles could possibly have been. Besides that, he is warlike and revels in his role as commander-in-chief of predatory tribes to which he promises all the spoils of conquest that might be expected to accrue to any attacker backed by the Lord: "The Lord is a man of war." *Ex. 15:3* "It is the vengeance of the Lord." *Jer. 51:11* The Jews of the Old Testament had a book called The Wars of the Lord referred to in *Numbers 21:14.*

The writers of the New Testament at times make a brave attempt, furthered by the Church, to unscramble the compassionate caretaker from the heartless avenger, and for Christians they seem to pull it off. It's quite a trick.

⇒•◆•⇐

Like the pagan gods, the unpredictable swift-to-anger God of the Bible has to be feared and appeased, by sacrifices and constant down-on-the-knees worship and petitioning. He is the enthroned king and humanity his self-deprecating subjects. He is the Master; they are the slaves, abject and ridden by guilt and fear, grateful for any show of leniency.

Although animal sacrifices are supposedly substituted by the Mosaic law for the human sacrifices demanded by Baal and Moloch, the idea of human sacrifice persists throughout the Bible and becomes the precept upon which Christianity is founded. God orders the unquestioning altar-slaying of Isaac by his father, and when he makes the same requirement of child-sacrifice by Jephthah, he doesn't relent. One belief behind animal and human sacrifices was that blood could purify.

The seven sons of Saul are hanged to appease the Lord. *II Sam. 21:1–9* A demand for human sacrifice is actually clearly outlined in the Mosaic law: "Notwithstanding no devoted thing, that a man shall devote unto the Lord of all that he have both of man and beast . . . shall be redeemed but shall surely be put to death." *Lev. 27:28,29* Christianity, evolving as it did from bloody practices of religions built upon superstition and fear, is a theology of human sacrifice, torture, death, and cannibalism, coupled with blind obedience to an autocratic despot who decreed it all. Even Paul demands that bodies be living sacrifices to God. *Romans 12:1*

⟫⟫◆⟪⟪

If not an actual racist, God certainly shows partiality. He is the God of the Jews, and he makes no bones about it. He chooses them to be forever his people, and the Old Testament is the story of the wars instigated by God to bring this about, his guidance of the Jews in all that they undertake, and the detailed rules he lays down to govern them. When he orders them to invade Canaan and wipe out idolatry, he wants all Gentiles annihilated: "Thou shalt utterly destroy them." *Deut. 20:17*

Like Jesus in the New Testament, he has contempt for the Gentiles, and he makes that very clear: "Saith the Lord, the lion is come up from his thicket, and the destroyer of the . . . Gentiles is on his way." *Jer. 4:7* Jesus later lays it on the line to the disciples: "Go not into the way of the Gentiles . . . but rather to the lost sheep of the House of Israel." *Matt. 10:5,6*

God chooses Abram to be the father of that greatest nation on earth and changes Jacob's name to Israel, making Jacob's sons the founders of the 12 tribes of Israel: "For thy people Israel didst thou make thine own people forever; and thou, Lord, becamest their God." *I Chron. 17:22* These are the words of David.

The Lord tells Moses: "And I will walk among you, and will be your God, and ye shall be my people." *Lev. 26:12* The prophets echo God's prejudice: "You only have I known of all the families of earth." Thus God speaks to Israel through Amos 3:2. And God tells Ezekiel: "I will dwell in the midst of the children of Israel forever." *Ez. 43:7* When the prophets foretell the last days to come at the end of the Babylonian captivity and the establishment of Zion in Jerusalem, the subjection of the Gentiles is always projected.

God is also partial in smaller ways than those that involve the whole of civilization. He is such an admirer of Abel that Cain is driven to kill his brother in a fit of jealousy. And although Jacob is more at fault than Esau in the matter of the birthright and parental blessing, God excuses Jacob to such an extent that: "Jacob have I loved, but Esau have I hated." *Romans 9:13* If anyone doesn't treat David just right, that person is in trouble with God: "And it came to pass that the Lord smote Nabal that he died." *I Sam. 25:38* Nabal had made the mistake of refusing to pass out a lot of food to David and his men, total strangers to Nabal. (His widow then marries David.) God isn't kidding when he says: "For I set all men every one against his neighbor." *Zech. 8:10*

⟫⟫◆⟪⟪

Vengeance wreaked by God is really drastic. He sells Israel to the king of Mesopotamia for eight years, because the Israelites intermarried with Gentiles and worshipped idols. *Judges 3:8* He "smites" Israel and delivers the Jews to the Moabite kings for 18 years. *Judges 3:14* He sells the Jews to the king of Canaan for 20 years. *Judges 4:2* He delivers the Jews to the Midianites for seven years. *Judges 6:1* He allows Jerusalem and Judah to fall into the hands of the Philistines for 40 years and to be under the rule of Babylonia for 70 years. *Judges 13:1*

God treats Moses spitefully for a minor display of temper and forbids him to enter the Promised Land, including Aaron in the punishment. Most of the Jews liberated from Egypt are not permitted by God to live to occupy Canaan, because they were fearful about invading it when God wanted them to.

At one time God strikes thousands of innocent persons dead because some men looked into the Ark of the Covenant. The sort of behavior on the part of the Most High displayed in these instances goes on and on and culminates inevitably in the retention of hell as the ultimate revenge for all who commit the awful (in God's eyes) sin of disbelief.

⋙◆⋘

The unspeakable cruelty of the Christian God, manifested in his sentencing of a man who picked up sticks on the Sabbath to be stoned to death and his predilection for mass slaughter, reached its height when he destroyed all the inhabitants of the earth except for one family of his own choosing. Christians tell this flood story as if it is beautiful because of the rainbow ending and God's promise never to commit wholesale murder again in exactly that way. One woman's abortion today they consider a crime, but they worship a deity who drowned all children and pregnant women at one fell swoop and later thought nothing of putting to the sword all the first-born of Egypt (human and animal) after first setting up an excuse for such savage conduct by causing Pharaoh to refuse to "let my people go." To such a monster they build cathedrals.

⋙◆⋘

The God of the Bible is a sadist. He creates hell, and its first occupants are the angels who started an insurrection in heaven, an insurrection in God's own domain, which apparently he was powerless to prevent and which was perpetrated by imperfect beings he created. The Bible gives no account of God's creation of the angels, although it must have been before he made the universe, for Satan has already fallen from grace and is present in the Garden of Eden as a serpent when Adam and Eve arrive. Yet God created heaven and earth at the same time! *Gen. 1:1*

Bible readers are told at times that the revolutionist angels are already smoldering in hell, but other passages claim that their cubicles equipped with chains are being reserved for them. And certainly Jesus and the apostles have to deal with evil spirits still on the loose, including Satan, whom they very often mention as their opposition.

Perhaps by using the plumbline he frequently holds in biblical visions, God has fashioned a torture chamber large enough to accommodate for eternal occupation another group of miscreants besides rebellious angels: the vast majority of doomed humanity not destined for heaven. "For many are called but few are chosen." *Matt 22:14* To fill up every fiery corner (or every boiling wave) God declares everyone a sinner because Adam and Eve learned to tell the difference between right and wrong, although such ability would seem to be a desirable trait in the eyes of a deity so hung up on behavior patterns.

Next he declares every kind of natural conduct a sin and now has a sufficiently large if unenthusiastic population for his vast Hades (furnace, lake of fire, gate-enclosed smoking pit). Conscripted caretakers will probably be Shadrach, Meshach, and Abednego, all known for their god-given gift of withstanding warm temperatures.

With hell an accomplished fact in God's bag of infamous tricks, there is need of a Savior; God himself (as Jesus) is it, and one had better believe it. Those satisfied not to ask questions or express doubt in the setup are now perfect candidates for faith. But there is a catch here, a snag of such magnitude that it entangled even Paul's line of thought and one that makes Christian theology senseless. The word is, as Unity likes to say, "responsibility."

Throughout the pages of both Testaments God causes certain events to take place and people to behave in particular ways. He tempts and proves: "God did tempt Abraham." *Gen. 22:1* And: "For the Lord your God proveth you." *Deut. 13:3* The entire book of Job is based on the proving by God of one of his masochistic servants. Even the Lord's Prayer pins this sly behavior on the beseeched: "And lead us not into temptation." *Matt. 6:13*

When God (Love) showered fire and brimstone down upon Sodom and Gomorrah and the surrounding plain, hopefully all the cremated children and embryos were sinners of their own accord and were not innocents slaughtered in revenge for a hard heart solidified by God, as were the Egyptian first-born at a later date. The entire situation of the enslavement of the Jews in Egypt and the misery resulting from it are direct results of another of God's manipulations. He causes Joseph to be sold into slavery by his brothers and carried off to Egypt, allowing them to feel guilty for years and causing much grief to Jacob. This cruel plot on the part of God led to long years of suffering by the Jews as slaves to the Pharaohs and to their years of deprivation in the Wilderness. Moses is on to God's deceitfulness: "Fear not: for God is come to prove you, and that his fear may be before your faces, that ye sin not." *Ex. 20:20* Thus he clues in the Israelites.

In the New Testament, everything that happens in connection with the ministry of Jesus has been fore-ordained, according to Jesus and the apostles. When the appointed time came for crucifixion, Judas was the traitor, the Jews the perpetrators: "But all this was done, that the scriptures . . . might be fulfilled." *Matt. 26:56*

Other Bible passages carry out the idea that God is responsible for everything that happens, and the Church often faces a dilemma when today horrendous disasters must be laid at God's door and their value in the scheme of things painted as unfathomable by the human mind. At times Satan gets the blame as the agent of some deed whose assignment to God's instigation would be an embarrassment to the dedicated followers of a benign deity, thus bringing into question the power of God to overcome evil.

The prophets do not hesitate to put both good and evil at God's command: "I make weal and woe, I am the Lord, who do all these things." *Isaiah 45:6,7* "Is it not from the mouth of the Most High that good and evil come?" *Lam. 3:38* And: "Does evil befall a city unless the Lord has done it?" *Amos 3:6* Ezekiel describes the awful brand of evil God imposes upon urban areas: "Therefore thus saith the Lord God: Woe to the bloody city! I will make the pile for fire great. Heap on wood, kindle the fire, consume the flesh, and spice it well, and let the bones be burned." *Ez. 24:9,10* Not content to call for the eating of human flesh, the God of the Bible gives instructions for seasoning it and disposing of the bones!

The moral question of humankind being blamed for pre-ordained "sin" puts God in need of an apologist, and he finds an inept one in Paul. Faced with the accusation that it is unfair of God to doom people to hell through no fault of their own, the apostle can find no way out: "For the scripture saith unto Pharaoh, Even for this same purpose have I (God) raised thee up, that I might shew power in thee, and that my name might be declared throughout all the earth. Therefore hath he mercy on whom he will have mercy, and whom he will he hardeneth. Thou wilt say (you bet) then unto me, Why doth he yet find fault? For who hath resisted his will? Nay, but O man, who art thou who repliest against God? Shall the thing formed say to him that formed it, Why hast thou made me thus? Hath not the potter power over the clay, of the same lump to make one vessel unto honour, and another unto dishonour?" *Romans 9:17-21* (Can "logic" be more revolting than this?)

Is there a concept more corrupt or more repellent to any fair-minded person than that humanity should be held responsible for behavior prompted and imposed upon it by its accuser? With God the perpetrator, human behavior must be blameless, and a God who is guilty of entrapment may exist, but adored, or even admired, he cannot be. And there is yet another moral question involved, for if God can make people act according to his will, it is an evil God who will make them behave otherwise and end up in hell. Finally, the conclusion must be drawn that if an all-powerful Creator doesn't make everything perfect, he has not acted responsibly and can hardly expect imperfect human beings to do so.

⟹◇⟸

The Christian God is now on his second attempt to create a world to his liking, and heaven has already been the scene of civil war. Can the "saved" be assured of a perfect eternal home? Will it even be an *orderly* Utopia?

⟹◇⟸

The unfairness of God prevalent in the pages of the Bible (starting with the idea of original sin) reveals itself again in the theory that the good deeds of individuals will count for nothing, if they are not believers in everlasting life and Jesus as the Savior: "He that believeth on the Son hath everlasting life; and he that believeth not the Son shall not see life; but the wrath of God abideth on him." *John 3:36* With the biblical God, unbelief is the greatest sin (or disobedience of the command to believe). Only faith is required for salvation and thus becomes the highest morality, at least in this passage of the scripture.

Achievements in this world, even if they promote the welfare of humanity, are pointless, and honors and recognition for the advancement of human knowledge are meaningless in God's massive bookkeeping system. Spiritual life is the only measure of a person's worth when heavenly rewards are bestowed: "For what shall it profit a man, if he shall gain the whole world, and lose his own soul?" *Mark 8:36* Paul has all the inside information, as always, of the kind of human intelligence acceptable to God: "For it is written, I will destroy the wisdom of the wise, and will bring to nothing the understanding of the prudent . . . For ye see your calling, brethren, how that not many wise men after the flesh, not many mighty, not many noble, are called . . . He that glorieth, let him glory in the Lord." *I Cor. 1*

Under these standards, quite a few benefactors of humankind won't qualify for passage through the heavenly portals, for with this God all is black and white. When it comes to fair-minded justice, he is so rigid and unwilling to recognize moral worth or mitigating circumstances that one would hope he could not qualify to fill a bench in the judicial court system of the United

States. And for his companions in eternity he *prefers*, not the accomplished, not the brilliant, not the stimulating, not the outstanding achievers who may not conform, but the docile, the gullible, the child-like, the nondescript nonentities with nothing to recommend their selection but blind belief.

⇒·◆·⇐

Moral indignation on the part of God is rather easily aroused toward some practices of society such as trimming the hair or the beard, adorning the body, eating of certain kinds of food, noncircumcision, working on the Sabbath, prostitution, and homosexuality, but toward many *injustices* sometimes prevalent in a culture he seems to adopt a tolerant attitude. For instance, *slavery*, common among the Jews and other peoples in Bible days, he not only condones but sets up rules to cover. *Ex. 21* and *Lev. 25* He holds that a man's slaves are his money. *Ex. 21:21* And he gives permission for a man to sell his own children or to buy an impoverished brother, and even priests may buy slaves.

Abraham and other wealthy Old Testament Jews had many bondmen and bondwomen, as they were sometimes called, who were bought and sold and considered as the property of the owners to be handed down to the heirs. Jesus tells parables about slaves and selling human beings without once condemning the practice or expressing any indignation. Nowhere in the Bible is to be found any remonstrance against slavery at all. On the contrary, in this book which is heralded as the embodiment of the highest ethics to which humankind can aspire, such "servants" are ordered to be subservient to their masters, and Jesus and the apostles echo God's demand for total obedience on the part of the enslaved: "Servants, obey . . . your masters." *Col. 3:22*

The Bible has been used to justify slavery throughout the world, especially in the Deep South of America and the early colonies, and it must bear responsibility for the dehumanization of a portion of the human family. It intensified racial prejudice, because the God revealed in its pages chose to put the stamp of approval upon the pitiless practice of the enslavement of human beings by their fellow-man. In like fashion, this Master treats *his* servants: "Thou art the master. I am the slave."

Vast inequality in the distribution of wealth also fails to get God's dander up. Although poverty makes it easier to get into heaven, according to Jesus, who warns that riches will make it almost impossible, such is not the opinion of the Old Testament Lord: "For it is the Lord thy God who giveth thee the power to get wealth." *Deut. 8:18* As a result: "The rich ruleth over the poor." *Prov. 22:7*

Jesus's attitude toward riches would, if taken seriously by Christians rather than lightly by them like many of his teachings, make wealth a hot potato to be tossed from hand to hand, since its possession is a sure ticket to perdition. (At one time the Ark of the Covenant was so treated because of the death and pestilence sent by God as punishment for its slightest misuse. No one wanted to keep it.)

Although God's indignation may not be aroused by social ills such as slavery and the unfair distribution of wealth, it is another story when laxity is shown by the Jews in the matters of biblical killing and conquest. In one especially barbarous instance, God's servant Moses sends the Jewish forces back to finish off the male children and women of Midian but to save the girl babies and virgins, of which the Lord then gets his share. And poor Saul just isn't bloodthirsty enough for God. Although God has chosen him to be the first Jewish king, Saul loses favor because he has failed to kill all the Amalekites, as God had ordered: "It repenteth me that I have set up Saul to be king." *I Sam. 15:11* (So much for New Testament orders to Christians to obey rulers because they are all well-chosen by God.)

God doesn't take kindly to it, either, when King Azariah fails to get rid of all the altars to idols. He turns Azariah into a leper. He did the same thing to Miriam when she rightly criticized Moses for marrying a heathen. That temper of God's is far-reaching: "Who gave Jacob for a spoil, and Israel to the robbers? Did not the Lord?" *Isaiah 42:24*

⟫⟩◆⟨⟪

Some of God's remarks about sex would not meet the decency standards of many communities, and his explicit language might shock parents who censor what their children read. Judges know that strict censorship laws would immediately force the Bible from library shelves and ban it from book stores.

He addresses himself to Nineveh in these words: "I will discover thy skirts upon thy face, and I will show the nations thy nakedness and the kingdoms thy shame. And I will cast abominable filth upon thee." *Nahum 3:5,6* His lascivious intentions toward the "haughty" daughters of Israel are transmitted to Isaiah shamelessly: "Therefore the Lord will smite with a scab the crown of the head of the daughters of Zion, and the Lord will discover their secret parts." *Isaiah 3:17* Then this poorly-disguised sex maniac issues a unique order: "Thou shalt pluck off thine own breasts." *Ez. 23:34*

This Christian God, like deities of other religions and mythologies, comes to earth and "helps" women have children, but in spite of a great many instructions about sex, God pretends little use for it when others engage in it and has a special place in his heart for all who refrain from it: "For thus saith the Lord, unto the *eunuchs* that keep my Sabbaths, and choose the things that please me . . . even unto them will I give in mine house . . . a place and a name better than that of sons and daughters. I will give them an everlasting name." *Isaiah 56:4,5* These scriptures probably hang in needle-point on the cell walls of monks, priests, and other celibates.

—————

There are other times when God could sound more refined. He refers to Miriam: "If her father had but spit in her face, should she not be ashamed seven days?" *Num. 12:14* And: "Behold, I will corrupt your seed, and spread dung upon your faces, even the dung of your solemn feasts." *Mal. 2:3* (The priests addressed probably planned only frivolous feasts from then on.)

Ezekiel quotes God freely, that God's inspirational remarks might not be lost to posterity: "The Lord commanded: And thou shalt eat it as barley cakes, and thou shalt bake it with dung that cometh out of man, in their sight." *Ez. 4:12* Again God warns: "I . . . will cut off from Jeroboam him that pisseth against the wall." *I Kings 14:10* Such words are not used in church-service responsive readings.

Astonishing words of the Christian Deity:

Leviticus Chapter 26 contains 33 verses of descriptions in God's own words of unbelievably dreadful consequences which will result if the Jews incur his displeasure: "I will even appoint over you terror, consumption, and the burning ague, that shall consume the eyes, and cause sorrow of heart . . . and I will bring a sword upon you . . . I will send the pestilence among you . . . I will also send wild beasts, which shall rob you of your children." He lives up to that last threat when he sends the she-bears to devour 42 children who are playfully teasing Elisha.

"And thou shalt eat the fruit of thine own body, the flesh of thy sons, and of thy daughters which the Lord thy God hath given thee." *Deut. 28:53* These words are usually included in some of God's recommended menus.

No priest having any blemish may approach the altar of the Most High, according to his instructions to Moses: "For whatsoever man he be that hath a blemish, he shall not approach: a blind man, or a lame, or he that hath a flat nose, or anything superfluous, Or a man that is broken-footed, or broken-handed, Or crookbackt, or a dwarf, or that hath a blemish in his eye, or be scurvy, or scabbed . . . he shall not come nigh unto the altar." *Lev. 21:18–23*

Deuteronomy Chapter 28 contains 53 consecutive verses devoted to the many persecutions God will visit upon the Jews who serve other gods. The Jews at this time worshipped many gods as often as they acknowledged Jehovah, and such backsliding is one of the primary concerns of God throughout the Old Testament and of Jesus and the apostles in the New. Chapter 32 sums up God's intended punishment for disloyalty to him: "I will heap mischiefs upon them; I will send mine arrows upon them. They shall be

The Judeo-Christian God   43

burnt with hunger and devoured with burning heat, and with bitter destruction: I will also send the teeth of beasts upon them, with the poison of serpents of the dust. The sword without, and terror within, shall destroy both the young man and the virgin, the suckling also with the man of gray hairs." (Did anyone get left out?) The Pentagon would drool over God's arsenal.

The writings of the prophets overflow with words of God that ought to make the very churches tremble.

The following are all from Jeremiah:

"Behold, I will fill all the inhabitants (Jews) of this land, even the kings . . . and the priests and the prophets with drunkenness. And I will dash them one against another, even the fathers and the sons together, saith the Lord: I will not pity, nor have mercy, but destroy them."

"And shall not my soul be avenged on such a nation as this?"

"For behold I will send serpents, cockatrices among you and they shall bite you, saith the Lord."

"Behold, I will feed them, even this people, with wormwood, and give them water of gall to drink." He'll do it all for you-oo-oo.

"Behold, I will punish them: the young men shall die by the sword; their sons and their daughters shall die by the famine." God promises this treatment for the enemies of Jeremiah.

"And I will appoint over this people four kinds, saith the Lord: the sword to slay, and the dogs to tear, and the fowls . . . and the beasts . . . to devour and destroy."

"For who shall have pity upon thee, O Jerusalem? I will bereave them of children . . . and the residue of them will I deliver to the sword." Beginning to sound a lot like Hitler.

"And I will cause them to eat the flesh of their sons and the flesh of their daughters, and they shall eat everyone the flesh of his friend in the siege and the straitness." If only someone other than God could plan the diet!

"For I will punish them (migrating Jews) that dwell in the land of Egypt as I have punished Jerusalem, by the sword, by the famine, and by the pestilence."

"For I will call for a sword upon all the inhabitants of the earth." Just in case anyone feels left out.

"Fear and the pit and the snare shall be upon thee." God curses the Moabites.

"It shall be a desolate heap, and her daughters shall be burned with fire." God is referring to the land of the Ammonites.

"Bosrah shall become a desolation, a reproach, a waste, and a curse, and all the cities thereof shall be perpetual wastes." Believe it. Look at Sodom,

Gomorrah, and Jericho.

"Therefore the young men shall fall in her streets." Damascus might prefer to be included out.

"Also Edom shall be a desolation: everyone that goeth by it shall hiss at all the plagues thereof." Edom is poor Esau's territory.

"And Hazor shall be a dwelling for dragons." Send for St. George.

"And I will send the sword after them till I have consumed them." This time it's the Elamites.

"And Chaldea shall be a spoil." God's not through yet.

"All ye that bend the bow, shoot at her, spare no arrows." Babylon is the target.

"Take vengeance upon her; as she hath done, do unto her." What became of "Love thine enemies" and "Do unto others"?

"Go up against the land . . . waste and utterly destroy after them." Somebody called that making it "crystal clear."

"Spare ye not her young men; destroy ye utterly all her host . . . this is the time of the Lord's vengeance." Remember last year's score.

"Make bright the arrows . . . gather the shields."

"Thou art my battle axe and weapons of war, for with thee (Israel) will I break in pieces man and woman and with thee will I break in pieces old and young." Gentiles don't hold this against God. Anyone can have a bad day.

"The daughter of Babylon is like a threshing floor, it is time to thresh her." The *floor?*

"I will bring them down like lambs to the slaughter."

God communicates to Ezekiel in similar tone:

"For thus saith the Lord . . . they shall slay their sons and their daughters."

"Therefore the fathers shall eat the sons." A Father and Son banquet?

"Thus shall my anger be accomplished . . . and I will be comforted." God has his own Valium.

"So will I send upon you famine and evil beasts." God's gift packages contain different combinations of goodies.

"And I will lay the dead carcasses of the children of Israel before their idols; and I will scatter your bones." Saves the cost of a funeral.

"I will accomplish my fury upon them . . . Neither will I have pity."

"Slay utterly old and young, both maids and little children, and women. . ." After all, that's what God does.

⟫◇⟨

The God of the Bible is a demon with no moral standards. He orders atrocities and condones injustice and unfairness. The world he created is full of natural disasters that bring terrible destruction, and nature at its best is the enemy of life much of the time. Humankind has had to struggle constantly to survive. Disease and suffering are its lot, and alleviation of them eludes it.

Every reprehensible kind of human being exists and threatens the helpless. Hunger and poverty are present everywhere in the world. If the Christian God is good and the cause of everything, then everything must be good, but people cannot be credited with having, or being able to exercise, moral judgment, if God's "good" behavior does not seem so to them but, on the contrary, seems the epitome of evil.

Besides, the Lord has a history of being devious. He lets Ezekiel in on one of his tricks: "If the prophet be deceived, I the Lord have deceived that prophet and will stretch out my hand and destroy him." *Ez. 14:9* Another time God puts a lying spirit into the mouths of some prophets in a plot to cause the death of King Ahab. *I Kings 22:23*

God also makes use of evil spirits. He sends one upon Saul, and David has to come and play and sing for the king in order to cure him. Another evil spirit from the Lord causes Saul to hurl a javelin at David. *I Sam. 19:9* Earlier, God assists Jacob in a scheme to help Jacob get possession of much of his father-in-law's livestock. *Gen. 30*

Christians want a God of love, and there are continuing attempts to revise the Bible in order to give them one. Confronted with the ferocious deity of their Holy Book, believers speak of the vast "mysteries" of the supernatural, to which, according to Jesus and Paul, only a few are privilege. Paul writes of the acknowledgment of the "mystery of God, and of the Father, and of Christ." *Col. 2:2*

The Old Testament Lord was a flawed deity with all the characteristics, not necessarily admirable, of human beings. He was tyrannical and vengeful, a god with whom the Jews often argued and disagreed, but he had chosen them as his special people, and they were expected to obey the rules. For falling away they were made to suffer, but there was always the promise of re-instatement into his good graces and eventual triumph over the Gentiles on the Day of the Lord. The whole system was simple, except for the laws the Lord transmitted to Moses, which were complex beyond belief and invaded every area of the Jews' existence. The Pharisees gradually came to believe in resurrection of the body, but the Lord of the Old Testament does not promise an after-life. Proper conduct on earth brings favor and approval of the Jews' Jehovah, which will lead to the fulfillment of the prophecies about a deliverer and the eminence of the Jewish Zion. No matter what disasters were permitted to befall the Jews throughout the centuries, the Lord always preserved a "remnant" that seemed to verify the covenant made with Abraham.

Then the Christians took this Yahweh for their deity and made him into a god acceptable to all degrees of definition and to all sects from Catholic to Orthodox to Protestant and from the Fundamentalist to the Christian Scientist. The writers of the New Testament took an almighty Creator and Manipulator, invented by superstitious and ignorant people of an ancient age, and with the aid of myth ideas, fashioned a multi-faceted god-head that is adaptable to any one of various roles.

First, they nullified the covenant with Abraham in favor of a new covenant of everlasting life offered in the person of a sacrificed human savior-god who then rose from the dead to complete the pattern delineated in many pagan mythologies. To retain the monotheism which by then had become traditional among the Jews, as well as among some Gentiles, they came up with a Trinity and special angels (later added saints). John was not satisfied even with a trinity, but made God into a six-pack: "For there are three that bear record in heaven, the Father, the Word, and the Holy Ghost: and there are three that bear witness in earth, the Spirit, the water, and the blood, and these three agree in one." *I John 5:7,8*

By becoming a human sacrifice in the guise of his own son, the New Testament God offered eternal life in heaven in return for belief in himself as a savior. Non-believers would go to hell. The Mosaic law was no longer the way into God's favor, now called "grace." Some Jews were willing to accept this Savior as the fulfillment of the prophecies about a Messiah, but the Jews as a whole were not. So gradually this salvation was extended to the Gentiles, mainly through real or invented apostle-evangelists.

God became the Father exhibiting universal love, but the vengefulness remained in the concept of hell, on the theory that fear is more persuasive than love. Although the Christian deity became more and more abstract and non-corporeal after the resurrection, many human qualities had to be retained in the framework for the sake of comprehensibility by people who do not deal in the infinite. It is impossible, furthermore, to speak or write of the thoughts and deeds of gods, unless one conceives of these thoughts and actions as being similar to those experienced by humans. The Christian God had to remain human in many respects. In identical situations, God still reacted with less compassion than most human beings would.

The apostles could not abandon Judaism enough to deny that the Jews were still the Chosen People, and it was difficult for them to let the Gentiles be "grafted" in. *Romans 11* All the new converts became the "chosen" people to the degree that the apostles warned them about associating with unbelievers: "Now we command you, brethren, in the name of our Lord Jesus Christ, that ye withdraw yourselves from every brother that walketh disorderly, and not after the tradition he received of us." *II Thess. 3:6*

Not satisfied with sanctimoniously separating themselves from infidels, the New Testament writers went even further by claiming that the saved had been predestinated from the beginning of the world. Bad enough to give Bible readers a god who was responsible for people's behavior and then blamed them for wickedness that might result, but New Testament theologians make eight or nine statements about predestination that are so assertive, some sects have been founded on the principle or at least include it in their dogma. "Whom he did predestinate, them he also called, and whom he called, them he also justified: and whom he justified them he also glorified." *Romans 8:30* And: "Who shall lay anything to the charge of God's elect?" *Romans 8:33* One passage of scripture combines both ideas of behavior influence and predestination: "What then, Israel hath not obtained that which he seeketh for; but the election hath obtained it, and the rest were blinded according as it is written, God hath given them the spirit of slumber, eyes that they should not see, and ears that they should not hear." *Romans 11:7,8*

Such a God is the personification of unfairness and partiality. Fundamentalists no doubt have their own apologies for such Bible passages, but scriptures like these have been carefully glossed over by the cosmic cosmetics applied in the New Testament epistles to the *over-all* portrait of the Christian divinity. Mysticism is the ingredient of the cosmetic. The Old Testament Lord needed little of it, but when Judaism became more and more exposed to the mythological and "mystery" religions of other countries through increased contact and communication, the word "mystery" begins to appear in New Testament scripture: "But we speak the wisdom of God in a mystery, even the hidden wisdom, which God ordained before the world unto our glory." *I Cor. 2:7* Within the framework of this new theology, God becomes part of an extra-terrestrial hierarchy who still appears occasionally in typical biblical visions, but no longer in person.

Bible prose written after the alleged ascension became rich with ideological concepts, imaginary abstractions, and use of mystical metaphors, and God gradually became the embodiment of word images such as Wisdom, Love, Power, Faith, Grace, Hope, Knowledge, Nature, Force, Charity, Mind, Truth, Health, etc., as intellectual philosophers made peace with the Bible.

So today it is almost impossible to express disbelief in "God," because of the many conceptual ways in which God is comprehended. G-O-D is no longer identifiable nor required to be so. From the awesome lawgiver who wrote on tablets of stone with his finger, God has become a vast cosmic presence enveloping the universe and answering to any noble logo or title that connotes some limitless virtue or inimitable relationship with humankind.

It has become expedient to forget that the Word of God contains a description of his fiendish anticipation: "Behold, the day of the Lord cometh, cruel both with wrath and fierce anger, to lay the land desolate: and he shall destroy the sinners thereof out of it . . . Everyone that is found shall be thrust through; and everyone that is joined unto them shall fall by the sword. Their children also shall be dashed to pieces before their eyes; their houses shall be spoiled, and their wives ravished." *Isaiah 13:9,15,16*

It has become expedient to forget that the Word of God says that he conditions behavior in order that he might have the pleasure of punishing wrong-doers: "Notwithstanding they (Eli's wicked sons) hearkened not unto the voice of their father, because the Lord *would slay them*." *I Sam. 2:25* And Paul, with unbelievable insensitivity, makes the assertion that God ordained the Mosaic law so that increased offences would make it possible for more grace to be granted. *Romans 5:20,21* As if it were not enough to malign his God in this way, Paul adds to the libel by claiming that the Christian God deals "to every man the measure of faith" according to which he is expected to conduct his life. *Romans 12:3*

It has become expedient to forget all this and to obscure the basic idiocy that underlies Christianity as presented in the Word of God—namely, that the God of the Bible first created human beings imperfect and permitted his son Satan to cause their downfall, after which he would re-instate them only when he had forced them to kill him, ingest his body, and rejoice in this plan for salvation. To make such a plan plausible and less repugnant to thinking persons, the New Testament treats of the Word of God as a "mystery," which cannot be understood by reasonable creatures but can be accepted by "babes" and by any mature individual who is willing to become childlike.

⟹⧫⟸

The Christian God is unbelievably impulsive, and there seems to be no purpose in any of his far-reaching innovations. No motivation lies behind the Creation of the World, and human beings are *afterthoughts*. He is not seen contemplating his *plan* for salvation, and there is no impetus for this sudden reversal of policy other than *whim*. And what a sadistic whim it was!

As pictured in Christian dogma, their God is the fiend of all time, and although Christians choose to call him a Savior, he is by his own admission a Torquemada whose beneficent New Testament gesture will culminate in eternal anguish for all except a small portion of humankind: "Because strait is the gate, and narrow is the way, which leadeth unto life, and *few* there be that find it." *Matt. 7:14* Where is the milk of human kindness, which is credited to Christians in abundance, that they find this situation anything but atrocious? It is not a beautiful plan—it is a horrid plan. To attribute it to a Heavenly Father is a travesty against parenthood. What human father would subject his children to a proving ground, where their relationship with him would be the criterion which would determine that most of them would be found wanting, and for this failure be sentenced to eternal agony in a place the father had fashioned ahead of time? Such a parent would not be lionized and enthroned as the author of love and compassion, surely.

Salvation should be examined for what it really is in the New Testament. It is not salvation. It is damnation, for most of humanity, and the New Testament God has the nerve to say so and even claim that the few who will benefit from the plan have been chosen from the beginning of time. St. Paul makes that very clear: "But ye are come unto Mt. Sion, and unto the city of the living God, . . . to the general assembly and church of the firstborn, which are written in heaven, . . ." *Hebrews 12:22,23* And St. John has a vision depicting the suffering of all whose names were not written in "the book of life from the foundation of the world." *Rev. 17:8* There are several other references to predestination in the Holy Book.

To assure that eternal life in some perfect heaven would be enjoyed by all, required only that God's Truth be equally apparent to and thus accepted by every human creature who ever lived or ever will live. Instead of making that Truth (if there is such a truth) self-evident, God, Christians will have it, arranged that a bloody plan for salvation, pagan in nature, should be dramatized on earth in relative obscurity, with himself as chief actor, and in such a manner that at the time there was little agreement about it or belief in it and ever since nothing but controversy about it.

How could the Christian God have expected such a "truth" to be widely and quickly spread? (Surely speed and diversity were of the essence where the final assignment of souls was concerned.) Most people of that day were, as are many today, illiterate. There were, and are now, hundreds of languages and innumerable nuances inherent in them. There was very little written communication and even less travel, and some areas of the world were not yet "discovered." 2,000 years have elapsed, and most people are still destined for hell, either because they have not heard of Christianity or because the salvation legend is especially vulnerable to skepticism. Revealed religions are per se hearsay religions with all the courtroom problems of hearsay credibility.

The Christian God, as the New Testament portrays him, is not a candidate for admiration, if only on the basis of his long-range design for humankind that is implicit in the plan for salvation. If the depth of his love is to be measured by that design, the measuring stick need not be of great length. Yet Christians proselytize for acceptance of a theology built around such a god. This theology makes salvation necessary because Adam and Eve were not aware of divine truth, through no fault of their own. For God's refusal to make them aware of it they are cursed, and their descendants along with them, until, with either cruel intent or owing to failure to consider the inevitable outcome, he comes up with a repulsive device to save a few and damn many.

Taught, nevertheless, from childhood, to pledge allegiance to this figment of the supernatural, Christians have chosen to devote every energy and bend every effort to turning aside his wrath and bowing to his volatile will, in the hope that, if their god is happy, they will be, too.

CHAPTER TWO

The God From Galilee

Others said, This is the Christ.
But some said, Shall Christ come out of Galilee?
—John 7:41

Jesus bases his ministry upon the assumption that the end of the world is imminent and that he will return shortly and establish the kingdom he preaches. In the gospel of Matthew alone, Jesus refers to this concept at least six times. "From that time Jesus began to preach, and to say, Repent: for the kingdom of heaven is at hand." *Matt. 4:17* These words of warning are an exact repetition of those of John the Baptist, whom many mistake for the Messiah. *Matt. 3:2*

Sending his disciples out onto the circuit, Jesus reminds them: "For verily I say unto you, Ye shall not have gone over the cities of Israel, till the Son of man be come." *Matt. 10:23* Again Jesus asserts: "There shall be some standing here, which shall not taste of death, till they see the Son of man coming in his kingdom." *Matt. 16:28* He makes it clear, after describing his early triumphant return: "This generation shall not pass till all these things be fulfilled." *Matt. 24:34*

In Galilee Jesus repeats: "The time is fulfilled, and the kingdom of God is at hand." *Mark 1:15* "The hour is come, and now is, when the dead shall hear the Voice of the Son of God." *John 5:25* Finally: "If I will that he tarry till I come, what is that to thee?" *John 21:22* Here Jesus speaks of the disciple John to Peter. Paul and the other evangelist apostles take up Jesus's clarion prediction, still echoed today.

As a natural accompaniment to the wording of impending doom, verbal pictures of the End are majestically painted by Jesus on several occasions. His second coming will bring about the redemption of the Jews from the Gentiles, and the establishment of the Jewish kingdom of God. In the words of Jesus: "And when ye shall see Jerusalem compassed with armies, then know that the desolation thereof is nigh. Then let them which are in Judea flee to the mountains . . . and let not them that are in the countries enter thereinto. For these be the days of vengeance, that all things which are written may be fulfilled. But woe unto them that are with child and to them that give suck (the usual biblical disregard for women) in those days; for there shall be great distress in the land, and wrath upon this people. And they shall fall by the edge of the sword and shall be led away captive into all nations: and Jerusalem shall be trodden down by the Gentiles, until the time of the Gentiles be fulfilled." *Luke 21:20–24* Jesus's narrow world surfaces. He limits the area of his second coming to Jerusalem and a tiny Judea, as he gives details.

The recital of this Armageddon is somewhat different in Matthew and also elaborates upon the accompanying condition of the heavens. After the terrible tribulation (for which some religious sects store up provisions) the sun and *moon* will be darkened, and the stars shall *fall*. Then all shall see (with no light?) the Son of man coming in the clouds. His angels shall come with trumpet sounds (and flashlights?) and gather up the elect from the four winds. *Matt. 24*

These descriptions by Jesus point up the fact that he was abysmally ignorant of science and the universe and was no more cognizant of knowledge to be discovered later than the average superstitious Jew of his day. He makes no mention of atomic power; the armies will use swords and have no air cover; stars can fall and the sun lose its heat and light, and life will still remain on the earth and clouds in the heavens, upon which he can float down into the four winds. As the Son of God, or God if you will, he has none of the information which people have been able to acquire through their own efforts during the centuries since then (in spite of the opposition of the Church). Why didn't Jesus know everything there is to know?

He doesn't even seem to know the season or day of his return to earth, for he says the elect should pray it is not in winter or on the Sabbath; yet they do not take these predictions of Jesus concerning the last days seriously, or they would all move near mountain ranges, and Christian women would hesitate to bear children as they prepare for the imminent end of all things. Jesus was not omniscient, obviously.

Jesus's description of the day when he will return to establish his mythical kingdom is almost word-for-word repetition of these passages attributed to the prophet Zechariah: "Behold, the day of the Lord cometh, and thy spoil shall be divided in the midst of thee. For I will gather all nations against Jerusalem to battle; and the city shall be taken, and the houses rifled, and the women ravished; and half of the city shall go forth into captivity, and the residue of the people shall not be cut off from the city. Then shall the Lord go forth, and fight against those nations . . . And ye shall flee to the valley of the mountains . . . yea, ye shall flee . . . and the Lord my God shall come, and all the saints with thee. And it shall come to pass in that day, that the light shall not be clear . . . And the Lord shall be king over all the earth." *Zech. 14*

Joel also foretells the Day of the Lord when the Gentiles shall come under the domination of Jehovah: "For the day of the Lord is near in the valley of decision. The sun and the moon shall be darkened, and the stars shall withdraw their shining. The Lord shall roar out of Zion, and utter his voice from Jerusalem; and the heavens and the earth shall shake . . . Judah shall dwell forever, and Jerusalem from generation to generation." *Joel 3:15,16,20* (Judah fell 2600 years ago.)

Almost all the prophets predict such a Day of the Lord when the new kingdom of Zion will be accomplished, whose subjects shall include all other nations under the God of the Jews. Familiar with these traditional expectations, Jesus with his customary respect for the Old Testament, coupled with his goal of clothing himself with the prophecies, feels compelled to make his statement: "that all things that are written may be fulfilled." *Luke 21:22*

He is bound always to address himself to the establishment of a *kingdom*, since a kingdom with a descendant of David as ruler is what the prophets all promise and what the Jews all expect will be the ultimate future stronghold of a triumphant Jewish nation (Zion). Jesus could not have laid claim to the Messiahship without portraying himself as the king-to-be when Israel would be redeemed from the domination of her conquerors. His reference to the days of vengeance are directly from the prophets: "For the day of vengeance is in my heart, and the year of my redeemed is come." *Isaiah 63:4*

Either Jesus patterned his Second Coming after the prophetical Day of the Lord, or the prophets had been given inside information about it several hundred years before even the *birth* of the self-proclaimed Redeemer.

Statements of Jesus about what the Church chooses to call Judgment Day make one wonder if definite plans for it have been formulated. Conflicting verses of scripture leave the questions of when, where, and by whom judgment will take place unanswered. Jesus says in Luke 13:28: "There shall be weeping and gnashing of teeth (sure thing) when ye shall see Abraham, and Isaac, and Jacob, and all the prophets, in the kingdom of God, and you yourselves thrust out." To the unsaved whom he is addressing it would appear that the Jews mentioned have already been judged or that they were admitted to heaven without benefit of judgment. (Incidentally, the spiritual bodies Jesus says the elect will have are apparently identifiable, if further conclusions are drawn from these words of Jesus, words which Paul later ignores when he maintains that none who lived before Christ is eligible for eternal life.)

Referring again to a Jewish patriarch, Jesus says that he will not accuse people to the Father but that Moses will: "Do not think I will accuse you to the Father: there is one that accuseth you, even Moses, in whom ye trust." *John 5:45* In Moses Jews are given for a judge a murderer, a military leader who ordered the slaughter of innocents and the wresting of lands from their rightful inhabitants, and a man not deemed fit enough by God to set foot in the Promised Land.

Although Jesus has claimed in the above statement that he himself will not accuse, he later says: "But whosoever shall deny me before men, him will I also deny before my Father which is in heaven." *Matt. 10:33* Jesus repeats the claim that he will do the judging: "When the Son of man shall come in his glory, and all the holy angels with him, then shall he sit upon the throne of his glory: And before him shall be gathered all nations (quite a crowd): and he shall separate them one from another, as a shepherd divideth his sheep from the goats." *Matt. 25:31,32* Again: "For the Son of man shall come in the glory of his Father with his angels; and then he shall reward every man according to his works." *Matt. 16:27* Yet again: "The Father . . . hath given him (the Son) authority to execute judgment." *John 5:27*

Retreating from his role as judge, however, Jesus on another occasion gives the job to the angels: "The Son of man shall send forth his angels, and they shall gather out of his kingdom all things that offend, and them which do iniquity; And shall cast them into a furnace of fire: then shall be wailing and gnashing of teeth." *Matt. 13:41,42* (Will parents be snatched from children and children from parents?)

Finally, to add to the confusion, Jesus delegates the disciples: "Ye shall also sit upon twelve thrones, judging the twelve tribes of Israel." *Matt. 19:28* Apparently judgment of Gentiles is of little concern, and that will certainly cut down on a very crowded calendar. (Population of this world is already several billion.)

Jesus has much to say about judgment and eternal punishment in order to establish fear as a motivation for belief in his role as Savior of a sinful humankind, thus coupling fear of physical punishment with a sense of guilt, two powerful persuaders in any cause. It is somewhat of a contradiction to believe that judgment of human behavior will even be necessary, since one message of the gospels is that belief in Jesus as the Redeemer is all that is required for salvation: "For God so loved the world, that he gave his only begotten Son, that whosoever believeth in him should not perish, but have everlasting life." *John 3:16* Judgment as portrayed in the New Testament is immediate once it starts, without trial or consideration of contributing conditions, a system with no bill of rights and no degree of guilt or punishment, although there do seem to be lesser and greater rewards. Here on earth judges often find it difficult to pronounce sentence fairly, and long jury trials are frequently necessary to determine guilt, but divine judgment is cut and dried, and the accused before the throne of *grace* can expect no mercy or pity from their heavenly father, no consideration of heredity or environmental influence.

⇒◆⇐

Jesus tries to convince John the Baptist that he (Jesus) is the Messiah by buttering John up and speaking highly of him to the people, although in some passages of the gospels John seems to accept without question that Jesus is such, especially when God as a pigeon lands on Jesus's head. John could be expected to recognize the Messiah with ease since John supposedly has been given the privilege of announcing the long-awaited arrival of the Redeemer. But Jesus passes out compliments: "Verily, I say unto you, Among them that are born of women (includes nearly everyone) there hath not risen a greater than John the Baptist." *Matt. 11:11* He says John is a prophet risen from the dead (Jews expected prophets to re-appear in this way), but John denies that he himself is either a prophet or the Messiah, as many think.

It is possible that Jesus sees John as a rival; at least he does not seem very upset when John is beheaded. In some scriptures, John is not all that convinced that Jesus *is* the Messiah, as he sends from prison to ask Jesus if he is. Jesus then instructs these inquirers to tell John of all the great works that have been done: "Then Jesus answering said unto them, Go your way, and tell John what things ye have seen and heard: how that the blind see, the lame walk, the lepers are cleansed, the deaf hear, the dead are raised . . ." *Luke 7:22* and *Matt. 11*

Jesus doesn't seem to know whether he will get more followers by preaching heaven or by preaching hell. He is not very specific in his descriptions of either one. Heaven is a very desirable place with unimagined delights and supposed to contain many mansions which Jesus himself is going to prepare. (This finishing project ought to insure some construction workers getting through the pearly gates early.) When Jesus is questioned about human relationships that will prevail in Paradise, he gets by with an explanation that the bodies will be angelic: "They are as the angels of God in heaven." *Matt. 22:30* Because angels are able to function as human beings and are sometimes mistaken for them, the saints may expect to appear much as they did on earth, with the possible addition of a halo and a bunch of feathers at each shoulder, but whether in the buff or robed in white perma-press is not clear.

Christians pretend little interest in details about their everlasting fate, but each probably has "a little list" of questions too frivolous, in his or her estimation, to admit. Jesus says they will recognize each other, but will they have any kind of relationship with one another? (There will be no marrying or giving in marriage.) If there is no relationship, what is the appeal of heaven, and if there is, will the saved miss their skeptical relatives in hell? (There shall be no sorrow.) Will the resurrected be the age they were at death—newborn, a senile 95? Will they have bodily functions? (They will live in mansions and eat at tables.)

Will they have shape and form? (Otherwise how recognize each other?) Will faces have wrinkles and lines; will bodies be chubby, skinny, short, tall, male, female, of different races? (All Bible angels are male.) Will lost limbs be replaced, infirmities erased, ugly features beautified, emaciated bodies restored? Jesus says that occupants of heaven can converse with occupants of hell (*Luke 16:19–25*), but Paul would seem to make that impossible by saying that Jesus descended into the "lower parts of the earth" (hell) before he ascended "far above all heavens." *Eph. 4:9,10* Will children go to hell, as the early Church fathers taught (graphically describing their agony)? If not, what is the cut-off age?

With so little knowledge of the heavenly abode, Christians still make sacrifices (no longer literally) in order to reach it. Of the tortures of hell Jesus is more informed, and he regularly foretells of the weeping and wailing and teeth-gnashing awaiting all who deny him as the Savior even John the Baptist was not sure Jesus was.

Making it plain that he considers Satan a rival, Jesus admits his existence, is carried through the air and tempted by him 40 days, and refers to him often: "Simon, behold, Satan hath desired to have you." *Luke 22:31* He cures a woman whom he says: "Satan hath bound, lo, these eighteen years." *Luke 13:16* Jesus also declares that hell was prepared for the devil and his angels, of which there are vast hosts. *Matt. 25:41* Jesus makes it clear that they are powerful antagonists of God. Satan actually is treated by Jesus and the apostles as an evil and dangerous "he's everywhere" mischief-maker who vies with God for the hearts of men, most of the time successfully. Hell is described as having gates and as being both a lake and a furnace.

⟫◦⟪

Jesus spends much of his brief ministry casting out devils or unclean spirits. He is not very knowledgeable about medicine, attributing many ailments from epilepsy to insanity to the possession of the body by spiritual demons. He has power over them and tries to give some of his followers the same power, although the disciples are not always successful at exercising it. At times the touch of Jesus's hands will heal, also; then again at other times a little spit works, or the hem of his garment. (Such transference of power is a concept originating in pagan magic.)

Many unlikely stories abound in the gospels of Jesus's experiences with healing by the banishment of devils that inhabit people of that day. One of the most elaborate accounts is found in Luke. Shortly after the episode in which he calms the waves, Jesus enters a city and meets a man "which had devils a long time," a man who lived in no house and ran around naked (a not uncommon biblical practice). Jesus commands the unclean spirit to come out of the sufferer, but the spirit cries out (oh, yes, they can speak): "What have I to do with thee, Jesus, thou Son of God most high?" (The man's name is Legion, because so many devils possess him.)

The devils beseech Jesus to cast them into a herd of swine, and after he does so, the swine "ran violently down a steep place into the lake and were choked." *Luke 8* (Quite a loss to the owner of the pigs, whether a Gergesene or a Gadarene!)

Continuing in this vein, the disciples try to heal a child possessed of a devil and fail. Jesus impatiently asks that the child be brought to him. "And as he was yet a coming, the devil threw him (the child) down and tare him. And Jesus rebuked the unclean spirit, and healed the child." *Luke 9:38–42* Again: "And devils also came out of many, crying out, and saying (devilishly), Thou art Christ the Son of God. And he rebuking them suffered them not to speak: for they knew that he was Christ." *Luke 4:41* But: "Unclean spirits, when they saw him, fell down before him, and cried, saying, Thou art the Son of God." *Mark 3:11*

Obviously these unclean spirits (the devil's angels who used to live in heaven?) are a good source of miracle-working for Jesus, and it is handy that they frequently announce his identity. E.g., some of them make their home in a man in a synagogue (of all places), saying: "Let us alone; what have we to do with thee, thou Jesus of Nazareth? Art thou come to destroy us? I know thee who thou art, the Holy One of God. And Jesus rebuked him, saying, Hold thy peace and come out of him. And when the unclean spirit had torn him, and cried with a loud voice, he came out of him . . . And immediately his fame spread abroad." *Mark 1:23–28*

Jesus seems to have no difficulty "casting out" these little devils, but one wonders where they go when no unfortunate animals are nearby. Into other persons, apparently, for Jesus tells the disciples to "raise the dead, cast out devils." *Matt. 10:8* How easy can it be?

Some contemporaries thought Jesus to be just another prophet: "And the multitude said, This is Jesus the prophet of Nazareth of Galilee." *Matt 21:11* And: "Many of the people therefore when they heard this saying, said, Of a truth this is the Prophet. Others said, This is the Christ. But some said, Shall Christ come out of Galilee? . . . So there was a division among the people because of him." *John 7:40–43* "Search and look," said the Pharisees, "for out of Galilee ariseth no prophet." These words spoken to Nicodemus are indicative of the problems faced by Jesus in proving that he fulfilled the prophecies foretelling of a Messiah. Jesus could hardly breathe in and out once without remarking that some occurrence or occasion fulfilled an Old Testament prophecy. Throughout the gospels he makes a conscious effort to establish that he is the awaited Redeemer (whom the Jews expected to save them from the Gentiles).

In Matthew alone Jesus alludes to these prophesies 31 times. He also admits that he follows certain patterns of behavior *purposely* to fulfill a familiar-to-all prophecy of a Messiah-to-come, forecast by the fortune-teller prophets of the Old Testament: "I am not come to destroy, but to fulfill." *Matt. 5:17*

Jesus is thought at times to be a prophet risen from the dead: "And they said, Some say that thou art John the Baptist: some say Elias (Elijah); and others Jeremias (Jeremiah), or one of the prophets." *Matt. 16:14* Jesus also thinks of himself as a prophet, or at least takes seriously this belief of some of his fellow Jews, for he says at one time: "Nevertheless I must walk today, and tomorrow, and the day following: for it cannot be that a prophet perish out of Jerusalem." *Luke 13:33* Can he be both prophet and God?

⋙·◆·⋘

The disciples, who are frequently skeptical although they hear even *devils* identify Jesus as the Son of God, confront Jesus with a prophecy from Malachi that says Elias must return before the Messiah comes, but Jesus answers that: "Elias is come already, and they knew him not." *Matt. 17:12* Here Jesus is claiming that John the Baptist was Elias. In fact, he so states while John is still alive: "This is Elias which was for to come." *Matt. 11:14* But John tells the priests: "I am not the Christ. And they asked him, What then? Art thou Elias? And he saith, I am *not.* Art thou that prophet? And he answered, No." *John 1:20,21* Jesus describes himself many times as the Son of man, a title applied to prophets, of whom Elijah was traditionally supposed to be the one who would recognize and identify the Messiah.

Throughout the gospels Jesus stresses that he is both the Son of God and God himself: "He that believeth on the Son hath everlasting life." *John 3:36* And: "All things are delivered to me of my Father." *Luke 10:22* But: "I and my Father are one." *John 10:30* And: ". . . even as we are one." *John 17:22*

Jesus and God and the Holy Ghost make up the Trinity, that dogma of the Church which became necessary to retain the monotheism of Christianity. It was one of the mystic concepts invented to clothe the Christian religion with that "mystery" of which the New Testament is enamored. Such enigmas are meant to put comprehension of Christian theology out of reach of the masses, who are summarily commanded to "avoid foolish questions" and fall back on puerile trust, leaving the intellectualism and privilege which are required for understanding, to the clergy.

Without the Trinity, Christianity might be seen as having three gods, and Satan, seemingly more powerful than all of them, might have to be allowed to be the fourth. Indeed, some scriptures challenge the Trinity quite effectively: "My Father is greater than I." *John 14:28* And: "I love the Father." *John 14:31* These statements are attributed to Jesus.

⇒◆⇐

Jesus is often confronted by the question of how his teaching relates to the Mosaic law and to secular law. Throughout the gospels he struggles with answers. Finally, in a superficial manner, he tries to solve the whole problem with one brief remark: "Render unto Caesar the things which are Caesar's." *Mark 12:17*

Such a stand leaves a great deal open to further question as to separation of Church and State, and the argument about whether the Church should take political attitudes remains a bitter one today.

At times Jesus preaches that God must have the highest allegiance, in connection with which idea he says that up until the time of John the Baptist the law prevailed, but since then the "kingdom of God" is taught. In line, however, with his predilection for contradicting himself, he on another occasion assures the Pharisees (strict adherents to the God-given Mosaic law): "Think not that I am come to destroy the law or the prophets." *Matt. 5:17* He expands this theme: "Till heaven and earth pass, one jot or one tittle shall in no wise pass from the law . . ." *Matt. 5:18* To add to the confusion, he then proceeds to defend the disciples when they break the Mosaic law, and at times he amends it to excuse his own actions.

The conflict which arises between the "morality" of obeying civil law and the "morality" of following religious beliefs when the two are in opposition is recognized by Jesus, but he does little to resolve it: "In vain do they worship me, teaching for doctrines the commandments of men." *Matt. 15:9*

⇒◆⇐

Jesus does not sanction any challenge of the State by its citizens, although it is clear from his words that a very oppressive class system existed among the Jews of his day. New Testament scriptures teem with talk of kings, rulers, lords, and masters, and their servants, many of whom are slaves. The teaching of Jesus is concerned with instructions of how all members of that society should conduct themselves in their present situation. No one in servitude is encouraged to rebel against it, and the division of the culture into the rich and the poor, also obvious from Jesus's words, is not considered by him to be a situation that should be changed, except by reliance upon charity and welfare.

The unique appeal of Christianity to early converts was the promise that the next world would be a place where the class ranking would be reversed. In the meantime, the underprivileged, subservient, and poverty-stricken were to content themselves with their social position and not threaten the hierarchy. Jesus repeatedly reprimanded the scribes and Pharisees for their ill-treatment of the laity, but reform was to be voluntary and undertaken as a way of avoiding hell.

Jesus addresses himself to the Hebrew class system which imprisoned his contemporaries: "The servant is not greater than his lord . . . If ye know these things, happy are ye if ye do them." *John 13:16,17* Bible attitudes would not be popular with labor organizations today. John the Baptist advises: "Be content with your wages." *Luke 3:14* Servants have no civil rights in the parables he tells. Speaking of the need to be on watch for the last days, he paraphrases: a servant who, failing to anticipate his master's return, and "shall begin to beat the men servants and maidens, and to eat and drink and be drunken; the lord of that servant will come in a day when he looketh not for him, . . . and will cut him in sunder . . . and that servant, which knew his lord's will, and prepared not himself, neither did according to his will, shall be beaten with many stripes. But he that knew not, and did commit things worthy of stripes, shall be beaten with few stripes." *Luke 12:45–48*

Such scriptures give a vivid impression of Jesus's attitude toward the working class. Their bodies belonged to their masters, who were free to mete out corporal punishment to suit their own sadistic tendencies. The gospels contain much talk of high and low rank. Jesus tells a parable in which the following instruction is offered: "When thou art bidden of any man to a wedding, sit not down in the highest room; lest a more honorable man than thou be bidden of him . . . For whosoever exalteth himself shall be abased; and he that humbleth himself shall be exalted." *Luke 14:8–11* Jesus was prone to take advantage of every opportunity to "put down" people of importance when he was describing Paradise. At other times they are often heroes of his narratives.

Several parts of Jesus's Sermon on the Mount give much consolation to servants, and also the poor. The effect, if not the purpose, of many of the teachings, is to keep the underdogs in their miserable estate and reasonably resigned to it. The poor especially have little chance of acquiring any assets, and Jesus declares their situation hopeless—there will always be poor people. There certainly always will be if Jesus's recommendations for dealing with poverty are followed.

His primary palliative is for the rich to give everything they have to the poor. In spite of the fact that Jesus holds out heaven as the reward for compliance, no one seems to take him seriously, probably not seeing what will be gained by creating a surrogate group of indigents. Having abandoned the poor to their fate, Jesus defends Lazarus's sister when she pours on his head a whole box of "ointment of spikenard very precious." When there is a murmuring that the ointment might have been sold and the proceeds given to the poor, Jesus chides: "Let her alone; why trouble ye her? she hath wrought a good work on me. For ye have the poor with you always . . ." *Mark 14:3–7*

Another time he has kind words for a poor widow who puts two mites in the temple treasury, choosing to ignore the observation of some spectators that it may be unfortunate that the temple to which she has just contributed "all the living that she had" was "adorned with goodly stones and gifts." *Luke 21:1–5*

Jesus sees the poor as objects of charity. They can serve as a stepping stone to Paradise for all those who take pity on them: "But when thou makest a feast, call the poor, the maimed, the lame, the blind: And thou shalt be blessed, for they cannot recompense thee: for thou shalt be recompensed at the resurrection of the just." *Luke 14:13,14* Paul later echoes this sentiment when he says it is better to give than to receive. That may be, but it is also much less humiliating. Neither Paul nor Jesus considers the psychological plight of those who must always be the *objects* of that commendable charity. Their degradation does not detract from the rewards their benefactors will enjoy in the next life.

To be fair, Jesus does seem to indicate that just the fact of being poor will assure one of a place in heaven. He tells a story of a rich man "which was clothed in purple and fine linen" and a beggar at his gate who waits for crumbs from the rich man's table. When the scene changes, the beggar is in Paradise, and the rich man is—in that place where all persons cursed with wealth will eventually be. *Luke 16:19–31* Heaven and hell are not reward and punishment! They are equalizers!

⇒•◇•⇐

That his teaching was intended strictly for the Jews is the obvious conclusion reached from the emphasis Jesus placed on the audience he sought. To the Samaritan woman (Samaritans were descendants of Jews who had intermarried with people of Mesopotamia and Asia Minor) Jesus flatly asserts: "For salvation is of the Jews." *John 4:22* He has little time for the Gentiles, although he occasionally associates with some of them.

An episode related in the scriptures is cruel proof of the fact that the Jews were his chosen audience: Jesus refuses to listen to a Gentile woman (or to answer her) when she begs him to heal her daughter. Pressed, he finally explains: "I am not sent but unto the lost sheep of the house of Israel. It is not meet to take the children's (Jews') bread and to cast it to dogs (Gentiles)." After she further humiliates herself, he finally agrees to heal the child. Not satisfied with being rude and practicing heartless discrimination, he then exploits the occasion by delivering a speech on the power of faith (and persistence?). *Matt. 15:22–28* (Christians worship a God who refused to heal a *sick child*, until he was pressured!)

In John 12:15 it is said that Jesus fulfills the Old Testament prophecy (always does): "Fear not, daughter of *Zion:* behold, *thy* King cometh, sitting on the ass's colt." And Jesus also gives definite instructions to his workers when he sends them out to spread the word: "Go not into the way of the Gentiles . . . but rather to the lost sheep of the House of Israel." *Matt. 10:5,6* At the Last Supper Jesus limits the realm to come: "And I appoint unto you a kingdom . . . that ye may eat and drink at my table in my kingdom and sit on thrones judging the twelve tribes of Israel." *Luke 22:29,30* Just prior to this, he has described the behavior of Gentile kings and told the disciples: "*Ye* shall not be so."

Belatedly the authors of the gospels have Jesus, just before the ascension, instruct the disciples to enlarge the audience: "And he said unto them . . . that repentance and remission of sins should be preached in his name among all nations." But this change of policy must be suspect, for Jesus throughout almost his entire ministry says that he has come as the Messiah of the Jews.

———⟫◆⟪———

Jesus likes to tell stories to prove a point, and these stories the Bible calls parables. He may have gotten the idea from Ezekiel, whose contemporaries remarked upon this habit of his that manifested itself during Ezekiel's few waking hours. The disciples are curious about why Jesus uses this method of communication, and his answer is that *they* may know the *mysteries* of heaven but that others are not given that knowledge—all this in spite of the likelihood that the disciples were not for the most part known for their perceptive qualities. And, of course, they are all men—no woman could be expected to be able to comprehend anything as complex as the mysteries of heaven. And with the disciples and Jesus no longer around, *no one* on earth can, apparently, understand them. (How could Paul?)

From these words of Jesus to the disciples one gathers not only that God is so complicated that he is unfathomable but that favoritism is shown in the revelation of the intricacies of everything pertaining to the divine: "Therefore speak I to them in parables: because they seeing see not; and hearing they hear not, neither do they understand." *Matt. 13:13* Why bother to preach at all, if it is futile? Not to mention the put-down of his contemporaries by a "man" who is himself apparently not well-educated and whose intelligence is poorly-rated by his neighbors and fellow-citizens: "And the Jews (of his hometown) marvelled, saying, How knoweth this man letters, having never learned?" *John 7:15* and *Mark 4:33*

Jesus as much as says that people can't understand anything but storytelling. Even so, several of the parables are foggy and meaningless, so much so that even the privileged disciples have to ask for explanations: "His disciples came unto him saying, Declare unto us the parable of the tares of the field." *Matt. 13:36* Jesus also admits that he speaks in parables to fulfill a prophecy. *Matt. 13:35* There must be *some* reason to speak in such a manner that the truth is obscured.

The contents of the parables are frequently characterized by violence and injustice. Jesus does not disapprove of social conditions inherent in the contents as long as they make a point. E.g., Jesus tells a parable about a king who *sells* a man who owes him money and at the same time *sells* the debtor's wife and children. Although he uses the parable to make some comment on forgiveness, Jesus expresses no moral indignation whatever toward the selling into slavery of human beings. *Matt. 18* Another time he tells a story of an employer who becomes angry at the protests of workmen who receive the same pay for working all day as those who work one hour. The employer is supposed to represent the kingdom of heaven where "the last shall be first and the first last." *Matt. 20:16* No unfairness is attributed to the employer by Jesus, even though the employer arbitrarily states that he will pay as he pleases. Jesus seems to feel that such an attitude is just.

If rewards in the next world are as inequitably distributed, it would seem repentance at the last minute would be the wise course to follow. This same unfairness is inherent in the parable of the prodigal son. *Luke 15* Certainly any father would be happy to see a philandering son return to the fold at long last, but his prejudice, while understandable, is hardly admirable, and the loyal son would have just cause for indignation.

One of the most violent and unfair of the parables and one of the most far-fetched is the story of the marriage feast which servants do not wish to attend and for which reluctance they are massacred. This grisly tale continues, as "guests" are forced in from the street to view the wedding rites. One such kidnapped soul who understandably is not attired in a wedding suit is bound and cast into darkness for being improperly clad. *Matt. 22:1–14* The moral of this tale of atrocities is again that many are called but few are chosen!

That Jesus should use such reprehensible deeds to illustrate his principles tells the reader something of his personality. Episodes of bestial behavior and occasions for revenge have a fascination for him. Such an impression is compounded not only by his choice of material but to an even greater degree by a realization that he feels no repugnance for it. The performers in some of his parables are liars, assassins, wealthy oppressors, ingrates, con-artists, slave-beaters and slave-merchants, autocrats, and torturers. Victims of the wickedness present in all this do not win Jesus's sympathy. They are pawns in the literary conceit he has chosen to employ, and he occasionally endorses the villain of the piece. The parable that tells of the householder and the husbandmen in Matthew 21 is especially gory.

Even the parable of the Good Samaritan is about highway muggers. Here again there seems to be acceptance of the crime, and Jesus ignores the racist bigotry of the Jews of his day, who made it unlawful to associate with Gentiles and despised Samaritans. The point he seems to belabor here is that the object of the racism is to be commended for not harboring resentment.

After completing one of these gruesome sermonettes, Jesus usually departs abruptly, leaving his audience to contemplate as much on the horrid details as on the murky moral.

At the conclusion of one parable, the final words of a nobleman (!) are: "Unto everyone which hath shall be given; and from him that hath not, even that he hath shall be taken away from him. But those mine enemies, which would not that I should reign over them, bring hither, and slay them before me." Jesus invents this parable to illustrate his own philosophy, and he deliberately puts these words into the mouth of a despot who is punishing his servant (slave) for an honest error in judgment, an error which represented a financial loss to his master. This king's retaliatory treatment of the erring servant, and his concluding edict proclaiming death by the sword for any disobedient subject, has been described by Jesus to serve as an illustration of recommended behavior. (This nobleman had become the ruler of his "enemies" by going into a far country to "receive for himself a kingdom.") *Luke 19:11–27*

In several of the parables one looks in vain for any compassion and understanding, for any trace of ordinary human kindness. The humans aren't very kind, and the story-teller doesn't come off very well, either. These parables are brutalizing. They cannot be told to children (which is why Sunday Schools must dwell on Old Testament fairy tales and Jesus the Magician). In no way can they ennoble. Even hardened adults will shudder at their ferocity, and sensitive readers will look elsewhere for inspiration.

The few women who appear in the stories Jesus tells are usually victims of slave-masters and kings, but at least one parable mirrors the position held by women in Palestine. *Ten virgins* await their one bridegroom, but five of them fail to bring extra oil for their lamps and have gone to buy more when the tardy bridegroom arrives. These "foolish" virgins implore the bridegroom, sequestered with the other five: "Lord, Lord, open to us." He, self-righteous to a fault, makes a very formal reply, under the circumstances: "Verily I say unto you, I know you not." Jesus is the steely fellow, for whose arrival at the end of the world all must be prepared. *Matt. 25:1–13* This allegory is played out by Christian congregations in which at a certain age young girls become "brides of the Church."

When Jesus is not proclaiming his divinity to anyone who will listen, he enigmatically sometimes conceals it and asks others to do so: "Then charged he his disciples that they should tell no man that he was Jesus the Christ." *Matt. 16:20* After his transfiguration, he cautions: "Tell the vision to no man, until the Son of man be risen again from the dead." *Matt 17:9* Again, upon another occasion: "And he straitly charged them that they should not make him known." *Mark 3:12* At times, after performing miracles, he asks for secrecy: "And he charged them straitly that no man should know it." These were his orders after he had raised the daughter of the synagogue ruler from the dead. *Mark 5:43*

Following the healing of a deaf mute: "He charged them that they should tell no man: but the more he charged them, so much the more a great deal they published it." *Mark 7:36* Perhaps in that admonishment lies the chief purpose behind the pretended desire for secrecy. There are two other possible reasons for Jesus's request that healings not be aired about. One is fear for his life and another is to keep doubt at a minimum.

Whatever the reason, the secrecy itself is contrary to his command: "Let your light so shine before men that they may see your good works, and glorify your Father which is in heaven." *Matt. 5:16* And the following claim of his would seem to belie hiding his light under a bushel: "The works that I do in my Father's name, they bear witness of me." *John 10:25*

⟫•◈•⟪

Despite belief to the contrary prevalent today, Jesus was not a booster for family life. In the scriptures he treats his mother and siblings with something less than affection and respect. He does not marry or father children. After laying down rules about adultery and divorce, he proceeds to predict some rather astonishing effects that belief in him will have upon the family as an institution: "For I am come to set a man at variance against his father, and the daughter against her mother, and the daughter in law against her mother in law. And a man's foes shall be they of his own household." *Matt. 10:35,36* From the time he is 12 years old and doesn't bother to tell his mother that he is remaining in the temple, he seems to have no close ties to his family and discourages his converts from having any with theirs.

He demands that they drop everything immediately to become his followers: "And he said unto another, Follow me. But he said, Lord, suffer me first to go and bury my father. Jesus said unto him, Let the dead bury their dead . . . And another also said, Lord, I will follow thee; but first let me go bid them farewell, which are at home at my house. And Jesus said unto him, No man, having put his hand to the plough, and looking back, is fit for the kingdom of God." *Luke 9:59–62* Two of his disciples actually leave their father mending the fishing nets. *Matt. 4:21,22*

It is a real puzzle where Christians today get their exalted view of the Christian family. And few Bible readers will understand the worshipful position accorded to Mary, for Jesus was rude to his mother at the marriage feast: "Woman, what have I to do with thee?" *John 2:1–4* And he was even more uncivil when she and his brothers waited at the edge of a crowd to speak to him, posing a question to his disciples: "Who is my mother? And who are my brethren?" and indicating that the disciples were now his family. *Matt. 12:46–49* Then he added that all who do the will of God, "the same is my brother, and sister, and mother."

The attitude of Jesus toward women in general is ambiguous in the extreme. At times he seems to regard them as they exist under the Mosaic law. Again, he upholds them. Sexism on his part cannot be condoned, since he supposedly came to earth as the moral example for all time to come, and bias that prevailed in the treatment of women during the period of time he spent as a human being should not have influenced him to conform to it. Although such treatment might have been the custom of that day, Jesus's behavior standards should surely have been timeless.

He has a touching scene with *children*, in which they get just about as high an approval rating as it is possible to award, since everyone else is cautioned to be as naive as they are, but woman receives little praise and that only when she is performing some act of servitude, such as pouring oil on Jesus's head or washing his feet and drying them with her hair, or even giving her last mite to the poor. *Mark 14:3–9 John 12:3* Or not ceasing to *kiss* Jesus's feet. *Luke 7:45*

It's what Jesus *doesn't* say that is more a key to his attitude toward women than what he says or does. For instance, he doesn't say that Eve was wrongly blamed, he doesn't say that the Mosaic law is cruelly demeaning of women, he doesn't say that women need not submit to their husbands in everything, he doesn't say that wives may ever divorce their husbands or marry again if their husbands divorce them for "fornication," he doesn't say that there are no witches and in any case they should not be burnt to death, he doesn't say that a hapless girl thought not to be a virgin when she is wed should not be stoned or burnt to death (and her despoiler go free), he doesn't say that ten virgins should not belong to one bridegroom.

The gospel of John tells a story of a woman caught "in the very act" of adultery, who is brought before Jesus in the temple. The self-righteous scribes and Pharisees, whom Jesus habitually labels adulterous, prepare to stone her according to the Mosaic law. Jesus looks up from scratching in the dirt with his finger and admonishes: "He that is without sin among you, let him first cast a stone at her." *John 8:7* These scribes and Pharisees, as well as most other Hebrew men, did not think of themselves as sinners, so it was a risky proposition that really changed nothing about the status of women in Jewish society of the time.

It would have been a wonderfully opportune occasion for Jesus, since he was surrounded by people listening to him teach, to have spoken out against the inexcusable cruelty of a law that would kill a woman in an excruciating way for a minor "sin" that was indulged in by even the temple priests. By not doing so, he failed to protect any other women in a similar situation, who might even be falsely accused. He had succeeded only in saying: Judge not.

Jesus was not moved to inquire about the other partner in the act, who had been permitted to go free, and he asked for no details, such as whether the woman had been a victim of force or held at knife point. It is all too obvious that Jesus spoke the truth when he said he came to uphold the law of Moses.

He makes snide remarks about harlots and, according to John 4:29, he knows every woman's marital status and sexual secrets, but he is big-hearted about female sexual peccadilloes and frequently blames them on possession of women's bodies by devils, which he expels. In Jesus's eye, as with his contemporaries, the *man* is seldom at fault in any sexual situation, and the woman has to promise never to be naughty again.

It must be concluded that Jesus was the usual male chauvinist of his day. Although he travelled about with women, none was a disciple, and none will sit at his table in heaven. Finally, it is clear that he shared the sexist conviction of Jewish men of Bible days that sexual relations with women were unholy, for he gives extra commendation to eunuchs, especially those who castrate themselves "for the kingdom of heaven's sake." *Matt. 19:12*

⇒•◆•⇐

At times Jesus gives cryptic answers and at times he is very wrong. When certain church elders among the Jews ask by what authority he preaches, a natural enough question, he replies by in turn asking them a question which puts them on the spot in such a way that they refuse to answer it. His verbal shrug follows: "Neither tell I you by what authority I do these things." *Matt 21:27* Most of the time he is repeatedly naming God as his authority, without even being asked.

In another instance, when asked for a sign, although he habitually describes many happenings as signs and can hardly make a move without declaring it a sign, he says to the Pharisees and scribes: "An evil and adulterous generation seeketh after a sign; and there shall be no sign given to it, but the sign of the prophet Jonas." *Matt. 12:39* By this answer Jesus says he meant that he would be in the earth three days just as Jonah was in the whale's belly three days. Actually, Jesus was to be in the grave a little over one day and two nights.

Cryptic replies to earnest questions when it would seem clarity would better serve a sincere advocate are difficult to justify. They are in the same key as some of Jesus's behavior and instructions, often mysterious, and the gospels are packed with discrepancies and errors concerning him. Perhaps the most obvious error that can be attributed to Jesus's teaching and ministry, however, has to lie in his prediction that he would return to earth within a very short time and before his generation should pass away.

⇒•◇•⇐

The manner in which Jesus chooses his disciples is incomprehensible and surely open to criticism when one considers that care and discrimination would ordinarily be shown at such a time. Apparently he picks them up, total strangers or at the most mere acquaintances, as he is strolling about the countryside. Several are fishermen, one is a publican, and that is about all one is given to know about them. The gospels do not even agree upon their names. One is left to wonder what Jesus knew about their background and to conclude he wasn't interested in finding out very much about them. That one of them proves less than loyal is not surprising.

Jesus himself loses patience with the disciples several times for their lack of faith, failure to understand, and inability to perform miracles. He is driven to cursing them and calling them names. Not exactly a model of patience himself, he vents his wrath upon them: "O faithless and perverse generation, how long shall I suffer you?" *Matt. 17:17* Acts 4:13 says they were "unlearned and ignorant men."

One gospel gives a list of their names but not of their occupations, although most seem to be of humble origin, admittedly uneducated and simple, thus readily fitting into the ideal mold for Christians as outlined by Jesus and later by the apostles. They seem to be completely irresponsible, for they traipse along with a total stranger (?) at a moment's notice, dropping everything, quitting their employment, gathering no belongings, not worried about a livelihood, and not permitted by Jesus to say goodbye to their families or make provisions for them. The two brothers who abandon their father in the fishing boat don't give him a backward look.

Although they are unable to understand Jesus at times, he doesn't hesitate to tell them that they are privileged to have knowledge of spiritual enigmas that cannot be mastered by others. And their possibly rather limited mental capacities will not preclude their enthronement in heaven as the judges of the Jews. When Jesus sends them and 70 other followers out as missionaries to those fellow Jews, he instructs them to sponge off friends and sympathizers for food and lodging, as he does. It is possible to be even nervier, and Jesus is, criticizing his hostess Martha for working in the kitchen (probably preparing a spur-of-the-moment repast for her unexpected guest) instead of listening to an egotistical Jesus utter words about mansions in heaven, in the kitchens of which she has a hunch she is really going to be stuck.

Since not only the disciples but most if not all of the leaders of the new sect are probably, to put it generously, not exactly pillars of wisdom, it is to be expected that Jesus will gear his preaching to all who are willing to become child-like and to accept him on faith that requires the abandonment of reason and of truth: "Verily I say unto you, Except . . . ye become as little children, ye shall not enter into the kingdom of heaven." *Matt. 18:3* Jesus makes a further case for ignorance: "I thank thee, O Father . . . that thou hast hid these things from the wise and prudent, and has revealed them unto babes." *Luke 10:21* Education and knowledge gained from maturity lead to eternal damnation, because they threaten blind faith, and achievement in this world assures one a place far down on the class scale in heaven, as the first shall be last and the last shall be first.

The faith of the disciples in Jesus as the Messiah is so precarious, even after months of close association with him, that their belief does not solidify until they are partaking of the Last Supper: "Now are we sure that thou knowest all things, and needest not that any man should ask thee: by this we believe that thou camest forth from God. Jesus answered them, Do ye now believe?" *John 16:30,31* The final days of destiny give the disciples an opportunity to show themselves to be men of integrity, but they desert Jesus to a man, after one of them betrays him.

Peter comes off the worst, and his three-times denial of Jesus is reminiscent of two former occasions when Jesus lost his temper with Simon Peter: "Get thee behind me, Satan: thou art an offence unto me." *Matt. 16:23* But Jesus says he will build his church upon Peter, even though Peter is not the most beloved of Jesus, and Jesus knows in advance that Peter will deny him three times.

Women follow Jesus and the disciples from city to city (fan-club groupies?) and Jesus, if he had been a good judge of character, should have made some of them disciples, as they courageously remain loyal and believing, coming to the scene of the crucifixion and meeting Jesus the morning of the resurrection. They received few accolades, but the snivelling, cowardly disciples sit on heavenly thrones.

⟹⬦⬤

"For I am meek and lowly in heart." *Matt.* 11:29 Jesus may have thought of himself that way, but these are not adjectives which come to mind when reading the account of his ministry in the gospels. He continually makes it abundantly clear that he has been sent by God, is God, and will return in clouds of glory to claim a kingdom. That's meek?

He has no patience whatsoever with anyone who doesn't listen to him and unhesitatingly pronounce him the Messiah, although some pretenders at the time claim the same title. Others have continued to do so. He even warns of false Messiahs, so it is not to be wondered at that the Jews wanted a little proof, especially the priesthood which he was trying to unseat or reform.

He calls unbelievers fools, wicked, perverse, adulterous, and "whited sepulchres" and with relish assigns them to eternal torment. If his contemporaries believed with the ease he expected of them, the Jews probably would have accepted a Messiah long before Jesus appeared on the scene. To anticipate instant belief and welcome on their part was naive and showed little understanding of human nature by Jesus. His quick temper, impatience, and resort to violence on occasion, along with his contemplation on the fate of the unbelievers, sometimes make it impossible for the love to show through, although the gospel of John tries to smooth it all over and give the world a Savior full of loving compassion.

Christianity was established by the sword, and Jesus brought it: "I came not to send peace but a sword." *Matt.* 10:34 The Jews had a history of violence, and Jesus was well-versed in that history. He doesn't hesitate to pick up a whip and drive the merchants and moneychangers from the temple area. These capitalists were assigned a permanent place in the temple courtyard where they sold pigeons and animals for the sacrifices demanded under the Mosaic law, as a convenience to worshippers. Far better if Jesus had condemned the whole idea of the useless slaughter of innocent creatures to appease a vindictive Jehovah.

He calls all who pray on street corners hypocrites, but ministers pray in public today, even at football games, and no doubt some of them are sincere; surely not all are "serpents" and "vipers." They might be incensed at being so described.

Another show of temper and violence occurs on a walking trip when Jesus, suddenly hungry, finds a fig tree bearing no fruit (Mark 11:13 says it is out of season). Furious, Jesus curses it: *"Let no fruit grow on thee hencefor-ward forever."* The innocent tree proceeds to wither away on the spot. *Matt. 21:19*

Not satisfied to downgrade *individuals* who don't believe, Jesus damns whole cities which fail to put out the welcome mat: "Woe unto thee, Chorazin! Woe unto thee, Bethsaida! . . . And thou, Capernaum . . . shalt be brought down to hell." *Matt. 11:20–23* All of this hardly sounds like the "Prince of Peace."

Any humility which might surface is properly smothered in such pro-nouncements as: "In this place is one greater than the temple." *Matt. 12:6* And: "Behold, a greater than Jonas is here." *Matt. 12:41* And: "Behold, a greater than Solomon is here." *Matt. 12:42* These are all words spoken by Jesus to describe himself.

Afore-mentioned parables of horrendous bloodiness and pointless bru-tality fall from the lips of this self-proclaimed deity and would match any presentation on television today; yet Christian groups trying to sanitize cur-rent entertainment keep the Bible accessible to all ages.

⟹•◇•⟸

Jesus is addicted to making rash promises which involve conditions and occurrences contrary to what most people regard as natural laws. Such seem-ing order is sufficient evidence for many persons to envision some sort of supernatural being. Some consider it to be, for them, the *supreme* evidence. Jesus seems to fail to understand that reliance upon so-called miracles might tend to foster doubt and questioning about whether a hoax could have been perpetrated. "Unnatural" happenings depend for their verification on wit-nesses, whose reliability, of necessity, is open to doubt. Witnesses may be vic-tims of their imaginations, gullibility, or intentions, or even of poor eyesight and faulty hearing, and they may not be accurate reporters.

Perhaps Jesus does realize that miracles arouse suspicion in rational minds, and thus his insistence upon faith and child-like confidence. Categorically, at any rate, he assures: "Whatsoever ye shall ask the Father in my name, he will give it you." *John 16:23* He proceeds to elaborate upon this by saying that faith as large as a mustard seed will move mountains. But bull-dozers and dynamite are still being manufactured, and few have seen a large mound of earth and rock moved without them. The idea that any favor sin-cerely requested of God will be granted is rather frightening, and one can only hope that all requests are of a benevolent nature. The validity of the promise would surely be put to the test should two mustard-seed faith-pos-sessors want an identical mountain moved in opposite directions at the same time.

A God whose mind is so easily influenced is a God without plan or wisdom or ability to see into the future, a God who, contrary to some scripture, *is* after all changeable. Such a deity precludes any conception of order in the universe, although human experience has been that some kind of order and natural law exist.

Besides giving his disciples, and 70 other appointed missionaries, the ability to raise from the dead and drive out those elusive evil spirits, Jesus gets carried away and expands: "Behold, I give unto you power to tread on serpents and scorpions . . . and nothing shall by any means hurt you." *Luke 10:19* Just before he is taken up into heaven, he goes even further: "In my name shall they (the saved) cast out devils; they shall speak with new tongues; They shall take up serpents; and if they drink any deadly thing, it shall not hurt them; and they shall lay hands on the sick, and they shall recover." *Mark 16:17,18*

Unrealistic claims such as these, added to the suggestion that becoming a eunuch is considered worthy in the kingdom of heaven (*Matt. 19:12*) and that offending eyes should be plucked out, sinful hands and feet chopped off, and families forsaken (*Matt. 19:29*), have led to lonely lives spent in monasteries and convents, self-mutilation, faith healers, and weird cults among those who take these words literally, and to apologetic shrugs among those who pick and choose what they consider to be practical and admirable in the teachings of Jesus. Thousands of suicides and willing martyrs, taking the promises and instructions of Jesus seriously, sought to assure themselves of a heavenly abode. Many even included their children in this plan for salvation.

⇒◆⇐

Christians like to speak of being "born again" in the "spirit" and many say it is a universal requirement for that "pie in the sky." True, Jesus does make that assertion, but, as he often does, he then contradicts himself and says: "I came not to call the righteous, but sinners to repentance." *John 3:3* and *Mark 2:17* Many times his actions are opposed to his teaching, some blatantly so, such as shortly after telling listeners not to call anyone a fool (*Matt. 5:22*), he himself says to his pet targets, the scribes and Pharisees: "Ye fools and blind." *Matt. 23:17*

At least once he is intentionally devious. His brothers plan to attend the Feast of the Tabernacles in Jerusalem and urge Jesus to accompany them and perform some of his miracles. Unbelievers in him themselves ("For neither did his brethren believe in him."), they suggest that he "shew himself to the world." But Jesus, saying his time has not yet come, tells his brothers to go without him, leading them to believe he does not plan to attend. After they leave, however: "Then went he also up unto the feast, not openly, but as it were in secret." He preaches there in the temple, but he is not captured for the same reason that his time has not yet come. *John 7:2–14* It is little wonder there is so much disagreement about the character of Jesus that arguments persist, even among theologians.

His teaching of the need to be born again denies the ability of God to create perfection at the first attempt; all born of God are imperfect and need to be improved. Since heaven was the scene of civil war and considering that the first generations of humankind had to be destroyed as faulty, God begins to come across as a consummate blunderer. Actually, Paul implies that rebirth is meaningless, when he says the New Jerusalem is populated by the "firstborn," who have always been of the "elect." *Hebrews 12:22,23* Predestination scripture negates any need for rebirth.

<hr />

The span of human lifetime has increased greatly since Bible days. Some persons are living even into their nineties, and they are spending those years in a material world and environment. Adjustment to that world so that reasonable contentment if not enjoyment is possible would seem to be of necessary concern to material bodies requiring material things. Yet Jesus teaches that life here on earth is of secondary (actually *little*) importance and that all time and energy should be expended in preparation for an ill-defined eternal existence in heaven.

The small amount of information about the reward he holds out for abandoning earthly pursuits seems to suffice for Christians. He tells them that they will be subjects of a kingdom where some will be greater than others (just like earthly monarchies) and that all will be able to see him. Other than that, Jesus lets the chief attraction of heaven be that it is not hell.

The instinct of self-preservation is so strong in humanity that any promise that abolishes death "has a wondrous attraction" for them, as the old hymn observes. The idea that existence of any sort should continue *forever,* though, would seem to be mind-boggling, if not terrifying, and can Christians be happy in this world living in fear that loved ones are damned? Or will the ecstasy of heaven be all the more intense as the saved contemplate their better fate in contrast to that of their more unfortunate fellows? The Revelation says they will shout Alleluia. *Rev. 19:3*

One must keep in mind when reading the admonitions of Jesus that he labored under the illusion that life in this world was nearly over for everyone. Just as soon as he finished preparing those mansions, he intended to come back and gather up the saints, or let the angels do it. So perhaps the following statements of his are understandable, after all: "He that hateth his life in this world shall keep it unto life eternal." *John 12:25* "And every one that hath forsaken houses, or brethren, or sisters, or father, or mother, or wife, or children, or lands, for my name's sake, shall receive an hundredfold and shall inherit everlasting life." *Matt. 19:29* "Whosoever he be of you that forsaketh not all that he hath, he cannot be my disciple." *Luke 14:33* (Why such contempt for the world that God created?)

Jesus discourages any ambition other than this attainment of future reward: "For what is a man advantaged, if he gain the whole world, and lose himself . . . ?" *Luke 9:25* Any position of importance achieved in this world will be a liability in the next, for "the first shall be last." Jesus outlines the goal of every Christian: "Seek ye first the kingdom of God." *Matt. 6:33*

⋗◆⋖

Luke traces Jesus's genealogy through 75 generations back to Adam (although anthropologists have found evidence that human beings were around a bit previous to that time). Jesus claims, however, that he existed before the world began. It is incomprehensible that Jesus as God should even have a genealogy, but it was necessary, to establish him as the Messiah, that his ancestry should extend to David, at least. Jesus as both divine and the heir (by succession) to the throne of a reunited Jewish nation is a throwback to pagan human-god mysticism, but the Jews have refused to accept him as either God or king. (The Hebrew Messiah is nowhere *clearly* defined as to concept in the Bible.)

⋗◆⋖

At times Jesus must have exuded charm and authority, for he is said to attract *multitudes* and worshipful followers of both sexes. Far from having the gentle personality traditionally attributed to him, however, he is often overbearing and condescending in the scriptures, with traits not usually associated with the sublime deity of love and compassion. Although he does exhibit these latter traits at times, an impartial student of his sometime behavior might apply other adjectives to the Jesus of the Bible: impatient, heartless, imperious, vengeful, vain, rude, misinformed, quick-tempered, inconsistent, given to violence upon occasion, smug, and scornful. From the gospels, the reader can fashion a Jesus to his or her liking.

A parasite upon society during his ministry, he is at the same time a welcome guest. He is appealing, and he repels. He soothes, and he stirs up. He makes sense, and he rants. He weeps at the death of a friend, and he consigns untold numbers of his "children" to *eternal* torment. He curses his disciples, and they lean on him lovingly. He gives good advice, and he recommends impractical behavior. He loves, and he has "enemies." He brings the Word, and he comes with a sword. He bears a promise of joy, and he bestows a terrible burden—fear and guilt.

—————◆◆◆—————

Several hundred years, which saw much controversy (even persecution) over the identity and doctrines of Jesus, produced the final New Testament, although even then not one acceptable to all. And the final agreement upon the Creeds had brought the warring factions into a semblance of a whole, which has not prevented almost continuous formation of sects whose adherents translate the faith as they see it into various rules for sipping, nibbling, kneeling, sprinkling, dunking, babbling, fasting, tithing, ring-kissing, bell-ringing, healing, snake-handling, self-chastising, aisle-rolling, confessing, and supplicating, the lot linked up with other complex guidelines for dress and diet, ad infinitum.

—————◆◆◆—————

Metaphorical and analogical descriptions of himself are characteristic of Jesus's preaching. In the gospel of John, alone, he uses over 20 complimentary cognomens:

THE SON OF MAN	1:51
THE SON OF GOD	3:18
LIVING WATER	4:14
SPIRIT	4:24
THE MESSIAH	4:26
CHRIST	4:26
A PROPHET	4:44
THE BREAD OF LIFE	6:35
LIGHT OF THE WORLD	9:5
THE DOOR	10:9
GOOD SHEPHERD	10:11
GOD	10:30
THE RESURRECTION AND THE LIFE	11:25
THE WAY, THE TRUTH, AND THE LIFE	14:6
PRINCE OF THIS WORLD	12:31
MASTER	13:13
LORD	13:13
SPIRIT OF TRUTH	14:17
HOLY GHOST	14:26
THE COMFORTER	14:26
THE TRUE VINE	15:1
THE HUSBANDMAN	15:1

—————◆◆◆—————

Many of the behavior rules laid down by Jesus are guilty of an impractical morality that would make of human beings spineless, passionless, unresponsive robots. Some of the more traditional rules for good conduct, if not all, are borrowed from the Mosaic law and from the book of Proverbs, which may have been appropriated from the Gentiles, and from philosophers such as Confucius, Plato, and Aristotle, who lived a few hundred years before Christ.

Jesus softened some of the harsher demands of the Mosaic law, stiffened the one about divorce, and got into trouble when he undermined the authority of the Jewish tribal priesthood. The Sermon on the Mount (or on the Plain, where Luke 6:17 locates it) contains most of Jesus's moral precepts and is so long it is thought to be a summary of several dissertations. To follow these precepts literally one would have to be a person practicing no discrimination or evaluation based upon reason or experience.

Here are some ways Jesus tells people to act:

1. Accumulate no wealth or possessions. There is no need for them. Besides you would run the risk of getting rich. If you do, be sure to give it all away.

2. Make no plans. Give no thought to the morrow. Do not buy groceries or cook. Don't buy patterns or sew. Just stand there like a lily. God will feed and clothe you.

3. Be gloomy and mournful.

4. Be self-righteous and put-upon, holier than thou. Parade your perfection in such a way as to invite persecution.

5. Be smug and know that you are the salt of the earth and the light of the world. Let everybody know this.

6. Do behave so you can be high up in the class system in heaven.

7. Think of yourself as a gross sinner. Nearly every thought you have and almost everything you do must be regarded as a sin that will require repentance and forgiveness.

8. Take no pleasure in this world. Constantly point toward the kingdom of God, the coming of which is imminent.

9. Be sure to *believe* that someone else bought your way into heaven by being tortured to death, a death in which you had a hand. Be comfortable in that concept of salvation.

10. Agree with everyone else.

11. Don't admit to having sexual urges. If a sight of a member of the opposite sex arouses you, pluck out your eye.

12. Be a eunuch, if you want to win special approval of God.

13. Don't have *deep* love for your family. Abandon them, if you want to receive an "hundredfold" and attain everlasting life in heaven for sure.

14. Be retiring, do not lead, take a back seat, do not assert yourself. Be a jellyfish. Do not be proud of your accomplishments.

15. Love everybody. Have no special feeling for those who might otherwise endear themselves to you.

16. If a criminal robs you of $50, give him another $50.

17. Don't use your reason or your mind. Remain as a child, with no moral sense, ability to discriminate or make rational decisions, or experience to guide you.

18. Be gullible and credulous. Do not question or philosophize.

19. Don't resist any attacker. Let him abuse you again.

20. If you lose a lawsuit, pay double what you are assessed.

21. If someone kidnaps you and takes you five miles, offer to go ten.

22. Love all those who mistreat you. This will encourage them to continue, since they have now discovered how to win your admiration and affection.

23. Don't declare your charitable giving for income tax credit.

24. Avoid the "dogs" and "swine" of this world. Save your uplifting thoughts for worthy persons.

25. Don't worry or rebel at misfortune (which will be your special lot). Be content and passive, confident you have a heavenly father who loves you so much that if you don't grovel, he'll throw you into a furnace (lake?) of fire forever.

26. Behave as you please most of your life and say you're sorry at the end. That way you'll get your reward before more exemplary persons at the seat of judgment.

27. Do not achieve prominence in this world, for the first shall be last in the next.

28. For special approbation, refrain from eating, pour oil on your head, and wash your face. Then take a gift to the church.

⇒•◇•⇐

Jesus spoke many harsh words. Several examples follow:

1. "Ye serpents, ye generation of vipers, how can ye escape the damnation of hell?" (To the scribes and Pharisees) *Matt. 23:33*

2. "Woman, what have I to do with thee?" (To his mother) *John 2:4*

3. "O faithless and perverse generation, how long shall I suffer you?" (To the disciples) *Matt. 17:17*

4. "Who is my mother, and who are my brethren?" (To the disciples when his family waits to speak to him) *Matt. 12:48*

5. "Let the dead bury their dead." (To a disciple who wants to bury his father) *Matt. 8:22*

6. "Woe unto thee, Chorazin! Woe unto thee, Bethsaida! . . . And thou, Capernaum . . . shalt be brought down to hell." (To unfriendly cities) *Matt. 11:21–23*

7. "An evil and adulterous generation." (Of the scribes and Pharisees) *Matt. 12:39*

8. "And he that hath no sword, let him sell his garment, and buy one." (To the disciples at the Last Supper) *Luke 22:36*

9. "And whosoever shall not receive you . . . when ye depart out of that house or city, shake off the dust of your feet." (To the disciples) *Matt. 10:14*

10. "And the brother shall deliver up the brother to death, and the father the child: and the children shall rise up against their parents, and cause them to be put to death." (Speaking of the dissension to be caused by Christianity) *Matt. 10:21*

11. "But whosoever shall deny me before men, him will I also deny before my Father . . . Think not that I am come to send peace on earth: I came not to send peace but a sword. For I am come to set a man at variance against his father, and the daughter against her mother, and the daughter in law against her mother in law. And a man's foes shall be they of his own household." *Matt. 10:33–36*

12. "O generation of vipers, how can ye, being evil, speak good things?" (To the Pharisees) *Matt. 12:34*

13. "The Son of man shall send forth his angels, and they shall gather . . . all them which do iniquity; and shall cast them into a furnace of fire: there shall be wailing and gnashing of teeth." *Matt. 13:41,42*

14. "I am not sent but unto the lost sheep of the house of Israel . . . It is not meet to take the children's (Jews') bread, and cast it to dogs (Gentiles)." (To a Canaanite woman who asks him to heal her child) *Matt. 15:26*

15. "Wherefore if thy hand or foot offend thee, cut them off, and cast them from thee: it is better for thee to enter into life halt or maimed, rather than having two hands or two feet to be cast into everlasting fire. And if thine eye offend thee, pluck it out." *Matt. 18:8,9*

16. "Let no fruit grow on thee henceforward forever." (To a fig tree that bore no fruit out of season) *Matt. 21:19*

17. "Woe unto you that laugh now! for ye shall mourn and weep." and "Woe unto you, when all men shall speak well of you!" (To a multitude) *Luke 6:25,26*

18. "Ye fools and blind." (To the scribes and Pharisees) *Matt. 23:17*

19. "And woe unto them that are with child, and to them that give suck in those days." (Speaking of the last days) *Matt. 24:19*

20. "For, behold, the days are coming in the which they shall say, Blessed are the barren, and the wombs that never bare, and the paps which never

gave suck." (To his female friends, warning them of the last days) *Luke 23:29*

21. "Then shall he (the Son of man) say also unto them on the left hand, Depart from me, ye cursed, into everlasting fire, prepared for the devil and his angels." *Matt. 25:41*

22. "Get thee behind me, Satan: thou art an offence unto me." (To Peter) *Matt. 16:23*

23. "If a man abide not in me, he is cast forth as a branch . . . and men cast them into the fire, and they are burned." *John 15:6* These words became the justification (command!) for burning heretics alive.

⟫◇⟪

According to the Bible, Jesus and the devil are in constant competition for the "souls" of humankind. So the legends behind Christian theology imply and so Jesus himself teaches. He repeatedly warns against Satan and temptation, and he dies to bring about Satan's death. If this goal had been achieved, all who lived after Jesus's death would have been saved, but a literal or figurative devil is still very much alive and active in Christian dogma.

The Bible implies that Satan has a large host of angels or spirits at his command, dedicated to the task of abetting human beings in disobeying or disbelieving God. The Bible reader must ask himself or herself which is the more powerful today—Jesus or Satan (if all persons who are not Christians are considered to be in the hands of the devil). Although the largest single religion, Christianity in its three divisions of Eastern Orthodoxy, Roman Catholicism, and Protestantism, claims only about one-fourth of the world's population today. That leaves approximately three billion people alive at the present time, including all members of other religions, destined for hell. And the fastest-growing religion today is Islam.

The devil of the Bible was able to change himself into a snake, bring sin into the world and turn every human creature away from God, and make it necessary for a Supreme Deity to be tortured and killed. He could perform miracles—fly through the air, transport God to the tip of a steeple, find a mountain that overlooked the entire earth, possess that world and offer it to God in return for his allegiance, and get into people's bodies and speak aloud. He made the earth to tremble and shook kingdoms, made the world a wilderness and destroyed cities. He challenged God and escaped from the "pit."

The lesson of the New Testament is that Satan made everyone evil, and God had to come up with a scheme to redeem man from Satan's clutches. But so far Satan is still far ahead, and if Jesus should return today, he would be able to claim for his kingdom only one person for every three belonging to Satan, even assuming that every Christian will be saved.

The existence of hell, as long as it has even one occupant, attests to the victory of Satan over God. And as of today, Satan is three times as powerful as God in the struggle for the souls of his own creatures. Chains may await Satan, but he will share them with most of humankind, according to the Christian Bible.

The victories that *are* won by God through Jesus must be gained entirely by the sole efforts of those who believe in the sacrifice described in the New Testament, since God either cannot or does not choose to banish Satan and sin from the earth by himself.

⟹⟶◆⟵⟸

A direct corollary can be drawn between Jesus as Savior and the tradition of Judaism and the Mosaic law whereby the sins of the congregation of Israelites could be expiated by transferring them to an animal, which was then put to death on the altar. *Lev. 4:13–21*

Jesus may also be seen as the embodiment of the primitive practice of transferring the sins of a group to an animal or human scapegoat which then was banished or even put to death as a means of expelling all past wrongdoing committed by members of a society, a custom which often took place once a year at the beginning or end of a season. That animal or human being was sometimes endowed with divinity, and thus a man-god might die as a scapegoat and become a "redeemer." The Jewish Day of Atonement on the tenth day of the seventh month of every year was ordered by God to be set aside for a ceremony wherein the priest (originally Aaron) should "lay both his hands upon the live goat, and confess over him all the iniquities of the children of Israel, and all their transgressions in all their sins, putting them upon the head of the goat, and shall send him away by the hand of a fit man into the wilderness." *Lev. 16:21*

Mythology documents many pagan customs involving the killing and "resurrection" of incarnate gods for purposes other than the expiatory ones of some human sacrifices, and the sacramental eating of the body of Christ in the Eucharist and Communion rites is reminiscent of a heathen tradition of dining on the effigy of a tribal god and thus becoming partly divine. Just so Christians today either figuratively or in fact believe that they enter into a mystical union with the body of Christ by eating his flesh and drinking his blood (so instructed by Jesus himself). *Luke 22:19,20*

⟹⟶◆⟵⟸

Pagan religions in different parts of the world embraced many suffering saviors and many virgin births. And the "death" and "resurrection" of vegetation were symbolized in practices which found their counterparts in Christian legends. Nature, the heavens, the waters, the earth, and the seasons controlled by the sun combined in the minds of superstitious savages and in the rituals of even advanced cultures to nurture beliefs in magic and in religions characterized by mysticism.

Any even cursory examination of mythology throughout the world will reveal an astonishing similarity between the traditions and dogma surrounding Christ and the Church and the ancient superstitions of paganism. Peoples throughout the ages came to invest the elements and nearly every common plant and animal, as well as many hypotheses, with spirits, which gradually took on ever more human characteristics, sometimes metamorphosing into actual human beings and often eventually into gods and goddesses. The bull, ram, calf, and lamb were all deities at times. In such a way Jesus may have been perceived as the lamb of God.

The old songs which tell of being "washed in the blood of the Lamb" are possible plagiarisms from these heathen ceremonies which deified animals and used their blood to purify people, buildings, and altars. The Old Testament Jews sprinkled the blood of sacrificial animals upon the altar and vail of the tabernacle in the belief that such blood would cleanse and sanctify.

Jesus was depicted in early Christian art as a fish, and Christianity still uses the fish in its symbolism, seemingly unaware of the pagan origin of such display. The Nature worship common to pagan cultures in some instances imparted divine power to water as necessary to life. It was natural to transfer this power to creatures associated with streams, lakes, and seas, and fish became sacred. Much of the New Testament relates to water, fish, fishermen, boats, and storms at sea. Jesus describes himself as Living Water and promises to make the disciples "fishers of men."

Tree worship also evolved from nature worship, and gods were envisioned as the trees themselves or as fastened to them, just as imaginary spirits were believed to inhabit other natural objects. The idea of a god hanging on a tree was the inevitable heritage of descending superstitious generations who were bound to inject it into their own worship systems. Jesus used the tree analogy (vine) to depict himself and spoke of believers and unbelievers as branches in different conditions: "That ye bear much fruit, so shall ye be my disciples." *John 15:5–8* This analogy was also used by Paul: "For if thou wert cut out of the olive tree which is wild by nature, and wert graffed (sic) contrary to nature into a good olive tree: how much more shall these, which be the natural branches, be graffed (sic) into their own olive tree?" *Romans 11:24* There are numerous references to "hanging on a tree" in the scriptures of both Testaments, and even the crucifixion is referred to as "hanging on a tree." The cross of Christianity, in any case, is a familiar pagan symbol that has existed in some form in almost every society, including the most primitive.

The theory has been debated that Christ was manufactured as a Sun god, a theory which has a direct tie-in with pagan worship built around the seasonal cycles of nature and vegetation. And Christ's resurrection is linked to the season of rebirth. Upon such a possibility and upon the related Zodiac and its twelve signs, familiar to the "wise men" of Babylonia, Egypt, and Assyria, it has been widely claimed may rest the foundation for yet another explanation of Jesus being symbolized as the Light of the World with twelve disciple satellites, and for other facets of both Judaism and Christianity.

It is obvious from examination of mythology and paganism that Jesus Christ may be a myth or that he has been so clothed in the vestments of magic and fable that his resemblance to the myth saviors and heathen gods-incarnate cannot be ignored. Certainly the above theories do not prove that Jesus did not live as a real person in the Holy Land 2,000 years ago, but it is impossible not to be influenced by the paucity and fragility of the evidence that Jesus existed as a Palestinian Hebrew.

Historical data on Jesus is admittedly meager and open to dispute, unless one accepts the contradictory and undocumented gospels as proof. Scarcely a line about Jesus's physical appearance or every-day life beyond incidents which relate specifically to his ministry or role as savior can be found in *any* part of the New Testament, let alone the gospels. There is no "homey" discourse about him as a growing child or maturing adult and hardly anything at all about his family or family life, and the reader must inevitably wonder— was there really a person Jesus? Or was there just a Christ cult that had been building at a time when cultism and mysticism were flourishing in the Middle East?

The part which mythology plays in Christian theology and the unsubstantial proof of a Jesus who sojourned on earth must in the long run be evaluated by interested parties to their personal satisfaction.

=➤·◆·◄=

Consideration of the biblical Jesus logically leads to an assessment of the God of Christians as he emerges in the New Testament personification. The conclusion reached could conceivably be that by bringing their god down to earth for an extended time as a human being, by making their deity flesh and blood, they have diminished "him" with the brush of myth and superstition. Just who "they" are probably cannot be specifically determined, but must include every assenting Christian to a certain extent.

Christendom has not only a human god (like pagan deities) but a supernatural god whom it is possible to describe and delineate in terms of human attributes, a god who can never differ from a human being, or super-human being at best. By bringing him down from the upper regions assigned to the good guys, by divesting him of his infinity and majesty and godliness, and by assigning to him human characteristics, Christians tarnished the divinity of their deity. The traits attributed to him as a human being remained the divine traits of their God, who could not escape humanness or be superior to it, for he had already exhibited himself in the flesh. And those who choose to depict Jesus as the epitome of compassion and sweetness of character ignore the claim of Jesus himself that he was the incarnate Old Testament Lord, with all of Yahweh's meanness, partiality, jealousy, and vengefulness—the deity who chose to show special consideration to one people, who slaughtered thousands, drowned and tortured babies, violated women, expressed admiration for merciless despots and ruthless conquerors, rewarded villainous deeds, abetted duplicity, and forced his behavior rules upon a helpless nation.

Christians are obligated to obey that Mosaic law also, for it was bequeathed by their God and categorically endorsed by Jesus, who said he came to fulfill it and that not one tittle of it should fail. He made his position very clear: "For had ye believed Moses, ye would have believed me: for he wrote of me. But if ye believe not his writings, how shall ye believe my words?" *John 5:46,47*

By upholding the Mosaic law Jesus sanctioned slavery; sacrifices; the burning of witches; the stoning of young women, disrespectful and stubborn children, heretics, and Sabbath breakers; circumcision; polygamy and concubinage; and innumerable other discriminatory and heartless acts. But the Old Testament Lord was not yet monstrous enough for Christianity—no, he must debase himself further by fashioning a place of eternal pain for all those who choose to deflate his precarious ego. Hanging on a cross as a man, he had to bring further proof of his depravity to a people already his slaves. That the majority of this people refused to believe he would so disgrace himself should have been no surprise to an omniscient deity.

The God of the Christians and the *mother* of their God belong to a Semitic race which comprises less than one percent of the world's population, and 12 thrones in the Christian heaven are occupied by twelve more members of that race. The Christian deity and the Christian heaven are very provincial in the sense that they pertain to any one particular race or nation, but the Christian God was not only a human Jew but chose to show partiality to the people of that race.

The Christian God was *dead* for part of three days. "He" wears clothes, eats at a heavenly table (kosher), and lives in a mansion with many angel-servants. A favored few of his saints will be greater than others. This God is superstitious and ignorant of science—he was an exorcist who thought the sun could stand still and the moon had light of its own. He was a tempter and tricker, even a deceiver.

He makes threats. He is partial to one sex and actually refused adamantly for a time to heal a Gentile. He belittles family life and relationships. He encourages people to mouth nonsense, handle snakes, drink poison, and mutilate their bodies. He curses cities, even a tree, and persons who don't agree with him. He destroyed 2,000 pigs without paying for them. More importantly, the Christian God seems incapable of banishing evil from the world, or doesn't choose to, teaching that bloodshed redeems.

It is possible that any attempt by a people to define its gods automatically detracts from their godliness.

⟫◆⟪

Before he departed this vale of tears, as God's habitat for humanity this side of the grave has been described, the Savior of the entire world might have been expected to leave very lucid instructions as to how salvation might be achieved. And from his lips on various occasions do fall words that supposedly pinpoint "the way." Such words should leave not the smallest doubt, for they deal with *everlasting* happiness or inevitable *everlasting* torment. Let these words be examined!

When a lawyer questions Jesus about the requirements for eternal life (in heaven, one assumes), Jesus asks the lawyer what "the law" says, no doubt referring to the Mosaic law. The lawyer answers: "Thou shalt love the Lord thy God with all thy heart, and with all thy soul, and with all thy strength, and with all thy mind; and thy neighbor as thyself." Jesus replies: "Thou hast answered right: this do, and thou shalt live." *Luke 10:25–28*

No mention of belief in himself as the Son of God or the Redeemer of the world from sin! In other words, one does not have to be a Christian to be saved. Love for God and fellow beings suffices.

Consider, then, Jesus's words at another time: "He that believeth on the Son hath everlasting life; and he that believeth *not* the Son shall not see life; but the wrath of God abideth on him." *John 3:36* To Nicodemus Jesus also expounded: "He that believeth on him is not condemned; but he that believeth not is condemned already, because he hath not believed in the name of the only begotten Son of God." *John 3:17,18*

No mention of love of God and neighbor! Unquestioning belief is all that is necessary for salvation. There are no other stipulations.

Jesus's above statements are categorical, but in at least one sense the two requirements are at odds, for Deism and Christianity are not one and the same in every case, not by far. For, although Christianity may imply love of God and one's neighbor, such love does not necessarily imply Christianity. Thus, Jesus himself is presented in the scriptures as denying the need of anyone for a Savior.

But that is not yet the end of the puzzle. Jesus continues to put up conflicting guideposts: "The hour is coming, in the which all that are in the graves shall hear his voice, and shall come forth; they that have done good, unto the resurrection of life, and they that have done evil, unto the resurrection of damnation." *John 5:28,29* No mention of belief in Jesus Christ or of love of God and neighbor! Now only good deeds assure one of "life." No need here, or in above rules, to be reborn!

Perhaps Jesus intended to leave the impression that love of God and humanity, *plus* belief in himself as the Savior and Son of God, *plus* good deeds, are *all* necessary for assignment to heaven. But he comes a long way from claiming that. Each requirement stands alone in the course of his ministry. And those other admonitions about being born again and being converted simply make the conditions mandatory for salvation the more perplexing. If there are cut-and-dried rules for playing the game of life (and there should be when the stakes are so high that defeat leads to damnation), the referee fails to transmit them to the players.

<hr />

Christianity chooses to include the virgin birth of Jesus in its dogma, but biblically it is a circumstance narrated in only two of the gospels and completely ignored in the rest of the New Testament. Not only ignored, but denied! and denied so explicitly that it is obvious that paganism, whose gods were frequently born of virgins, was parent to the idea. Matthew and Luke are responsible for the claim that Jesus's mother was a virgin, impregnated by the Holy Ghost, but then both of these gospel-writers are brazen enough to give the Bible reader long (and completely different) genealogies of Jesus from Joseph to David and beyond.

Matthew wanted to make Jesus more authentic by tying in a virgin birth with a prophecy from Isaiah, but that same virgin birth was not compatible with the Jewish tradition (and with other prophecies) that the Messiah would be of the house of David. Matthew has a special gift for concocting stories to fit prophecies; perhaps that talent makes it possible for him to go to a great deal of trouble to establish Jesus's descendancy from David, without an apology, just before he gives his account of the virgin birth, concluding the genealogy thus: "So all the generations from Abraham to David are fourteen generations; and from David until the carrying away into Babylon are fourteen generations; and from the carrying away into Babylon unto Christ are fourteen generations." *Matt. 1:17* This genealogy serves no purpose, if Jesus was not the son of Joseph.

Luke recognizes his own dilemma, at least, and adds a parenthetical aside to his introduction of Jesus's genealogy (which lists 15 more generations to David than were named by Matthew): "And Jesus himself began to be about thirty years of age, being, as was supposed, the son of Joseph." *Luke 3:23* Mark describes a scene that takes place when Jesus visits his own country. His former neighbors exclaim: "Is not this the carpenter, the son of Mary, the brother of James, and of Joses, and of Juda, and Simon? and are not his sisters here with us?" *Mark 6:3* No one recalls on this occasion or even hints at anything unusual about Jesus's parentage. How did Matthew and Luke know about a virgin birth? Was it revealed only to them?

John realized the peril involved in the claim of a virgin birth (or he was also not aware of such a claim) for he not only makes no mention of it but promotes the counter-claim—that Jesus was descended from David. *He* reports Jesus's countrymen saying: "Is not this Jesus, the son of Joseph, whose father and mother we know?" *John 6:42* John also gives an account of another incident: "Philip findeth Nathanael; and saith unto him, We have found him, of whom Moses in the law, and the prophets did write, Jesus of Nazareth, the son of Joseph." *John 1:45* John even suggests that Jesus was not born in Bethlehem, when he repeats the arguments of a group of doubters: "Hath not the scripture said, That Christ cometh of the seed of David and out of the town of Bethlehem, where David was?" *John 7:40–43* The story used by the gospel of Luke to have Jesus born in Bethlehem was that Joseph had to pay his taxes in the city of David, because Joseph was "of the house and lineage of David." *Luke 2:4* Apparently the populace believed that Jesus was born at home in Nazareth. Deliberate mishandling of facts surrounding Jesus's birth reeks of invention, even fraud.

The conflict about Jesus's origin was so embarrassing that Peter and Paul both denied the virgin birth indirectly, and in fact no biblical mention is made of it beyond what appears in Matthew and Luke. Here are Peter's words: "Men and brethren, let me freely speak unto you of the patriarch David . . . knowing that God had sworn with an oath to him, that of the fruit of his loins, according to the flesh, he would raise up Christ to sit on his throne." *Acts 2:29,30* Paul has no doubts of Jesus's lineage: "Of this man's (David's) seed hath God according to his promise raised unto Israel a Savior, Jesus." *Acts 13:23* And: "Concerning his son Jesus Christ our Lord, which was made of the seed of David, according to the flesh." *Romans 1:3* Paul was not one to glorify womanhood by painting Mary as a virgin.

In all fairness to Peter and Paul, it is possible that the virgin birth became a figment of the imagination after their time, if the gospels were written later than Acts or the epistles. A real or imaginary hero becomes more fabulous with the passage of the years. But that still does not explain the fact that Luke, author of a genealogy of Jesus in the book that bears his name, is also supposed to have been the author of the book of Acts, in which the virgin birth is not spoken of, and in which both Peter and Paul flatly assert that Joseph was Jesus's natural parent.

Jesus would seem to settle the whole issue when he speaks to St. John in The Revelation: "I Jesus have sent mine angel to testify unto you these things in the churches. I am the root and the offspring of David . . ." *Rev. 22:16* It's a wise child that knows its own father, perhaps, but Jesus was a very wise child. *Luke 2:40*

⇒◆⇐

Jesus as the human sacrifice offered up by his father was the duplication of an ancient pagan practice of offering the firstborn son to be put to death as an act of homage and appeasement to tribal gods. This tradition and custom was supposed to be the target of the Lord's wrath in the Old Testament that was directed against the worshippers of Baal and Moloch. Elimination of the "groves" and altars where children were made to "pass through the fire," and eradication of this abominable ritual, along with the gods who demanded it, were given as the justification for and purpose of the Jewish conquest of Palestine. Worship of the monotheistic, "nice" Hebrew Lord was to be substituted for heathen ways.

Nevertheless, scripture says that the ancient Hebrews themselves frequently ascribed to the frowned-upon method of worship, and the Old Testament God required it for himself on occasion, as for instance when Abraham was told to sacrifice Isaac, and Jephthah was made to burn his only child to death. *Judges 11:30–39* The prophet Micah reveals how this concept of child-by-the-father human sacrifice persisted in Jewish tradition at the time parts of the Old Testament were written: "Wherewith shall I come before the Lord, and bow myself before the high God? shall I come before him with burnt offerings, with calves of a year old? Will the Lord be pleased with thousands of rams, or with ten thousands of rivers of oil? shall I give my firstborn for my transgression, the fruit of my body for the sin of my soul?" *Micah 6:6,7*

Although dedication of the firstborn to the Lord as a human sacrifice to atone for sin was gradually replaced by dedication of the firstborn male offspring to serve in the temple or in some related religious capacity, the idea of actually putting the victim to death lived on to its final conclusion—the Son offered up by the Father in an act of atonement for sin. Thus the God of the Bible, who is portrayed in the Old Testament as the relentless enemy of human sacrifice among the heathen, turns himself, in the shape of his own son, into the *New Testament* equivalent.

Behavior that is hideous and reprehensible in part of the Bible becomes in a later part an act of divine love and beauty. But the Christian Redeemer is the same human sacrifice of those pagans who practiced infanticide as a necessary part of their religion, and there is no escape from that fact. The derivation of Christian doctrine from paganism is too obvious to admit of argument. The human sacrifice of Jesus is just one evidence of it.

———⟫◆⟪———

Jesus has taken on a benignity and a gentle sweetness in societies which seek the lost cohesiveness of other days. He is the sympathetic companion who proffers the love and support which could formerly be extracted from the mutual empathy felt by people in a less harried, more personal era. But, how did Jesus himself want to be visualized? Here are his instructions: "But I will forewarn you whom ye shall fear: Fear him, which after he hath killed hath power to cast into hell; yea, I say unto you, Fear him, . . ." *Luke 12:5*

Jesus must inevitably emerge from the scriptures as the angry rejected prophet of doom who looks forward to having his revenge. That he had an abrasive side to his personality is obvious not only from the fact that he could not get along with his own family and was often at odds with the disciples but also from the evidence that he was not even liked or respected by his Nazareth neighbors. One would have thought that such a wondrous child who had arrived with an angelic fanfare, who had been announced as the Savior of the whole world, and whose destiny had been sensed by distant Zoroastrian priests, would have been carefully watched in awe during his childhood and youth, but among his own family and townspeople he enjoyed no deference. The attitude of the latter is so humiliating to him that he is unable to perform any miracles among them. He explains that a prophet is without honor in his own land and in his own house. *Matt. 13:54–58*

Such treatment may have accounted for his bitterness and readiness to assign his detractors forevermore to hell. It is ironic that this self-proclaimed Messiah of the Jews should find himself today still rejected by his own people and proprietor of a heaven where few of his fellow Jews will spend eternity with him. He will have the obligation of committing *them* to the flames, while he welcomes to his kingdom a preponderance of Gentiles, who received little of his attention on earth.

But surely the omniscient Lord of the Old Testament Jews (the Chosen People) could foresee this outcome of his new promise!

CHAPTER THREE

The Mosaic Law

Where to Find the Law Laid Down by God:

Exodus, 13 chapters

Although God has suffered from a prolonged case of laryngitis ever since Bible days, Moses traditionally received word for word from the mouth of the Lord all these complicated and detailed rules while he was in the desert and on Mt. Sinai, at Horeb and in Moab, playing Indian-guide to the Jews in the Wilderness. The tools for writing being what they were in those days (God wrote on tablets of stone with his finger) it is hard to imagine Moses recording these endless instructions, many of which are almost impossible to obey.

Moses does not complain about the task, or indeed even mention it often, but the enormity of it is apparent when one considers that six entire chapters of Exodus are required to set forth minutiae of how to build the Ark of the Covenant and the tabernacle and of how priests should dress and make offerings. All of the strict and involved picayune rules transcribed by Moses have to be read to be believed, and it is not surprising that Jewish temple scholars today constantly study the Torah and the Talmud. Elaboration and interpretation are endless.

Jesus lived under this Mosaic law, breaching it on only a few occasions and changing it slightly only where two or three of the most controversial rules were concerned. To those who feared he wanted to abolish it, he reassured his fellow Jews: "It is easier for heaven and earth to pass, than one tittle of the law to fail." *Luke 16:17* Yet Christians today who want to emulate Jesus leave the Mosaic law to the Orthodox Jews, except when parts of it apply to their own purposes and prejudices.

All who shudder at the ferocity of these biblical precepts should realize that they are still very much a part of the Word of God and may be put in force at any time when prejudice and purpose prevail.

Several of the Most Controversial Laws

1. He that curseth his father or mother shall surely be put to death.
2. He that smiteth his father or mother shall surely be put to death.
3. If thou buy a Hebrew servant, six years shall he serve.
4. If a man knows his ox is vicious and the ox kills someone, the owner shall be put to death.
5. If a man kills his slave by striking him, he shall be punished, but if the slave doesn't die at once, there shall be no punishment, for "he is his money."
6. Thou shalt not suffer a witch to live.
7. After engaging in the sex act, both partners are unclean until evening. They must bathe.
8. If a man has intercourse with a menstruating woman, he is unclean for seven days, and so is the bed.
9. Wizards shall be stoned to death.
10. Anyone who worships other gods shall be stoned to death.
11. An adulterer shall be put to death.
12. A girl not a virgin when she marries shall be stoned at her father's door.
13. A man may divorce his wife with a written notice to her.
14. A blasphemer shall be stoned to death.

15. A priest with a blemish may not approach the altar.

16. A priest shall not go near a dead body. Dead bodies defile.

17. If a man have a stubborn son, then shall his father and his mother bring him unto the gate and all the men of the city shall stone him that he die.

18. Thou shalt not sow a field with mingled seed.

19. No work whatsoever may be done on the Sabbath.

20. Thou shalt not stew a kid in its mother's milk.

21. Of the heathen shall ye buy bondmen and bondmaids, and of the children of strangers among you shall ye buy, and they shall be your possession forever and an inheritance for your children.

22. Your impoverished brother may be bought and forced to be your hired servant.

23. A priest may buy a slave.

24. A garment of both linen and wool combined may not be worn.

25. Homosexuality is an abomination.

26. Blood in any form may not be eaten.

27. Every male child must be circumcised.

28. Life for life, eye for eye, tooth for tooth.

29. Marine life without scales or fins may not be eaten.

30. Only animals that both chew the cud and part the hoof may be eaten.

31. Do not plow with an ox and an ass together.

32. A man must be the sexual partner of his brother's widow, if his brother left no heir.

33. Ye shall not round the corners of your heads, neither shalt thou mar the corners of thy beard.

34. Anyone who touches a dead body is unclean for seven days.

35. If a man is discovered raping a virgin who is not betrothed, he must buy her for his wife.

The Ten Commandments

From the mass of intricate behavior rules with which the books of the law are filled, scripture readers can barely manage to extricate the fabled Ten Commandments, which they have heard glibly referred to all their lives as if these orders stand alone and clearly-defined in the Holy Book. On the contrary, they are intermingled with many other instructions straight from the mouth of the Lord, and always in somewhat different form. As a result, several branches of the Christian Church, let alone Judaism, ascribe to different Decalogs the label of legitimacy.

The two most clearly-defined are to be found in Exodus 20:1–17 (repeated with elaboration in Deuteronomy 5:6–21) and Exodus 34:14–26.

The first and more familiar one was inscribed on the tablets which Moses broke in anger when he found the Israelites worshipping the golden calf (fashioned from jewelry stolen from the Egyptians). When the Lord repeated the "testimony" and re-carved it with his finger on two new tables of stone which an 80-year-old Moses had hewn and carried to the top of Mount Sinai, he failed to hand down the same ten commandments. Yet these latter tablets of stone remained intact, at least for a time, and safe from Moses's temper.

But even if one insists upon the pre-eminence of the traditional Decalog, it becomes apparent that only six of the commandments are concerned with morality. The first four address themselves to the manner of worship of the Hebrew deity—almost half of them, in fact. As to the remaining six . . . are they at all striking in originality and nobility, or do they chiefly stress property-protection and merely mandatory behavior for members of any society that wished to endure? And has not the categorical way in which they are stated necessitated their refinement and expansion whenever they are put into practical usage? Thou shalt not kill. Not even in self-defense or in war? Thou shalt not steal. Not even to obtain food for a starving child? And it scarcely would require divine guidance and a law degree to give *birth* to the last six commandments. They are not in the range of the profound, nor are they all-encompassing.

Jesus passes over them in a hurry and in several different arrangements in the New Testament, and the Bible reader may notice that in no part of the New Testament do the Ten Commandments appear in their entirety. Paul also pays them little regard in Romans 13:9 wherein he maintains they are all covered by "love one another." And, although Jesus mentions them variously in passing, in Matthew 19:18,19 and Mark 10:19 and Luke 18:20, he also seems to feel that they are superfluous.

When a lawyer asks Jesus which is the greatest commandment, Jesus replies: "Thou shalt love the Lord thy God with all thy heart, and with all thy soul, and with all thy mind. This is the first and great commandment. And the second is like unto it. Thou shalt love thy neighbor as thyself. On these two commandments hang all the law and the prophets." *Matt. 22:35–39* He implies that these two are sufficient.

The Golden Rule and the principles of the last six commandments have been inculcated in several social systems, some of which antedated Judaism. They were not and are not today unique to Christianity.

CHAPTER FOUR

Biblical Cruelties

Although Adam and Eve have no sense of right and wrong when they eat of the tree of knowledge, God accuses them of sinning and drives them from the Garden of Eden to prevent their partaking of the fruit from the tree of everlasting life. Pre-judging the human race, he then decrees it shall suffer for this "sin" by returning to the dust from which Adam was made. *Gen. 3*

Cain kills his brother Abel, because God is partial to the altar sacrifices of Abel, preferring animals to grain. God then banishes Cain. *Gen. 4*

At the time of the Flood, a disaster not uncommon to the traditions of other religions, Noah (an imbiber) and his family are the only persons God deems righteous enough to be saved from drowning. All other inhabitants of the earth, including infants and children and pregnant women, are given no opportunity to survive the merciless rising waters. *Gen. 7,8*

Again attributing sin to innocents, God fails to find even ten persons, or embryos in any stage of gestation, saintly enough to escape the fire and brimstone (biblical napalm) he rains down on the entire population of Sodom and Gomorrah, once more with no warning except to a few of his favorites. As they flee, God turns Lot's wife into a pillar of salt for looking back in horror at where her friends and neighbors are perishing in a fiery holocaust. *Gen. 19* Today many Christians oppose the abortion of any fetus as God-forbidden murder.

Abraham is certainly willing to do whatever deed the Lord orders of him and thinks up some not too honorable on his own. Told by God to sacrifice Isaac, Abraham has a knife at the bound boy's throat, before he hears an angel's voice telling him God is now satisfied that Abraham really loves him. *Gen. 22* Fortunately, this temptation of Abraham by God, as the Bible calls it, comes out all right, for Abraham was old and might have been deaf, and the angel was calling from heaven.

When jealous Sarah insists, God instructs Abraham to send Hagar and their 14-year-old Ishmael away into the desert alone, where they nearly die. *Gen. 21*

Pharaoh orders midwives to strangle all newborn Jewish children in Egypt. When they hesitate, he decrees that all male babies born to the Jews be cast into the river. *Ex. 1:18,22* Christian parents of the present time deny their children blood-curdling television viewing and give them Bibles.

Moses kills an Egyptian deliberately for beating an Israelite. *Ex. 2:12* He becomes God's law-giver. One of his commandments, straight from God, is "Thou shalt not kill."

God tries to kill Moses, because his son by a Midianite woman is not circumcised. His wife, angered, circumcises the child with a sharp stone and casts the foreskin at the feet of Moses. God then lets Moses go. *Ex. 4:24–26* God's *priorities!*

After first *purposely* hardening Pharaoh's heart so that he will not set the Israelites free, God, through the black magic of Aaron's rod, visits upon the Egyptians ten terrible plagues. *Ex. 7–11* Even the animals are victims.

The needless, brutal slaughter on Passover night is the intended result of another "hardening" of Pharaoh's heart by an egotistical maniacal God who wishes to parade his power. *Ex. 12:29* Thus God continues his propensity of making the innocent suffer for the guilty which culminates in the crucifixion.

More of this heart-hardening on the part of God causes Pharaoh to pursue the Israelites and fall victim to the waters of the Red Sea, along with his charioteers. *Ex. 14:28*

With no justification whatsoever, God orders Moses and the Jews to overrun and seize for themselves seven nations in the land of Canaan and promises his dedicated assistance: "And I will send hornets before thee which shall drive out the Hivite, the Canaanite, and the Hittite . . . By little and little I will drive them out from before thee, until thou be increased, and inherit the land." *Ex. 23:28,30*

He then instructs Moses on proper treatment of the victims: "And when the Lord thy God hath delivered it into thy hands, thou shalt smite every male thereof with the sword. But the women and the little ones, and the cattle, and all that is in the city, even all the spoil thereof, shalt thou take unto thyself . . . But of the cities of these people which the Lord thy God doth give thee for an inheritance, thou shalt save alive nothing that breatheth: But thou shalt utterly destroy them; namely, the Hittites, and the Amorites, the Canaanites, and the Perizzites, the Hivites, and the Jebusites; as the Lord thy God hath commanded thee." *Deut. 20:12–17*

For "offering strange fire before the Lord," two sons of Aaron, priests of the tabernacle, are struck dead: "And there went out fire from the Lord and devoured them." *Lev. 10:1,2* The vacancies created may have been hard to fill.

A blasphemer curses the name of God in the wilderness camp, and God orders him put to death by stoning: "And the children of Israel did as the Lord commanded Moses." *Lev. 24:23* The rocky terrain of Palestine brooded ill for miscreants.

In order that the camp will be clean enough for the Lord's presence, Moses expels from it, besides every leper, everyone who has an issue of blood, and everyone defiled by the dead. *Num. 5:24*

Israelites who complain, with good reason, in the desert, are burned with fire by God in the uttermost parts of the camp. *Num. 11:1*

Seeing that the Jews are dissatisfied on their journey to the Promised Land because they have no flesh to eat as they had in Egypt, the Lord typically loses his temper and sends a vast excess of quail, enough to cover the ground a day's travel in each direction from the camp and to stack up to a height of more than three feet. As the people start to eat what they have worked hard to gather, God "smote them with a very great plague." *Num. 11:31–33*

God turns Miriam into a leper, after she criticizes Moses for marrying an Ethiopian. Such unions were contrary to Jewish custom and also disapproved of by God for everyone except Moses. *Num. 12:10*

The Israelites are forced by God to wander forty years in the Wilderness in order that all those who are over a certain age will die before the land of Canaan is reached. Spies had been sent there by Moses to survey the possibilities of conquest, and when their report showed a reluctance to embark upon this venture immediately, God was furious and sentenced the entire congregation to wander one year for each of the forty days the spies had spent on their reconnoitering expedition. *Num. 14*

A man caught picking up sticks (!) on the Sabbath is ordered by God to be put to death, and the wandering tribes comply: "And the Lord said unto Moses ... all the congregation shall stone him with stones without the camp." *Num. 15:35,36*

Challenge of the authority of Moses by anyone always brought out the worst in God, and he buries *alive* the wives and children of two princes guilty of it. *Num. 16:32,35*

After striving to reach it many years of their lives, Moses and Aaron are told by God that they may not enter the Promised Land, because Moses had struck a rock in *anger* to obtain water, although God had instructed him to get water from a rock once before. Moses is allowed a glimpse just before he dies. *Num. 20:11,12 Deut. 34* The Lord might have shown some compassion for Moses, who was probably at his wit's end.

Tired of manna and short on bread and water, the Israelites understandably murmur against both God and Moses, although they should have known punishment from the Lord would be dire and swift: "And the Lord sent fiery serpents among the people, and they bit the people; and much people of Israel died." The plague is not stayed until, at God's instructions, Moses makes use of Old Testament magic and fastens a brass serpent to a pole, the sight of which proves to be a snake-bite cure. *Num. 21:5–9*

Zimri, the son of an Israelite prince, and Cozbi, a Midianite (Gentile) princess, are slain by a priest before the people in the camp so that God will end another plague which is punishing Baal-worshippers: "He took a javelin in his hand ... and thrust both of them through, the man of Israel, and the woman through her belly." God is so pleased by this display of righteous wrath that he declares: "Behold I give unto him (the priest) my covenant of peace ... because he was zealous for his God." *Num. 25:8,13* It may be recalled that Moses's first wife was a Midianite, and that her family was kind to him when he fled Egypt as a murderer.

After a gory attack upon the Midianites, ordered by God, the Jewish forces are questioned by bloodthirsty Moses: "Have ye saved all the women alive? Now, therefore, kill all the males among the little ones and kill every woman not a virgin. Keep the virgins and girl children for yourselves."

The Lord then tells Moses to divide the spoil and levy a tribute to the Lord of persons and animals captured. God's share is 675 sheep, 72 cattle, 61 asses, and 32 *persons.* The jewels and gold taken are then given to the temple as an offering worth 16,750 shekels (a shekel was a gold or silver coin weighing 1/2 oz.). The priests bring it into the temple. *Num. 31*

Both Testaments speak of slavery many times and express no disapproval of it: "If the priest buy any soul with his money . . ." *Lev. 22:11* "Both thy bondmen, and thy bondmaids, which thou shalt have, shall be of the heathen . . . of them shall ye buy . . . as an inheritance for your children . . . they shall be your bondmen for ever." *Lev. 25:44–46* An impoverished *brother* may be purchased and forced to serve his sibling. *Lev. 25:47,48* Jesus tells a parable about slavery without condemning this human condition. *Matt. 18:23–27*

Sacrificial killing of literally thousands of animals and birds in both Testaments, especially the Old, is an inexcusably inhumane religious ritual. (Only certain portions of the meat could become food for the temple priests.) This widespread practice was carried out at the command of the Christian God and can be condoned only from the standpoint that it supposedly replaced the human sacrifices that are a part of Bible lore.

When Solomon dedicates the temple at Jerusalem, he offers up before the Lord 22,000 oxen and 120,000 sheep. The altar proves not large enough to accommodate the massive slaughter and burning. *I Kings, 8:63,64*

Moses relays God's instructions: "If thy brother . . . or thy son, or thy daughter, or the wife of thy bosom, or thy friend which is as thine own soul, entice thee secretly, saying Let us go and serve other gods . . . thou shalt surely kill him . . . and thou shalt stone him with stones that he die." *Deut. 13:6,9,10*

Not satisfied with destroying whole cities by his own hand, the Lord several times has his chosen people do it for him. Joshua is selected to level Jericho, although a lady of the evening and her family are spared for aiding the Jewish spies. "The Lord was with Joshua." *Josh. 6* Prostitutes are often Bible heroines.

Secretly taking some spoil for himself in the battle of Jericho, Achan, a Jewish warrior, is found out. His punishment? All Israel stoned and burnt him *and all his family*, then raised an altar to the Lord over their bodies. *Josh. 7:24–26*

Answering an appeal for aid in battle voiced by Joshua, God intervenes: "And the sun *stood still*, and the moon *stayed*, until the people had avenged themselves upon their enemies." *Josh. 10:13 Everything* comes to a halt to permit biblical revenge.

Gideon, a cruel warlike man, tortures the elders of Succoth: "And he took the elders of the city, and thorns of the wilderness and briers, and with them he taught the men of Succoth." *Judges 8:16* Hotel Bibles are named for him.

Jephthah is forced to kill his only child, a daughter, because of a deal he made with God by which he agreed, in exchange for victory in battle, to sacrifice the first thing to meet him upon his return home, expecting it to be a dog. God is relentless and refuses to release Jephthah from his bargain. *Judges 11:39* This is another of the human sacrifices which led up to the crucifixion. ("Kill" meant "burn.")

Unprecedented cruelty to animals is displayed by Samson when he sets fire to the tails of 300 foxes, which he has first tied up two by two, tail to tail. He then proceeds to send them out to burn down the fields of the Philistines, who really haven't treated him very well. *Judges 15:4,5* Samson always gets his revenge. A dissolute but physically mighty man who can kill a lion with his bare hands and carry off the gates of Gaza on his shoulders, he is the typical biblical character who achieves eminence, ruling Israel twenty years as a judge.

Because Samson's father-in-law has kindled Samson's wrath by giving away Samson's wife to her husband's friend, the Philistines burn the woman and her father alive. *Judges 15*

The Philistines put out Samson's eyes and enslave him, owing to the blandishments of Delilah, who worms out of him the secret of his God-given strength. *Judges 16*

The death of Nabal is engineered by God, because Nabal has refused to provide food for David and his men, strangers to him. David then marries Nabal's widow. *I Sam. 25:11,38*

Saul and three of his sons all die during the same battle.

God drives Saul to suicide, because Saul fails to carry out an assassination God wanted accomplished. The suicide was a further frustration for God, who had intended for Saul to fall at the hands of the enemy because Saul "executedst not his (God's) fierce wrath upon Amalek." Saul had been forewarned of his pre-destined fate when at his request the witch of Endor called up Samuel's ghost. The prophet's spirit let the cat out of the bag, adding, "therefore hath the Lord done this thing unto thee this day." *I Sam. 28:18,19* and *I Sam. 31:4*

A young man who claims responsibility for Saul's death, hoping to win favor with David, is sentenced by David to the same fate. *II Sam. 1* Intrigue is common in Old Testament royal courts but swiftly dealt with when discovered.

David promises a reward to the man who will "smite the lame and the blind who are hated of David's soul." *II Sam. 5:8* The crippled, handicapped, and deformed were despised by Old Testament Jews, an attitude encouraged by the Lord, who did not permit them to approach the tabernacle altar.

Forgetting momentarily that the Ark of the Covenant must not be touched by human hands, Uzzah saves it from tipping over. God's appreciation comes in the form of instant death for the well-meaning unfortunate. *II Sam. 6:6,7* To David's credit, God's conduct does anger him.

Having made Bathsheba pregnant, David plots to have her husband Uriah slain in battle: "Set ye Uriah in the forefront of the hottest battle, and retire ye from him, that he may be smitten, and die." *II Sam. 11*

With his unique sense of justice, God says he will *give* David's wives to David's neighbor and cause the death of David's innocent child born of the union of David and Bathsheba, as punishment for David's sin. *II Sam. 12:11–14* In God's court of law, the innocent and exploited usually share or bear the entire burden of God's reprisals.

Absalom's head is caught in a tree. One of his father's (David's) men thrusts three darts into the young man, and ten armor-bearers finish Absalom off. All of this torture and agony are the culmination of an underhanded attempt by Absalom to wrest the throne from David. *II Sam. 18* Relatives of Old Testament monarchs will stop at nothing to unseat those in power. Often they are abetted by God or some prophet.

The appeasement of a fierce Lord is frequently necessary in the pages of the Holy Book. He brings a three-year famine (one of his favorite forms of punishment) upon the Israelites, because Saul had killed some Gibeonites. To induce God to relent, David turns over to the Gibeonites seven sons of Saul. They are hanged up unto the Lord. *II Sam. 21* Such atrocities are further instances of human sacrifices being used to satisfy the whims of a capricious deity, making it not too surprising that the New Testament crucifixion finally occurs for the same reason.

David says of the Lord: "He teacheth my hands to war." And: "Thou hast also given me the necks of my enemies that I might destroy them that hate me." *II Sam. 22:35,41*

The unforgivable sin of taking a census is committed by David, and God gives him a choice of three punishments, thus presenting David with another opportunity to be selfish. The wrong-doer chooses a pestilence on Israel instead of a seven-year famine or three months of fleeing before his enemies, with his usual concern for himself. Finally, sort of conscience-stricken in spite of himself, David builds one of those altars which diminish God's fury by feeding his ego, and the famine abates. *II Sam. 24*

Solomon gets rid of his enemies with a hit man, who, among others, kills Solomon's brother Adonijah for him and a man who had taken refuge in a temple. *I Kings 2:25,28–34*

The Lord causes the son of King Jeroboam to die, because Jeroboam worships idols, as many of the Jewish kings continue to do. *I Kings 14*

A prophet tells King Ahab that God is angry because Ahab has failed to kill the king of Syria: "Thus saith the Lord, Because thou hast let go out of thy hand a man whom I appointed to utter destruction, therefore shall thy life go for his life, and thy people for his people." *I Kings 20:42* Many of God's punishments visited upon the Jews work in reverse and benefit persons and countries which do not acknowledge him as the one true God.

Piqued when some enemy troops question whether he is a man of God, Elijah calls down fire from heaven to consume them. *II Kings 1* Some time before that he had with God's cooperation produced a three-year drought, and these were only two instances of his detestable behavior. *I Kings 17:1*

The teasing from a group of children about his bald head so infuriates Elisha that the prophet curses them and calls down the shocking anger of God upon them. *II Kings 2:23,24*

The king of Moab, at war with Israel, uses his oldest son as a burnt offering. *II Kings 3:27* Stories of such a practice form some of the reading material of the Bible.

The prophet Elisha turns a man into a leper. *II Kings 5:27*

"Strike them blind!" Elisha asks God, indicating a great host of Syrians. The

Lord doesn't hesitate. *II Kings 6:18*

During a famine in Samaria, a woman boils her son as food for herself and a female friend. She complains when the friend refuses to live up to an agreement to boil her own son next. *II Kings 6:28,29*

King Jehu of Israel orders the widowed Queen Jezebel thrown from a high window by some eunuchs. He then drives his chariot over her body to no purpose, and leaves it to be eaten by the ever-present dogs. God had decreed all this in a cryptic way. *II Kings 9:32–37*

By killing her grandchildren, Athaliah assures her succession to the throne of Judah for six years. One grandson, however, had managed to escape and is finally made king by the priests in the true spirit of biblical fun and games. The priests order Athaliah put to the sword, and the new king then steals all the hallowed fittings from the temple before his servants kill *him*. *II Kings 11,12* God has quite a bit of trouble with his Chosen People, which may not say much for his foresight. His anointed monarchs especially engage constantly in intrigue and assassination.

All the servants who murdered his father King Joash come under sentence of death from Amaziah, but he doesn't kill their children, restrained supposedly and at long last by the Ten Commandments. *II Kings 14:5–7*

The Lord makes King Azariah into a leper (leprosy being the most dreaded disease of Bible times) for being lax in destroying altars to idols. *II Kings 15:4,5* God's greatest concern, expressed frequently in both Testaments, is that the Jews will defect and worship other gods, and they often did. Even those who professed loyalty to Jehovah were quite likely to have a secret store of idols and images. Perhaps they wanted to touch all bases, but their faith in one god was tenuous.

"All the women therein that were with child he ripped up." Thus the Bible describes the conduct of King Menahem of Israel after he smote, through conspiracy and murder, a neighboring country. *II Kings 15:16* Embryos are expendable in the Bible.

Ahaz, the king of Judah, makes his son "pass through the fire." *II Kings 16:3* The Jews of that day frequently sacrifice their children to Baal. *II Kings 17:17*

Being eaten by lions is the Lord's way of annihilating Gentile captives from

Assyria who have been sent to Samaria. They incur his undeserved ire by not being aware of the fact that they are supposed to worship him. *II Kings 17:26*

King Manasseh makes his son "pass through the fire." *II Kings 21:6* Although Manasseh permitted idol worship and displeased the Lord, he withstood God's anger and reigned 55 years over Judah. One of God's threats: "Behold, I am bringing such evil upon Jerusalem and Judah, that whosoever heareth of it, both his ears shall tingle . . . and I will wipe Jerusalem as a man wipeth a dish, wiping it, and turning it upside down." *II Kings 21*

After being captured by the army of the Chaldees (under King Nebuchadnezzar of Babylon), Judean king Zedekiah sees his sons slain before his eyes just before he is blinded by his captors. He is imprisoned in Babylon. *II Kings 25:7*

Jacob's grandson Er is killed by God: "Er was evil in the sight of the Lord and he slew him." God also kills Er's brother Onan for refusing to mate with Er's widow, as was the Jewish custom when there was no heir. *I Chron. 2:3 Gen. 38:7,9,10*

King Asa, a man of God, decrees that whosoever would not seek the Lord God of Israel should be put to death, whether man or woman. *II Chron. 15:13*

With typical biblical unthinkable behavior, Jehoram, the son of King Jehosaphat of Judah, slays his brothers with a sword to strengthen his claim to the throne. *II Chron. 21:4 (Everyone carries a sword.)*

After the Jews who re-settle Jerusalem following the captivity marry heathen wives, Ezra persuades them to abandon their legal partners and their families, to please God. *Ezra 10*

Challenged in a petty argument with Satan, God permits him, to prove Job's loyalty, the freedom to persecute this sinless, God-fearing man. Job's children and servants suffer death, his wealth is lost, and he himself is covered with supperating sores and boils. *Job 1,2*

"Happy shall be he that taketh and dasheth thy little ones against the stones." *Psalms 137:9* The "little ones" are the children of Babylon. The words— God's.

The Lord makes dire predictions to Isaiah: "Everyone that is found shall be thrust through; and everyone that is joined unto them shall fall by the sword. Their children also shall be dashed to pieces before their eyes; their houses shall be spoiled, and their wives ravished." *Isaiah 13:15,16* Not surprising, perhaps, that such a God should think up a hell.

To Jeremiah the Lord says of the Ammonites: "Her daughters shall be burned with fire." *Jer. 49:2* The books of the prophets abound with such threatening promises from the mouth of the Lord.

Ezekiel receives similar confidences: "Thus saith the Lord God; As I live, surely they that are in the wastes shall fall by the sword, and him that is in the open field will I give to the beasts to be devoured, and they that be in the forts and in the caves shall die of the pestilence." *Ez. 33:27*

Men who plot against Daniel are cast into a lions' den, along with their wives and children. ". . . and the lions . . . broke all their bones in pieces." *Dan. 6:24* Daniel is one of the prophets of the Lord and enjoys his protection.

Incineration by the heat of the furnace is the heaven-sent fate that befalls the strong men who throw Shadrach and his friends into the flames. *Dan. 3:20–22*

Parental love in the Bible cannot be described as sublime or steadfast: "And it shall come to pass, that when any shall yet prophesy, then his father and his mother that begat him shall say unto him, Thou shalt not live, for thou speakest lies in the name of the Lord; and his father and his mother . . . shall *thrust him through* when he prophesieth." God is addressing Zechariah. *Zech. 13:3* Under the Mosaic law, stubborn children had to be stoned to death. In the meantime orders to parents were: "Thou shalt beat him with the rod, and shalt deliver his soul from hell." *Prov. 23:14*

Dreadful words of God about treatment of some of his Chosen People are graphic: "O Princes of the house of Israel, who pluck off their skin from off them, and their flesh from off their bones: who also eat the flesh of my people, and flay their skin off them; and they break their bones and chop them in pieces, as for the pot, and as flesh within the cauldron." *Micah 3:2,3* Such passages fill the Holy Book.

Matthew is the only gospel which tells the horrid story of Herod slaying all the children of Bethlehem and the nearby coasts, up to two years of age, because he so fears the birth of one child. *Matt. 2:16* Matthew had the holy family flee to Egypt to fulfill a prophecy that actually referred to the Exodus: "Out of Egypt have I called my son." *Matt. 2:15 Hosea 11:1*

Descriptions provided by Jesus of hell and the end of the world are gruesome and vengeful and sound as though they were delivered with flashing eyes and clenched fists: "So shall it be at the end of the world: The angels shall come forth and sever the wicked from among the just; and shall cast them into the furnace of fire; there shall be wailing and gnashing of teeth." *Matt. 13:49,50*

Some of the parables Jesus is fond of relating contain elements of discrimination and cruelty, which sometimes escape his condemnation. Most such parables can be found in Matthew.

The Last Supper, whether eaten as the Passover (Luke) or the evening before (John), provides a scene of what is actually cannibalism borrowed from mythological beliefs that to eat part of a god would make the diner god-like: "Except ye eat the flesh of the Son of man, and drink his blood, ye have no life in you." *John 6:53*

The capture, torture, and crucifixion of Jesus are horrible, but even more revolting is the concept that blame for them should be placed upon humankind, let alone the Jews. God causes all this ghastly panorama in order to fulfill the prophecies, from the betrayal of Judas to the final horror scene (according to the gospels). All who took part were mere pawns, but, not satisfied with making *them* killers of a heaven-sent Savior, the Bible tars all humanity with the same brush.

Jesus is a human sacrifice in the tradition of mythology and idol-worship. The practice is thought to have developed in part from a need to feed the spirits of the departed and in part from the assignment to gods the responsibility for disaster, which led to the subsequent conclusion that these gods could be appeased by offering them the lives of mortal creatures. Another factor lay in the hope that the bodies of freshly-killed human beings could serve as sustenance to preserve the strength and power of the tribal gods. The Jews of the Old Testament sometimes sacrificed their own children, and even those who accepted the Jewish Lord substituted animals for humans, although the demand of the Mosaic law that the first-born male belonged to the Lord has been interpreted by some Bible students to mean human sacrifice (as in the story of Abraham and Isaac).

Human beings have been the victims of offerings to such an extent that it is now known that the Aztecs, for instance, sacrificed thousands of persons a year. Priests took the victims, thought to have been only enemy captives, to the tops of their pyramids and cut out their hearts, which they offered to idols. After the arms and legs were roasted and eaten (just as in the Bible cannibalism is resorted to during famines), the skulls were placed in public view. They made a grisly sight for the Spaniards who easily conquered the Aztecs.

Some say these bloody rituals, depicted in Aztec paintings, were necessitated by hunger, as well as by the custom of sacrifice to the gods.

Ananias, a new convert after the death of Jesus, sold his land and failed to turn over every cent to the apostles. Peter accuses him of letting Satan make him *lie to the Holy Ghost*. Ananias is so frightened that he falls down dead! Peter's young men throw him into a grave without telling his wife what has happened. Three hours later she comes to look for her missing husband. Peter, without any remorse so far, accuses her also of lying about the amount held back and says spitefully: "Behold, the feet of them which have buried thy husband are *at the door.*"

The poor woman is so terrified and shocked that she follows her unfortunate husband's example and also expires on the spot. The same young men summarily throw her into the ground, too. *Acts 5* Peter is to become the first pope.

The adamant intolerance of the biblical deity is duplicated in the personality of the Christian advocate Paul. He drags followers of Jesus from their homes to prison and as a member of a lynch mob helps to stone Stephen to death. (Stephen has just seen Jesus in heaven at God's right hand, Trinity or no Trinity.) *Acts 7:54–60*

Even after his conversion to the doctrine of universal love, Paul proves to be as fanatical and mean as ever. "Filled with the Holy Ghost," he sets his eyes upon a "false prophet" Barjesus and hurls these words at him: "O full of all subtilty, thou child of the devil, thou enemy of all righteousness, wilt thou not cease to pervert the right ways of the Lord? And now, behold, the hand of the Lord is upon thee, and thou shalt be blind . . ." Immediately darkness fell upon him. *Acts 13:6–12* Paul's brand of evangelism sets the standard of behavior for the Christian Church toward all holding a different doctrine. Many would have to pay in blood for not accepting Christian dogma.

The book of The Revelation describes many vicious indecencies, whose repulsiveness is not diminished by John's explanation that they are all a vision sent by Jesus.

As a final comment upon this incomplete list of cruelties from the scriptures, the last verse of Deuteronomy will serve: ". . . all the great terror which Moses shewed in the sight of Israel." *Deut. 34:12* And to open readers' eyes to the reprehensibly dire threats of the Lord to be found in the Bible, they might consider the perusal of Leviticus 26, verses 16 through 39. More of these cursings may be digested, if readers have strong stomachs, by reading Deuteronomy 28, verses 15 through 68.

⇒◆⇐

Any treatise dealing with biblical cruelties might understandably remark upon the cruel hardship encountered by anyone who tries to write about the Christian Holy Book, a hardship naturally inherent in the difficulty of examining vagaries comprehensively, specifically the vagaries which are a large part of Bible contents. It is enough of a challenge to try to grasp the Hebrew Lord with his many forms and moods, his partiality and prejudices, but Christianity in the New Testament imposes almost insurmountable problems for the delver because of the monotheism which it projects, the ambiguous God-is-three monotheism consisting of an actual assault upon the Jewish tradition of "Hear, O Israel, the Lord our God, the Lord is one." Early Christendom split, ironically, over whether *Jesus* was *one* or *two!*

Owing partly to the continuing impact upon Judaism of the pagan mysticism practiced by neighbors and conquerors of the Jews, the New Testament produced a human god who was at once God himself, the Son of God, and an even more spiritual Holy Ghost. These three were both separate entities and identical with one another. God was Jesus, the father of Jesus, and the Holy Ghost. Jesus was God, the son of God, and the Holy Ghost. The Holy Ghost was God, the father of Jesus, and Jesus. Although the three were one, they frequently acted upon one another. Such a state of affairs produced a Trinity, supposedly compatible with monotheism.

This multiple identification of God and Jesus and the Holy Ghost is a barrier to any consideration of each or all of them and almost necessitates that each discourse contain an introductory explanation of which perception of any or all three is being currently employed. Thus, if one treats of the underlying legend of salvation (the core of the Christian religion) using the premise that Jesus is the *son* of God, the legend becomes one of such deplorable cruelty that only insensitive, misguided persons would be willing to accept their god as the instigator of it. For it features a Supreme Being so angry at his own creation humankind that he is willing to forgive its sins only if it kills his Son, which he then forces it to do.

There is no element of good or beauty in such a story, unless one is able to see worth in the idea that a father would dictate execution of his child as the only means of softening his own heart. God says to man: I am angry at you, but after I make you torture and kill my only son, I will not only find it in my heart to patch up a long-standing feud with you but will actually reward you by letting you move in with me forever. There is no other way that you and I can be reconciled!

Chapter Five

Mass Killings Ordered, Committed, Or Approved By God

The entire population of the earth at the time of Noah, except for eight survivors, in a flood. "And every living substance was destroyed which was upon the face of the ground, both man, and cattle, and the creeping things, and the fowl of the heaven; and they were destroyed from the earth: and Noah only remained alive, and they that were with him in the ark." *Gen. 7:23*

Every inhabitant of Sodom and Gomorrah, and of the surrounding plain, by "brimstone and fire from the Lord out of heaven." *Gen. 19:24* Lot's family fled.

All the first-born of every family in Egypt, including children of those in the dungeons and the successor to the throne of Egypt's Pharaoh, by God on the first Passover night. *Ex. 12:29*

All the hosts of Pharaoh, including the captains of 600 chariots, who drown in the Red Sea while pursuing the Israelites. ". . . and the Lord overthrew the Egyptians in the midst of the sea." *Ex. 14:27,28*

Victims who perish in the conquest of seven nations in Canaan by the Jews under God's guidance so that the Jews can occupy their lands as God had promised Abraham. "When the Lord thy God shall bring thee into the land whither thou goest to possess it, and hath cast out many nations before thee, the Hittites, and the Girgashites, and the Amorites, and the Canaanites, and the Perizzites, and the Hivites, and the Jebusites, seven nations greater and mightier than thou; And when the Lord thy God shall deliver them before thee; thou shalt smite them, and utterly destroy them; thou shalt make no covenant with them, nor shew mercy unto them." *Deut. 7:1,2*

Amalek and his people, by the edge of the sword. "Because the Lord hath sworn that the Lord will have war with Amalek from generation to generation." As long as Aaron helped Moses to hold up his hands, the Israelites prevailed. *Ex. 17:11,16* At times of crisis, the Lord often waxed whimsical.

3,000 Israelites, massacred by their Levite tribe at the command of the Lord for worshipping the golden calf. "Take every man his sword by his side, and go in and out from gate to gate throughout the camp, and slay every man his *brother*, and every man his companion, and every man his neighbor." *Ex. 32:27* These were the orders of a God who would brook no disloyalty, a self-styled "jealous" God.

Rulers of Israel, 11 in number, who refused to invade the Promised Land after they had spied on it for 40 days. God kills them with a plague. *Num. 14:37*

250 Levite princes of the Jews who challenged the leadership of Moses. God would have killed the whole congregation, if Moses hadn't pointed out the injustice of such a course of action. Owing to Moses's plea for sanity, the Lord *repented* somewhat and re-fashioned the punishment. Letting his compassion prevail, he proceeded to open up the earth and bury alive "the wives, sons, and little children" of two of the princes, then sent a fire that consumed the remaining princes. The rest of the congregation, properly terrified, next made a covering for the altar out of their incense braziers. *Num. 16:1–40* God was finally mollified.

14,700 Jews in a plague, because they rebelled against Moses after the killing of the 250 princes. At last Aaron makes atonement with incense to stop the plague. *Num. 16:41–49*

The Canaanites at Hormah, utterly destroyed by the Lord at the request of the Jews. *Num. 21:3*

The Amorites at Heshbon. Israel "took all these cities." Moses summed up the slaughter: "We . . . utterly destroyed the men and the women and the little ones." *Num. 21:25* and *Deut. 2:34*

All the sons and subjects of Og, about whom the Lord said to Moses: "Fear him (the king of Bashan) not, for I have delivered him into thy hand." None was left alive. *Num. 21:34,35*

24,000 Israelites who co-habited with Moabite women and worshipped Baal. "And the Lord said unto Moses, Take all the heads of the people, and hang them up before the Lord against the sun . . ." *Num. 25:4,9*

All the males and kings of the Midianites, because they worshipped idols, and all their wives and male children. "And the Lord spake unto Moses, saying, Vex the Midianites, and smite them. *Num. 25:16,17 Num. 31:7,8*

The subjects of two kingdoms on the east side of the Jordan, in order that Reuben and Gad might seize these realms for their own as a gift from God. *Num. 32*

The Ammonites, decimated by the Lord so that Lot might possess their land. *Deut. 2:19–21*

The Horims, slain by God in order that Esau might acquire their land. *Deut. 2:22*

All the citizens of Jericho, except for a prostitute and her family. "And they utterly destroyed all in the city, man and woman, young and old, and ox . . . with the edge of the sword." *Josh. 6* "They" make a grisly game of it, using the superstitious number "7" popular in the Bible, trumpet blasts, and marches around the doomed city. Joshua competes with Moses, the leader he replaced, for title of No. 1 Murderer (God's hit man) of the Old Testament, as he follows God's orders.

Men of Ai, and the women and children, 12,000 in all (and the city burned), in a treacherous ambush conceived and directed by God. Joshua and his men smote them with the "edge of the sword." With the usual biblical hocus-pocus, Joshua held out his spear at arm's length until all the inhabitants were killed, then built an altar and sacrificed to God to celebrate the victory. (God always *has* demanded recognition of his beneficence!) Joshua hanged the king of Ai on a tree. *Josh. 8:1–30* (Jesus was also to be "hanged on a tree." The precedent builds.)

The armies of five kings of the Amorites, who beseiged Gibeon. "And the Lord . . . slew them with a great slaughter." He then chased the survivors and killed more of them with hailstones. *Josh. 10:10,11* (The rest of the world apparently had to muddle along the best it could, while the Supreme Being was pre-occupied with the war games of some Semitic tribes. "You only have I known . . ." *Amos 3:2*)

The five kings of the Amorites after being shut up in a cave and then brought before the congregation. Joshua exhorted his fellow Israelites to: "Come near: put your feet upon the necks of these kings. Thus shall the Lord do to all your enemies." He then slew all five and hanged their bodies. *Josh. 10:16–26* The Bible specializes in such horror tales and yet is considered a proper book for children, in full confidence of its not being read.

All the people of Makkedah, and their king hanged, by Joshua. *Josh. 10:28*

All the people of Libnah. Not a soul remained; all were delivered to Joshua by the Lord. *Josh. 10:29,30* Joshua and God were agreed upon capital punishment.

All the people of Lachish, by Joshua. *Josh. 10:32*

All the people of Gezer. "And Joshua smote him and his people, until he had left him none remaining." *Josh. 10:33* Joshua continues to display the sterling qualities that win favor with the Boss.

All the people of Eglon. "They left none remaining." *Josh. 10:34,35* (The Old Testament is a mixture of brutal history, poetry, narratives, and philosophy.)

All the people of Hebron. "All the cities and souls that were therein." *Josh. 10:36,37*

All the inhabitants of "the country of the hills, and of the south, and of the vale, and of the springs and all their kings; he left none remaining but utterly destroyed all that breathed, as the Lord God of Israel commanded." *Josh. 10:40* God's communications with Joshua usually took the form of military communiques, and Joshua was nothing if not a "clean sweeper."

All 31 kings and inhabitants of their countries, of the hills and south country and land of Goshen and the valley and the plain and the mountain of Israel and the valley of the same from Mt. Halak to Mt. Hermon. "As God commanded Moses." *Josh. 11:12,16,17* and *12:24* Joshua was happy to do Moses' dirty work, but the logistics must have been mind-boggling.

The inhabitants of Gaza, Askelon, and Ekron, killed by Judah and Caleb. "And the Lord was with Judah." *Judges 1:18,19*

10,000 Moabites, by the Israelites. "...and there escaped not a man." *Judges 3:29*

10,000 Perizzites and Canaanites, conquered by Judah and Simeon. *Judges 1:4* (Whoever did the body-counting always came out with a nice round figure.)

600 Philistines, slain with an ox goad by Shamgar. *Judges 3:31*

All the hosts of Sisera. "And all the hosts of Sisera fell upon the edge of the sword." *Judges 4:16* (Old Testament swords all had *edges*, no *points*.)

120,000 Midianites by Gideon and his 300 men. *Judges 8:10*

All but one, who managed to escape, of his 70 step-brothers by Abimelech, the son of one of God's favorite torturers, Gideon, in order to gain for himself the throne of Israel. *Judges 9:5* Like father, like son.

30 young Philistines by Samson, furious after they guess his riddle. "The spirit of the Lord came upon him." *Judges 14:19*

Many Philistines with a "great slaughter" by Samson, because they burned his former wife and her father to death to avenge Samson, mistakenly thinking to win his approval. *Judges 15*

All the lords of the Philistines and a houseful of men and women, including 3,000 on the roof, who perished when Samson pulled down the pillars, after calling upon God to restore his strength. "So the dead that he slew at his death were more than they which he slew in his life." Samson's bloody score included 1,000 Philistines slain with the jawbone of an ass when "the spirit of the Lord was upon him." *Judges 15:14* and *16:27,30* (Is this the *Holy* Spirit that enchants the clergy?)

25,100 Benjamites, who, with God on their side, fought against their fellow Jews. *Judges 20:35*

50,070 people of Bethshemesh, struck dead by God, because a few of them who were working a field happened to glance into the Ark carrying the stone tablets of the Ten Commandments. "And the people lamented, because the Lord had smitten many of the people with a great slaughter." *I Sam. 6:19* God kept grave-diggers of the Old Testament working overtime burying innocents.

Philistines killed under Samuel. "And the hand of the Lord was against the

Philistines." *I Sam. 7:13* (Does God really like anybody?)

Philistines killed by Saul and Jonathan. "For the Lord hath delivered them into the hand of Israel." *I Sam. 14:12,13,20*

The Ammonites who threaten Jabesh, slain by Saul and the children of Israel "so that two of them were not left together." *I Sam. 11:11*

All the Amalekites killed by Saul upon God's orders. "Slay both man and woman, infant and suckling. . ." *I Sam. 15:3,7* (Bottle feeding was definitely recommended.)

Thousands of Philistines slain by David's armies. "Saul hath slain his thousands, and David his ten thousands." *I Sam. 18:5,6,7* and *23:5 II Sam. 5:25* and *8:1*

200 Philistine men, killed by David to obtain their foreskins with which to purchase Saul's daughter to be his wife. *I Sam. 18:27* (But that's *minor* surgery!)

The Geshurites and the Gezrites and the Amalekites slain by David, "leaving neither man nor woman alive." *I Sam. 27:8,9* (What about the infants and sucklings?)

The Jebusites, killed by David when he captured Jerusalem from them. ". . . and smiteth the Jebusites, and the lame and the blind . . ." *II Sam. 5:6,7,8*

The Moabites and 22,000 Syrians by David. "And the Lord preserved David." *II Sam. 8:2,5,6,14*

40,000 horsemen of the Syrians, killed by David. *II Sam. 10:18* (The horses, too?)

The children of Ammon, by David's men. *II Sam. 11:1*

The Ammonites of Rabbah and other cities, *tortured* to death by David. "He put them under saws and under harrows of iron and made them pass through the brick kiln." *II Sam. 12:31* (David, today the patriarch most revered by the Jews, was a man who lived by the values and customs of his age.)

Every man in Edom, killed by Joab and David. *I Kings 11:15*

The murderers of one of Saul's sons, sentenced to death by David. "And David commanded his young men, and they slew them, and cut off their hands and their feet, and hanged them up over the pool . . ." *II Sam. 4:7,12* Such deeds are typical of the behavior of God's favorites in the Bible. Even though it was *customary* behavior at the time, surely Almighty God's standards of morality should not fluctuate.

70,000 victims of a pestilence sent by the Lord, because David chose it as *his* punishment for taking a census. *II Sam. 24:15*

450 prophets of Baal, killed by Elijah. "And the hand of the Lord was on Elijah." *I Kings 18:40,46* (God's motto was "better dead than mis-led.")

100,000 Syrian footmen, slaughtered in one day by the children of Israel. "Thus saith the Lord, Because the Syrians have said the Lord is God of the hills, but he is not God of the valleys; therefore will I deliver all this great multitude into thine hand . . ." A wall falls on the 27,000 who are left. *I Kings 20:28,29,30* (That certainly got God the valley vote!)

100 Moabite troops, consumed by fire from heaven called down by Elijah when they question whether he is a man of God. *II Kings 1* Wholesale murder is proof of Godliness in the Bible.

42 children eaten by two bears, after Elisha curses them in the name of the Lord for making fun of his bald head. *II Kings 2:23,24* (Similar nightmarish tragedies happen in fairy tales, but there they aren't perpetrated by God.)

All who died in a 7-year famine sent by the Lord on Samaria. *II Kings 8:1*

70 children of King Ahab of Israel, and all the rest of Ahab's "house," after God decreed they should all be destroyed. The heads of the children are put into baskets at the gates of the city. *II Kings 9:8* and *10:1–11* (Baskets full of heads!) All of this was engineered by Jehu, whom God had chosen to succeed Ahab to the throne.

42 children of the king of Judah, by their uncles, at Jehu's command. Elisha is the medium through which God communicates his inhuman demands for the annihilation of these entire families, and Jehu is all too eager to comply: "Come with me, and see my zeal for the Lord." For all his savagery he wins the praise of the Lord: "Thou hast done that which is right in mine eyes and hast done unto the house of Ahab according to all that was in mine heart." *II*

Kings 10:12–17,30 The God of the Christian Bible has little regard for the family as such.

All worshippers of Baal in Samaria and Israel by 80 guards at the direction of Jehu. The victims were tricked into attending a Baal-worship service where they were all butchered. "And they smote them with the edge of the sword." *II Kings 10:18–25*

185,000 Assyrians slain by *one angel* overnight. Thus the Lord defended Jerusalem. *II Kings 19:35* The *Christian* conception of an angel puts a halo (much-needed) on the Old Testament variety.

All the priests of heathen gods in Judah, slain by King Josiah. *II Kings 23:20*

500,000 men of Israel by King Abijah of Judah and his men. "God smote . . . all Israel before Abijah and Judah." *II Chron. 13:16,17,18* This atrocity was the result of civil war between Israel and Judah.

10,000 Edomites killed by Amaziah's men, who then carried away 10,000 more and "brought them to the top of the rock, and cast them down from the top of the rock, that they were all broken in pieces." *II Chron. 25:11,12* Amaziah accepted the Lord's advice on this campaign.

120,000 Judeans, massacred in one day by King Pekah of Israel, "because they had forsaken the Lord God." He also took 200,000 women and children captive as bondmen and bondwomen. These are all fellow Jews. *II Chron. 28*

500 subjects of a Persian king and the ten sons of Haman who meet death as the result of the machinations of Queen Esther on behalf of her Jewish countrymen. Haman suffers the same fate. Esther's uncle Mordecai and the other Jews throughout the kingdom had refused to abandon their Mosaic law. *Esther 3:5,8* and *7:10* and *9:1–14*

75,000 Persian subjects of King Ahasuerus by the Jews, urged on by Esther and Mordecai. *Esther 9:16* Esther's part in this is celebrated by a festive Jewish holiday, in which she is honored for saving her fellow Jews. It is called Purim.

Job's children and servants by God in a contest with Satan over Job's loyalty to God. *Job 1:13–19*

CHAPTER SIX

Discrepancies And Contradictions In The Scriptures

The Christian concept of an all-powerful God constantly trying to overcome an enemy which he himself created is a natural result of the biblical history of Satan, otherwise known as the devil, the fallen angel, Lucifer, and the Adversary. Jesus even calls Satan Beelzebub.

According to the scriptures, Satan is the angel who leads other angels in a revolution in heaven. Heaven as the scene of dissatisfaction and civil war is in itself a contradiction of the picture of heaven held by those who strive to attain it, but from it rebellious angels had to be cast out. Just when this uprising took place the reader is not informed, and just when it *could* have is a puzzle, since heaven and earth were both created at the same time, all within a few days, and Adam and Eve were placed in the Garden almost immediately, only to find Satan already there in the shape of a serpent. And he had already escaped from his prison!

Since God created the angels as his special band, it is contradictory to assume that he cannot control them, but it is just as contradictory for an all-good Almighty to allow angels to sin and to invade the earth and persuade humankind to sin. The struggle between good and evil common to many religions is not commensurate with belief in one omnipotent Deity, a God who should be able to vanquish any evil force he desires to eliminate. Instead, God, the Bible will have it, permitted Satan to cause the downfall of the human race, and from then on the biblical Satan is on a par with that God, vying for man's loyalties and very souls. Indeed, he might be regarded as the fourth god of the Christian religion, so mighty is he and so necessary to it.

Actually, the Old Testament does not make much mention of Satan. The book of Job calls him a *son of God* who comes to present himself before the Lord: "And the Lord said unto Satan, Whence comest thou? Then Satan answered the Lord, and said, From going to and fro in the earth, and from walking up and down in it." *Job 1:6,7*

Isaiah calls Satan Lucifer (to bear the light of knowledge was the epitome of evil from the very beginning): "How art thou fallen from heaven, O Lucifer, son of the morning! How art thou cut down to the ground, which didst weaken the nations! For thou hast said in thine heart, I will ascend into heaven, I will exalt my throne above the stars of God . . . I will be like the most High. Yet thou shalt be brought down to hell, to the sides of the pit. They that shall see thee shall narrowly look upon thee, and consider thee, saying, Is this the *man* that made the earth to *tremble*, that did shake kingdoms . . .?" *Isaiah 14:12–16* A powerful rival, for sure!

In the New Testament, to Jesus and the apostles and the early Christians Satan is very much a real entity who roams the world, frequently overcoming good and taking possession of all nations, which he offers to Jesus. Jesus contends with devils many times, conversing with them and casting them out of persons possessed by them (seven out of Mary Magdalene). He gives his disciples power over all of them. *Luke 9:1* And he says that hell was prepared for the devil and his angels. *Matt. 25:41* (Jesus got many of his ideas from Old Testament writings.)

During Jesus's ministry, Satan desires to have Peter and enters into Judas. Paul subsequently claims that the devil has, and practices, the power of death, and that Jesus through his own death hoped to destroy him. *Hebrews 2:14* Here is the contradiction again of God having to die to prevail over a being of his own invention, and incidentally failing, for Satan is still in the Church's vocabulary, and Peter tells converts: "The devil walketh about." *I Peter 5:8*

Paul warns repeatedly of Satan's powers: "Lest Satan should get an advantage of us: for we are not ignorant of his devices." *II Cor. 2:11* Contradictorily, Peter claims that the fallen angels are in everlasting chains under darkness. *II Peter 2:4* Unknown to him, the chains were loosed, permitting the forces of evil to contend, even today, with the forces of good. The battle is joined, and the Bible does not leave one confident of the outcome but rather with a suspicion that, like Dr. Frankenstein, God may have lost control of his "monster."

Hell is not the *realm* of the devil and his angel conspirators, as is often imagined, but was originally the pit described by Isaiah in which Satan and the fallen angels were to end up. In the Old Testament, hell, like Satan, is infrequently mentioned and not clearly described. Hell in that part of the Bible is not even a specific place, although at times a "pit" is spoken of as a place into which certain persons are to be cast as punishment from God. Human misery in various forms or violent early death are usually fates of those who disobey the Lord.

In the New Testament, however, with the concept of eternal life stressed by Jesus, it became necessary to provide motivation for belief, and fear was introduced in the form of a place of eternal torture for all who rejected him. Since the vague idea of the "pit" was already an accepted myth, it was easily taken over as the destination of all the recalcitrant. This "pit" gradually underwent a metamorphosis. Unquenchable fire was added, and it became a furnace, lake, or enclosure with gates, depending on which Bible verse is being read.

It certainly became a very real place in the teaching of Jesus and of the apostles who established Christianity. It produces "weeping and gnashing of teeth," a state of human suffering which Jesus regards as a proper fate for all who can't see a Jewish carpenter as a king or God. But Satan and his wicked spirits will be *unwilling* companions of the unsaved in this misery, if and when God finally succeeds in coming out on top of the contest between good and evil.

Heaven is ever-present in the pages of the Old Testament but not as a designated future home for all the righteous after death. Eternal life in heaven or hell is said to be the new promise of God with the coming of Jesus, but at least a favored few Old Testament figures *have* made it to heaven. God lives there in the Old Testament heaven along with the angels, some of them less than angelic, for lying spirits and evil spirits are available there for God's dark purposes.

Actually, the Old Testament Lord and angels don't spend much of their time in their heavenly abode, preferring to appear bodily on earth in clouds, smoke, bushes, wrestling matches, with swords, on mountains, and in innumerable dreams and visions. Jesus used to exist there with God before the world began and *now* sits there on the right hand of the throne, according to the New Testament, which pictures heaven as the ultimate home of the saints and saved.

Although not described at all in the Old Testament, heaven rates *some* description in the New, and a muddled version of it emerges. It is "up," a class system prevails there (Jesus says: "The same is *greatest* in the kingdom of heaven." *Matt. 18:4*), the twelve disciples (Judas, too?) will have thrones there, Jesus will be there awaiting the signal to return to earth and gather up the believers, the Holy Ghost leaves it to violate virgins and perform various other tricks, it contains many mansions for incorruptible spiritual bodies, untold delights await there for the blessed, and prophets call it home.

There is no marriage or giving in marriage, and living there together may really be "heavenly." In any case, there is not a great deal of room in the New Testament heaven, so it is just as well that "few are chosen." The Revelation gives the exact measurements of the New Jerusalem as 12,000 furlongs wide, long, and high. *Rev. 21:16* Since 4 billion persons now populate the earth, and human life is millions (some scientists say more than a billion) of years old, it is fairly obvious that hell will have to be a good deal larger than heaven.

Which heaven can be aspired to is also contradictory, since more than one is spoken of in the scriptures. And if there are some who are convinced that heaven is their destination, they'd best be prepared for a temporary stay, in spite of all the promises of eternal life, for Jesus says: "Heaven and earth shall pass away." *Matt. 24:35* and *Luke 21:33*

<hr>

One of the greatest theological contradictions found in the Bible is embodied in the idea of original sin. Jesus says in John 15:22 that: "If I had not come and spoken unto them, they had not had sin." But Paul says in Romans 5:19 that: "For as by one man's disobedience many were made sinners, so by the obedience of one shall many be made righteous." (This is the only time, by slip of tongue or pen, that Adam is the culprit.)

From Jesus's statement it might be assumed that humankind was better off before he came, since it didn't have to bear the burden of sin and be in danger of damnation. Paul found it necessary, however, as has the Church, to label all persons sinners because of the disobedience of Adam and thus in need of a savior who would make atonement for those sins to an angry God.

Paul maintains that up to the time of Christ all suffered death but that Jesus brought the hope for eternal life. The concept involved in all this is that God found it desirable finally to release man from the curse he imposed in the Garden of Eden by coming to earth himself as a lowly human being and having himself tortured to death on a cross, thus saving man from the death God had himself decreed. To put it more succinctly, God made atonement to himself. Paul puts it this way: "Therefore as by the offence of one, judgment came upon all men to condemnation; even so by the righteousness of one the free gift came upon all men unto justification of life." *Romans 5:18*

God's words in the Old Testament, which he repeats many times, would seem to uphold the idea of original sin: ". . . for I am a jealous God visiting the iniquity of the fathers upon the children." *Ex. 20:5* In one sense the concept of original sin seems to be supported by Jesus: "Except a man be born again he cannot see the kingdom of God." *John 3:3* Apparently God cannot create an unflawed person.

Paul, with his attitude toward women showing, places the blame for original sin belatedly upon Eve, with the theological quibbling at which he is the master: "And Adam was not deceived, but the woman being deceived was in the transgression." Then his big heart just will win out: "Notwithstanding she shall be saved in child-bearing, if they continue in faith and charity and holiness with sobriety." *I Tim. 2:14,15* Finally Paul defines the whole

Christian doctrine as he ordains it: "But the scripture hath concluded all under sin, that the promise by faith of Jesus Christ might be given to them that believe." *Gal. 3:22*

—————⟹◆⟸—————

Another theological contradiction perhaps equally as important as that surrounding original sin is that concerning the Trinity. The following verses graphically represent the dilemma of the Church: "For there are three that bear record in heaven, the Father, the Word and the Holy Ghost, and these three are one." *I John 5:7* "He that hath seen me hath seen the Father." *John 14:9* "My Father is greater than I." *John 14:28* "And whosoever shall speak a word against the Son of man, it shall be forgiven him, but unto him that blasphemeth against the Holy Ghost it shall not be forgiven." *Luke 12:10*

Continuing: "But the Comforter, which is the Holy Ghost, whom the Father will send in my name . . ." *John 14:26* "As thou, Father, art in me, and I in thee . . . that they may be one even as we are one." *John 17:21,22* "I and my Father are one." *John 10:30* "And Jesus said unto him, Why callest thou me good? none is good, save one, that is, God." *Luke 18:19* Jesus even prays to God: "Father, forgive them." *Luke 12:34*

Further, Jesus as the Son of God was born of a woman impregnated by the Holy Ghost (with her handy consent). The angel Gabriel so tells Mary: "The Holy Ghost shall come upon thee, and the power of the Highest shall overshadow thee; therefore also that holy thing that shall be born of thee shall be called the Son of God." *Luke 1:35* It's sort of a case of "I'm my own Grandpa." But the Church, through its creeds, has opted for the Trinity, thus placing upon humankind the burden of guilt for having, both by sin and actual fact, caused the humiliating death of God, and leaving the question hanging of why God should pay atonement to himself with his own blood after turning himself into a circumcised human male.

—————⟹◆⟸—————

Contradictory to every moral law is the theory that an innocent should face the consequences for the misdeeds of another, a theory embodied in the Christian dogma that Christ died to make reparation for the world's sins and to reconcile God and his children. Most persons prefer to pay for their *own* mistakes and would not welcome *rewards* belonging to another. Such miscarriages of justice would hopefully leave them with feelings of remorse, yet Christianity demands acceptance of the idea that God himself died at their hands to pay for their sins, and asks them to anticipate the consequence of their act—eternal bliss in the company of their victim!

This "proxy" concept of expiation is straight from the old Jewish and pagan customs of sacrifices and offerings of humans, animals, and harvest fruits, and to most persons the practice of putting an animal to death for purposes of atonement is preferable to the human sacrifice commemorated in the Mass and the cannibalistic Communion and Eucharist. The whole bloody basis of the Christian religion and the use of the torture-cross symbol are so repulsive that adherents try to make things cheerier with new wardrobes, breaking of fasts, and colored eggs, when Easter season comes around, but children whose parents strive to shield them from the shocking cruelty of which the human race is capable are exposed by the Church to stories and pictures of betrayal, suffering, and death and told that they helped to drive nails into the hands and feet of someone who loves them. To make matters worse, they are taught that all these deeds comprise a *beautiful* story.

Many *pagan* religions have been characterized by ceremonies built around the precept that an innocent should die to redeem the guilty, but the Bible has no shame: "While we were yet sinners, Christ died for us . . . through our Lord Jesus Christ, by whom we have now received the atonement." *Romans 5:8–11*

⟹◆⟸

God's threat to Adam that Adam would surely die the very day he ate of the tree of knowledge (*Gen. 2:17*) is not carried out. Actually Adam is to live 930 years. Finally, death does catch up with him, and the reader is told by Paul that it is an eternal death. Hope for *everlasting* life comes only with belief in Jesus Christ. The promise of eternal life is the second covenant given by God to the Jews, the covenant of circumcision having been negated by the failure of the Old Testament Jews to please God during the time they lived by the law handed down from God to Moses. Thus the Bible contains both the Old and New Testaments.

God sentenced Adam to return to dust, and Paul, self-appointed interpreter of all God's intentions, leads one to believe that such was the fate of all generations of Jews from Adam through Moses: "Nevertheless, death reigned from Adam to Moses, even over them that had not sinned after the similitude of Adam's transgression." *Romans 5:14* Paul doesn't explain in what way they *had* sinned, and he later contradicts himself by recalling that Enoch was taken to heaven without suffering death, before Moses was born. *Hebrews 11:5*

Paul wades into deeper theological depths and finds himself in the whirlpool churned up by the conflict between the *law* by which Jews had lived from the time of Moses and the new *faith* in Jesus Christ required of all converts. Jews who had patterned their lives after the teachings of God through the Mosaic law are now told that that is no longer sufficient or whol-

ly necessary. Salvation is now imperative in order to achieve the new promise of everlasting life. Righteousness once attained through observance of the
law now could be acquired only by *grace* which came on the heels of belief.
Paul ascribes even more unfairness to God by claiming that God actually created the Mosaic law in order to increase *offences* so that more *grace* might be
needed. *Romans 5:20,21* (God should have felled Paul again!)

This replacement of the *law* by *faith* and *grace* confronts Paul with the
question which naturally arises of whether the generations of the period
from Moses to Christ are eligible for everlasting life. Paul hopes so but
doubts it. His reasoning is embodied in the following scriptures and they are
indicative of the many times Paul is hoist on his own petard.

First Paul speaks for God about the Jews who escaped from Egypt:
"Wherefore I was grieved with that generation and said, They do always err
in their heart, and they have not known my ways. So I sware in my wrath,
They shall not enter into my rest." *Hebrews 3:10,11* Then his dissembling
encompasses all the Jews from Moses to Jesus: "But Israel, which followed
after the *law* of righteousness, hath not *attended* to the law of righteousness.
Wherefore? Because they sought it not by *faith*, but as it were by the works
of the *law*." *Romans 9:31,32* In the same epistle he writes: "Brethren, my
heart's desire and prayer to God is, that they might be saved." *Romans 10:1*
But Paul judges them unworthy, in spite of himself: "They being ignorant of
God's righteousness, and going about to establish *their own* righteousness,
have not submitted themselves unto the righteousness of *God*. For *Christ* is
the *end* of the *law* for righteousness." *Romans 10:1–4* It is rather presumptuous of Paul to criticise the righteousness of the Mosaic law, since God transmitted it to Moses in person after going to quite a bit of trouble to turn this
murderer into a law-giver.

But Moses isn't around to defend himself, and Paul goes even further.
Speaking of some favored and revered descendants of Abraham down to
Christ, he says: "And these all having obtained a good report through faith
(contradicting himself) received not the promise: God having provided some
better thing for *us*." *Hebrews 11:39,40* The *better* thing is of course everlasting
life in Paradise. Paul leaves the explanation of God's unkind partiality up to
his readers.

Peter makes his own claim as regards the question of life after death for
pre-Christ Jews: "For David is not ascended into the heavens." *Acts 2:34* But
Jesus said: "When ye shall see Abraham and Isaac, and Jacob, and all the
prophets, in the kingdom of God . . ." *Luke 13:28* Peter's contention and that
of Paul that the Jews up to the time of Christ were not admitted to heaven,
is also contradicted by scriptures which describe the presence of Abraham
there and the appearance of Moses and Elijah with Jesus at the time of the

Transfiguration. *Luke 16:22–31* and *Matt. 17*

——>·◇·<——

Having sat out the Old Testament, the Holy Ghost and its machinations are suddenly everywhere in the New, but the references to it (him) are so contradictory that one can have no clear idea of just what it (he) is supposed to be, although the Church, in spite of dissension, has settled the transcendental enigma, declaring the Holy Ghost to be God. God might wish to file a protest, and he would be justified, for the Holy Ghost is the buttinsky of all time, giving advice and warnings, planning people's itineraries, causing them to talk in gibberish, falling upon them, dwelling in the hands of a designated few (Paul and the other apostles), being breathed onto people by Jesus, carrying on conversations, and impregnating virgins (sometimes obligingly sending the angel Gabriel ahead to announce his arrival).

Just about the time the Bible-reader has the Holy Ghost pegged, along comes John, the touch-up artist of the New Testament, who turns the Holy Ghost into the Spirit of Truth and the Comforter which Jesus will ask the Father to send in his place to the disciples, a Comforter only they can know and that will dwell in them forever. *John 14:16,26* Strange, then, that the Holy Ghost can be transmitted.

Peter tries to inject the Holy Ghost into Jewish history by claiming: "For the prophecy came not in old times by the will of man: but holy men of God spake as they were moved by the Holy Ghost." *II Peter 1:21* The prophets themselves, however, didn't give the Holy Ghost credit for their impassioned ravings.

The Bible, so freely populated with angels, devils, spirits, wild-eyed fortune tellers, witches, seers, wizards, disembodied voices, burning bushes, pillars of smoke, blooming rods, and magic, wouldn't have been complete without a full-fledged ghost, but to turn God into a spook took considerable theological craftsmanship. Incidentally, the faithful can receive the Holy Ghost through prayer and sometimes, but not always, by baptism, if they haven't already had a surprise visit from him.

——>·◇·<——

Although the God of the Old Testament is very concerned about how the Jews live in this world, Jesus and the apostles stress the need to reject the world and concentrate on the hereafter totally. Christians are required to deny themselves all earthly pleasures in preparation for everlasting life in an ill-defined next realm: "For the flesh lusteth against the Spirit, and the Spirit against the flesh: and these are contrary the one to the other: so that ye cannot do the things that ye would." *Gal. 5:17*

Jesus's attitude toward worldly and heavenly pursuits which called for a choice between them is echoed by Paul in another letter to one of his con-gregations: "Set your affection on things above, not on things on the earth." *Col. 3:2* Having warned converts to deny themselves gratification of earthly desires, Paul then tells them how they may find *acceptable* enjoyment: "Therefore I take pleasure in infirmities, in reproaches, in necessities, in per-secutions, in distresses . . ." *II Cor. 12:10* Paul is the New Testament Job, and Christians glory in the afflictions assigned to them. Self-chastisement and self-denial are marks of piety and sanctification.

There is no tragedy, misfortune, sorrow, or disaster shattering enough or pointless enough to make believers rebel, even today: "For whom the Lord loveth he chasteneth, and scourgeth every son whom he receiveth." *Hebrews 12:6* "For I reckon that the sufferings of this present time are not worthy to be compared with the glory that shall be revealed in us." *Romans 8:18* Masochists make good candidates for believing that the reward for which they have been waiting 2,000 years will ultimately materialize, although there *has* been at least one impatient nameless complainer. He or she made the oft-quoted remark that it is no wonder God has so few friends, consider-ing how he treats them.

⇒◇⇐

God in the Old Testament was very vehement about forbidding the eating of blood, and the promise that it would be no part of the Jewish diet was part of God's covenant with Noah and Abram. But Jesus at the Last Supper offers his blood symbolically to be drunk by the disciples: "And he took the cup, and gave thanks, and gave it to them, saying, Drink ye all of it. For this is my blood of the new testament, which is shed for many for the remission of sins." *Matt. 26:27,28* Drinking the blood of a god, a pagan ritual, thus became a Christian one, but before blood can be drunk, it must be shed. Paul writes categorically that: "Without shedding of blood is no remission." *Hebrews 9:22*

Paul probably made this assertion in an attempt to justify the crucifixion, at best a distasteful means of paving the way for forgiveness of sin, if forgive-ness is necessary. The crucifixion revived the heathen ritual of human sacri-fice which the Old Testament Lord condemned Baal worshippers for prac-ticing.

⇒◇⇐

If God had been looking for a nondescript people by whom to introduce the Savior of the entire world, he could hardly have found one of less importance than the Jews of that day. And to have made them his Chosen People centuries before is even more difficult to understand. Jews of the early Old Testament were relatively few in number, idol-worshipping, nomadic, simple, and bereft of a homeland; and their main occupation was agriculture. At the time Jesus was presumed to have lived, they were under Roman rule and so unprepossessing as to rate scarcely any recognition by historians of the day.

The Roman Empire was widespread and powerful, and the Greek and Roman languages the common ones into which other languages were translated. And some nations which conquered the Jews were far more cultured and advanced than their Jewish neighbors. For instance, the Babylonians and Chaldeans and Egyptians were skilled in agriculture, architecture, commerce, law, handwriting, astronomy, the Zodiac, government, mathematics, and banking. The status of women in these countries, in contrast to their position of inferiority among the Hebrews, was high, and they engaged in business. The Assyrians were the first to use iron and were more gifted in the arts than even the Babylonians.

The city of Babylon was extraordinarily beautiful, with hanging gardens and lovely architecture, and even contained libraries, at the time of the Jewish captivity. Zoroastrianism was the uplifting religion of the Persians. It taught that life was a battle between storm and sunshine (good and evil). The good, Ahura Mazda, would eventually triumph, but everyone must continually fight on one side or the other. The sacred book, the Avesta, presented a highly idealistic way of living, stressing good thoughts, behavior, and words, thus contradicting the Old Testament view that all Gentile religions were degenerate. The Magi were the priestly and learned caste of Zoroastrianism. The Ten Commandments repeat Zoroastrian principles.

Out of all these possibilities, however, to say nothing of the ancient cultures of the Far East, the Almighty of the Bible made a few barbaric Semitic tribes his Chosen People. The standards he used for such a selection are obscure and contradictory, if he intended to start a religion for the whole world. Judaism has remained a religion for some people of Semitic origins, for the most part, and Christianity not only did not take hold among *them* but required over 300 years to become an established religion. Is God incapable of being revealed equally to all?

⇒•⇐

The Bible asserts in several places that Jesus existed before the world began. Jesus himself so claims: "And now, O Father, glorify thou me with thine own self with the glory which I had with thee before the world was." *John 17:5* His birth on earth then created one of the many contradictions that caused dissension among early Christian churchmen and led to Councils and violent arguments, even fist fights. These arguments included disagreements over the Trinity doctrine, of course, besides one of how Jesus could be anything but human, and another that asked if Jesus was divine, when did the divinity begin? Some antagonists maintained that during Mary's pregnancy, Jesus *dribbled* down from heaven over a period of nine months. And yet another horrendous difference arose over whether God and Jesus were made of the same material or only similar material, when Jesus became a god.

To answer charges that the persons who won the arguments and made the final theological decisions had no special qualifications to do so, squirming believers claim that each Council was under the guidance and inspiration of God, just as they also claim that those who put the New Testament together in its entirety could make no errors because of divine control. Strange, then, that contradictions are so prevalent in the Holy Book that division, often bloody, has been the history of the One True Religion divinely revealed. (Over 250 Protestant sects, alone, exist). The young Church declared some bishops heretics and decided the Word of God by vote.

—————◈—————

The particular Jews to whom the biblical God gives his approval and blessing and to whom he assigns positions of eminence are for the most part not highly admirable persons. The first man and woman he created couldn't wait to get into trouble. Noah, one of only eight human beings righteous enough to be saved from the Great Flood, later becomes a drunkard and lies around naked, the butt of derision on the part of his son. Abraham passes off his wife as his sister twice, allowing her to be taken into the households of two rulers and by this deceit acquiring wealth. He appears willing, without protesting, to kill his favorite child by slitting its throat and sends another son Ishmael along with the child's mother into a vast desert alone.

Lot, who with his family was the only worthy enough to be rescued from Sodom and Gomorrah, later practices incest with his daughters while he is intoxicated. Earlier, he has offered them, virgins, to men of the city who threaten his home and demand that he send out to them the male angels spending the night there.

Jacob tricks Esau into selling him his birthright and also disguises himself to fool his father, for which duplicity, with a perverted sense of fairness, God hates *Esau* forever. Later, Jacob, that schemer who is to become the father of the twelve tribes of Israel, carries out a plot by which he obtains an unfair share of his father-in-law's livestock. *Gen. 30*

Moses has to flee as a murderer, then as God's hatchetman, along with Joshua, slaughters untold thousands of Gentiles in order to take possession of their land. King Saul is so dissolute he tries to kill his own son with a javelin and David in any way he can and finally has to be driven to suicide by God, who made him king.

David is less than honorable in his love life and is forbidden by God to build the temple because of his immoral behavior. Solomon does everything to excess and whiles away his time with 700 wives and 300 concubines. Most of the ensuing kings revert to idol worship and sacrifice their own children, when they are not engaged in plots and assassinations to win or hang onto the throne.

Of all the aforementioned, David becomes the most-admired patriarch by those who forget that he offered to turn traitor and fight with the Philistines. Properly white-washed, he becomes the king whose descendant will emerge as the Messiah, according to the prophets, who gloss over his role as torturer and wife-stealer.

All these giants of the two nations of Israel and Judah are the highly-praised exemplars often referred to in awe by Jesus and the New Testament apostles. For instance, Peter calls Noah a "preacher of righteousness." He describes Lot as a just and righteous man and dubs David a patriarch. *Acts 2:29 II Peter 2:5 II Peter 2:7,8* They deserved to be Jewish heroes, perhaps, but singled out by God?

⇒·◇·⇐

When God created the world, he decreed *light* the *first* day and the sun and the moon and the stars on the *4th* day. *Gen. 1* The Bible does not explain how God existed in a state of total darkness prior to that. Or *where* he existed. Or who and how many existed there with him. Or how his existence came about.

⇒·◇·⇐

God's covenant with Abraham, the covenant of circumcision, was to be permanent, according to God's promise; yet in the Wilderness, at the end of his patience with the Israelites, he offers to make Moses the father of the Jewish nation. Later, the *new* covenant of everlasting life replaces the first covenant, with the coming of Jesus. *Gen. 12:2* and *Ex. 32:10,11* Abraham failed to get a signature on his contract with God, and God feels free to break it with impunity. God's word was not good.

⇒·◇·⇐

Although God pledged himself to establish the Jewish nation *forever* and promised Palestine to the Jews, he leaves some nations unconquered by Moses and Joshua in order to *prove* the Jews and teach them war. He allows these four nations to enslave the Jews 63 years. He also causes Jerusalem and Judah to fall into the hands of Babylonia under Nebuchadnezzar for 70 years and Israel to be absorbed by her conqueror Assyria. The prophets predicted the reunion of Israel and Judah, but it did not take place, and the ten tribes of the North and the southern two remained separate, as they had become after the death of Saul. Instead of remaining one nation, ruled by David's line, as the prophet Nathan had foretold, the Jews were absorbed, scattered, and persecuted.

⇒◆⇐

Jesus is supposed to be of the house of David, in order to fulfill the prophecy that the Messiah would come from that line. Throughout the New Testament this lineage is assigned to Jesus, but in fact it is Joseph who is descended from David, and Joseph is not Jesus's father. By making Jesus the son of a god, in the tradition of other mythologies, the writers of the New Testament got themselves into a theological bind. *Matt. 1:1–16 Luke 2:4 Luke 3:23–31*

⇒◆⇐

Fear that the end of the world was at hand and that some frightful Judgment Day was at the dawning was an attention-getter first used in the New Testament by the Essene John the Baptist, who terrified even some of the Pharisees and Sadducees with talk of "the wrath to come." *Matt. 3:7* Jesus wasn't above using the psychology of fear and sounded the same note over and over: "Verily I say unto you, This generation shall not pass away, till all be fulfilled." *Luke 21:32* He made his second coming so terrifying and so imminent that the apostles were convinced of its prompt occurrence and eagerly anticipated being among the first occupants of the "kingdom of God."

Witnesses in courtrooms on earth today who are shown to be unreliable in one area are not given much credence in other areas, but this discrepancy in the teachings of Jesus, made manifest by the fact that all the disciples are dead and the Church is still using the same scare tactic about the end of the world, doesn't seem to have made his other pronouncements suspect. It does attest to deliberate misleading on the part of God or to a God who cannot see into the future or shape it.

⇒◆⇐

The Bible is a book about the Jews, their history, customs, lifestyle, superstitions, and religion; it is a contradiction that Gentiles should find much meaning in it for them. Locating a good word for Gentiles in the Old Testament is a nearly impossible feat. The Jews hold them in as much contempt as God does. Their ultimate annihilation is described by the prophets in such brutal language, and their treatment by Israelite armies at the direction of the Lord is so vindictive it should cause any Gentile reading the Bible to pitch the whole ponderous tome onto the nearest trash heap.

Jesus was a Jew who claimed to be that Gentile-despising God of the Old Testament. He said he came to preach to the Jews, and that is almost totally what he did and instructed his disciples to do. He called Gentiles "dogs." Outside of a few remarks about carrying the gospel to the Gentiles (which were so understated that visions were required after his ascension to convince Peter and Paul and the other apostles that salvation was intended for Gentiles as well as Jews), he is concerned with the Jews, their laws, their marriages, their diets, their relationship with their God, their prophets and prophecies, their history, and their salvation. Jews see the risen Christ, Jews see the ascension (unless the two white-clad men in Acts [*Acts 1:10*] were Gentile angels).

The Bible is an ego trip for Jews. They are the Chosen People and the people designated by God to give origin to the *new* faith. The apostles tried to spread the word strictly among the Jews at first, tardily to the Gentiles. Even then, much of their argumentation concerned such Jewish behavior as the practice of circumcision and obedience to every aspect of the Mosaic law.

Both the Old and New Testaments have little that is intended for the Gentiles, but Gentiles chose to appropriate what little there was. The God of the Old Testament considered the Gentiles idol-worshippers, although many of them were not. Some worshipped deities more idealistic than the Lord of the Jews. Nevertheless, that Lord had no use for them, although he allowed Gentile nations to take the back-sliding Jews captive as punishment for disobedience.

Paul had great success with the conversion of Gentiles, but his words express his true feelings: God will give "glory, honour, and peace, to every man that worketh good, to the Jew *first*, and also to the Gentile." *Romans 2:10*

———⋙⋅◇⋅⋘———

There are many blatant contradictions between scriptural passages from the Old and New Testaments. A limited number of examples will serve to pinpoint the stark differences in context:

"In righteousness shalt thou judge thy neighbor." *Lev. 19:15* So God orders in the Old Testament, but Jesus teaches "judge not that ye be not judged." *Matt. 7:1*

"Thou, Lord, art seen face to face." *Num. 14:14* But Jesus contradicts Moses: "Not that any man hath seen the Father." *John 6:46*

"The rich man's wealth is his strong city." *Prov. 18:11* But Jesus teaches: "It is easier for a camel to go through the eye of a needle, than for a rich man to enter into the kingdom of God!" *Mark 10:25*

"The earth abideth forever." *Eccles. 1:4* "The earth . . . and the works that are therein shall be burned up." *II Peter 3:10*

"Remember the Sabbath day to keep it holy." *Ex. 20:8* But Paul equivocates: "One man esteemeth one day above another; another esteemeth every day alike. Let every man be fully persuaded in his own mind." *Romans 14:5*

"An eye for an eye and a tooth for a tooth." *Ex. 21:24* But Jesus urges, turn the other cheek. *Matt. 5:38,39*

"Thou shalt not kill." *Ex. 20:13* This commandment was relayed by a leader who had murdered an Egyptian and who went on to master-mind the slaughter of thousands in the long march to reach Palestine. It wasn't long after laying down this law to the Israelites that Moses ordered: "Thus saith the Lord of Israel, Put every man his sword by his side, and go in and out from gate to gate throughout the camp, and slay every man his brother, and every man his companion, and every man his neighbor." *Ex. 32:27* And even Jesus says: "And he that hath no sword, let him sell his garment and buy one." *Luke 22:36*

"The son shall not bear the iniquity of the father." *Ez. 18:20* But God told Moses: "I, the Lord thy God, am a jealous God, visiting the iniquity of the fathers upon the children unto the third and fourth generation . . ." *Ex. 20:5*

"Ye have kindled a fire in mine anger which shall burn forever." *Jer. 17:4* But John gets his re-touch tools out again: "God is love." *I John 4:16*

"As it is written, Jacob have I loved, but Esau have I hated." *Romans 9:13* This quotation of God's words by Paul jars, not only because of the context, but because Paul has just claimed: "There is no respect of persons with God." *Romans 2:11* God's antagonism toward Esau is inconsistent with the behavior of the twin brothers. Esau is a good-natured, forgiving, naive person who was the victim of Jacob's duplicity.

"Now go and smite Amalek, and utterly destroy all that they have, and spare them not, but slay both man and woman, infant, and suckling." *I Sam. 15:3* "And it came to pass that at midnight the Lord smote all the firstborn in the land of Egypt . . ." *Ex. 12:29* These Bible verses concern the God who came to earth as Jesus Christ, of whom James says: "The Lord is very pitiful, and of tender mercy." *James 5:11* Those who see wholesale bloodshed of babies as an act of pity and mercy adore this God in places of worship and sing paeans of praise—"How Great Thou Art!"

To the Romans again Paul speaks of: ". . . the god of Peace." *Romans 15:33* And Christians refer to Jesus as the Prince of Peace in a prophecy-fulfilling effort, but Jesus himself said: "I came not to send peace, but a sword." *Matt. 10:34* And: "He that hath no sword, let him sell his garment and buy one." *Luke 22:36* The Old Testament had its own definition of the Almighty:

"The Lord is a man of war." *Ex. 15:3*

"And Elijah went up by a whirlwind into heaven." *II Kings 2:11* Also Enoch was taken bodily to heaven at the age of 365. *Gen. 5:24* But Jesus claims the distinction for himself: "No man hath ascended up to heaven, but he that came down from heaven, even the Son of Man." *John 3:13*

—————◆—————

Are human beings responsible for their behavior? The person who believes what the Bible says in some passages need not think so, although it is taught and assumed as basic to Christianity that all are sinners and must accept blame for being such. But several verses of scripture contradict this assumption and project the thought that not only has behavior been conditioned by God but that the saints have already been chosen and the fate of many, if not all, predestined. Furthermore, helpless humanity is trapped and tempted. By Satan? Often, by God.

Jesus himself with no compunction whatever, in explaining why he tells so many parables, imparts this reason to astounded readers: ". . . all these things are done in parables: that seeing they may see, and not perceive; and hearing they may hear, and not understand; lest at any time they should be converted, and their sins should be forgiven them." *Mark 4:11,12*

Paul muddies the waters even further with his special gift for squarely being controversial: "God shall send them strong delusion, that they should believe a lie: That they all might be damned who believed not the truth." *II Thess. 2:11,12* With his "potter and clay" equivocation to the Romans, he embroiders the theme of God as the shaper of man's character: "Therefore hath he mercy on whom he will have mercy, and whom he will he hardeneth." *Romans 9* He even uses the word "predestinated": "He hath chosen us in him before the foundation of the world . . . having predestinated us unto the adoption of children by Jesus Christ." *Eph. 1:4,5*

Predestination from the time of the creation of the world is also claimed in passages from The Revelation: "And they that dwell on the earth shall wonder, whose names were not written in the book of life from the foundation of the world." *Rev. 17:8* "And whosoever was not found written in the book of life was cast into the lake of fire." *Rev. 20:15* Christians may be able to induce God's secretary to add a name or two, unless the entries were made with God's finger.

Since the Lord's Prayer with its plea to "lead us not into temptation" impugns temptation on the part of the Lord, and the Bible says he tempted Abraham and "proved" the Israelites, God's behavior is often hard to distinguish from that common to Satan. James furnishes the inevitable biblical contradiction this time: "Neither tempteth he (God) any man." *James 1:13*

Because the Bible says that few will be allowed to pass through the traditional gates of pearl, the benevolence of God in cancelling his first promise and replacing it with the second promise of everlasting life is doubtful. When asked if only a few would be saved, Jesus confirmed the questioner's premonition and cautioned: "Strive to enter in at the strait gate: for many, I say unto you, will seek to enter in, and shall not be able." *Luke 13:24* If, knowing the future, God was conscious of the fact that many more would be damned than would be saved, even going so far as to prepare a list of the fortunate, the Bible makes him sound downright malicious.

⟹◆⟸

The Mosaic law and the teaching of Jesus sometimes conflict. Jesus and Paul spend considerable time trying to reconcile the two, not always successfully, and always with the new admonition in mind that since John the Baptist the Jews were no longer under obligation to obey any law and need answer only to God, as they are "justified by faith": "By him all that believe are justified from all things." *Acts 13:39*

This doctrine, held by many today, puts religious belief above obedience to the law and could be a dangerous one. It has been used by the Church and fanatics to excuse atrocities and crimes, as well as by the opportunistic. The argument persists of whether one is obliged to obey a law which violates one's religious convictions. Even the Bible is not clear on the question (not an unusual situation), but with the contradiction inherent in scripture after scripture, the apostles demand respect and obedience to every ordinance of kings and governors. *I Peter 2:13–17*

⟹◆⟸

Jesus makes the statement in the *New* Testament, repeated by the apostles, that unless one becomes as a child, he cannot enter the kingdom of heaven. *Matt. 18:3* But the attitude toward children in the *Old* Testament shows somewhat less admiration for their ability to discriminate: God refers to "your children which in that day had no knowledge between good and evil." *Deut. 1:39* Paul himself admits: "When I was a child, I spake as a child, I understood as a child, I thought as a child: but when I became a man, I put away childish things." *I Cor. 13:11* To instill into the young a course of action like this one of Paul's is the goal of educational systems in civilized countries. Choosing a philosophy of life such as a child without guidance might select is not a course that has an appeal for mature adults. Indeed, the progress of any society is usually measured by the degree in which rationality prevails in it.

The great mass of perplexing contradictions and errors which assaults anyone who has the stamina to plow through the Bible has necessitated a complicated theology that challenges the thinking processes of an adult. The untried mind of a child, though, peopled as it is with images of Santa Claus and Tinker Bell, may after all represent just the level of thought processes required for acceptance of a religious system which has its roots deep in superstition and mythology.

An in-depth study of the history of magic and religion throughout the world cannot help but reveal the fact that the facets and components of Christianity have evolved from the worship systems of primitive peoples and pagan cultures. From the first assignment to the supernatural of responsibility for whatever could not be controlled, to the Christian "mysteries" of heaven, the same elements of horror, cruelty, fanaticism, and mysticism that characterize some pagan religions, in company with much of their pageantry and beauty, have marked the doctrine and spread of Judaic-Christianity. And Judaism and Christianity both still employ magic.

The myth of the soul, originating in savage tribes, is one of the oldest traditional beliefs to find its way to Christianity, and its assignment to various parts and secretions of the human body led to hair-worship (Samson), heart-worship (cannibalism of the Eucharist and Communion), saliva-worship (spit-healing by Jesus), etc., and to the body-soul concept (guardian angels and ghosts). In ancient religions, soul(s) and body could be separated at death, but both were eligible for resurrection and a heavenly home, often preceded by a Judgment Day.

The Creation and Adam and Eve in a garden did not originate with Judaism. They were borrowed ideas, as were Satan (linked to snake worship, in turn to sexuality, in turn to Eve and serpent), original sin, angry gods who withdraw from fallen mankind, savior gods to reconcile it and be crucified, and various hells.

Other concepts and practices common to mythology which Judaism and/or Christianity embrace include: gods who travel between heaven and earth, virgin-born humans and gods, gods who mate with maidens to produce demi-gods, gods who must be appeased, gods who rise yearly with the season, Messiahs, eating the body of a god, animal sacrifice, human sacrifice and sacrifice of a proxy (son for father), blood as a purifier, devil-possession, exorcism, miracles, immortality as a gift from the gods, licentious rites and filthy gods and goddesses (Revelation), baptism, celibacy, confession to priests, absolution, sacramental bread and wine, penances, extreme unction, spirits, demons, monotheism, a Trinity, temptation undergone by gods, the uncleanness of sexual union and menstruation and childbirth, religious ecstasy, the glow of righteousness, reliance on legends such as The Deluge and Confusion of the Tongues, fetishes (relics, medals), sun worship (Sunday,

Jesus as halo-adorned life-giving Christ), Zodiac worship (Jesus as a fish or Lamb of God, twelve tribes, twelve disciples, mansions in heaven), revelation in holy books, worship at altars and temples, use of candles and bells and feast days, asceticism, supplicating, anointing, and exclusion of women from religious rites.

Zoroastrianism, e.g., along with the religions of Greece, Egypt, Assyria, and other countries "neighboring" Israel, is thought to be a possible source of much Christian doctrine. As described in preceding pages, it, like Christianity, embodied belief that good persons would go to heaven. At the end of 12,000 years Ahriman (Satan) would be overthrown; then the Savior Saoshant would be virgin-born and the dead rise, as hills became molten metal to destroy the wicked. Ahriman and his demons would occupy hell, loved ones would be reunited, and the righteous would enjoy eternal bliss in their heavenly home. All this is almost Christianity to a "T."

⟫•◇•⟪

Belief in God and Jesus as the Savior is the only way for man to escape damnation, says the Bible, but Paul claims it is impossible to comprehend his God: "How unsearchable are his judgments, and his ways past finding out." *Romans 11:33* Jesus, himself, explains to his disciples that he has to speak in parables, for it is not given to listeners other than they to understand his teachings. *Matt. 13:11* This image of a human race as basically incapable of grasping concepts is a fit companion for the Christian requirement that people accept Christianity on faith alone. Hunger for knowledge caused the *downfall* of the human race.

The idea of faith, which is not based on knowledge or experience or rational thinking arising from doubt, replaces the search for truth. The putdown of intelligence and use of the mind in any way is so woven throughout the New Testament that one must finally conclude that people should strive to be stupid and unquestioning, and that those who are not are doomed. Intelligence paves the way to hell-fire: "For it is written, I will destroy the wisdom of the wise, and will bring to nothing the understanding of the prudent." *I Cor. 1:19* And: "God hath chosen the foolish things of the world to confound the wise." *I Cor. 1:27* Paul, not content with belittling those with a high I.Q., proceeds to insult the clergy: "It pleased God by the foolishness of preaching to save them that believe." *I Cor. 1:21*

The conclusion necessarily drawn from these scriptures is that, since "imprudent" and gullible persons are the most likely to accept illogical ideas or unnatural "facts," the Christian religion risks rejection by anyone who chooses to use his or her gray matter. Education, then, is the enemy of humankind, since it will surely lead to damnation. Such, at least, are the implications of the Gospel, and in fact the Christian Church was for many centuries the greatest barrier ever erected against learning and research, including progress in medicine and surgery. Compelled finally to abandon this sterile position as indefensible, it then adopted the stand that all knowledge, scientific or otherwise, always enhances the teachings of the Bible and the Christian Church. Before this attitude was assumed by the Christian hierarchy, "heretical" scientists were burned at the stake or made to recant.

⇒·◇·⇐

Jesus, verbally picturing his magnificent and terrifying Second Coming, says the people will *see* him arriving in the clouds, although the sun and *moon* (!) are darkened and the stars have fallen. *Matt. 24:29,30*

⇒·◇·⇐

Failure of Christians to follow many of the moral precepts laid down by Jesus is understandable when one studies the rules individually (keeping in mind that the Golden Rule was the basic doctrine of a score of religions) and comes to the realization that observance of the more unworkable ones would cause havoc in any society. The ethical worth of many of them is doubtful, to be kind. A few examples make the point.

"Turn the other cheek" encourages cruelty to others. "Judge not" eradicates the use of any moral evaluation. Such a practice would overthrow entire legal systems and lead to a takeover by criminal elements. "Be as children" negates the whole field of reason and experience as useful to humanity in making decisions that govern personal behavior, and eliminates the need for education of any kind. Children cannot distinguish between reality and fantasy, and their minds are immature and not trained to consider and arrive at reasonable conclusions.

"Have no care for personal needs" would put everybody in care of the State, which would have no tax-base, as the economy and financial support for government would evaporate. "Give all you have to the poor" would reverse the distribution of wealth without changing anything. "Take no thought for the morrow" would sound the death-knell for capitalism and individual enterprise and wipe out all opportunity for employment.

"Servants, obey your masters" and "Citizens, obey your rulers unquestioningly" would (and did for centuries) encourage every slavemaster and budding despot. There would be no need for elections and no opportunity to criticize oppressive employers or dishonest government officials. "Children, obey your parents slavishly" would result in gross exploitation of children in undesirable ways.

"Love your enemies" (the Bible is infested with talk of enemies) would make love meaningless. Inherent in the very word is a sense of evaluation and appreciation and spontaneous response to both. If forced, it is worthless. Also, the idea that spontaneous feelings can be controlled by will-power is contrary to the findings of psychology, and would result in sterile, non-creative mental lethargy. People would be robots with identical reactions and carefully-controlled emotional responses. Refreshing personality differences would disappear. Today, charismatics and born-again Christians feel obligated to present a benign facial expression and nothing-is-rotten attitude every waking hour. They have resurrected Pollyanna.

"Cut off your hands and feet and pluck out your eye," besides resulting in horrible disfiguration, actually practiced in the past, wrongly implies that the extremities and the eyes act independently of the brain. Instructions such as these were taken literally many times, and Jesus himself made no distinction between those that were to be so regarded and those that were figurative.

Though some of the more praiseworthy behavior rules preached by Jesus are considered unique, they actually echo those of other earlier religious systems and of philosophers such as Confucius, who lived 500 years before Christ. Greek moralists had recommended them, also, and they were not original with Jesus.

�='◇'=

After carrying on without ceasing about the kingdom of God which will be established at the end of the world, Jesus reneges: "For, behold, the kingdom of God is within you." *Luke 17:21*

�='◇'=

Although religion and ethics are one in the Bible, it is entirely possible to abide by a system of ethics and not be a religionist. The Christian religion teaches that unbelief is in itself immoral, when actually mere belief in a religious dogma has little to do with morality: "Whatsoever is not of faith is sin." *Romans 14:23*

To make mere belief a standard of ethics is unrealistic, yet belief in Jesus as the Savior is all that is required by Christianity for achievement of the highest reward: "He that believeth on the Son hath everlasting life." *John 3:36* Unbelief is sufficient in itself to send the doubter to hell: "He that believeth not the Son shall not see life; but the wrath of God abideth on him." *John 3:36* Jesus emphasizes again: "Except ye be converted . . . ye shall not enter into the kingdom of heaven." *Matt. 18:3*

Faith or belief in a religious system is in itself not a measurement of a person's ethical behavior. Surely a more uplifting standard for human actions should prevail, such as adherence to a system of rational morality whereby people function to achieve a harmonious society. Blind belief in Christianity as well as other religions has visited immeasurable oppression and persecution upon conformers, as well as dissenters, in the form of inquisitions, crusades, fanaticism, alliance of Church and State, and the suppression of scientific investigation and discovery, hand in hand with the downgrading of education.

The basic teaching of Christianity cannot be disguised—believe or be damned. But *morality* concerns *behavior,* not unquestioning acceptance. It cannot be defined as conformity to dogmatic direction and submitting to threats.

———⊳◆⊲———

Instead of uplifting humanity, the Bible saddles it with a picture of itself as being base and sinful, thus doing documented harm to the psyche: "O wretched man that I am!" *Romans 7:24* "Who shall deliver me from the body of this death?" *Romans 7:24* "Who shall change our vile body?" *Philip. 3:21*

By calling almost every harmless and natural act a sin, the Bible and Church have reduced everyone to the status of "such a worm," as the hymn declares. Friedrich Nietzsche said of "sin": "That par excellence of the self-violation of man was invented to make science, culture, every kind of elevation and nobility of man impossible; the priest (Church) rules through the invention of sin." Perhaps that is why Satan is permitted to "walk about."

———⊳◆⊲———

Despite the seal of approval put upon women through admiration of the Virgin Mary by the Church, especially the Roman Catholic, the Bible is not concerned with the image women may have of themselves. By the time they have been told to shut up and submit to the opposite sex, found themselves referred to as whores over a hundred times, had their sexual relationship with men downgraded and every bodily function peculiar to them pronounced unclean, they have little self-respect left. After Paul gets through telling men to be celibate, woman can't be blamed for wondering how future Christians will be produced, and how the lauded Christian family will "long endure," if she rebels at her child-birth pain punishment.

———⊳◆⊲———

Jesus tells his followers that: "Whatsoever ye shall ask the Father in my name, he will give it you." *John 16:23* The way to ask is by prayer, but petition prayers cannot be reconciled with a God who should be able to handle things without suggestions and requests from mortals. Besides, God says assertively in the Old Testament: "I am the Lord, I change not." *Mal. 3:6*

Jesus promotes the idea that God is a year-'round Santa Claus who will grant the faithful anything: "Ask, and ye shall receive." *John 16:24* If every plea from believers changes God's mind, the picture arises of a vacillating, purposeless, undependable Almighty, and responsibility for the course of events belongs to people, not God. Either he manages the world in the best possible way or he lets prayer influence him to manage things in a different way.

Ability to change the mind of the Most High or to help him make decisions is heavy stuff for people who feel they have to tell God his business. "Guide us, bless this food, lead us not into temptation, abide with me," and all such mouthings, to say nothing of specific requests for special personal favors from the trivial to the serious, are insulting to an all-knowing, all-wise deity. And one cannot help but appreciate the dilemma of a God presented with conflicting solicitations. When two Catholic University athletic teams compete and send up prayers for victory, God has a headache on the way. Both may ask, but both cannot receive.

Prayers of thanks are just as pointless to a totally unselfish God. It is even contradictory for God to demand recognition and constant worship for his gift of his own death at human hands. Jesus made it clear that gifts should be anonymous and alms done in secret. *Matt. 6:3,4* He then contradicted himself by making belief in this "perfect gift" of his blood so important that rejection of such belief condemns the unbeliever to hell. Human parents who make sacrifices for their children don't demand that the children say thank you for the rest of their lives on their knees. And constant paeans of praise embarrass most benefactors.

Groups and organizations exist which will pray for favors if asked to, and they will offer the prayer for a specific length of time, as if God is hard to convince or his attention is difficult to capture. Not bad conclusions, perhaps, when one considers the task of a deity bombarded by tens of thousands of prayers at once in many different languages. Time-off for prayer consideration has to be found by a God already busy running the world and heaven, over-seeing nature, creating every new-born, managing 4 billion lives and finding husbands and wives for the ones who marry, supervising everyone's death at the proper time, and still trying to rest every seventh day. All this is handled perfectly by a biblical Creator who couldn't arrange a sacrifice that his Chosen People would believe.

⇒◆⇐

Madison Avenue would blanch at the manner in which events surrounding the "God-Messiah" were handled. If the desire was to make it all hard to believe, the fulfillment of the expectations of the Jews could hardly have been managed more expeditiously. Concealment rather than publicity seemed to be the goal, and a public relations expert could have been put to good use. Instead, God ended up with his chosen tribes rejecting all of the new promise that Jesus represented, besides denying his divinity and destiny as the Messiah and Savior king of the Jews. Jesus didn't become that king of the Jews, although right in their midst he was born miraculously, rose from the dead, and was lifted up into heaven. Still, his fellow Jews said, "No way."

To achieve this negative result, God might have adopted the following set of rules, drawn up especially for him:

(1.) Rules for Keeping News of Your Earthly Arrival from Spreading:

a. Have the angel Gabriel tell a virgin that she's going to be your mother and that you will be your own father. She'll be reluctant to impart the improbable information that she will soon be the very *Mother of God*, who up to that time hadn't needed one.

b. Tell her fiance by means of the same angel that the little embryo involved will someday save his people from their sins. Have him be nonchalant, telling as many persons as will believe his story about his pregnant fiancee.

c. Arrive in a stable (Luke) or house (Matthew) in a little town in a tiny country with no one present except the "father" and mother.

d. Have an angel or two tell a few shepherds in a field (Luke, only) in the middle of the night about your birth. Have them check out the story, and "make known abroad" that the people's Savior, Christ the Lord, has arrived. Have the people "wonder," so that no one will be convinced that God himself is growing up in a Nazareth carpenter's family, from infancy to age 30.

e. Put a bright star in the sky at a height of only a few thousand feet so that it can be followed, have it travel at the speed of a camel, make it descend to a position of about 100 feet over the birthplace, and have three Zoroastrian Magi (well-versed in astronomy) trace it and not be agog over this astral phenomenon to the extent that they so much as comment upon it.

(2.) Rules for Playing Down the Resurrection:

a. Don't announce beforehand the time and place to anyone who might assemble witnesses.

b. Arrange to rise from the dead before the sun is up (John) in a deserted spot where only a few friends will shortly arrive. Have them not tell anyone except your immediate followers.

c. Make no public appearance after leaving the tomb, such as on the temple porch where a large number of doubters would surely be present.

d. Do not visit your mother or sisters who might spread the thrilling news.

e. Be careful not to mingle with any of the Jewish priesthood who might become convinced of what you had been telling them. Do see and converse with only a few believers, in secret rooms, on a lonely beach, and along a country road.

(3.) Rules for Ascending into Heaven So It Will Hardly Be Noticed:

a. Do it in three different places casually at a moment's notice in the presence of no more than eleven persons, all sympathetic to you.
b. Have no special announcement made about it.

———————

To prove his Messiahship to the Jews, Jesus repeatedly made the claim that almost every move he made and everything that happened to him fulfilled a prophecy, but apparently one important prophecy proved to be a challenge he could not meet, namely that Christ could not come out of Galilee. Nicodemus, who was defending Jesus's cause, was confronted by Pharisees who were trying to have Jesus arrested: "Search and look: for out of Galilee ariseth no prophet." *John 7:52* Earlier, when Philip tried to convince Nathanael that Jesus was the Messiah, Nathanael seemed to have this prophecy about Galilee not producing Christ in mind when he questioned Philip: "Can there any good thing come out of Nazareth?" *John 1:46*

Jesus made no attempt to counteract the charge that he could not be the Messiah because he was from Nazareth, but the gospels of Matthew and Luke try to make everything proper by having Jesus born in Bethlehem. Luke is the only one, however, who bothers to come up with a reason for Bethlehem being the birthplace. On the other hand, Matthew is the only gospel containing the story of the flight to Egypt, which is supposed to fulfill another prophecy.

The Jews believed that the prophets had foretold the return from the skies of Elias (Elijah) *before* the coming of the Messiah. Jesus tried to latch onto this affirmation by declaring that John the Baptist was Elias, but John the Baptist denied that he was Elijah and was even skeptical, while in prison, about whether Jesus actually *was* the promised Redeemer.

———————

Believers place a great deal of their faith in Jesus as God on his singularity. They hold that he was unique in the following ways: he was immaculately made (although Mary underwent the Jewish purification rites for childbirth) of the union of a god and a maiden, he cast out devils, he was a healer, he raised the dead, he said he was God, he forgave sins, he performed miracles, he arose from the dead, and he ascended into heaven.

Every one of these wonders connected with him have been (or are being) duplicated, either in mythology and pagan religions, in Bible stories about other personalities, or in present-day life. Mythological gods habitually came to earth and fathered children of virgins. Jupiter, for instance, had many offspring. Even more *claimed* or were *proclaimed* to be the children of gods. Exorcists were part of the medical profession in Jesus's day and still ply their occult trade. When David played and sang for Saul he drove out the evil spirits, as did the 70 other followers Jesus sent out to preach. The disciple John even complained to Jesus of some outsider who was casting out devils in Jesus's name, and Jesus did not object. *Luke 9:49,50* Paul healed and drove out evil spirits just by means of aprons and handkerchiefs that had touched his body. In one specific instance he healed a cripple, and Peter's shadow had healing powers. Long before, Elisha cured leprosy. Philip healed people of unclean spirits, palsy, and lameness.

Elisha brought the child of a Shunamite woman back from the dead, Paul restored the life of a young man who had fallen from a window, Peter raised Dorcas. All these biblical characters rose from the dead, just as Lazarus and the ruler's daughter whom Jesus resurrected. The Witch of Endor called Samuel back to earth, and Moses and Elias appeared in the Transfiguration. Rising from the dead was not the impossible feat it is considered today. The Jews expected Elijah to return to earth and thought all the prophets capable of it, so Jesus's promise of a second coming was not a new idea for them nor a unique one. Herod suspected Jesus of being John the Baptist newly-risen from the dead, and others thought Jesus to be Jeremiah or Elijah. Both resurrection and return to earth from the realm of the dead did not represent the impossible to the superstitious people who inhabit the Bible. The Pharisees *believed* in *resurrection* of the body.

Many persons have proclaimed themselves gods, and some in Jesus's very lifetime asserted that they were the Messiah. Jesus himself predicted that many in the future would claim to be gods. Throughout the intervening years and even today persons occasionally have deified themselves.

The Bible is full of miracle-workers. The Old Testament had more than its share. Moses and Aaron had a miraculous rod, but Pharaoh's sorcerers could perform some of the same wonders the rod accomplished. *Ex. 7:11,12,22* Moses cured pestilence victims with a brass snake, and he got water from a rock twice, to say nothing of parting the Red Sea. Although Jesus fed the multitudes with a small number of loaves and fishes, Elijah and Elisha beat him to it by multiplying both oil and meal. Elijah, Elisha, and Joshua all three parted the waters of the Jordan, and Elisha made iron float. Jesus walked on the water, but Peter also took a few steps before he sank.

Jesus cast out devils, but so did almost a hundred others. All the miraculous powers of Jesus were bestowed upon the disciples by Jesus before the ascension.

Enoch went up to heaven from earth without even dying first, and Elijah was carried alive into the clouds by a flaming chariot. Perhaps that is why Jesus's ascension is lightly and contradictorily treated in the Bible, and why the apostle evangelists barely mention it. To the Jews of that day it wasn't such a miracle.

The forgiveness of sin in the Old Testament was accomplished by sacrifices. Today some divisions of the Church give their clergy the power to forgive sins, just as Jesus gave it to the disciples. And among some Christians, Mary plays an important part in obtaining absolution for sinners. Jesus's instructions for praying, embodied in the Lord's Prayer, indicate a direct line is open from mortals to the Great Scorekeeper in the sky and that forgiveness from God does not require a middleman, although the role of intermediary has been assigned to Jesus by the Church. Prophets sometimes assumed this function in the Old Testament. Supplicating God in Jesus's name is pointless when one considers the Christian concept of the Trinity, that three-equal-one dogma that fouls up any chance Christian theology has of making sense. God and Jesus being one and the same, there is nothing to be gained by entreating God in his own name. Not that all Christian sects acknowledge the Trinity, a concept deemed essential to monotheism by the majority of Christendom, however.

⇒⋅◇⋅⇐

Two different stories are told in the Bible about the fate of Judas. The first, related in Matthew, says that Judas hanged himself and was buried in Potter's Field, bought by the chief priests who hired him, such burial being carried out, as usual according to Matthew, to fulfill a prophecy. It is called the "Field of Blood" to this day, maintains Matthew. *Matt. 27:5–8* (Such expressions as "to this day" found in several biblical books, including the Pentateuch, suggest that the books were written at a date much later than would be consistent timewise with the alleged author.)

As told in Acts, however, supposedly written by Luke, Judas buys the field and bursts asunder in a fall, "and all his bowels gushed out" (entrails have a fascination for scripture writers) to fulfill a different prophecy found in Psalms, a biblical book of poetry that proves a prodigious source of dim forecasts that can be quoted to verify almost any circumstance. *Acts 1:18,19*

It would not be asking too much of biblical accuracy to assume that the true fate of Judas be known to two of his contemporaries who were considered reliable enough to write two of the gospels about Jesus. Even if the books were authored by the next generations, the death of Judas was hardly so obscure that facts about it could not be determined. Yet the bishops of the Church decided that the books of Acts, Matthew, and Luke were divinely revealed and the Word of God.

⟫⟪

Peter is chosen by Jesus to be the foundation corner-stone of the Church, although at one time he calls Peter "Satan." Peter unashamedly lies and denies Christ three times and later frightens two early converts to death. Hardly a rock on which to build anything. *Matt 16:18,23 Acts 5 Matt. 26:69–75*

⟫⟪

When Saul (Paul) is struck temporarily blind on the road to Damascus, the reader is told that the men accompanying Saul hear Jesus's voice, but Paul later says they did not. "And the men which journeyed with him stood speechless, hearing a voice, but seeing no man." *Acts 9:7* "And they that were with me saw indeed the light, and were afraid; but they heard not the voice of him that spake to me." *Acts 22:9*

This is not a trivial contradiction, considering that Paul later claims several conversations with Jesus by means of which Jesus reveals to Paul all the mysteries of heaven, bestows upon him an apostleship, and points him to the Gentiles. Paul heard this voice loud and clear, if no one else did, and proceeded to become the chief spokesman for the new religion to the extent that Christianity has, with some justification, been dubbed "Paulianity."

⟫⟪

Paul's moral standards, revealed in the epistles, could charitably be described as flexible, although he manufactures unbending rules of conduct for everyone else: "For though I be free from all *men*, yet have I made myself servant unto all that I might gain the more. And unto the Jews I became as a Jew, that I might gain the Jews; to them that are under the law, as under the law, that I might gain them that are under the law; to them that are without law, as without law . . . that I might gain them that are without law. To the weak became I as weak, that I might gain the weak: I am made all things to all *men*, that I might by all means save some." *I Cor. 9:19–22* How's that for integrity?

Perhaps he is even willing to shade the truth more than a little in order that he might "by all means save some" when he claims off-handedly that 500 persons saw Christ after the resurrection. *I Cor. 15:6* None of the four gospels numbers the privileged viewers at more than a few besides the disciples, but Paul, who wasn't one of them, feels no obligation to produce any details about this encounter, failing to indicate either where or when it occurred. If 500 Jews or Gentiles, besides the eleven, did see Jesus during the 40 days' interim between the resurrection and the ascension (a length of time recorded only in Acts), it must have been a ho-hum experience for them, as at the first meeting of the believers in Jesus held after the ascension, only about 120 were present. *Acts 1:15* These included the disciples and relatives of Jesus.

This total marked the number whom all the preaching and fantastic miracles, including the awesome sound of God's voice issuing from heaven several times, had managed to convince during a period of from one and one-half to three years. Evangelists capture that many converts at one service, now that brains have been properly washed throughout the centuries. The Jewish nation, who experienced all the anecdotes about Jesus first-hand, turned a cold shoulder on them all, but the older a miraculous story becomes, the easier it seems to be to accomplish belief in it.

By the time Paul labors and gives birth to a vast body of Christian dogma in Acts and the epistles, it is understandable that the Church has found it advantageous to establish Sunday Schools, Catechisms, Seminaries, Denominational Colleges, Bible Study Classes, and Religious Instructions. And bewildered Bible browsers vow that every Bible should come with a built-in interpreter.

Thousands of religious books have been penned that try to explain, prove, or apologize for the Christian Bible and as many to combat doubt and refute criticism of its inconsistencies and obfuscations, partly because of Paul's fast foot-work. It all began in the book of Acts, an assortment of blown-up fables and outrageous exaggerations that has not been surpassed by any book of fairy tales ever issuing from the fertile imaginations of the authors of make-believe. If Christ has a throne at God's (his own?) right hand, Paul certainly occupies the one on the left. That would make it very handy for God to lean over and ask Paul about Paul's claim made to the Roman congregation that: "Where there is no law (before Moses) there is no transgression." *Romans 4:15* That statement left an embarrassed God, it would appear, with no excuse for having destroyed almost all the earth's inhabitants in a deluge and for sending a downpour of fire upon Sodom and Gomorrah, to say nothing of visiting the sin of Adam and Eve upon all humankind.

Fortunately for Paul, he also not surprisingly made a contradictory statement: "There is none righteous, no, not one." *Romans 3:10* Paul really cannot be blamed for having difficulty with the way that sin, the Mosaic law, and grace inter-relate.

Paul's biography as outlined in Acts and his autobiography as written down in Galatians are completely contradictory and make it difficult to arrive at the truth about his activities and his very existence, just as his authorship of the Pauline epistles cannot be proved, and indeed the book of Acts makes no mention of him ever sitting down with pen in hand. Readers of the Bible, of course, realize that between its covers there rests not one book whose date and author are not subject to speculation. And even if the source could be established, the possibility, and, yes, likelihood of interpolation and fraud, added to the probability of translation error, must be admitted.

If Paul really was a Pharisee whose persecution of converts extended to literally dragging them from their firesides, it is a bit hard to swallow that almost overnight he was willing to bury the Mosaic law under a stack of gnostic mysticism a mile high. And to claim that among God's Chosen Jews, not one was righteous.

⇒•◆•⇐

Very little verification can be found in historical records for the existence of the person Jesus, and all of that verification has been challenged more or less successfully, and rightly or wrongly labelled fraud. Assuming that Jesus actually lived and trod the paths of Palestine, the Bible does not describe him physically and does not tell the reader anything about his parents or home or how he occupied himself before he began to teach, whether he attended school at all or was illiterate. His personality must be revealed from his own words recorded in the gospels and from the anecdotes told about him. All Bible students must then decide for themselves whether it is an appealing one, and whether it represents "perfection."

But the greatest contradiction concerning Jesus's sojourn on earth, if such be granted, lies in the various aliases he adopts or which are bestowed upon him. There is no consistency in his role or identity that emerges from the New Testament, and perhaps he was, like Paul, all things to all people.

As the anticipated Messiah of the Jews it is necessary to assign to him certain characteristics, because the mission of that Messiah lay in overcoming the Gentiles and ruling over a new kingdom of the Jews which would encompass all the Gentile world under the dominance of the Jews' Lord of the Old Testament. Enmity towards the Gentiles thus had to be a part of the makeup of Jesus, and he expressed that antipathy on several occasions. Jesus surely realized that the Jews of his day were not looking for a heavenly Redeemer so much as for a sort of superman Nation Builder descended from David. Of course, there is the possibility that a Supernatural Christ cult already was building among the Jews, perhaps led by the Essene hermits, as has been suggested. Within such a cult a fictional Jesus Christ could have been created. The fact that so little is known of Jesus as a person might be explained in this way.

Jesus as Savior of the Jews from their sins and bestower of eternal life upon them gives his role in the gospels another dimension and this time a rather narrow spiritual one. His partiality shown to the disciples and the twelve tribes of Israel when he talks about Judgment Day, the Kingdom of God, and eternal life in heaven helps to make him fit into this assignment very well.

When the Savior image is enlarged to encompass the entire world, his coat of many colors begins to be let out at the seams until finally, promoted from his part as *Son* of God, he wears the robe of "Jesus Christ Super Star"— God himself—who already holds sway over the kingdom of heaven but will with breathtaking speed set up for the "elect" a new and wonderful kingdom of God on earth, or in the skies, it isn't clear which, and who will with terrible dispatch, consign everyone else to eternal torment. Even in the character of One Supreme Deity without fault he must manage to portray compassion and care as Loving Father and couple it with the pitilessness of avenger and torturer.

Jesus plays all these parts in the New Testament—the Messiah of the Jews, redeemer of the Jews from the Gentiles, ruler of a worldwide kingdom of the Jews, mystical Savior of the Jews from their sins, ruler of a heavenly kingdom for Jewish saints, Savior of the world from sin as the sacrificed Son of God and Son of Man, and finally God himself who rules over an earthly and heavenly kingdom of God for the saved of the whole world, while still retaining his status as Son sitting on the right hand of the throne. To these portrayals is added the ones of reformer of the Jewish priesthood and moralist for humankind.

In most New Testament scriptures these varied roles intermingle and vie with each other, and it is seldom clear in any given instance just how Jesus sees himself or how others regard him. Apparently most of his contemporary Jews, and the Jewish remnant that remained after the sacking of Jerusalem in 70 AD, refused to see Jesus in any of his Supernatural garments, although they or their parents had personally seen or heard about the low-hung Star and host of angels, the waves that abated, the Devil flying through the Jerusalem sky transporting Jesus to temple pinnacles and mountain tops, unclean spirits identifying Jesus aloud as they tore the bodies of their victims and jumped into 2,000 pigs who couldn't swim, a swathed figure coming from the grave at Jesus's urging, money taken from a fish's mouth at Jesus's instructions, Jesus walking on water, multitudes fed by him twice with a few loaves and fishes, earthquakes and eclipses marking events in Jesus's life, risen saints walking about after the Crucifixion, Jesus's empty tomb and his reappearance as a talking and eating zombie, and his ascent into the firmament without benefit of space ship or rocket.

Today most of the world's Jews are willing to agree with Christendom that Jesus lived as an estimable man, and they make little objection, vocally at least, if Gentiles want to make a Jew their God. Jesus, however, was not able to "save" his countrymen, Jewry itself, from the eternal damnation he preached. The disciples will be very unhappy when they are required to judge the Chosen People.

⇒•◇•⇐

Witches, wizards, and their craft were anathema to the Old Testament Lord to the extreme that such magicians were to suffer death, although any hocus-pocus on the Lord's behalf always won his approval. New Testament figures operated on this principle with every sort of miracle-working, and Jesus's own wizardry was used to prove his divinity to people so accustomed to magic and trickery that it was difficult to stir up much astonishment. Miracles credited to Jesus and the prophets and apostles are governed by Frazer's (*The Golden Bough*) "mysterious law of spiritual economy" whose operation in the history of religion has decreed that the passage of time adds to the "worth" of miracles wrought by god-men.

That Jesus shared all the superstitions common to people of his time is obvious to any Bible reader. He produced healing miracles from the personal conviction that devil-possession was often the cause of bodily affliction, and he frequently spoke of portentous "signs," curses, and fortune-telling. He believed in spirits, ghosts, and visions and that "virtue" went out of him when a sick person touched his garment. He endorsed the sacrifices of fowl and beasts to appease the wrath of heaven. The book of Mark quotes Jesus's list of the sins to which God's children are prey: "for from within, out of the heart of man, proceed evil thoughts, adulteries, fornications, murders, thefts, covetousness, wickedness, deceit, lasciviousness, an *evil eye*, blasphemy, pride, foolishness." *Mark 7:21,22* Acceptance of superstitious belief is a prerequisite for belief in the biblical God.

⇒•◇•⇐

Some circumstances of the life of Jesus are related and referred to as though they were clearly recorded in the Bible, but nobody can come upon one that is described consistently in every, or even in most, detail. The revealed scriptures retain in the New Testament the reputation for contradiction earned in parts of the Old, and the discrepancies between the two Testaments are glaring. Most persons, unless they are Bible-educated, remain ignorant of them.

Some New Testament contradictions concerning the life of Jesus, by no means all, follow:

Genealogy

Matthew gives the ancestry of Jesus as comprising 28 generations from David, Luke as 43. No names are alike in the lists given, except for those of David and Joseph, Salathiel and Zorobabel. If Matthew is correct, each progenitor was 40 years of age at the time the next generation appeared. If Luke is correct, each was 26 years of age, since there was a span of about 1,080 years between David and Jesus. Joseph was not supposed to be the father of Jesus, in any case, according to Christian belief.

The Conception by a Virgin

Matthew and Luke are the only gospels which make this claim. Matthew says an angel told Joseph of it in a dream just in time to save Mary from being "put away," which under Jewish law probably meant death. Luke says the angel Gabriel appeared to Mary to announce the forthcoming "visit" of the Holy Ghost. It is not known by what authority Mary and Joseph were believed, if indeed they were. (It was common in heathen mythology for gods to come to earth and debauch virgins, and virgin-born saviors were not unique.)

Herod's Decree to Destroy All Children Two Years of Age and Under

This story is told only in Matthew. If such a horrendous atrocity was actually carried out, as this scripture says, all living in the vicinity at the time would have been affected by it or aware of it, but history records no such crime, common as inhuman orders are to the pages of the Bible.

Time of the Crucifixion

Mark says the third hour, or 9 a.m., but John says the sixth hour (noon) was when sentence was passed.

Inscription on the Cross

Matthew	This is Jesus the king of the Jews
Mark	The king of the Jews
Luke	This is the king of the Jews
John	Jesus of Nazareth the king of the Jews

Women at the Cross

Matthew says many stood afar off, including Mary Magdalene, Mary the mother of James, and the mother of Zebedee's children. Mark and Luke speak of many afar off, and Mark includes Mary Magdalene and Mary the mother of James the Less. John says Jesus's mother stood at the cross, along with her sister and Mary Magdalene.

Events at the Crucifixion

Matthew says the veil of the temple was rent, that there was an earthquake, that it was dark from the sixth to the ninth hour, the graves opened and bodies of the saints arose and went into Jerusalem, appearing to many (beating Jesus to the resurrection). Mark and Luke speak of darkness and the veil of the temple being rent but mention no earthquake or risen saints. John is the only one who tells of Jesus's side being pierced.

Burial of Jesus

Matthew says the Jews asked Pilate for a guard to prevent the body from being stolen by the disciples, and for the tomb to be sealed. All this was supposedly done, but the other gospels do not recount these precautions.

Time of the Resurrection

Matthew says Sunday at dawn, Mark says the sun was rising, and John says it was dark.

Those Who Came to the Tomb

Matthew says Mary Magdalene and the other Mary. Mark says Mary Magdalene, Mary the mother of James, and Salome. Luke says Mary Magdalene, Joanna, Mary the mother of James, other women, and Peter. John says Mary Magdalene alone and later Peter and John.

Angels at the Tomb

Matthew says there was an earthquake and an angel came down, rolled back the stone and sat upon it, then spoke to the women. Jesus appeared to them as they went to tell the disciples.

Mark says the women found the stone rolled away, entered the tomb, and saw an angel sitting on the right side. He talked to them, and Jesus then appeared to Mary Magdalene.

Luke says the women found the stone rolled away and entered the tomb. Two angels appeared to them.

John says Mary Magdalene found the stone rolled away and told Peter and John, who went to the tomb and entered it. Mary stooped down and looked into the tomb, seeing two angels, one at the head and one at the feet. They spoke to her. Jesus then appeared to her, but she failed to recognize him at first.

Belief That the Disciples Stole Jesus's Body

Matthew says the guard was paid to tell this story, but no other gospel makes such a claim.

Appearances of the Risen Jesus

Matthew says an angel at the tomb told the two Marys and that Jesus also told them, to tell the disciples to meet him in Galilee. The disciples then went to a mountain previously agreed upon, and met Jesus there. This was his only appearance, except to the women at the tomb. Matthew devotes only five verses to this visit with the disciples.

Mark says that Jesus walked with two of the disciples in the country, and that they told the rest of the disciples, who refused to believe. Later he appeared to the eleven disciples at mealtime.

Luke says two followers went, the same day that Jesus rose from the dead, to Emmaus, a village *eight miles* from Jerusalem, and there Jesus joined them but was unrecognized. While they ate a meal together that evening, they finally recognized Jesus, whereupon he disappeared. Returning at once to Jerusalem, they told the disciples their experience, and suddenly Jesus appeared among them, frightening them, as they thought he was a spirit. Jesus then ate some fish and honey and preached to them.

John says Jesus appeared to the disciples the evening of the day he arose, in Jerusalem, where they were hiding. He breathed the Holy Ghost upon them, but Thomas was not present and refused to believe. Eight days later Jesus joined the disciples again at the same place, and this time he convinced Thomas. Once more Jesus made an appearance to the disciples at the sea of Tiberias but again was not recognized. After telling them to cast their nets on the other side of the boat, Jesus becomes known to them and prepares bread and fish for them. They all eat together as they converse.

The Ascension

Matthew says nothing at all about it. Mark casually says that Jesus was received up into heaven after he finished talking to the disciples in Jerusalem. Luke says Jesus led the disciples to Bethany and that while he blessed them, he was parted from them and carried up into heaven. John says nothing at all about it. For a happening of such sensational significance its treatment in the Bible is so off-hand and perfunctory that the whole episode comes across as an afterthought. When only two of the apostles choose to tell about it, surely one could expect those two to get the *place* right!

―――⟫◈⟪―――

These contradictions, along with innumerable others understandably kept under wraps, would seem to argue, except to the most ardent apologist, that the persons, unknown, who wrote the gospels were not present at the happenings described, or that they were very careless about their facts. Less important events might not make an impression great enough to produce accuracy, but surely the crucifixion, resurrection, and ascension of the Savior of the World do not fit into that category.

The book of Acts further adds to the confusion. It says that Jesus showed himself to the apostles for a period of 40 days after his resurrection (thus contradicting Matthew, Mark, Luke, and John) and spoke to them of things pertaining to the kingdom of God: "And when he had spoken these things, while they beheld, he was taken up; and a cloud received him out of their sight. And while they looked stedfastly toward heaven as he went up, behold, two men stood by them in white apparel: Which also said, Ye men of Galilee, why stand ye gazing up into heaven? this same Jesus, which is taken up from you into heaven, shall so come in like manner as ye have seen him go into heaven." *Acts 1:3–11*

Paul outdoes every other "authority" by saying that Jesus was seen by 500 persons between the time of the resurrection and the time of the ascension, although he doesn't say where. He also claims that he himself "as one born out of due time" also saw Jesus. *I Cor. 15:6,8*

The description of the ascension in Acts does, at least, add a little belated and welcome drama to what could have been a compelling sight for one of those multitudes who, the New Testament states, were in attendance at several other occasions that marked Jesus's ministry but who dwindled to a pitiful few when the time came for the ultimate wonders. And believers still wait for the fulfillment of the promise made by the two "men in white."

The Christian religion designates the Bible as the revealed Holy Word of God, and fundamentalists at least profess to believe every word of it, but the many contradictions and discrepancies in the scriptures would seem to make it impossible to deny that error pervades them. How excerpt it and leave the truth intact?

⇒•◊•⇐

The Christian Church feels no necessity to answer the charge that Jesus's virgin birth and miraculous parentage by a god in the form of a ghost are nothing but myths borrowed from pagans, but the Bible itself does little to refute it. After Matthew and Luke tell their fabulous and contradictory stories of such an origin for Jesus (in an attempt to make him fulfill vague Old Testament prophecies), no further reference to his supernatural parentage or unnatural birth appears in any other scripture. In fact, the remaining New

Testament goes to great pains to depict Jesus as the son of Joseph in order to fulfill another set of predictions.

Jesus himself asserts that he was a descendant of David and yet continued to say that he was the Son of God. In the biblical sense that everyone is a "child of God," Jesus may have been divine, but he claimed to have had totally human parents like everyone else and to be in need of baptism to take away the stigma of having been born human under the curse of original sin. *Rev. 22:16*

———◆———

One of the most amazing contradictions of the Bible may lie in the dramatic reversal of the roles played out in it by Jews and Gentiles. The Chosen People of the Old Testament gloried in a Creator who showed partiality for them out of all the world's millions. The Jews basked in his promise to be their special Lord forever, at the Gentiles' expense. The New Testament then has this God break his contract with the Jews and make Gentile believers his Chosen People, while consigning his former favorites to burn in hell for continuing to trust in the Old Promise.

Christianity asks not only that faith be put in such a two-timer but that the wondrous "love" he exhibits in the Bible be made manifest in human beings, who are then expected to find happiness in the knowledge that most of their fellow creatures, including the Jews, will spend eternity in agony. Paul paints the picture of adherents to the new theology as a smug assembly of holier-than-thou favorites of an ethereal Light-God who chose them ahead of time to be his companions in an eternal Paradise while the damned (from the beginning) writhe in hell.

New revelations from this changeable God continue to be experienced, if one believes Joseph Smith, and Mohammed wiped out the New Promise for a still newer one.

———◆———

The book of Matthew claims that 63 generations lived out the time span between Adam and Jesus. *Matt. 1* Allowing the scriptural testimony concerning the long lives of Adam (930 years), Methuselah (969 years), and other ancient oldies, any Bible reader who does not reject the sciences of anthropology, archaeology, and geology completely, must encounter a scriptural-acceptance problem of some magnitude.

———◆———

The many contradictions in the contents of the Bible both as to "fact" and as to concept gradually impose upon the reader the uneasy realization that ideas do not evolve logically in the pages of the Holy Book. "That just doesn't make sense!" is the reaction that even an avid proselytizer must feel at times and that some religious philosophers have voiced.

It has been noted that most members of religious communities prefer to have their spiritual manna spoon-fed to them than to try to gather it for themselves. To try to gather it from the Bible is admittedly a time-consuming, mind-boggling, frustrating, and finally faith-shaking enterprise.

The plight of the delver into the scriptures of both Testaments is inevitably linked in great part to the legends upon which the very foundations of Judaic-Christianity rest. True, some of these legends are not taken seriously by anyone except so-called fundamentalists and are regarded as "allegorical fairy tales" by sophisticated believers who prefer a mystical approach to their faith. Still, the fabulous legends are the core of the Christian religion and comprise an integral part of the revealed Word of God.

The Bible *opens* with a legend, a murky, inept description of the creation of the world and its first inhabitants which admits of no purpose or intent on the part of the Creator. With no fanfare: "In the beginning God created the heaven and the earth." It must have been find-a-new-interest week, for in some nowhere a possibly jaded God had been passing time which hadn't yet begun, with the unreliable angels who proved to be his first bungled creatures. (The Bible says that Jesus was there, too, in a sort of Siamese-twin relationship.) Unable to control these "angelic" ingrates, God is forced to put down a revolt by several of them, but instead of destroying them, poor foresight leads him to throw them into an ill-conceived pit from which they proceed to escape. The cause of the uprising was their leader Satan's ambition to be equal to God (or the gods). This bad scare causes God to be ever-watchful that the same aspiration does not rear its head again, which accounts for his hard line with Adam and Eve. Satan is now free to come to earth, after the Creation, and cause the downfall of man, as a duplication of his own disgrace.

In one section of his new toy-world God has fenced off a Garden of Eden, and just because this paradise needed a gardener he decided on impulse to fashion Adam, a carbon copy of himself, and give him a companion that resembled some of the other gods: "Let us make man in our image, after our likeness . . . male and female created he them." *Gen. 1:26,27—Gen. 2:15*

With his liking for putting people to the test, which surfaces frequently in future Bible episodes, the Lord has provided the Garden of Eden with temptation in the shape of two trees bearing luscious fruit. Then he forbids Adam and Eve to eat the fruit of the tree of knowledge of good and evil, thus giving them freedom of choice instead of exercising control over their behavior, while at the same time refusing to furnish them with the means of making judgmental decisions—a sense of right and wrong. In spite of their vulnerability, the serpent Satan has been allowed into the Garden to *force* them to make a choice they were not prepared to make.

When, egged on by the serpent, the two "malefactors" disobey God, they could not know it was "wrong" to do so, but God is infuriated and calls their disobedience a "sin" anyhow. This "sin" was the unforgivable one of acquiring a conscience, and its enormity caused God to place a curse upon its perpetrators and all their descendants whereby this "sin" was to become a part of the heritage of the whole human race and be responsible for human destiny—death.

The Bible is a book supposedly dedicated to dictating the behavior of suffering humanity. The New Testament is devoted to influencing every citizen of the world to act in such a way as to gain heaven and avoid hell. The assumption is that people are free to do as they please but must suffer the consequences. Surely fairness demands that, having been shanghaied to sail on the ship of life and in danger of shipwreck, each crew member would at least be furnished with a lifejacket, in this case a knowledge of the difference between right and wrong.

Yet God chose to declare it a sin to acquire this awareness and for commission of this sin by two unlucky victims in a bucolic setting, he condemned human beings to their ultimate extinction. Indeed, this sin was so hideous in God's eyes that God himself had to die at human hands in order to pardon humankind for committing it. He then promised everlasting life to his murderers, in heaven with him if they believed they had killed him—in hell if they refused to believe it. This was the same everlasting life that God had taken great pains to deny his children until they nailed him on a cross.

The story of this denial is part of the legend of the Garden of Eden, and it reveals even more pettiness on the part of God. It surfaces right after he "runs up" coats of skins to cover the nakedness of the mother and father of the human race, who now recognize, after eating the forbidden fruit, how vile is the naked body given to them by God. Adam had named his wife-without-benefit-of-clergy "Eve," "because she was the mother of all living," although as yet Adam had acquired no sex education and Eve not only didn't know she was enceinte but up to then had not given birth to anything except the downfall of man. *Gen. 3:20,21*

God is apparently explaining his bizarre behavior to the other gods (Genesis can't decide how many there are): "And the Lord God said, Behold, the man is become as one of us, to know good and evil." *Gen. 3:22* With these words addressed to his fellow gods, the Creator admits that fear of a challenge from earthlings similar to the challenge Satan had presented is the basis of God's curse on his children, which eventually necessitates a Savior.

He was afraid they would become god-like, a fear which shows up again in the legend of the Tower of Babel. *Gen. 11*

Wait a minute! If an understanding of right and wrong makes human beings equal to God, then wouldn't most persons, including Adam and Eve from the time they ate the no-no fruit, be on a par with God? God so states in the scripture quoted above, and this equality now achieved by them in the Garden of Eden leads to God's next move—banishment of the two first culprits from the garden to prevent them from eating of the fruit from the tree of everlasting life: "Therefore the Lord God sent him forth from the garden of Eden . . . Lest he put forth his hand, and take also of the tree of life, and eat, and live forever." *Gen. 3:22,23* This first book of the Pentateuch gives the world a deity (or deities) in such a precarious position that he must provide for the fate of death for the creatures who comprise the threat to his omnipotence. The irony of the legend reposes in the fact that he brought it all upon himself by bringing them into existence in the first place, the consequences of which he should have been able to foresee.

By this time, the mind of the average reader in search of biblical truth is reeling. But there is more to come, for after many more-or-less successful years of dominion over his Chosen People, God suddenly decides to force everlasting life upon all the world's billions whether they want it or not. Why it is suddenly okay by God for them to live forever when that was considered risky to God's prestige centuries before is a question the Bible doesn't answer.

The legend becomes even more legendary when God unveils his plan for letting people back into his good graces. Christendom calls it salvation, and it involves the death of God in human form at the hands of a depraved (sinful) humankind, who will then be rewarded for this murder by living forever in heaven, provided they believe that their victim was actually a Savior. If they find this legend distasteful and highly improbable, they will spend this eternal life, newly granted them, in hell, which, frankly, sounds like a proper fate for those who own up to the torture and execution of their redeemer and are happy to have had the assignment.

While God is using this means of giving people absolution for being born human, Jesus at the point of death is asking God to forgive them for this latest crime, which was all part of the plan. No crucifixion—no salvation.

Salvation and the Savior are traditionally two parts of an appealing legend, but the scriptural Savior holds out salvation only to those who acknowledge him. Thus he is a savior if he exists as such in the mind; otherwise he is the opposite of a savior—a merciless judge who consigns more people to torment than the Savior grants eternal bliss. For Jesus himself says: "Because strait is the gate, and narrow is the way, which leadeth unto life, and few there be that find it." *Matt. 7:14*

Before this plan for salvation was inaugurated, all suffered the same fate (death) because of the curse put upon two of them for being too ambitious, but after the coming of the Savior, a favored few would now be admitted to Paradise, while the great majority would be damned forever. And the Bible goes so far as to say that those few have been selected from the beginning of time.

If predestination is part of the legend, and the saved are already chosen, what does that make the Bible as far as Christians are concerned? A book with little relevant religious significance, some feasible and some impractical but few original moral observations, just another collection of fables (and anecdotes that may or may not be true mattering little either way), and featuring some commendable prose and poetry and some abominable literary garbage, the whole interspersed with ancient history of more or less accuracy. (To various researchers it means much more.)

But if the predestination and pre-ordination passages can be the "skeleton" kept in the closet because the laity fails to open the closet, the laity may then assume that they have free will, and it would in turn be very fortunate for them that Adam and Eve learned to distinguish between good and evil. In both Testaments God provides various punishments for unwise behavior choices. And the final choice, of whether to believe in a savior or not, can lead to eternal damnation. The first woman's sin thus contradictorily made salvation both needed and possible. Still, the concept of a deity at the helm of everything cannot be reconciled with the ability, even duty, of human beings to act according to their own decisions. How can God run things, if human decisions interfere? How *can* humankind have freedom of choice?

Can it be that God's will and human will are in *competition* with each other? If such be the case, then in the matter of belief in Jesus as Savior, humankind seems to be winning the competition, since only one-fourth of the world is Christian. If it is God's wish that the whole human race *believe*, he is far behind in getting his way. Human will is triumphing over God's will. And it follows that in any given situation, if human will is free, the two wills must always contend, and any plan made by the Christian God would be subject to frustration because of the *exercise* of humankind's free will.

The riddle evolving from all this is as old as Christian theology, and the confusion born of the difficulty of solving it is profound. If A murders B, is it God's will? Or should blame be placed in both instances on human decisions? Where does human will leave off and God's will prevail? Didn't the murderer commit a sin by exercising his free will to kill? And what about the builder of the dam, who may have willfully used faulty materials? And yet, after preventable disasters, there are always those, starting at the pulpit, who will say without indignation that it was the will of God.

One may argue that human destiny is in its own hands and still admit that God's will wins out in the end when all who chose not to believe and all who were not given an opportunity to believe are all thrown into hell, but if, as is taught (or assumed from the concept of a God of love) God's benign plan and desire is for all his children to share eternity with him, he is bound, as of the present, to mourn the enormous failure of his intentions to be realized. His goal, in fact, can never be met, for already only a minority (probably small) have been saved. God must be doomed to suffer frustration and sorrow.

The religionist tries to align his will with that of a supernatural being, but even that aim relies for its fulfillment on God's will being revealed to everyone alike, if he or she seeks it. Yet no one can deny that disagreement necessarily arises over the content of such revelation. Not even the most devout interpret God's will alike, as can be shown by the many sects born through the years from difference of opinion. And apparently God not only cannot be relied upon to impart his will explicitly but cannot be trusted to wield it unless asked to. "Thy will be done" the Lord's Prayer implores, and in such fashion most *public* prayers at least are concluded. Even Jesus prayed: "Nevertheless not as I will, but as thou wilt." *Matt. 26:39* A traditional feature of prayer is a petition to God begging him to reveal his will. The clergy exists partly because the laity sees them as channels through which God transmits his will to them and their will to God.

The history of the Christian hierarchy records many attempts to keep people from interfering with the will of God. Medical research, even anaesthesia, were opposed as instruments for impeding God's plan. Some sects today still hold this point of view. Scientific discoveries of all kinds met with opposition of the Church for hundreds of years, and courts still must overrule prejudice against the healing arts.

The Jews of the Old Testament argued with God to get him to change his mind, and he frequently did. (Moses seldom hesitated to set God straight.) They imposed their will upon his, even though they might pay for it, and that is basically what prayers of petition try to do. Such attempts further show that there is conflict between the two wills—divine and human.

The fact of temptation, a biblical reality, adds to the contradictory problems of good and evil and freedom of choice as they tend to build in the scriptures. Acknowledgment of the existence of temptation implies that human beings may either bow to it or resist it. Jesus had a choice of behavior several times while under great temptation. The legend of Satan tempting him for 40 days is built on the presumption that Jesus could have committed a sin, and in the Garden of Gethsemane he successfully resisted temptation again, after an angel boosted his morale: "Nevertheless, not my will, but thine be done." *Luke 22:42*

Here is biblical proof again that human will and God's are at war incessantly, and that sin is committed when human will is at odds with God's. Temptation is an effective cause of what the Bible calls sin, and Jesus warns of temptation many times. Just before the crucifixion, he finds one last opportunity to caution the disciples about it: "Pray that ye enter not into temptation." *Luke 22:40* Here God is given credit for helping people to avoid temptation, but at other times scriptural passages infer that he is a tempter himself: "Lead us not into temptation." Yet, if sin results when human will is contrary to God's, temptation would seem to be a tool of the devil and might be said to represent Satan's will.

When human will does not agree with God's, the New Testament especially claims that people are performing the will of Satan. Perhaps, then, there is after all no such thing as human will, but only God's and Satan's. And the bewildered scrutinizer of the scriptures is now back to the concept of the continuous struggle between God and Satan, which Satan seems to be winning.

It is hard, in the face of the biblical legends, to find an area where God's will does operate freely and completely, and how can these areas be identified with certainty? Even in the area of nature, people interfere increasingly in various ways, or is pollution willed by God? What judgment can people use to designate areas totally under God's control, if many tragic events and circumstances seem to contradict the New Testament image of God as a loving Father who is all-good? Perhaps the relentless Jehovah of the Old Testament is a more believable deity than the laundered one of the New Testament, although in the final analysis it is scarcely possible to be more relentless than the consigner to hell portrayed in the gospels (glad tidings).

The ultimate contradiction of a good Almighty God with dominion over a world teeming with misery intrudes upon any consideration of God's will. A beneficent deity would appear to be the antithesis of any prevailing condition of suffering or evil in his domain, and vice-versa. Piety attributes every occurrence to God's master plan, adding that "God moves in mysterious ways," but such claims lead to understandable criticism concerning supernatural priorities. When will disease and hunger be eradicated? When will disasters be curbed? Why did Jesus point out: "Ye have the poor with you always"? *Mark 14:7* Did he mean that God would make no effort to improve unhappy human conditions? Or that he *could* not?

<hr />

The Old Testament Lord and the New Testament God are in many ways a contradiction of each other. Vengeful, cruel, and unfair as the Old Testament Yahweh might be, he didn't trifle with his own majesty. There was no doubt whatever that he was always the Supreme Commander whose awful punishments for any challenge to that supremacy arrived promptly. True, many persons, such as Abraham, Jacob, Sarah, Noah, Moses, Hannah, and Samson's parents, to name a few, had personal experiences with him, but he retained his divinity.

The God of the New Testament, however, supposedly this same egotistical despot, arrives on the scene, after announcing himself, as a human embryo; is born in a smelly stable of questionable parentage; spends at least a year as a circumcised, nursing, diapered infant and 16 or 17 more as an immature youth in the care of his parents; and finally, after hiding out like a criminal, dies the death of a thief and lies in a tomb for almost two days.

⟫◆⟪

It was certainly not an original idea (rather, a pagan commonplace) for a god to come to earth or for mortals to declare themselves gods or be so designated by other mortals, and when there were several gods, the absence from their duties of a few of them was not disastrous. The Hebrew Lord and the New Testament Master, however, were heads of monotheistic systems; yet both elected to spend years on earth concerned with only a small segment of humanity. The Lord of the Jews hovered over them in the Wilderness for a period of 40 years, as a pillar of cloud during the day and a pillar of fire by night. The New Testament God, too, like his counterpart of the Old Testament, chooses to leave the store unkept in order to live approximately 33 years as a human being. Either no one was in charge during that time, or, under the Trinity, government of the earth and heavens by the supernatural was at two-thirds efficiency. And fortunately Jesus rose from the dead and got back up to the throne, or the world might still be godless or at the same depleted level of management. Even so, the question remains of why the biblical deity should concentrate, in both Testaments, so long and so hard on the Jews exclusively, leaving the rest of the world to bungle along, with its various gods.

⟫◆⟪

That any one True God of the Universe should stoop to carry out the legendary New Testament plan for salvation that made complicated and humiliating manipulation necessary, when it was within his power to "save" in any fashion he chose, is an enigma. Such a scheme can do nothing but detract from the dignity of any God who might command the respect of humankind. Even if the ambiguous role of Savior is played by a Son, the ignominy is the same, and it is all the more contemptible on the part of a father to use his son as a needless sacrifice. Father Arranges Son's Execution!

It has been said with justification that anything can be proved by a Bible quotation, if the Bible is accepted as an authority, but this assertion necessitates the presence in the Holy Book of a host of contradictory passages and errors. In fact, several thousand have actually been pointed out by critics. Since the cornerstone legends themselves contradict one another, each dogmatic position makes nearly every other untenable. The deeper the probing, the greater the frustration experienced by the inquirer. Theological rationalizing, however, is seldom called for, as biblical illiteracy on the part of the laity is not regarded as a matter for concern but rather as a plus, if faith is to be sustained.

One final area of Christian theology upon which there is little agreement and which remains cloudy even after a careful reading of the Bible addresses itself to the requirements for salvation. For although some scriptures say that only belief is necessary, other passages say that faith without works is worthless: "He that believeth on the Son hath everlasting life: and he that believeth not the Son shall not see life; but the wrath of God abideth on him." *John 3:36* These are Jesus's very words, but James contends: "Faith without works is dead." *James 2:26*

Jesus here is categorical about the chances of an unbeliever entering the kingdom of heaven. The alternative destination is hell. One naturally must then consider the problem of those who have had no opportunity to believe. After all, the missionary goal of saving souls assumes that those who have not heard and been converted are destined for damnation. If this is *not* a legitimate assumption, then missionaries and gospel-spreaders of all varieties, who carry the message and introduce the salvation plan of the Christian faith, run the risk of being responsible for the consignment to hell of all who reject the proselytizers' "good tidings."

The dogma that everyone who has even heard about Jesus only to deny him will suffer eternal torment ought to give the zealots pause, for surely no *just* God would damn persons for non-belief in a legend unfamiliar to them. If those who have not heard of Jesus as the Savior don't go to hell, then they must go to heaven, so are they not better left alone? Or do missionaries feel that believers will be in trouble with the Almighty if they do not carry the Word to all nations and for that reason are willing to place others in jeopardy?

Besides, there are people everywhere who have physical and mental infirmities which prevent them from hearing, reading, or understanding. What is their fate? And at what age are children judged to be responsible for making their own decisions about religion? Are they, born sinners, expected to arrange their own baptism?

All of this argues against the whole Christian plan of salvation. It is unconscionable to think that on such an important issue as punishment or reward in a life after death, any personal God would not provide for one universal all-encompassing theology within the grasp of the loneliest human creature in the remotest part of the universe. Salvation, if such there be, should not depend upon one incident, knowledge and recognition of which are not freely available to all.

Actually, humanity should not even be in need of salvation from the punishment of death, as claimed by Christianity, for the scriptures relating to the predicament of Adam and Eve in the Garden of Eden would seem to indicate that the biblical Creator intended, even before the "sin" of disobedience was committed, that humankind should suffer permanent extinction. To live forever was the privilege of the gods, and for fear that Adam and Eve would eat of the fruit from the tree of everlasting life they were driven from the Garden.

Because he had attempted to be as the gods, *Satan* was driven from heaven, and it follows that a jealous Creator would not tolerate the same aspiration on the part of his two earthly counterparts who had already frustrated his intention that they remain forever ignorant. "And the Lord God said, Behold, the man is become as one of us, to know good and evil: and now, lest he put forth his hand, and take also of the tree of life, and eat, and live forever; Therefore, the Lord God sent him forth from the Garden of Eden." *Gen. 3:22,23* The Bible gives no motivation for God's sudden reversal, in the New Testament, of the decree of eternal death, the fate planned for all from the Beginning.

Either the premise of such an intention on God's part must be granted, or it must be acknowledged that he would have permitted Adam and Eve to eat of the tree of life only on the condition that they not also eat of the tree of knowledge. To put it another way, people would have been spared eternal death, if they had remained in abysmal ignorance.

Either way, there is no question of salvation and no need for a religion founded upon such a concept. There is only the question of a god changing his mind (that God who "changes not"), a god manufactured in the way gods and goddesses have been for many thousands of years, patterned to satisfy the superstitions, allay the fears, and fulfill the "needs" of countless breeds and civilizations.

But if theologians and the clergy still insist that death was imposed upon human beings as punishment for sin and that their God actually intended for them to live *forever*, although Genesis scripture makes it clear that all were created mortal and the Creator *feared* that these mortals would *try* to be as immortal as the gods, let them consider the alternative—that God foresaw their destiny as free of any form of death. A mental picture then looms of a teeming globe inhabited by billions upon billions of human beings, many of whom are millions of years old, packed body to body in a hideous endurance contest, until they can't stand the sight of another unwelcome human creature and are screaming and pleading for death. Any savior then would have to present himself as a wholesale executioner.

———◇———

The mass of baffling contradictions that go to make up "God's Plan" as conceived by Christian theology is staggering, but from scriptural murkiness the realization inevitably emerges: that some impulsive three-in-one godhead created (1.) for a reason never unveiled, a world so ugly and meaningless that Christians must shun every appealing facet of it and regard it as a loathsome way-station on the road to possible damnation, meanwhile spending all their time helping themselves and their fellows "overcome" it, as Jesus did; and (2.) specifically to till the land, human beings so imperfect that every god-given passion and instinct which enabled the human race to survive a hostile environment with a minimum of comfort (and to produce those additional farmhands as ordered) must be condemned as a degrading defect, the indulgence of which paves the way to hell. Since godliness and worldliness are antitheses and since "servants cannot serve two masters," only *denial* of God's masterpiece the World, along with repression of God-endowed "human nature," will lead to heavenly rewards.

Jesus did not advocate enjoyment of worldly pleasure or worldly achievement, but rather recommended things of the spirit, going so far as to demand that man "forsake all that he hath." And Paul required that every thought be directed heavenward and that all things of the flesh, especially, be scorned: "Set your affection on things above, not on things on the earth." *Col. 3:2* Calling for mortals to be "long-suffering" (*Col. 3:12*), he elaborated: "For in this earthly house we groan, earnestly desiring to be clothed upon with our house which is from heaven." *II Cor. 5:2* He glorified the miseries of earthbound humanity and viewed misfortune as chastisement visited by God upon special favorites.

What possible purpose formed the impetus for creation of a world destined to be considered as a gauntlet which people must run to reach their final goal—heaven? What reasoning lay behind the creation of human wretches doomed to spend their earthly lives welcoming the lash and, in extreme fear of *eternal* punishment, resisting the temptations of God's own son Satan (*Job. 1:6*), whom Jesus called "the prince of this world" (*John 12:31*) and because of whose blandishments the world's first population had to be drowned without warning to make way for a new crop of human puppets at the same mercy of God and Satan? Of that new crop, more than three-fourths alive today are headed for the fires of hell, under the New Testament plan for salvation, although these second-edition children of God are presumably an improvement over the inhabitants of Noah's day, whose destruction was supposed to banish wickedness from the earth. God can't seem to succeed in anything he undertakes.

If human beings were created to spend eternity gazing upon their Creator, then God's plan has been a massive failure, and they, instead of benefiting from it, have in the main been the victims of it. The idea that any plan of an omnipotent deity could go awry, however, is unacceptable, and it must be assumed not only that everything happens according to divine plan but that every development of the plan gratifies its originator. The God of the Bible, on the other hand, frequently does suffer frustration (to the extent that he has periods of regret and repentance described in the scriptures), so once again Bible browsers will discover themselves face to face with another of those numerous contradictions which they have learned to expect to encounter in the pages of the Holy Book, a book which teaches that two know-nothing human beings were able to upset the Almighty's applecart in the very beginning and drive him to suicide.

CHAPTER SEVEN

Treatment Of Women In The Sweetest Story Ever Told

Woman's sense of her own worth is not enhanced by the biblical account of her creation as an afterthought mate for man from one of his ribs. *Gen. 2*

———◆———

Blame for the introduction of sin into the world being placed upon a woman who had no knowledge of right and wrong and who in no way was any more at fault than the man, is typical of the attitude of the Old Testament writers toward the female sex. *Gen. 3* Because an innocent woman "sinned" once, humankind was made subject to death.

According to Christian dogma, Eve's punishment for causing the downfall of the human race—subjection to her husband and bearing children in sorrow—became a curse upon all women for all time to come. *Gen. 3:16* In all fairness, however, Eve should be *enshrined* by the Christian Church, rather than maligned, for without her there would be no Christian religion. Christianity is based on atonement made necessary by the "fall of man." Had there been no "fall," for which Eve was responsible, there would have been no need for atonement and salvation.

———◆———

Sexual relations with women are unclean for men throughout the entire Bible. Although delights of the female body are stressed in some books such as Song of Solomon and Proverbs, the general attitude toward the sex act in the Holy Book is that it is an *enjoyable evil*. Refraining from sexual activity is a mark of purity and piety on the part of men.

The male sex is the chief concern of the Bible, the female sex being almost totally subordinate to it, with a few exceptions. Her role is usually conceived as wife, mistress, concubine, or mother of prominent men. The earliest indication of the uncleanness-of-women theme which is to prevail in both of the Testaments may be found in the words used to describe the purification by Moses of the Israelites in preparation for God's visit to them at Mt. Sinai: "Come not at your wives." *Ex. 19:15* The last: "they which were not defiled with women." *Rev. 14:4*

———⟫◆⟪———

The Mosaic law ordained by God through his servant Moses could scarcely be more degrading to women. Some examples of specific rules include the following:

1. The wife of a slave and her children shall be her master's possessions. If the male slave leaves, he leaves alone. *Ex. 21:4*

2. If a man sell his daughter to be a maidservant, she shall belong to her master forever. *Ex. 21:7*

3. If a woman has borne a *man* child, she shall be unclean 7 days, and she is separated for her *infirmity*. She shall continue in the blood of her purifying 33 days; she shall touch no hallowed thing, nor come into the sanctuary, until the days of her purifying be fulfilled. *Lev. 12:2–4*

4. But if she has borne a *maid* child, then she shall be unclean 2 weeks and must purify for 66 days, and she must then make a *sin* offering as an atonement for bearing a female. *Lev. 12:5*

5. A woman is unclean until evening after engaging in the sex act. She must bathe. *Lev. 15*

6. A menstruating women is unclean for 7 days. She shall be put apart. Anyone who *touches* her will be unclean until evening and must bathe. Furniture she sits upon is unclean until evening. *Lev. 15*

7. After sexual intercourse with a menstruating woman, a man is unclean for 7 days. So is the bed. *Lev. 15*

8. A woman is unclean if she has any bleeding after menstruation. Seven days of separation are required to cleanse her, after the bleeding stops. Furniture she sits upon is unclean, and so is anyone who touches that furniture. That person must bathe and wash his clothes. The offending woman must make a *sin* offering. *Lev. 15*

9. "And whosoever lieth carnally with a woman that is a bondmaid betrothed to her husband; *she* shall be scourged." *Lev. 19:20*

10. A prostitute daughter of a priest shall be burnt to death. *Lev. 21:9*

11. Witches shall be stoned to death. *Lev. 20:27*

12. The worth of persons who make singular vows to God is estimated by the priest. A male from age 20 to 60 is valued at 50 shekels of silver, a woman in that age span 30 shekels. A male from 5 to 20 years is worth 20 shekels, a female 10 shekels. A male from 1 month to 5 years is worth 5 shekels, a female 3 shekels. A male above 60 is worth 15 shekels, a female 10 shekels. *Lev. 27:2–7*

13. Women accused of adultery are brought before a priest and made to drink water mixed with dust in order to determine their guilt. There are no such tests for men, and no woman could pass such a test. *Num. 5*

14. A girl not a virgin when she marries shall be stoned to death at the door of her father. *Deut. 22:21*

15. A man may divorce his wife with a paper, a bill of divorcement, which he hands to her, whereupon she must leave his house. *Deut. 24:1*

16. A divorcee may not re-marry the husband who divorced her. *Deut. 24:4*

—◆—

The treachery often attributed to biblical women is illustrated by the following Old Testament tale. At the close of a battle, Sisera is pursued by the Israelites and is invited into the tent of Jael, his friend's wife, to take refuge. She gives him milk to drink. When he is sleeping under the delusion that he is safe, she drives a huge nail into his forehead, fastening his head to the ground. *Judges 4* Such women are Bible heroines. ("Milk" was sexual favors, in the original text.)

—◆—

The only two books of the Bible named for women seek to glorify members of their sex who deserve little admiration. By trickery and use of her feminine charm, Esther is made queen of a Persian kingdom and saves many of her fellow Jews at the expense of the lives of 500 subjects of the king and those of the ten sons of Haman, who are hanged at her request. *Esther 1–10*

Although the book of Esther is an Old Testament book, its salacious, undercover narrative, which ends with the conforming woman triumphant, is built upon the unequal relationship between the two sexes that predominates throughout the entire Bible. Esther is the stereotype of the kind of woman who meets with Bible approval. Her qualities are typical, and include possession of the seductive beauty that whetted the hearty sexual appetites of male members of both Gentile and Hebrew societies of Bible days. Along with her physical attributes, she also is still blessed with the virginity demanded by the double-standard morality of the Bible. She exhibits acceptance of the Mosaic perception of the female as unclean, along with the talent common to biblical women for occasionally bending men to their will by making use of their one weapon—sexuality. And she is not above making use of that talent, with a result which is understandably appreciated by her fellow Jews.

Esther is introduced into the story of the Persian king Ahasuerus (Xerxes) as a conspiring vamp. Queen Vashti has threatened the supremacy of the entire male population of a vast kingdom by starting her own woman's liberation movement and refusing to parade her charms before a husband and a crowd of leering gluttons who had been drinking and feasting for seven days. The king's henchmen, alert to the far-reaching consequences of permitting a woman to defy her master, and fearing a domino reaction from one end of the realm to the other, persuade the king to issue a decree that "every man should bear rule in his own house."

Vashti is dethroned and the king forced into the inconvenience of trying out a panel of the "fair young virgins from all the provinces of his kingdom," a process which cannot begin, however, until precautions have been taken to prevent any possibility that Ahasuerus might be contaminated by these candidates for the recently-vacated queenship. To accomplish their purification, six months with oil of myrrh, and six months with sweet odours (and with "other things for the purifying of the women") are required.

Esther is a true woman of her time, and so enthusiastically does she compete, that she wins out in both the sanitation department and in the contest for the king's favor, the latter lasting only one night in contrast with her 12-month warm-up stay in the locker-room showers. *Esther 1–10*

⇒>◈<⇐

That "whither-thou-goest" daughter-in-law Ruth deliberately entices Boaz by sneaking into the place where he sleeps (in a drunken stupor) and lying down at his feet. "And it came to pass at midnight, that the man was afraid, and turned himself: and, behold, a woman lay at his feet. And he said, Who art thou? And she answered, I am Ruth thine handmaid: spread therefore thy skirt over thine handmaid." *Ruth 3:8,9* (Behold!) (And even Lo!)

She is put up to this seduction by her mother-in-law Naomi, who has thanked the Lord for bringing Boaz into their lives. Ruth and Naomi, and Esther, too, may be excused for what seems demeaning behavior, when the dependence of biblical women upon men for support and protection is considered. Because of their subjugation to husband, father, brother, and kinsman, their behavior should be judged accordingly.

⇒>◈<⇐

"Have they not divided the prey; to every man a damsel or two?" *Judges 5:30* These are the words of Sisera's mother, as she seeks an explanation for his failure to return from battle.

Men are *holy* who stay away from women. This principle is upheld again in a situation using unusually lucid scripture, even for the Word of God, but the Bible has a way of not shrinking from calling a spade a spade. The priest who offers David and his men hallowed bread to eat makes sure they are in the proper condition to eat it: "There is hallowed bread; if the young men have kept themselves at least from women. And David answered the priest, and said unto him, Of a truth women have been kept from us about these three days, since I came out, and the vessels of the young men are holy, and the bread is in a manner common, yea, though it were sanctified this day in the vessel." *I Sam.* 21:4,5

Solomon has 700 wives and 300 concubines. He is one of God's special favorites, whom God has blessed with wisdom. Such is the morality of the Bible. *I Kings* 11:3

King Rehoboam has 18 wives and 60 concubines, 28 sons and 60 daughters. *II Chron.* 11:21

King Abijah has 14 wives, 22 sons, and 16 daughters. *II Chron.* 13:21 Piker!

"For the lips of a strange woman drop as an honeycomb. . . ." *Prov.* 5:3

"Let her breasts satisfy thee at all times; and be thou ravished always with her love." *Prov.* 5:19

"To keep thee from the evil woman, from the flattery of the tongue of a strange woman." *Prov.* 6:24

"Come, let us take our fill of love until the morning." *Prov.* 7:18

"As a jewel of gold in a swine's snout, so is a fair woman which is without discretion." *Prov.* 11:22 It takes the Bible to put it that way!

"It is better to dwell in the corner of the housetop than with a brawling woman." *Prov.* 25:24

"Give not thy strength unto women." *Prov.* 31:3

"Behold, thou art fair, my love; behold, thou art fair; thou hast doves' eyes within thy locks; thy hair is as a flock of goats, that appear from mount Gilead . . . Thy lips are like a thread of scarlet, and thy speech is comely . . . Thy two breasts are like two young roes that are twins, which feed among the lilies . . . Thou art all fair, my love . . ." *Song of Solomon* 4:1–7 Sex objects elicit eloquence in the Holy Book.

"How fair and how pleasant thou art, O love, for delights! . . . now also thy breasts shall be as clusters of the vine, and the smell of thy nose like apples." *Song of Solomon 7:6–8* After purification, that is!

————≈◆≈————

Women of the Bible even have to decide whether to fend off or submit to a deity who has lust not only in his heart but in his intentions. Before he proceeds to his ultimate goal, he must first tell Isaiah why the proposed female victims are in need of punishment from a well-meaning guardian of their morals. Isaiah makes sure the Hebrew women understand what punishment they may anticipate, as well as the justifiable reason for it: "Moreover the Lord saith, Because the daughters of Zion are haughty, and walk with stretched forth necks and wanton eyes, walking and mincing as they go, and making a tinkling with their feet: Therefore the Lord will smite with a scab the crown of the head of the daughters of Zion, and the Lord will discover their secret parts." *Isaiah 3:16,17*

The Lord is not yet finished with his scathing predictions of what shall befall seductive women: "And in that day seven women shall take hold of one man, saying, We will eat our own bread, and wear our own apparel: only let us be called by thy name, to take away our reproach." *Isaiah 4:1* Unlike the wanton woman, a man could have as many sex partners as he could not beat off.

The entire book of Isaiah reveals the Lord's mental image of the female repeatedly, but this seems to vacillate from one of unseemly aggression to one of scornful weakness. "As for my people, children are their oppressors and women rule over them." *Isaiah 3:12* And: "In that day shall Egypt be like unto women, and it shall be afraid and fear." *Isaiah 19:16*

————≈◆≈————

God recognizes the deviousness of women and makes use of it: "Thus saith the Lord, and send for cunning women." *Jer. 9:17*

The prophets are faithful in recording the Lord's propensity for humiliation of the female sex by comparing sinful cities and nations to it: "Jerusalem is as a menstruous woman." *Lam. 1:17* The Hebrew men didn't seem to realize that the bodily functions of women which they abhorred, added to the act of sexual union which they regarded as sinful and dirty, made possible their own reproduction and the birth of those sons and Jewish heroes who were able to win God's admiration, not to mention the fresh supply of virgins to serve the male libido. And the God of the Christian Bible despises his own handiwork manifested in the sexual drives and bodily functions of his own creation—

human beings. Yet, though he may deplore these human traits, he doesn't hesitate to tell people to "multiply"; in fact, he so instructs them several times. And although Paul says that man is the image and glory of God, that same deity and all his spokesmen on earth as portrayed in the Bible felt nothing but disgust for the way in which humankind reproduces itself.

The book of Ezekiel probably ranks first in its contempt for women as expressed in God's own words: "Slay utterly old and young, both maids and little children, and women: but come not near any man upon whom is the mark . . . fill the courts with the slain." *Ez. 9:6,7* "How weak is thine heart, seeing thou doest all these things, the work of an imperious whorish woman." *Ez. 16:30* "As a wife committeth adultery, which taketh strangers instead of her husband." *Ez. 16:32* "And they shall strip thee also of thy clothes and shall take thy fair jewels and leave thee naked and bare." *Ez. 16:39* "Neither hath come near to a menstruous woman." *Ez. 18:6* "Thus will I cause lewdness to cease that all women may be taught not to do after your lewdness." *Ez. 23:48* Jerusalem is the vile woman, as she often is in God's metaphors.

Hardly anything more scathing can be said in the Bible than, e.g.: "Behold, thy people in the midst of thee are women." *Nahum 3:13* Nineveh is the city to be pitied in this instance. God preferred the men of Sodom and Gomorrah, perhaps, but even in those cities, the biblical fire and brimstone fell on the women and children, as well as the perverts. All the embryos perished.

Even when God's favorite macho men are indulging in behavior frowned upon by the Lord, women who dare to criticize them are properly punished in the Bible. David's wife Michal reprimands her husband for dancing unclothed before the Ark of the Covenant in the sight of the maidservants. David's sassy rejoinder is eloquent evidence of the disdain biblical men felt for women: "It was before the Lord, which chose me before thy father, and before all his house, to appoint me ruler over the people of the Lord, over Israel: therefore will I play before the Lord. And I will be yet more vile than thus . . ." The next verse gives the sequel: "Therefore Michal the daughter of Saul had no child unto the day of her death." *II Sam. 6:20–23*

For speaking ill of her brother Moses, Miriam is made leprous. (Moses had married outside the law.) Both Michal's and Miriam's punishment came from the Lord. *Num. 12*

David's concubines are sexually used by his son Absalom. David, with typical

biblical justice, imprisons the *concubines* for life. *II Sam. 16:22* and *20:3*
David's behavior towards women doesn't keep him from being a great
favorite of the Lord and the fore-father of the prophesied Messiah.

Some women of the bible are painted as so vicious as to have no redeeming
qualities. Jezebel, a princess before she becomes the wife of King Ahab, is a
Baal worshipper and kills the prophets of the Lord. Shades of Eve, she is also
blamed for her husband's misdeeds and becomes the victim of an assassin
Jehu, who can match her cruelty for cruelty. *I Kings 21:25 II Kings 9:30–37*
The Bible persecutes Jezebel for defending her religion with the same zeal
shown by the Jews in establishing theirs, the difference being that their intolerance was decreed by the Lord.

Chivalry was waiting for knighthood. Lot offers his two virgin daughters to
the Sodomites in lieu of two male angels, later "sleeps" with the girls himself. *Gen. 19* To protect a male houseguest, a concubine is pushed out the
door, abused all night long, and found dead on the doorstep the next morning. *Judges 19:22–30*

Because men and women are both defiled by the sex act, according to biblical teaching, Jesus had to be born of a virgin, who was supposed to be thrilled
to find herself pregnant on her wedding night, never having slept with the
groom. *Matt. 1:18* Giving birth to God made it necessary for her to undergo the Jewish purification rites. *Luke 2:22* Since the baby Jesus was a male,
those rites required only 40 days.

Jesus is almost contemptuous of his mother. When she finally finds him in
the temple after anxiously searching for him for three days, this 12-year-old
withers her with the arrogant words: "Wist ye not that I must be about my
Father's business?" *Luke 2:49* At the marriage feast in Cana when his mother appeals to him, he replies to her in the following manner, before the
guests: "Woman, what have I to do with thee?" *John 2:4* (You're only my
mother!)
    During his ministry, when she and his brothers try to speak to him in a
crowd, he ignores them, saying that his family consists of those who do the
will of God. *Matt. 12:46–50* (So much for Christian family life.) Throughout
the gospels he seems to have no concern or interest whatsoever in his mother, with the single exception that John alone says she was present at the crucifixion and that Jesus, seeing her, puts her in the care of one of the disciples.
John 19:25–27 A last-minute, haphazard arrangement on the part of someone who knew exactly when he was going to die!

Woe to pregnant women and nursing mothers at the end of the world, warns Jesus. *Matt. 24:19* It would seem only fair to give women at least a nine-month warning.

Almost nowhere in the New Testament is the worth of woman acknowledged. Children get some special attention, but although Christ has female followers (at whose homes he sometimes lodges), for the most part the New Testament and indeed the Old are concerned with men. With some exceptions the important persons are men. It is true, Jesus does not bad-mouth women, yet neither does he dignify them. He seems to inspire loyalty among them, at one time defends a prostitute, and, disregarding Jewish custom, converses openly with the woman at the well. *John 4:6–29* But Jesus certainly did little to encourage reform in the treatment of womankind under the Mosaic law, and he was not enough incensed by her enforced servitude to men within the Hebrew culture of his day to become anything but a weak advocate of her liberation.

Confronted on every hand, as he must have been, by instances of mistreatment of the female sex, he does not become sufficiently indignant to denounce the sexism of Bible days, beyond making a few reproachful remarks on one or two occasions. He certainly could have found much that might have been expected to infuriate a God of love, such as the stoning and burning of women who were accused of being less pure than men were expected to be, or who were accused of being witches. He might have questioned the many laws of Moses that treated her as a sexual pariah and sexual love as an act of shame, and that bound her to her slave master.

He could have chided men for refusing to speak to women on the streets, and he could have told those same men that women were apt to be just about as worthy as they. He could have defended Eve, and . . . but why go on? If he had been emphatic about equality of the sexes, if he had taken a stand for women even as strong as the one he took for children, women would not still be struggling for equal rights in societies where the Bible has a large role in determining the status of the female. Rather than a tool in her subordination, the Bible might be a weapon in her battle for self-determination. It was Jesus's failure to be her champion plus her biblical heritage as first transgressor that encouraged her persecution by the Church and that still deny her equal rights with the male.

When, instead of teaching respect for the female sex, Jesus told stories such as the one in Matthew 25 about the ten virgins who await one bridegroom, he made it clear that his attitude toward women was not very different from that of his male contemporaries, who placed women's bodies at men's disposal.

Mary Magdalene, cured of seven (!) devils by Jesus, is one of several women who follow Jesus's entourage from place to place and are present at the crucifixion and resurrection, not deserting Jesus as the cowardly disciples do. (If even the most intimate of Jesus's associates falter, how can ordinary persons who have not met him and can't be expected to, be blamed if they are not steadfast believers?)

Although Jesus's women friends do remain loyal to the end, in contrast to the disciples, who don't seem to put any faith in anything Jesus predicted, they are not privileged to meet with him after the resurrection or to witness the ascension, and the mother and family of Jesus are not present at or after the resurrection. Here again, there is no record in the gospels of Jesus having any filial love for his mother, or anything but conflict with his brothers and sisters. He seems to go home but once, and then meets with such disrespect by his neighbors that he is unable to work any miracles (the prophet in his own land). Spending many hours wining (*Matt. 11:19*) and dining off his friends, apparently he doesn't even spend holidays with his mother. Mary could not have been treated with more deliberate neglect in the Bible, by Jesus and by the gospel writers, if she had been the mother of Satan, rather than the mother of God. *Matt. 13:57,58* Maybe Jesus didn't like chicken soup.

No specific praise is expressed in the New Testament for family life or woman's place in it, and the loose morals prevalent in the Old Testament, coupled with its sex-discrimination laws, do not speak for either. On the contrary, in the New Testament the family is seriously downgraded. Jesus opens a special path to heaven for all who *forsake* family completely, and he and his disciples, and later Paul, set the example. (Celibate nuns and monks and priests became numerous when Christianity flowered.)

The Old Testament *does* make it clear the Jewish family is traditionally strong, but Jesus seems to threaten it by saying: "If any man come to me, and hate not his father, and mother, and wife, and children, and brethren, and sisters . . . he cannot be my disciple." *Luke 14:26*

If members of the female sex are not disillusioned by the time they get to Paul, they may then prepare to encounter the proverbial straw. Although a woman-hater, he is willing to use her to support the Church. Churched women are still satisfied if they are tossed a bone once in a while, permitting themselves to be treated with insults and contempt when they dare to seek parity with men in the sectarian hierarchy. (Discrimination is explained by attributing it to Jesus.)

Except in a derogatory manner, Paul seldom mentions women. A typical quote from one of his wordy epistles to the early Christians: "To every *man* that is among you, not to think of *himself* more highly than *he* ought to think; but to think soberly, according as God hath dealt to every *man* the measure of faith." *Romans 12:3*

Paul gets off to a good start by calling many women lesbians. *Romans 1:26*

⋙⋯◆⋯⋘

In the spirit of the Mosaic law, Paul furthers the idea that sexual relations are unclean, probably recalling the words of Jesus: ". . . there be eunuchs, which have made themselves eunuchs for the kingdom of heaven's sake." *Matt. 19:12* Paul is more specific: "it is good for a man not to touch a woman . . . I say therefore to the unmarried and widows, It is good for them, if they abide even as I . . . Now, concerning virgins . . . I say it is good for a man so to be . . . Art thou loosed from a wife? seek not a wife." *I Cor. 7*

Married persons, claims Paul, care for worldly things while the unmarried care for spiritual things. He who has enough willpower to remain a virgin "doeth well." Anyone who gives not a woman in marriage does better than one who does. A woman whose husband dies *may* marry again, but she will be happier if she doesn't. Paul, forced to face up to the weakness of others, finally does concede: "But if they cannot contain, let them marry, for it is better to marry than to burn." *I Cor. 7* Marriage, to Paul, is just a barely sanctioned way out for the weak and undedicated, and he found nothing in the teachings of Jesus to make him think otherwise. The Church has laundered the scriptures, with its usual license, to make marriage a holy institution and even a sacrament, and today New Testament thinking on it is purposely obscured, while marriage and the family have become the "Christian," church-oriented way of life. (On earth, that is. In heaven there will be no marriage or family relationships. And none of those repulsive carnal pleasures, one infers. *Mark 12:25)*

The "pecking order" is precisely delineated by Paul in his crusade to see that men would dominate the new Church. A possibly lightning-struck fanatic, whose insecurity fosters speculation about his own sexual tendencies, his diligence in putting women in their place finds long-suffering church women today strangely free of indignation towards him and the Church. His words should not fail to raise the hackles of any self-respecting modern woman: "A man is the image and glory of God but the woman is the glory of man. For the man is not of the woman, but the woman of the man. Neither was the man created for the woman, but the woman for the man. But I would have you know that the head of every man is Christ; and the head of the woman is the man; and the head of Christ is God." *I Cor. 11* Well, there goes the Trinity, and one can see why Paul is the darling of the male-dominated Church.

In case any woman has a bit of pride left after all this, Paul humiliates her even further: "Let your women keep silence in the churches: for it is not permitted unto them to speak; but they are commanded to be under obedience, as also saith the law. And if they will learn anything, let them ask their husbands at home: for it is a shame for women to speak in the church." *I Cor. 14:34,35* How nice! Men know it all!

———=>·◇·=———

Paul instructs Timothy: "Let the women learn in silence with all subjection. But I suffer not a woman to *teach*, nor to usurp authority over the man." *I Tim. 2:11,12* Can woman hope for more respect in heaven? The book of the Christian woman's faith gives her short shrift on earth.

The further arrogance and contempt of Paul toward women in general and toward unfortunate women in particular, which is shared by the early founders of the Christian church, is heartlessly expressed again to Timothy. Of widows Paul writes: "Well reported of for good works; if she have brought up children, if she have lodged strangers, if she have washed the saints' feet, if she have relieved the afflicted ... But the younger widows refuse; for when they have begun to wax wanton against Christ, they will marry; having damnation, because they have cast off their first faith. And withal they learn to be idle, wandering about from house to house; and not only idle, but tattlers also and busybodies, speaking things which they ought not. I will therefore that the younger women marry, bear children, guide the house." *I Tim. 5:10–14* Here again marriage is a last resort, to prevent behavior that is even worse. The behavior of widowers is left to their own discretion. Perhaps they seldom gossip or visit their neighbors.

In general, biblical women fail to inspire admiration or respect. In the Old Testament they are frequently sex objects used in metaphorical descriptions repeatedly as "virgins," "whores," or "harlots." Quite a few (Old Testament) women are barren and require the aid of the Lord, an angel, or a prophet, or (in the New Testament) the Holy Ghost to produce the important-to-be off-spring. The results of such unions are usually male, of course, a nice trick still unfathomed by most of modern medicine.

Many uncomplimentary adjectives may be applied to women found in the pages of the Word of God, such as devious, incestuous, barren, sexually delinquent, seductive, submissive, and even murderous (Athaliah murders her grandchildren to gain the throne). They share their husbands with as many as 699 other wives and tolerate harems of concubines, also offering their maidservants to their spouses for sexual partners. They marry close kinsmen and are supposedly overjoyed to bear children when far past the child-bearing age and when they have been impregnated by unseen spirits demanding their consent.

If they are beautiful, their husbands may pass them off as their sisters instead of their wives. They may be the means by which their fathers acquire sons. They meekly suffer punishment for the slightest disobedience such as eating fruit or looking over their shoulders. They are painted as heartless and vengeful (the daughter of Herodias asks for the head of John the Baptist, and Sarah demands that Hagar and Ishmael be sent into the desert without water).

They are sex victims of close relatives (David's son Amnon compromises his sister Tamar). There are 19 specific cases of incest in the Bible, not counting the necessary shenanigans of Cain and Seth, and starting with Abraham's marriage to his half-sister Sarai.

Bible women plot and trick, tempt and tease. They often use their wiles in patriotic causes to trap deluded victims (devious Delilah finds womanizer Samson's Achilles' heel). They are accorded no respect and desire none. The Queen of Sheba could have been an exception, but the purpose of her visit to Jerusalem was to check out Solomon.

Whenever a group or multitude is counted or one of the frequent censuses taken, the total announced in the Bible is always the tally of the men, "besides the women and children." Counted with the juveniles, women rank even lower than they in the kingdom of God.

———⋙•◆•⋘———

Treatment of women in the Bible is characterized by such indecency and utter contempt that it is a travesty to call this book the Word of God. From the first, every natural function peculiar to their sex is deplored by the God-given Mosaic law and employed as the vehicle for labelling a woman unclean for a considerable part of her lifetime and even during the act of giving birth (although the process may have been the culmination of a visit from God in the form of the Holy Ghost, as myth gods were fathered by a golden cloud or by a feather pressed to the breast).

As if humiliation were not enough, the Lord decrees savage butchery of both women and children, especially throughout the pages of the Old Testament. Women, when not actually slaughtered, are consigned to rape and concubinage by this Christian deity, sometimes in public view: "Their children also shall be dashed to pieces before their eyes; their houses shall be spoiled, and their women ravished." *Isaiah 13:16* "Therefore I will give their wives unto others." *Jer. 8:10* "And the city shall be taken and the women ravished." *Zech. 14:2*

God's punishment for David's sexual misconduct with Bathsheba fell, with typical biblical precision, upon the innocent: "Thus saith the Lord, Behold I will take thy wives before thine eyes and give them unto thy neighbor, and he shall lie with thy wives in the sight of this sun." *II Sam. 12:11* Here God specifically condones polygamy, as well as public obscenity. The Mosaic law actually included rules for plural marriage: "If a man have two wives . . ." *Deut. 21:15*

Among God's cursings of Hebrews who do not abide by his grisly laws are the following: "Thou shalt betroth a wife, and another man shall lie with her." *Deut. 28:30* And: "Cursed shall be the fruit of thy body." *Deut. 28:18* And: "Thy sons and thy daughters shall be given unto another people." *Deut. 28:32* Blameless children, wives, and mothers all bear the brunt of God's strange system of justice. Could a heathen god of the most bestial kind conceive of more depravity? It is surely not surprising that many deists, atheists, and agnostics regard the Bible as the ultimate insult to a benevolent God! And to the reputation of the Christian God must be added his invention of a place of eternal torture.

The Bible perceives the female as the sexual toy of the male: "And seest among the captives a beautiful woman, and hast a desire unto her, that thou wouldst have her to thy wife; Then shalt thou bring her home to thine house; and she shall shave her head and pare her nails; And she shall put the raiment of her captivity from off her, and shall remain in thine house, and bewail her father and her mother a full month: and after that thou shalt go in unto her, and be her husband, and she shall be thy wife. And it shall be, if thou have no delight in her, then thou shalt let her go whither she will." *Deut. 21:11–14* There were few places a used woman could go, since virginity was so highly regarded by men of the Bible that a woman who did not possess it at the right time could be put to death. (The several tests for virginity common to the people of that day are frequently faulty.) In the above situation of the rejected slave-wife, the only restraint upon the male manipulator of the female puppet is that he may not *sell* his victim, because he has "humbled" her. Well, sort of.

———◆———

Jesus did not denounce the Old Testament law. How could he, since as God he had been the law-giver through Moses? He actually endorsed it emphatically: "For had ye believed Moses, ye would have believed me: for he wrote of me. But if ye believe not his writings, how shall ye believe my words?" *John 5:46,47* How, indeed?

Logically, then, indecencies toward women permitted or commanded under the Mosaic law appear to be sanctioned by Jesus, including the practice of Onanism, which enslaved Hebrew women as the sexual partners of the brothers of their heir-less dead husbands. Lack of respect in this field of treatment of women under the law of Moses is demonstrated dramatically and openly by Jesus in an episode related in chapter 12 of Mark, wherein some Sadducees tell a story about a woman forced to become the sexual property of *seven* brothers under the law of Onanism. "Whose will she be in heaven?" the Sadducees ask. In anyone with a sense of decency, such a question would have created at least a degree of embarrassment and indignation at this violation of the bodies and dignity of womankind, but Jesus regards the question as more important than the social implications involved in the law. He informs the Sadducees that there will be no marriage relationship in heaven, which may make it doubly attractive to the much-used woman involved. This is the manner of brief replies that people get in the New Testament to any inquiry about heaven. But Jesus can be even more flippant. He tosses out the information that there's no sweat, anyhow, because God is the god of the living, not the dead. (Not only is the chattel of the seven brothers abandoned in death, but so are all of the human race not saved by belief in Jesus.)

⇒◆⇐

As long as women fail to denounce the Bible, they are in danger from it, for it has long been and continues to be their oppressor. Its scriptures demean her and deprive her not only of her self-respect, but of veritable control over her body. The Bible makes her a slave, a piece of property at the mercy and whim of the male and in a state of total submission to her husband, who may even act as her abuser.

She is regarded by the scriptures as the receptacle of the male seed and the means of reproducing the human race, and this is her only function. Her position in the family is lower than that of the family dogs who infested the Holy Land. At least they didn't have to be separated from the family for days, at times when circumstances peculiar to women prevail.

⇒◆⇐

Here is an example from the Mosaic law of how she could be victimized: "If a man find a damsel that is a virgin, which is not betrothed, and lay hold on her, and lie with her and they be found; Then the man that lay with her shall give unto the damsel's father fifty shekels of silver, and she shall be his wife." *Deut. 22:28,29* (Forced to marry her rapist!) If a betrothed virgin is raped in the city and is not heard to cry out, she shall be stoned to death. No exception is allowed if her life has been threatened, and one gathers that if she had not been already another man's property, the rapist would have incurred no blame, although from then on she could be stoned or burnt for not being a virgin when she should be. *Deut. 22:23,24*

One of those required times was the wedding night. If the groom, who had probably not been a virgin for many a day, came to the girl's parents and claimed that their daughter had not been a virgin the night before, the parents were required to produce a bloody sheet to the city elders. If there was no bloody sheet (and more often than not there isn't) the unfortunate maiden must be brought to the door of her father's house, "and the men of her city shall stone her with stones that she die." *Deut. 22:21* It is awful to contemplate the atrocities committed in the name of God against innocent girls and those who had been brutalized. True, Jesus did on one occasion say to cast the first stone only if the accuser was without sin. (He also upheld every "jot and tittle" of the law.) *Sinless* accusers were free to proceed.

Christian women had better "pray without ceasing" that Jesus's Mosaic law never be enforced anymore than it already is. Much of that conduct-guide of antiquity remains mandatory behavior for Christians, e.g., the Ten Commandments, and many laws based upon other parts of it have been imposed upon those who reside in Christendom, no matter their belief. And, although other admonitions of the Hebrew law are discreetly considered unmentionable and outdated by present-day morals, even these rules remain part of God's Word and lie in wait between the covers of the Bible to be pounced upon and made to serve the dark cause of discrimination and abrogation of civil rights, as they have in the past.

＝＞・◇・＜＝

The Bible has been for too long a time the authority for legislating against women and for nourishing sexist attitudes that persecuted them and made them content with subjugation by the male and the Church. It still remains, abetted by the Church, one of the greatest threats to the rights and dignity of woman and is continually called upon to diminish her even further and to place her very body at the whim of the State. The question today, which inexplicably still threatens womankind wherever the Good Book is venerated, reads as it has for centuries: which words of God may be extracted from the Bible to subdue her next? The question has become one of urgency to all who have an interest in keeping women "barefoot and pregnant." Unfortunately, the Church, predicting the demise of "family" and "life," has always been in the vanguard of those who have a stake in propping up that traditional image. Woman must bend to the values set up by the clergy and gleaned by them from the pages of the Christian woman's manual. She must become the noble human sacrifice to God that Paul demanded, dedicating herself to the interests of others.

The Christian woman who tries to live by the Bible has the problem of ascertaining where she stands. The Old Testament laws were cognizant of the importance of *virtuous* women to the preservation and integrity of the Jewish family and tribe, but, beyond protecting that function, the Bible treats woman as little more than a sexual diversion for the profligate male. As wife and mother of heirs, she was allowed but one sexual partner, while plural marriage and concubinage made promiscuity socially acceptable for the foot-loose male. The rape and debauchery practiced by men of the Bible created the ambiguity found in societies which demand "purity" in the female at the same time these cultures tolerate attacks on that "purity" by virility cultism.

After changing the Mosaic laws about women in only one or two instances, chiefly in the area of divorce, and by contradicting himself even there, Jesus succeeded in befuddling the Christian woman still further in her search to determine how the Bible tells her to conduct herself. Where, before, men could simply hand their wives walking papers, Jesus is more strict, to be sure. But in Matthew 5:32 he rules that a man may divorce his wife for "fornication," while in Luke and Mark divorce is not permitted by Jesus for any reason, and, furthermore, "whosoever putteth away his wife, and marrieth another, committeth adultery: and whosoever marrieth her that is put away from her husband committeth adultery." *Luke 16:18*

Jesus does not allow the wife to get a divorce for any cause, even when he lets her delinquency be justifiable cause for her husband to get one, and Paul permits no divorce at all and remarriage by the woman only if her husband dies. *I Cor. 7:10–11,39*

As a result of such confusion, the Church can go to the Bible, sanctify any aim, and force its female faithful to continue happily as the "second sex" and to influence their sisters to agree that woman's destiny is to serve her God and husband and to reproduce the human race. Her chief duty in society, as seen by the Christian religion, is to serve as a baby machine, with or without her consent. But the Bible sentences her to play out even this role in "sorrow," because she was made to shoulder the blame for all the world's sins, even those of a male predator.

The clergy will find it profitable to refer her to Proverbs 31:10–31. This recital of the qualities of her sex which will win favor with the Lord begins with a question: "Who can find a virtuous woman? for her price is far above rubies." It then goes on to describe the virtuous woman. And before Paul has a chance to build a pedestal for *his* favorite *sexless* icon, Jesus tells her how to find happiness on the delivery table: "A woman when she is in travail hath sorrow, because her hour is come: but as soon as she is delivered of the child, she remembereth no more the anguish, for joy that a *man* is born into the world." *John 16:21*

Such Bible talk, plus God's curse on Eve, have been used by the early Church and are still employed by some fundamentalist sects to deny women any analgesics during childbirth. Not satisfied with making scripture into an instrument to add to woman's childbirth agony, Christianity waves the Bible before legislators to persuade them that women should be forbidden by law to exercise control over their bodies and be forced to risk health and peace of mind by making a baby out of every fertilized human egg.

If the Bible contains any direct admonition against abortion, it is not generally known, but, as always, there are scriptures that can be excerpted to make a case for "pro-lifers." "Be fruitful and multiply" is probably the favorite weapon, although there is no reason to believe that God ever said: "Be fruitful and multiply and multiply and multiply" or that it was ever intended that every square foot of earth have a human being standing on it. If that was God's intention, he abandoned it rather quickly by introducing death into the world in the Garden of Eden. Anti-abortionists can't be serious when they base their philosophy on the Bible. There is no other book between whose covers life is so cheap. The wholesale Hebrew massacres of thousands glowingly described in detail are outdone only by God's personal annihilation of entire cities, the first-born of a whole country, and on one occasion *everyone* on earth except for eight of his favorites. He demands human sacrifice on several occasions, and the Christian religion teaches that *death*, not life, bought salvation. Matthew claims that every baby in the Holy Land had to die because Jesus was born.

There must have been many children and embryos on the death lists following God's massive executions. The Bible tells the reader that *none* was left breathing, and that included pregnant women. His instructions to the Hebrews in their conquest of Canaan was to kill even the sucklings. *I Sam. 15:3*

Not only is the Bible itself a book of pro-death, but it has been used in the cause of death for centuries. The Crusades, Inquisitions, and Holy Wars are examples of Bible-inspired murder. The Church took seriously some words of Jesus: "I came not to send peace, but a sword." *Matt. 10:34* Many heretics were put to death to save their souls, and it is estimated that at least a quarter of a million witches were burned to carry out their sentence of death under the Mosaic law.

An argument could be made that no one should bring any child into the world, since Jesus said that many more souls would end up in hell than in heaven. Thus, the cards are already stacked against every human being at birth, and it might be better never to be born than to risk eternal damnation.

=>·◇·<=

The Bible is man-made, as are all religious Holy Books, so it is not surprising that its laws are to the advantage of the male sex. When women are willing to bow to the edict that God himself made those rules, she has put the shackles upon her own wrists. The next step is historically that she learns to love the shackles. Today, after 2,000 years of obeying the dicta of the clergy, many women in Christendom are proud to subordinate themselves and assume martyr-like roles for the purpose of saving their immortal souls and fulfilling what they have been indoctrinated to believe is their spiritual destiny. In this role, the Christian woman unprotestingly accepts the heritage of guilt which the Bible has handed down to her from Eve.

When the Lord placed all the future sins of humankind, both male and female, on Eve's shoulders, he set the stage for every kind of abuse of women in retaliation for Eve's transgression, and the chronicles of innumerable crimes against her person and psyche fill the pages of the Holy Book and the annals of history. Early churchmen held back nothing in their public verbal assault upon womanhood. Tertullian wrote: "You are the devil's gateway . . . how easily you destroyed man, the image of God . . . because of the death which you brought upon us, even the Son of God had to die." It could have been pointed out that Genesis 1:27 says that both men and women were to be created in the image of the gods.

Liberal theologians now admit, privately, that the "fall" of man is mythical. It is the hub of too many pagan religious systems to be preached as Christian dogma. And it is no longer acceptable to be so blatant in the condemnation of women as the Bible actually is. The soft pedal is down, and the finger doesn't point as openly. But the biblical Eve cannot be permitted to die, although her sex may have been allowed to discard (to all appearances, at least) the label of God-killer and executioner of the human race. This label works to the advantage of men throughout the Bible narrative too well for the Church patriarchy to lift it now. And every theologian and every member of the priesthood and clergy and Church hierarchy knows that without the "fall of man" there is no need of a redeemer.

The churchwoman is bound to wonder, in any case, just how much her status is changed. Holier-than-thou Church officials are still comfortable chiding her publicly for aspiring to positions of even semi-equality with them. Mouthing platitudes, they explain condescendingly to her that, much as they regret the situation, her body is shaped different from the male body and therefore unlike the body of Jesus and his disciples, and inescapably therefore at odds with the shape of God himself. It follows, as any dim-witted member of her sex should be able to see, that therefore she cannot be the representative of that God here on earth and unfortunately, too, not quite as holy. The Church must remain, essentially, a Brotherhood. (The female shape is admittedly well-suited to many chores connected with Church work, and uniquely-suited to child-bearing for the purpose of replenishing the pews of the sanctuary.)

It can only be concluded that women who let the Bible dictate their behavior have become so bowed-down under the weight of it that their self-evaluation is now measured by the degree to which they find pleasure in submission to the Master who rules humankind from its pages, after the manner in which Christian dogma chooses to interpret the scriptures. It is well-known that such interpretation is open to manipulation by any faction powerful enough to manipulate it and by every cult and denomination to whom that power is granted by its laity.

<hr />

Readers of the Bible cannot escape the impression that its theme is sin, blame, and punishment for most of the human race. Women seem still unwilling to denounce it as written by men whose purpose, in part at least, was to ensure masculine pre-eminence. At no time have women staged a concentrated rebellion against religion in general and cried, "Enough!" And until the Christian woman is ready to see the Bible for what it is, she won't have "come a long way, Baby." She will remain on "hold," vaccinated by spirituality against the sickness of striving for self-realization.

For the Word of God is not erasable, and it does not waver in its mandate to womankind: "Wives, submit yourselves unto your own husbands, as unto the Lord. For the husband is the head of the wife . . . Therefore as the church is subject unto Christ, so let the wives be to their own husbands in everything." *Eph. 5:22,24*

Chapter Eight

Vulgarity In The Word Of God

Language to be found in the Bible is often of such a nature that the Holy Book is seldom opened at random and read aloud in just any company. This fact has probably discouraged censorship of literature and publications, for those with knowledge of the coarseness common to scripture realize that strict enforcement of regulations against prurient and tasteless material would mean that the Bible could not be permitted to remain in public view. A cry would inevitably go up about tender minds being exposed to filth, if people were to brave the forbiddingly dull depths of the Good Book and discover what has been carefully kept from them by the clergy and teachers of religion.

When people are encouraged to read the Bible, be assured the proselytizer is praying inwardly that readers will do no more than scan a few familiar texts and leave the rest to the insiders.

There are many scriptural vulgarisms that those who write about the contents of the Bible do not want to use in a critique. These passages are often left to private scrutiny. Should curiosity lead to investigation, the outcome for the Bible illiterates would undoubtedly be astonishment and revulsion that such crudity should form part of a religious book that is touted as the source of inspiration to lift humanity to the highest of ethical and moral ideals and expression.

Throughout the Bible's lengthy and diversified substance, the descriptive language is nothing if not gross, with some limitations imposed upon it by translators who have come and gone, and new versions continue to appear regularly whose chief purpose is to make the family Bible, and that intrusive Gideon volume, more palatable.

Some examples of the Bible's coarse language:

"The Lord will smite thee with the botch of Egypt, and with the emerods, and with the scab, and with the itch, whereof thou canst not be healed." *Deut. 28:27*

"Thou art my God from my mother's belly." *Psalms 22:10*

"I will make mine arrows drunk with blood, and my sword shall devour flesh." *Deut. 32:42*

"My wounds stink and are corrupt." *Psalms 38:5*

"For my loins are filled with a loathsome disease." *Psalms 38:7*

"The righteous shall wash his feet in the blood of the wicked." *Psalms 58:10*

"Moab is my washpot." *Psalms 60:8*

"It shall be health to thy navel." *Prov. 3:8*

"He burst asunder in the midst, and all his bowels gushed out." *Acts 1:18*

"Woe to the bloody city, to the pot whose scum is therein." *Ez. 24:6*

"Much pain is in all loins." *Nahum 2:10*

"Behold, they belch out with their mouth." *Psalms 59:7*

"And he smote his enemies in the hinder parts." *Psalms 78:66*

"The spirit of man is the candle of the Lord, searching all the inward parts of the belly." *Prov. 20:27*

"As a dog returneth to his vomit." *Prov. 26:11*

"The blueness of a wound cleanseth away evil: So do stripes the inward parts of the belly." *Prov. 20:30*

"For all tables are full of vomit and filthiness." *Isaiah 28:8*

"Lo, I have given thee cow's dung for man's dung and thou shalt prepare thy bread therewith." God speaks to the prophet. *Ez. 4:15*

"Fill thy bowels with this roll that I give thee." Words of God to Ezekiel. *Ez. 3:3*

"Behold, I will corrupt your seed and spread dung upon your faces." *Mal. 2:3*

"Then Jesus saith unto them: Verily, verily, I say unto you, Except ye eat the flesh of the Son of man, and drink his blood, ye have no life in you. Whoso eateth my flesh and drinketh my blood, hath eternal life . . . so that he that eateth me, even he shall live by me." *John 6:53–57*

"They shall not satisfy their souls, neither fill their bowels." *Ez. 7:19*

"My bowels, my bowels! I am pained at my very heart." Words of God. *Jer. 4:19*

"He that believeth on me . . . out of his belly shall flow rivers of living water." Jesus's words. *John 7:38*

God predicts twins: "Two manner of people shall be separated from thy bowels." *Gen. 25:23*

Jesus asks Peter: "Do not ye yet understand, that whatsoever entereth in at the mouth goeth into the belly, and is cast out into the draught?" *Matt. 15:17*

"As a jewel of gold in a swine's snout, so is a fair woman which is without discretion." *Prov. 11:22*

"The wringing of the nose bringeth forth blood." *Prov. 30:33*

"Wherefore my bowels shall sound like an harp for Moab and mine inward parts for Kir-haresh." *Isaiah 16:11*

"I will take away the remnant of the house . . . as a man taketh away dung . . . Him that dieth . . . in the city shall the dogs eat: and him that dieth in the field shall the fowls of the air eat; for the Lord hath spoken it." *I Kings 14:10,11*

"Before I formed thee in the belly I knew thee." *Jer. 1:5*

"It is not meet to take the children's bread and cast it to dogs." The dogs specified are the Gentiles. It is Jesus's way of referring to people who are not Jews. *Matt. 15:26* The Mosaic law forbade the price of a "dog" bought as a slave to be brought into the temple.

"Therefore, behold, I will bring evil upon the house . . . and I will cut off from Jeroboam him that pisseth against the wall." *I Kings 14:10* The Lord is speaking.

"Hath he not sent me to the men that sit upon the wall, that they may eat their own dung, and drink their own piss with you?" *Isaiah 36:12*

CHAPTER NINE

Preposterous Passages From The Pages Of The Holy Book

Although God creates the Universe in six days out of *nothing*, he needs dust to make a mere man and one of Adam's ribs to fashion woman.

A talking *snake* in God's garden paradise leads to the downfall of *all* humankind, and a *bite of some fruit* provides the causation for the Christian religion. Of the first three humans in God's world (which he saw as very good), two almost instantly become the original sinners, and one kills his brother. *Gen. 3,4.*

World-maker, people-maker, surgeon—God is also a tailor. He makes coats of skins for Adam and Eve, evidently viewing Adam's fig-leaf "threads" with a jaundiced eye. *Gen. 3:21* (Doesn't every garden contain a pile of tanned skins?)

God's first specimens of humanity prove so wicked and flawed that they must all be destroyed, after only eight generations, with the exception of Noah (who is permitted to live 950 years), his three sons, and the four wives. God regrets the mistake he made in creating humankind, just as he must have had second thoughts about his angels when one of them became Satan. *Gen. 6*

The ark built by Noah and his sons is 500 feet long, 85 feet wide, and three stories high, with one door and one window. Noah has to find and take aboard 7 of every clean beast and 2 of every unclean, 7 of every fowl, and a male and female of each creeping insect. They all occupy the ark for 190 days. *Gen. 7,8* Unfortunately, Noah is very obedient and finds room for all the organisms that cause disease.

Noah's descendants anger God by building the Tower of Babel and a city.

Forced to come down to earth to see what is going on, God confounds their language and scatters them abroad. *Gen. 11* Such childish legends as this are the Bible's way of explaining complex problems of anthropology and other sciences.

In return for being made the father of a great nation, Abraham promises God that all male Jews will be circumcised, a minor surgical procedure which will ensure their favoritism with the Lord over Gentile uncircumcised "dogs." This lofty agreement is called the Covenant of Circumcision, the Old Testament. *Gen. 17:10*

Instead of seeking medical advice, Isaac's wife Rebekah asks the Lord about her pregnancy symptoms, and he bluntly diagnoses twins: "Two manner of people shall be separated from thy bowels." *Gen. 25:23* The Lord's bedside manner is peculiarly his own.

Jacob unknowingly wrestles with *God*, who touches Jacob's thigh, throwing it out of joint. Thus, either the hip or the knee was dislocated, both painful and disabling conditions, from which Jacob suffers no trauma. During the night-long struggle, Jacob *prevails* over God, and God asks Jacob to release him. Jacob demands and receives a blessing first, then claims he saw God "face to face." The Bible goes on to say that as a result of this incident, Jews to this day will not eat of "the sinew which shrank, which is upon the hollow of the thigh." *Gen. 32:24–32*

Moses sees an angel and hears God's voice coming from a burning bush on Mt. Horeb. Moses is instructed to remove his shoes, because he is on holy ground. The rest of his raiment is, fortunately, acceptable. *Ex. 3:2* Confrontations with God in the Bible frequently occur on mountains, in line with pagan superstition that heights brought one closer to the gods.

God tries to kill Moses, because Moses's son by a Gentile woman has not been circumcised. She is furious but takes care of the problem with a sharp stone. For such a petty reason was the chosen deliverer of the Jews and future law-giver almost eliminated. *Ex. 4:24,25,26* God's plans often go awry in Bible legends.

Moses and Aaron have just to hold out a rod to bring about the ten plagues visited upon Egypt by God. The black magic of Pharaoh's sorcerers could and did duplicate several of these wonders. *Ex. 7–11*

The Red Sea divides when Moses follows God's orders and holds out that rod again. *Ex. 14* The Jordan River parts several times, in later anecdotes.

Manna rains down from heaven and feeds the Jews for 40 years in the desert and wilderness. It is sweet and like coriander seed and can be made into cakes. *Ex. 16:15,31* Israelites who died on the way to Canaan, however, suffered more from pestilences sent by the Lord than from scurvy and rickets.

Moses is supposed to be the author of the Pentateuch, consisting of 187 chapters. Some chapters have as many as 50 verses, and some verses as many as 50 words. Traditionally, he received the Mosaic law straight from the mouth of the Lord, except for the Ten Commandments, which the Lord wrote on tablets of stone with his finger. From that method of jotting things down, one may form a mental picture of Moses with his Hebrew consonants and his clay tablets or scrolls of skins or papyrus (and precious little spare time) as he records five books of the Bible during nearly half a century in desolate country and in between fights with the natives and squabbles among the Jews. At the start of this chore Moses was 80 years of age. At the end he is able to write of his own death and burial and the mourning period. And it is assumed that in 586 B.C., when the Jews were driven from Jerusalem and the temple plundered, much of the old Hebrew literature was lost.

That magic wand which the Lord gave Moses comes in handy again in the desert at Horeb when Moses strikes a rock with it and water gushes forth. *Ex. 17:6*

God writes the tables of the testimony on both sides of two tablets of stone with his finger, twice. Moses carries these two stone slabs down the mountain on two different occasions at the end of a 40-day fast, and back up the mountain once. *Ex. 31:18* and *Ex. 32–34*

Throughout the pages of the Bible, God communicates directly with everyone concerned, sometimes in visions and dreams or through angels and the Holy Ghost, but usually no explanation of the means is given. "Thus saith the Lord" or "The Lord spoke to—" is sufficient to put him front and center, and different languages present no problem.

Moses talks God out of several harsh punishments decreed for the wavering children of Israel undergoing the hardships of the Wilderness. At one time the Lord is driven to distraction, however, and wants to make Moses the founder of the greatest nation instead of Abraham and Jacob. Moses sensibly points out that such a move won't look good to the Egyptians. The Old Testament Lord was not above taking advice when it was needed. *Ex. 32*

God sends a wind from the sea that brings an excess of quail, after the Israelites complain that they have no flesh to eat. The quail pile up almost *four feet* high around the camp and as far as a day's journey in each direction. *Num. 11:31*

Trivialities are so important to God that he tells Moses to order the children of Israel in the desert to make fringes on the borders of their garments with a "ribband of blue" to remind them of his commandments. The Jews throughout their wanderings have an understandable inclination to regress. *Num. 15:38,39*

God seems to spend the entire time period covered by the Bible exclusively looking after the Jews, one of the smallest nations then in existence. There couldn't have been many hours left over for the rest of the world.

The rod of the house of Levi buds, blooms, and produces almonds, just one of the Lord's ways of creating a "sign." *Num. 17:8* Portents, omens, and signs rated right along with prophecies as being full of occult meaning, in Bible days.

Following the Lord's instructions, Moses fashions a brass serpent and affixes it to the top of a pole. The sight of it cures bites from poisonous snakes. *Num. 21*

If a snake can talk in the pages of the Bible, a talking donkey should arouse no consternation. A seer by the name of Balaam shows none in the story of a donkey who saves Balaam's life by refusing to carry him past an angel trying to kill Balaam with a sword. (Angels are not sweet in the Bible; many of them are fierce and carry swords which they employ with great success.)

Balaam, who cannot see the angel and is obeying God's orders to join the king of Moab, beats the donkey. "And the Lord opened the mouth of the ass, and she said unto Balaam, What have I done unto thee, that thou hast smitten me these three times?" Understandably bewildered (Balaam has no way of knowing the Lord has changed his mind about what he is now supposed to do), Balaam still keeps his cool enough to carry on a conversation with the donkey. (Perhaps he has heard people make jackasses of themselves and sees nothing strange about the reverse happening.) His reply is: "Because thou hast mocked me: I would there were a sword in mine hand, for now I would kill thee."

At this rebuff, the donkey reminds Balaam of her past loyalty, and the Lord finally allows Balaam to see and talk to the angel. Poor Balaam has always been God-fearing and is more befuddled by the confusing directions from on high than by a murderous angel and a talking jackass! Balaam and the Lord finally conspire to trick Balak. *Num. 22,23* The biblical Lord is very devious, so this is nothing new. "Beautiful Bible Stories" such as this one of the talking donkey and the wise man are worthy of Uncle Remus.

Scouts for the Israelites advise against invading Canaan, because they have seen *giants* there. *Num. 13:33* Next week—Jack and the Beanstalk.

Joshua is such a great favorite with the Lord, probably because he is even more bloodthirsty than Moses was, that there is no end to the help the Lord provides him in his expeditions against the rightful owners of the lands of Palestine. On the day that Joshua defeats the five kings of the Amorites, Joshua for no apparent reason except perhaps that his helmet is getting a little small for his head, addresses himself to the heavens, thereby making a complete fool of himself and of Bible writers in general, whose knowledge of God is somehow perfect, but whose ignorance of astronomy and the universe is astronomical: "Then spake Joshua to the Lord . . . and he said in the sight of Israel, Sun, stand thou still upon Gibeon; and thou, Moon, in the valley of Ajalon. And the sun stood still, and the moon stayed, until the people had avenged themselves upon their enemies . . .

"So the sun stood still in the midst of the heaven, and hasted not to go down about a whole day. And there was no day like that before it or after it, that the Lord hearkened unto the voice of a man . . ." *Josh. 10:12–14* (And didn't tell him that for the sun to "stand still," at stagey orders from Joshua, the *earth* would have to.)

David, having killed a giant with a slingshot, then carries the *five-foot* sword of Goliath into battle. *I Sam. 21:9* Why, when he'd had such good luck with the slingshot?

The witch of Endor (bubble, bubble) calls Samuel back from the dead. He predicts Saul's death, because God made a mistake by naming Saul to be king. *I Sam. 28:7–19* Even the witches hated by the Lord can raise the dead, and somehow resurrection doesn't seem very miraculous.

The Holy Land is alive with every kind of soothsayer, seer, wizard, witch, prophet, false prophet, diviner, sorcerer, necromancer, and sons of the prophets. All manner of means are used by the lot of them to make predictions, such as musical instruments and animal entrails. They frequently cast lots to determine choice and guilt, and priests of the tabernacles of the Lord use various strange methods to discover "truths." Confidence in many magical carryings-on is easily imbued in such gullible and superstitious people as live in the pages of the Bible.

In the spirit of magic and fortune-telling, the Bible bulges with innumerable visions, dreams, sudden visits, and appearances involving angels, spirits, cloven tongues, devils, and ghosts. Many of the visions are very complicated, even containing detailed *measurements*, and strange beasts (but no pink elephants) usually with horns are among the phenomena which people these hallucinatory experiences.

Solomon, to build the temple to the Lord in Jerusalem, conscripts from among his subjects: 70,000 burden bearers, 80,000 hewers, 3,300 labor bosses, and 30,000 men to work in Lebanon part-time. He spends seven years building it and 13 years constructing a palace for himself and a house for his wife (only one of 700). Unbelievable amounts of costly stones and timbers, gold and jewels are used.

Solomon has 40,000 stalls of horses for his chariots and 12,000 horsemen. His provisions for one day are 30 measures of flour, 60 measures of meal, 10 fat oxen, and 100 sheep, besides wild deer and fowl. He is credited with composing 3,000 proverbs and 1,005 songs. *I Kings 4,6,7*

At the dedication of the temple, Solomon sacrifices 22,000 oxen and 120,000 sheep. The altar will not accommodate all the blood and flesh. *I Kings 8:62–64*

Jeroboam's hand dries up when he points at a prophet. *I Kings 13:4* (Don't *point.*)

Ravens feed the prophet Elijah bread and flesh after he brings a three-year famine upon the land. *I Kings 17:6* Other people are reduced to eating their own children, one of the examples of cannibalism carried out or prophesied in the Bible as punishments from the Lord.

The prophet Elijah brings a widow's son back to life. *I Kings 17:22*

When Elijah smites the River Jordan, the waters separate so that he and Elisha can cross. This is the second time the depths of the Jordan have parted to let someone get to the other side. (When the feet of the bearers of the

Ark of the Covenant touched the banks, Joshua led the children of Israel across a dry river bed into the Promised Land.) *II Kings 2:8 Josh. 3:17*

A flaming chariot carries the living Elijah to heaven in a whirlwind. *II Kings 2:11* At least, that is Elisha's story.

Elisha knows a good thing when he sees it and confiscates Elijah's mantle, which has escaped the flames. He smites the Jordan with it, and the river parts for the third time. Fifty "sons of the prophets" watch him do this. *II Kings 2:14* Only Cecil B. DeMille, however, has managed to figure out *how* it was done.

Elisha sweetens the waters of Jericho by casting salt into a spring and calling on God to heal it. *II Kings 2:20–22* (He was reaching for the sugar.)

Elisha is a guest at the home of a married couple. The wife, not surprisingly for Bible females, is barren, but Elisha, also true to Bible form, tells her she will have a son at a certain time. She does, and no questions asked, even by the husband, a trusting fellow indeed. *II Kings 4:16,17* One is given to ponder how these biblical predictors of births always know the number and sex of the fetuses.

Not to be outdone by several other biblical miracle-workers, Elisha brings a child back to life, who then sneezes seven times. *II Kings 4:35* Resurrectionitis?

Elisha provides many pots of oil from one pot so that a woman friend may sell it and keep her sons from being sold into slavery. *II Kings 4* It would seem that he could have eliminated a step simply by multiplying the money or making it grow on trees. With typical Bible morality, Elisha sees nothing wrong with slavery.

One-hundred persons need to be fed from a small supply of meal and water. Elisha to the rescue! *II Kings 4:43* Everybody beats Jesus to the punch.

An army captain of Syria would like to be healed of leprosy. Elisha tells him to dip into the Jordan seven times (the number seven keeps popping up in the scriptures) with the desired results. To make everything balance out, Elisha turns someone who displeases him *into* a leper. *II Kings 5*

Elisha makes iron float in the river. *II Kings 6:6* These old prophets run Jesus a close second in the miracle department. Is it any wonder he finds it difficult to impress his countrymen?

A man buried in Elisha's tomb comes into contact with Elisha's bones and returns to the land of the living. *II Kings 13:21* Will Elisha's wonders never cease?

An angel of the Lord all by himself (herself?) and in one night kills 185,000
Assyrians who threaten Jerusalem. "And when they arose early in the morning, behold, they were all dead corpses." *II Kings 19:35*

Isaiah, laying a salutary lump of figs upon the ailing Hezekiah, tells the king
he will die soon. The Lord, however, gives a sign that Hezekiah will recover, after all. The sign consists of letting the shadow on the sun dial go backward 10 degrees, after Hezekiah says that will be more convincing to him
than for the shadow to go forward. This phenomenon is supposed to mean
that Hezekiah will live 15 more years, owing to God's change of heart. *II
Kings 20* There don't seem to be any physicians in the Bible, except for Luke
(the *beloved* physician) who never is known to have office hours. As long as
figs are handy, who needs a doctor?

God's signs are not always popular with the Old Testament Jews. Not
only do they not trust God (he *does* have a habit of changing his mind) and
his portents at times, but sometimes they tell him they'd rather have no sign
at all.

God makes Ezekiel eat a roll (book) of lamentations. Ezekiel's directions
from the Almighty are a little crude: "Son of man, cause thy belly to eat, and
fill thy bowels with this roll that I give thee." *Ez. 3:3* (Who knows? Papyrus
may be a delicacy. Or a laxative?)

In one of Ezekiel's numerous and intricately constructed visions, God tells
him to lie on his left side (to bear the sins of Israel) *390* days, and on his right
side *40* days (consecutively, of course). God will bind him so that he cannot
turn over. (Talk about bed-sores!) He then tells Ezekiel how to eat during
this time. He is to bake his bread (lying on his side?) using man's dung (a
favorite four-letter word of God's) for fuel. When Ezekiel protests (whatever for?), God relents and says it will be okay to use cow's dung.

Continuing, God orders Ezekiel to cut his hair and beard and *weigh* the
hair, then burn *one-third* of it in the midst of the city, *smite* one-third of it
with a knife, and scatter the remaining third in the winds. But in the meantime, Ezekiel is to put a few left-over hairs in his skirt, then remove them and
burn them, too, symbolic of Jerusalem, a city which finds itself the subject of
many visions. *Ez. 4,5* (And this is the way God treats his *friends*.)

Daniel is able to describe and interpret the dreams of Nebuchadnezzar, although the dreams haven't been described to *him* by Nebuchadnezzar or by anyone else. *Dan. 2*

Three fellows survive in a fiery furnace that is so hot the men who throw them in are cremated. The Son of God is in the furnace with them. *Dan. 3*

A hand appears and writes on the wall before Belshazzar. The words are gobbledy-gook to everyone but Daniel, but he "figured it out" and put a real damper on the merry-making, saying they mean the kingdom will be overthrown. *Dan. 5*

Daniel is thrown into the lions' den (while the lions are at home) because he petitions God in violation of the law of the land. An angel saves him and his unique talents. *Dan. 6*

Jonah, a prophet trying to avoid the orders of God to go to Nineveh, hides out on a boat belonging to Gentiles. He sleeps through a terrible storm brought by God (storms at sea don't seem to wake up biblical characters) that threatens to sink the boat. Finally, the Gentiles discover by casting lots that Jonah is the cause, and they are compelled, against their will, to throw him overboard. Swallowed by a whale, he spends three days in its belly, constantly offering up irrelevant prayers. Finally, the whale can't stomach Jonah a minute longer and throws him up close to shore. *Jonah 1,2*

In one of those innumerable visions: "Behold the Lord stood upon a wall made by a plumbline, with a plumbline in his hand." *Amos 7:7*

Zechariah has heard of "You tell me your dream, I'll tell you mine." He sees Satan standing with Joshua (long-deceased) and an angel of the Lord. The Lord himself speaks, addressing Satan: "The Lord rebuke thee, O Satan." *Zech. 3:1,2* A most unlikely foursome but a very civil confrontation.

Joseph is not a bit upset or suspicious when Mary is found with child by the Holy Ghost, after an angel tells him Mary will have a son who will save his people from their sins. *Matt. 1:18–21* A less phlegmatic young man might have shown a little astonishment or had a few questions, but Joseph is anything but a wave-maker. He just quietly steals away in the scriptures. Now you see him, now you don't.

A star moves across the sky contrary to astronomical patterns. It is not labelled a comet. Wise men from Babylonia, a country very advanced in astronomy, accept this phenomenon and supposedly follow the star. *Matt. 2:9* In order to be followed on the ground, such a star could have been only a few thousand feet high and travelling at the speed of a camel. To mark a particular building, it would have to descend to a height of 100 feet or less.

Jesus is tempted 40 days in the wilderness by the devil and ministered to by angels. (That number 40 again!) He is set upon the pinnacle of a temple in Jerusalem by Satan and then at the top of a "very high" mountain from which he can see all the kingdoms of the world. Which mountain that could be in the Holy Land is not revealed. *Matt. 4:1–10* The devil can fly, because he is a bad angel who supposedly still has his "wings," but Jerusalemites are not impressed. (The devil, you say! Not again! We've got to find a way to keep him off that tabernacle pinnacle before he drops somebody and we have a lawsuit on our hands!)

Satan and his diabolical cohorts are not amorphous creatures of the imagination in the New Testament but very real personalities totally preoccupied with the corruption of everyone and in never-ending competition with God and Jesus and the Holy Ghost. A sub-title for that part of the Bible might well be: "Exorcism And How To Apply It." Jesus spends much of his time casting out devils and evil spirits that speak, from the bodies of tortured individuals, as do the disciples and apostles. Warnings of the insidious influence of Beelzebub and his demons fill the pages of this part of the Bible. (Beware of garrulous snakes!)

"He (Jesus) cast out many devils; and suffered not the devils to speak, because they knew him." *Mark 1:34* The Bible does not explain from whence came all these demons, although the reader must assume they are the angels who conspired with Satan to overthrow God, as described in Isaiah and the Revelation. Originally created by God, they, like another of his creations— humankind—soon failed to exhibit the perfection that might have been expected of God's handiwork.

Seven devils possess Mary Magdalene, and Jesus casts them out. *Luke 8:2* But that is certainly not a record, for, upon driving loudly-protesting devils out of only two sufferers, Jesus grants the wishes of the demons to be cast into a herd of 2,000 pigs (which then run into the sea and drown). *Matt. 8:28–33* and *Mark 5:13*

John the Baptist is rumored to be a prophet risen from the dead. *Matt. 14:2* Prophets were expected to rise from the dead and appear in visions and on mountain tops. (Jesus actually displays no powers not attributed in the Bible to Old Testament prophets.)

Jesus feeds two different multitudes (!) by augmenting a small amount of food. First, with five loaves and two fishes he feeds 5,000 men (besides women and children, who are seldom worth counting in the Bible). Twelve baskets of food remain. No explanation is given of how the victuals are cooked and served. The second time, he feeds 4,000 men (besides the usual nonentities), and seven basketfuls of food are left over. *Matt. 14:19–21* The disciples are slow to catch on how Jesus does this. (Hebrew grocers hoped that no one ever *would* catch on.)

To get to a boat containing the disciples, Jesus walks on the water during a storm, but they think he is a ghost, thus displaying the predilection of people of Bible days to believe in apparitions of all kinds. After Jesus speaks to them, Peter, according to Matthew (that weaver of fables), manages to take a few watery steps before sinking. *Matt. 14:22–31* (Actually, anyone can walk on water. It all depends on the temperature.)

Jesus turns water into wine. *John 2:1–10* If he did it today, many Christians wouldn't drink it. But Jesus would. He was called a "winebibber." *Matt. 11:19*

In a tableau called "The Transfiguration" by mysticists, Jesus takes Peter, James, and John to a mountaintop (luckily Holy Land topography permitted some lofty locations) where he glows, after the fashion of Moses and holy persons of other religions: "And his face did shine as the sun, and his raiment was white as the light." *Matt. 17:1–5* (Reminiscent of the Egyptian Sun gods.) Moses and Elijah join them and talk to Jesus, and a voice says the same words that were heard when Jesus was baptized. Peter, ever ambitious, suggests the building of three tabernacles, one each for Jesus, Moses, and Elijah. (Peter eventually was to get a rather impressive one of his own, in Rome.)

Admitting that different kinds of devils require different kinds of exorcism, Jesus tells the disciples: "Howbeit, this kind goeth not out but by prayer and fasting." *Matt. 17:14–21* (Feed a cold and starve a devil.)

The disciples are told by Jesus to find money in a fish's mouth. *Matt. 17:27* (They'd heard of a *piggy* bank, but this was ridiculous.)

Much of the morality taught by Jesus is impractical to the point of the absurd: Turn the other cheek, pay double damages, judge no one's behavior, go farther than *forced* to go, don't use your mind but be as children, sell *all* and give the proceeds to the poor (thus becoming poor yourself), have no thought for the morrow, make no plans, don't worry about food and clothing, be passive and meek, let everybody walk all over you, love people who persecute you as much as those who are kind to you and have regard for your feelings, be mournful, be smug and self-righteous and goad others into mistreating you, forsake everything of this world in preparation for the next, agree with everyone, deny sexual urges, mutilate yourself, have *no* deep love for your family and seriously consider deserting them, if you are robbed give the thief the same amount again, don't resist attackers but let them abuse you once more, avoid coarse people not on your level, accept every misfortune gratefully, don't share your culture with dolts, behave as you please as long as you finally repent.

The twelve disciples are to sit on twelve thrones in heaven and judge the twelve tribes of Israel. *Matt. 19:28* There is no "due process" in heaven, even for the Chosen People, but all the autocracy of a kingdom. (Why not a *Democracy* of Heaven?)

Jesus promises his "Second Coming" will be very soon, but, since he is only God, he really does not know the date or season. He cautions his listeners, however, to pray it doesn't happen in *winter* or on the *Sabbath*. And woe to pregnant women and nursing mothers, as it will be hard for them (even the elect) to flee to the mountains. *Matt. 24:15–35* It may be hard for quite a few persons to flee to the mountains, even non-pregnant men. Jesus's warning should make Christians reluctant to live on the plains, go to sea, or become residents of a space colony. And pregnant women and nursing mothers must be on needles and pins, if *they* are Christians.

The people shall *see* Jesus arriving in the clouds (at the second coming) although the sun and *moon* are darkened and the stars fallen. *Matt. 24:29–30*

An unfeeling story portraying the classic conception of heaven and hell is told by Jesus: A man already in hell (before Judgment Day?) asks Abraham in heaven to help him, but Abraham refuses and says no one can pass between heaven and hell. So the sufferer in hell asks Abraham to warn his five living brothers of their impending fate. Abraham has a hard heart, of which Jesus apparently approves. "They have Moses," Abraham pontificates, "and the prophets; let them hear them."

When the occupant of hell points out that it would be more convincing if one from the dead went to them, Abraham flippantly observes that if they won't believe Moses, they won't believe anyone. *Luke 16:22–31* This tale, like several of the parables Jesus tells, does not add to the reputation for mercy of the story-teller, and it hardly serves to explain why the resurrection of Jesus is supposed to be convincing or why the teaching of Jesus was supposed to be effective. Abraham in his remarks pronounces worthless any testimony that might follow that of Moses.

At a certain season, an angel moves the waters of a pool in Jerusalem, and the "sicky" who first steps into the pool every day is automatically healed. Quite a crowd of unfortunates hangs around the pool. *John 5:4* Twelve a.m. is splash time!

When Jesus makes a request: "Father, glorify thy name," a voice from heaven is heard to rumble: "I have both glorified it and will glorify it again." Some of the people standing nearby think it thundered. *John 12:28,29* Ancient tribes imagined thunder to be audible communication from the gods.

No account of Jesus's death and resurrection told in the gospels agrees with any other. The ascension is not even mentioned in Matthew and John and is told differently three other times. There is no agreement in the scriptures on the time that elapses between the resurrection and the ascension and on the identity and number of persons who see the risen Lord.

Since fish and fishermen play a prominent part in the little that the Bible reader is permitted to learn of Jesus's way of life and since the first symbol used for Jesus was a fish (Pisces of the Zodiac?), perhaps it is not surprising that he knows at any given instance exactly where a school of piscatorial creatures can be found. After he has risen from the dead, and some disciples are calmly pursuing their usual pursuits as though it is an everyday occurrence for the deceased to throw off their winding sheets and vacate their tombs, Jesus appears on the shore and tells them on which side of the boat to fish. "They cast therefore, and now they were not able to draw it for the multitude of fishes." They catch *153* fishes, and the net did not break. All except Peter (who swims to shore) keep their heads after recognizing Jesus to the extent that they drag all the catch to the beach. *John 21* And count it!

On the Day of Pentecost after the crucifixion, the disciples are all together, and suddenly came sound of a rushing wind . . . "there appeared unto them cloven tongues like as of fire, and it sat upon each of them. And they were all filled with the Holy Ghost and began to speak with other tongues." The ability to speak several languages is opportune now that the time has finally come to start saving people from hell, the other side of the "New Promise" coin that was minted when the Savior became a human sacrifice. "Speaking in tongues" becomes popular as a sign of special affinity with the Holy Spirit among the new converts, but Peter says on this occasion the "tongues" fulfill a prophecy about "the last days," which he and the other followers of Jesus expect momentarily, owing to the promise of Jesus made to them during his ministry. *Acts 2* This proves to be a tongue-in-cheek promise.

Almost everything that happens in the gospels is said to fulfill a prophecy. There are over 30 of such assertions in Matthew alone, most of them made by Jesus. He links almost everything he does to an Old Testament prophecy, thus strengthening his claim to the foretold (as believed by the Jews) Messiahship: "All this was done, that it might be fulfilled which was spoken by the prophet." *Matt. 21:4* Paul and the other apostles whose works are described in the New Testament books that follow the gospels can also shape everything that concerns Jesus to fit the prophecies and vice-versa. Jews as a whole apparently viewed this manipulation as preposterous.

When the apostles pray together, the building shakes. *Acts 4:31* (Sonic prayers!)

The apostles are able to heal at a fast rate. Even Peter's shadow can heal those sick and possessed of "unclean spirits." *Acts 5:15,16* (Pagan magic.)

An angel opens the prison doors for the apostles and tells them to go to the temple. *Acts 5:19,20* Webster's defines an angel as a messenger of God with wings and a halo. The word "imaginary" does not appear before the word "messenger." One must assume, from their scarcity today, that God abandoned the angels in favor of another means of communication and that, like the Pony Express, they became obsolete.

Stephen performs miracles because he is full of faith and the Holy Ghost. (It is rather strange, the reader may find, that the representatives of the Creator of Nature are made in the Bible to perform many acts contrary to nature with the intent of proving they represent that Creator.) Appointed as a food administrator among the early Christians, he says he sees Jesus sitting on the right hand of God. *Acts 6:8* The Trinity is going to make such a seating arrangement a bit of a trick.

After another angel of the Lord speaks to Philip and tells him where to travel next, "the spirit of the Lord caught away Philip that the eunuch saw him no more." Philip duly becomes visible again in Azotus. *Acts 8:26,39,40*

Paul (Saul) is a fanatical Pharisee who persecutes the early Christians. Not by studying the worth of their doctrine or its validity, but because of a terrifying experience (he claims) he suddenly becomes the mouthpiece of the future Christian faith. Struck prostrate and addressed by Jesus on the road to Damascus, he becomes the typical passionate convert and the self-appointed protagonist of the new Congregation. He hears the voice from heaven, so ever-present in the Bible legends, and from then on becomes the biggest know-it-all in history.

When he doesn't make satisfying headway with his fellow Jews, he abandons them for a richer lode, the Gentiles, and spends most of his time trying to reconcile the Mosaic law to the teachings of Jesus. He is not always successful, and finally throws up his hands and says there is no need to try to explain God's actions. God is the potter, and man is the clay, and that settles it.

His epistles to the early Church (if he actually wrote any of them) are now quoted as if they were written by Jesus, himself, who didn't write anything as far as is known (although once he scratched the dust with his finger). Paul doesn't state that he knew Jesus personally, and yet he makes a mysterious reference to having seen Jesus after the resurrection. Since he also says that Jesus was seen then by more than 500 persons, a claim not found in any of the gospels, one may be justified in being a little skeptical about other claims made by Paul. Such skepticism would be in line with that encountered by Paul in his competition with the other apostles and church leaders for recognition as chief interpreter of the words of Jesus. They regarded him as an interloper. *Acts and the Epistles.*

Peter raises Dorcas from the dead, joining such resurrectors as Jesus, Elijah, Elisha, and Paul. *Acts 9:40*

Cornelius, a Centurion, sees a vision of an angel of God who tells him to go get Peter, who at the time, the reader learns, is busy falling into a trance on a rooftop (next best thing to a mountain). Faint from hunger, Peter "sees" a sheet drop down full of four-footed beasts and wild beasts and creeping things and fowl. With the usual ease of communication of Bible days, the voice of the Lord gets right down to business and says: "Rise, kill, and eat." (The Lord has this weird preoccupation with the bill of fare all through the scriptures, which reached its peak in much of the Mosaic law.) Peter refuses to rise, kill, or eat, with the temerity displayed by the *Old* Testament Jews, because the animals are "unclean."

The voice is heard again, saying God has cleansed them and repeating the order three times. (Everything has to happen to Peter three times.) Peter is so slow to catch on that finally the *Spirit* gives up on him and tells him that *three* men sent by this Spirit are waiting to see Peter and that one of them is the Centurion.

Peter accompanies them to preach to the Gentiles, although it is an "unlawful thing" for a Jew to come unto one of another nation. Peter explains that God has shown him that he shouldn't call any man "common" or "unclean." The meaning of the dream has finally struck him, and he is just now learning tolerance, in spite of the fact that he has associated with Jesus for three years and might have been expected to have widened his horizons a little.

Peter continues: "Of a truth I perceive that God is no respecter of persons," and the crowd listens to him pave the way for the Gentiles to enter the fold. They are then fallen upon by the Holy Ghost (who is very unstable on his feet) and they all begin to speak with tongues in another of those nonsensical sessions of incoherency whose purpose is left to the imagination, as is the gist.

The whole infantile story of Peter's dream is a typical biblical device for getting a point across—in this case the need for the Gentiles as converts. Peter passes the new idea on to the disciples. *Acts 10*

An angel of the Lord (busy, busy) appears to Peter in prison, strikes off the chains, and takes him out through a locked gate. (Where is the obedience to the law preached by Jesus?) Peter knocks on the door of friends, who, thinking him still in the lock-up, believe it is his angel. *Acts 12* Apparently everyone has a heavenly counterpart. Or maybe just that much-spoken-of "elect" do.

Herod has a really bad day. He is making a speech and acting God-like, and "immediately the angel of the Lord smote him and he was eaten of worms and gave up the ghost (Holy?)." *Acts 12:23*

Paul, filled with the Holy Ghost, heals a cripple. *Acts 14:10* At times, the Holy Ghost seems to be more filling than at other times.

The Holy Ghost forbids Paul to preach in Asia and Bithynia. Orders of the Holy Ghost, however transmitted, come in very handy to sanction plans made for whatever reasons. At that time those were two areas Paul *feared* to visit. *Acts 16:6–7*

Paul is not to be left out in the vision department. Besides those in which Jesus appears to him in person, another dream features a Macedonian who asks him to come there and preach. *Acts 16:9* So do Christians today receive the "call."

Paul is right in there in the "unclean spirit" department, too. With these words he drives out one from a soothsayer: "I command thee to come out of her." And he came out the same hour. *Acts 16:18* (Takes a while to pack.)

A great earthquake (a natural-disaster type of emphasis that frequently accompanies stirring biblical events) occurs to free Paul and Silas from prison. All the doors fly open, and everyone's bonds are loosed. The jailor gets Paul to baptize him. *Acts 16:26,33* (An earthquake makes a handy ploy on quite a few occasions for the wonder-maker writers of scripture.)

Needing his spine stiffened, Paul has a vision in Corinth where God tells him not to be afraid. *Acts 18:9*

It is impossible to outdo Paul in any way. He works many miracles, so that the sick start bringing him handkerchiefs and aprons that can be used thenceforward to drive out evil spirits. *Acts 19:11,12* Paul the Witch Doctor hath "charms" to soothe.

Some exorcists try to cast out evil spirits using Jesus's name, but one of the spirits answers these exorcists scornfully: "Jesus I know, and Paul I know, but who are ye?" At this withering retort, the man afflicted with the sassy devil leaps on the exorcists so that they flee *"naked and wounded." Acts 19:13–16* There was no way of prophesying (a favorite biblical pastime) what might happen next on the streets of the Holy Land. The modern city scene just *pales.*

Paul lays his hands on the Ephesians (no need to worry about Paul with his asceticism), and the Holy Ghost (he's everywhere, he's everywhere) comes on them and causes them to speak with those "tongues" again and "prophesy." *Acts 19:6* Unfortunately, all such Bible gibberish has been lost to history.

Long-winded sermons had the same effect in Paul's time as they tend to have today. One of Paul's puts a young man to sleep, who proceeds to fall from a window and lose his life by defenestration. Paul stops talking long enough to restore the unfortunate church-goer to life. *Acts 20:10* This incident may have prompted the expression: "bored to death."

A prophet relays the words of the Holy Ghost to Paul, saying Paul will be bound in Jerusalem. *Acts 21:11* With all these timely warnings, why in the world was Paul ever in difficulty?

There will be a storm, warns Paul, speaking to some who are preparing a sea voyage. When it comes on the dot, he assures them all will be well, because "there stood by me this night an angel of God . . . saying, Fear not, Paul . . ." *Acts 27:22,23* Paul seems to need propping up just about all the time.

Using a new treatment for snakebite, Paul shakes off the culprit into the fire, and his hand doesn't even swell. *Acts 28:3–6* Cured without a *brass* snake.

Paul has a vision of a man in a *third* heaven. *II Cor. 12:2* But, after all, movies have been made about as many as seven.

The Book of The Revelation is the ultimate vision and the ultimate challenge and delight for theologians. Predicated, first of all, on a false premise (it describes "things that must *shortly* come to pass") and delivered to John from Jesus Christ by an angel, it finds John "in the spirit." After reading it and becoming more and more profoundly befuddled, the seeker-after-truth can explain this hodgepodge of mumbo-jumbo only by adding an "s" to what John found himself in.

The size of the New Jerusalem, assumed to be Heaven, is given in The Revelation. It is 1500 miles long, 1500 miles wide, and 1500 miles high. Therein will be the many mansions spoken of by Jesus, inhabited by "the flesh of the spirit" which must have housing and tables at which to eat. *Rev. 21:16* (Mention of "mansions" cannot help but trigger the realization that, significantly or merely coincidentally, there are twelve houses, or mansions, of the Zodiac.)

Finally, there could hardly be a more preposterous hypothesis upon which to base a religion than the one upon which Christianity is founded. Why have all the millions of Christian church edifices been erected, from St. Peter's at Rome to The Little Brown Church in the Vale? Why have authoritarian Christian clergy from Pope to pastor been permitted to dictate the lifestyles of millions of people and influence law-making to fit their personal convic-tions? Why have millions of lives been wasted in senseless dedication to Christian asceticism? Why have other millions died from martyrdom and persecution in the name of Christianity? Why have generations of Christians frittered away time, energy, and resources for 2,000 years in the worship of a purely mystical pagan Trinity? The answer is both simple and incomprehensible. It is because millions of people have been willing to believe that their God sacrificed himself to himself.

By any standards which rational human beings can bring to bear, such divine behavior makes the Christian God look a fool. Admittedly, the possibility exists that this Christian God's judgment of behavior does not conform to that of humankind. What appears ridiculous to earthlings, although they were created in his image and are always assumed to share the same thought processes exhibited by God, may make wonderful sense to the Christian Almighty.

In fact, a different way of judging behavior may explain the attitude of the Christian God which permits him to demand a perfection in the conduct of humankind which God himself does not exhibit. Human beings are warned to judge no one, cast no stones, love their neighbors as themselves, forgive totally, and exact no retribution. Yet that same God actually keeps score and looks (with what sometimes seems to be relish) to a final day of reckoning when all his "enemies" shall meet with their just deserts. And he grants forgiveness during human lifetime only if it is begged for.

The lives of God's children are relatively short at best, but the punishment is *eternal*. Jesus himself said that he would deny all those who denied him. Such vindictiveness on the part of the God of perfect love is not allowed to abide in the hearts of imperfect humankind.

CHAPTER TEN

Sex In The
Sacred Book

The first inhabitants of the earth, children of Adam and Eve, practice incest, as necessary sexual partners of their brothers and sisters. *Gen. 5*

Noah, drunk with wine made from grapes of his vineyard, which he apparently planted as soon as he stepped off the ark, is seen lying around naked by his son Ham, who tells his brothers. Angry, Noah curses Ham's innocent son forever. *Gen. 9*

Abraham passes off his wife Sarah as his sister to save his skin, as he fears being killed by men who lust after her. (Actually, his wife is his half-sister.) While they are in Egypt, Abraham permits Pharaoh to take Sarah (a 70-year-old temptress!) into his palace. Pharaoh gives Abraham many animals and slaves in return. The Lord is furious at Pharaoh (although Pharaoh has been properly deceived and has no idea that Sarah is married) and sends great plagues on Pharaoh's household. (God has a large variety of plagues on call, including some involving blood, frogs, lice, hail, fire, snakes, and cattle disease. For the slightest misbehavior, Old Testament sinners could expect to suffer the effects of one of these. Famine was another of the Lord's punishments. Thousands die when God lowers the boom.) *Gen. 12*

Sarah is barren (as are many biblical women, although biblical men are never sterile) so gives her maid Hagar to Abraham. Ishmael is born to them. *Gen. 16:1–4*

God tells Abraham that every male in his entourage (Abraham was wealthy and owned many slaves) must be circumcised. God stresses this mutilation so frequently and with so much vigor in the Bible that one wonders at his rather petty insistence on linking the condition of the human body to moral behavior. Gentile "dogs" are contemptuous in his sight for two reasons: they are uncircumcised, and they worship other gods. "And he that is born in the house or bought with money of any stranger, And he that is eight days old shall be circumcised among you." Circumcision is made the first condition of the covenant God makes with Abram to make him the father of a great nation that shall inherit the earth. *Gen. 17*

God tells Abraham just when to circumcise Jewish boys. That none who is uncircumcised may eat at the Passover feast in a Jewish home later becomes part of the Mosaic law. *Gen. 17:11–14*

"And Abraham was 99 years old when he was circumcised in the flesh of his foreskin." *Gen. 17:24*

God *seems* to play a role common to mythology of impregnating a mortal woman, this time Abraham's wife Sarah. She is barren and beyond child-bearing age, but God says to Abraham bluntly: "I will certainly return unto thee according to the time of life; and, lo, Sarah thy wife shall have a son . . . Is anything too hard for the Lord?" Further on the reader is told in no uncertain terms: "And the Lord visited Sarah as he had said, and the Lord did unto Sarah as he had spoken. For Sarah conceived." *Gen. 18:10,14* and *Gen. 21:1,2*

The wicked men of Sodom demand that Lot send out the two male angels staying with him "that we may know them." Lot, all heart, offers his two virgin daughters for their pleasure, instead. The invaders, however, refuse to accept the girls and try to break in. The angels strike them blind. *Gen. 19*

Lot's two virgin daughters plot to co-habit with their drunken father in order to give him heirs—the Moabites and the Ammonites. No disapproval is expressed or implied at this distasteful story of incest and intrigue. "Come, let us make our father drink wine, and we will lie with him." *Gen. 19:32* Peter later describes Lot as a "righteous man." *II Peter 2:8*

Abraham again passes Sarah off as his sister to King Abimelech for the same skin-saving reason as before. God, predictably, is angry at the wrong culprit again, although Abimelech has not touched Sarah. Abraham, who can do no wrong in God's sight, lamely defends his behavior by saying that Sarah really is his half-sister. In an attempt to appease God, Abimelech gives more livestock and servants to Abraham, and it is beginning to dawn upon the reader just how this favorite of the Lord has acquired his wealth. Still furious, God makes all the women of Abimelech's family barren. Abraham's belated intervention with God seems to avail, but Abimelech gets in the last word by telling Sarah that this "sister" act lets her misbehave. *Gen. 20* (Sarah was close to 90 years old and hadn't had a face lift.)

Men of the early Old Testament had sexual relations with their maid-servants as well as their wives, of which they usually had several, generally close relatives. Incest was common. Mates from the family of a close relative were often sought for young persons by their parents.

Isaac's wife Rebekah is barren (isn't everybody?). Barrenness of biblical wives makes way for all kinds of hanky panky with God and the Holy Ghost. This time, once more, the Lord, always on call, responds to Isaac's plea for an heir and "was entreated of him, and Rebekah his wife conceived." *Gen. 25:21*

To protect his own life, for he feared his neighbors would kill him to get at Rebekah, for she was beautiful, Isaac uses Abraham's ploy and passes her off as his sister (ho hum). Another King Abimelech, suspicious as well he might be, finds Isaac out and accuses him of a sordid masquerade. *Gen. 26:7–11*

The same old story of a barren wife whom God causes to conceive is pinned on Rachel, Jacob's wife. She follows the biblical custom of offering her maid to Jacob. (Morals were rather loose in those days, God's included.) Rachel bears a son Joseph, who is the only completely honorable and kind Jewish patriarch of the Old Testament, after getting off to a rather poor start as an arrogant teenager spoiled by his father. *Gen. 30* A dream-interpreter, he uses a divining cup. *Gen. 44:5*

Jacob's daughter Dinah is raped by Shechem, a prince of the Hivites, who then agrees to be circumcised, so he can marry her. Furthermore, all the males in Shechem's city undergo circumcision, so that they may dwell peaceably with Jacob's people, as Dinah's brothers Levi and Simeon lead them to believe. On the third day these two liars take their swords and slay Shechem and his father and all the men of the city. Still not satisfied, they plunder all the wealth and take captive the wives and little ones of their victims. *Gen. 34* Levi and Simeon are God-chosen.

Reuben, Jacob's son, takes his father's concubine for a sex partner. He, along with Levi and Simeon and nine more of his brothers, becomes a founder of one of the tribes of Israel. *Gen. 35:22*

Judah's daughter-in-law Tamar pretends to be a harlot to trap Judah, and she conceives by him and bears twins. *Gen. 38*

Onan, Jacob's grandchild, refuses to act as a sexual partner for his brother's widow and is killed by God for his reluctance. *Gen. 38*

Joseph is propositioned by Potiphar's wife. He rejects her advances, but when she falsely tells Pharaoh that Joseph forced his attentions upon her, Joseph is unjustly imprisoned for several years. *Gen. 39:12*

The Mosaic law contains explicit instructions and rules about sexual behavior. "None of you shall approach to any that is near of kin to him to uncover their nakedness . . . The nakedness of thy father, or the nakedness of thy mother, shalt thou not uncover . . . the nakedness of thy sister . . . the nakedness of thy son's daughter, or of thy daughter's daughter shalt thou not uncover . . . thou shalt not uncover the nakedness of thy father's sister . . . thy mother's sister, thy father's brother; thou shalt not approach to his wife . . . Thou shalt not uncover the nakedness of thy brother's wife . . . also thou shalt not approach unto a woman . . . as long as she is put apart for her uncleanness." *Lev. 18*

Adulterers shall be put to death. *Lev. 20:10–12* Homosexuals shall suffer death. *Lev. 20:13* A prostitute daughter of a priest shall be burnt to death. *Lev. 21:9* If a man will not marry his brother's widow, she shall come to him in the presence of the elders and loose his shoe and spit in his face. *Deut. 25:9*

Entering Canaan at last, Joshua circumcises all the male Jews who had been born since the flight from Egypt 40 years before. *Josh. 5:3*

Samson is fathered by an angel of the Lord. His mother was another of the Bible's barren women. *Judges 13:3*

Perversion and sodomy apparently were common in biblical times. One especially obscene story is told about some Israelite men who demand that a male house guest be brought out to them for sexual perversion acts. The host offers to send out his maiden daughter and his guest's concubine instead. The Israelites refuse the offer and insist upon the guest, but the concubine is pushed out the door. She is abused all night long and found dead on the doorstep the next morning. Angry, her master takes her body home, cuts it into twelve pieces and sends one piece to each of the tribes of Israel. As a result, there is a civil war in Israel, and 65,100 on both sides die in battle. *Judges 19,20*

Because the tribe of Benjamin needs wives, the Israelites attack one of their own tribes that fails to come to an assembly, and they proceed to kill men and women but take 400 virgins and bring them to a camp at Shiloh, where they give the girls to the Benjamites. More are needed, however, so prayer is offered to God for help. Then the Benjamites lie in wait at a feast of the Lord (in the vineyards) and capture the daughters of Shiloh as they come out to dance. *Judges 21* The Lord moves in mysterious ways.

Ruth, a widow, dresses and perfumes herself in an enticing way and sneaks into Boaz's bed on the threshing floor, as Naomi (her former mother-in-law) advises her to do. He is drunk (inebriation is commonplace in the Bible) and doesn't discover her till midnight. More honorable than she, he asks her to wait until he can make the proper arrangements with her nearest kinsman to marry her. *Ruth 3:4–8*

"And the Lord visited Hannah, so that she conceived and bare three sons and two daughters." *I Sam. 2:21* The Lord is kept very busy helping all these barren women become pregnant.

After God punishes captors of the Ark of the Covenant with an affliction of emerods (like boils), to appease him they must make a trespass offering of golden images of their emerods. *I Sam. 5* "They had emerods in their secret parts."

For the hand of his daughter, King Saul demands of David 100 Philistine foreskins. David generously slays 200 Philistines instead and delivers double the price. *I Sam. 18:25* (Gentiles had to be circumcised even if it killed them.)

King Saul strips naked and "prophesies" before Samuel. *I Sam. 19:24* Saul was chosen by the Lord to be the first king of Israel.

David marries Abigail after God has killed her husband for refusing to help David and after she makes a play for David by plotting against her spouse. *I Sam. 25*

Saul gives David's wife Michal to another man. *I Sam. 25:44*

David sees Bathsheba bathing, strikes up a relationship whereby she becomes pregnant, then plots to have her husband killed in battle. *II Sam. 11*

David's son Amnon pretends illness in order to trick his half-sister Tamar into waiting upon him, thus giving him an opportunity to force himself upon her, although she is a virgin. Tamar's brother Absalom has Amnon killed for his violation of Jewish law. *II Sam. 13* Family ties were as loose as the morals.

Absalom undermines his father David politically and sleeps with David's concubines in a tent on top of David's house. David later imprisons the *concubines* for *life*. *II Sam. 16,20* One might hope that justice on Judgment Day will be on a higher level of fairness than that exhibited in Old Testament scripture.

Age and infirmity are upon King David. His servants get him a young virgin "that my lord the king may get heat." *I Kings 1:1,2* Beats an electric blanket.

Solomon has 700 wives and 300 concubines, including many Gentiles. *I Kings 11:3*

Because she refuses to take part in a drunken brawl, Vashti is abandoned by her husband King Ahasuerus. Many virgins are sent for as candidates for queen to replace her. Esther, a Jewess, sneaks in among them. The virgins require twelve months for *purification* with oil and perfume. Then this king of Persia tries them all out. He makes Esther queen (no need to go into more detail). She tricks Haman, an enemy of the Jews, in such a way that he suffers the fate of execution by hanging. The Jews then kill 500 in the palace and 75,000 others, and Esther has the ten sons of Haman hanged also. This tale of murder, intrigue, and female heroism is a typical Bible narrative that features debatable morality. *Book of Esther*

Solomon is quite explicit: "My beloved put in his hand by the hole of the door, and my bowels were moved for him." *Song of Solomon 5:4*

Women of the Bible are temptresses: "Come let us take our fill of love until the morning: let us solace ourselves with loves. For the goodman is not at home . . . with the flattering of her lips she forced him. He goeth after her straightway, as an ox goeth to the slaughter." *Prov. 7:18–22* All men are helpless in the grip of the wiles of Bible women.

God's intentions are transmitted to Isaiah: "Therefore the Lord will smite with a scab the crown of the head of the daughters of Zion, and the Lord will discover their secret parts." *Isaiah 3:17* Lascivious old lecher licks his lips!

Isaiah is frank: "And I went unto the prophetess; and she conceived and bare a son." *Isaiah 8:3*

The Bible constantly speaks in voluptuous and cruelly extravagant language in describing the history, sins, and redemption of the Jewish nations. Glowing phrases are employed in referring to the escape from Egypt and the return of the Jews to Jerusalem at the end of the Babylonian captivity. Nations are compared to or metaphorically represented as whores, daughters, and virgins. (Thus when it is prophesied a virgin will have a son, that prophecy may well refer to Israel or Judah producing a king or prince.) "Thus will I cause lewdness to cease that all *women* may be taught not to do after your lewdness." *Ez. 23:48* "The virgin of Israel is fallen." *Amos 5:2* "The virgin, the daughter of Zion." *Isaiah 37:22*

The Old and New Testaments both praise eunuchs in the biblical tradition of the uncleanness of sexual relationships with women. "For thus saith the Lord, unto the eunuchs that keep my sabbaths, and choose the things that please me . . . even unto them will I give in mine house . . . a place and a name better than of sons and of daughters. I will give them an everlasting name." *Isaiah 56:4,5* Even Jesus, and Paul, John, and Peter further this idea in the New Testament. The purest piety can be achieved only through celibacy. Many have come to this conclusion.

"In thee (Jerusalem) have they discovered their father's nakedness . . . and one hath committed abomination with his neighbor's wife, and another hath lewdly defiled his daughter-in-law, and another hath humbled his sister, his father's daughter." *Ez. 22:10,11* (And another hath . . .?)

A parable told by God to Ezekiel: Two sisters committed whoredom in their youth in Egypt: "there were their breasts pressed and there they bruised the teats of their virginity . . . For in her youth they lay with her, and they bruised the breasts of her virginity and poured their whoredom upon her. And the Babylonians came to her into the bed of love, and they defiled her . . . Thus thou callest to remembrance the lewdness of thy youth, in bruising thy teats by the Egyptians for the paps of thy youth." *Ez. 23* Jerusalem is the whore, Judah one harlot, Israel the other. Allegories based on sex occupy a great part of the books of the prophets.

"Thou shalt pluck off thine own breasts," said the Lord God. *Ez. 23:34* Of sensual, pornographic phrases from the mouth of the Lord, typical of his revelations to the prophets, the Bible reader might well find the entire 23rd chapter of Ezekiel one of the best examples.

Perversion pervades the Bible: "And a man and his father will go in unto the same maid." This is the type of situation the Lord likes to describe for the benefit of the prophets. *Amos 2:7*

Saith the Lord to Nineveh: "I will discover thy skirts upon thy face, and I will shew the nations thy nakedness and the kingdoms thy shame. And I will cast abominable filth upon thee." *Nahum 3:5,6* Here Nineveh is portrayed as a shameless woman.

The Holy Ghost impregnates the Virgin Mary: "She was found with child of the Holy Ghost." *Matt 1:18* "The Holy Ghost shall come upon thee and the power of the Highest shall overshadow thee; therefore also that holy thing which shall be born of thee shall be called the Son of God." *Luke 1:35* (A "begotten" son must be sired.)

Herodias's daughter asks for the head of John the Baptist. Herodias is Herod's sister-in-law, whom John has told Herod he should not marry. John is in prison for incurring Herod's wrath. When Herodias's daughter dances for Herod and he grants her a request, she, at her mother's suggestion, asks for John's head and receives it on a platter. *Matt. 14* A typical biblical violent outcome of lust.

Mary Magdalene and other women follow Jesus and the disciples from city to city: "And it came to pass afterward, that he went throughout every city and village, preaching and shewing the glad tidings of the kingdom of God: and the twelve were with him, And certain women, which had been healed of evil spirits and infirmities, Mary called Magdalene, out of whom went seven devils, And Joanna the wife of Chuza Herod's steward, and Suzanna, and many others, which ministered unto him of their substance." *Luke 8:1–3* *Substance* means the physical material of a body.

In his book of The Revelation, St. John the Divine doesn't earn his title by the chaste content of his prose. He is preoccupied with whores and fornication, as are the prophets in the books attributed to them: "For all nations have drunk of the wine of the wrath of her fornication, and the kings of the earth have committed fornication with her." *Rev. 18:3* "Behold, I will cast her into a bed, and them that commit adultery with her." *Rev. 2:22* "And the ten horns which thou sawest upon the beast, these shall hate the whore, and shall make her desolate and naked, and shall eat her flesh, and burn her with fire." *Rev. 17:16* Sunday-School-lesson and catechism material?

———◇———

Any assessment of scriptural content dealing with sexuality must note the vast amount of it and the emphasis obviously placed upon that area of life by the ancient Hebrews of the Old Testament and the evangelists of the New

Testament. To Jesus himself it did not loom as very important, for although he mentioned sexual "sins" in passing, he had a tolerant attitude towards "sexual sinners." He actually seemed to flaunt a liberal attitude toward sexual morality, in contrast with the puritanical preachments of Paul.

The Old Testament Jews were no better than might have been expected as far as sexual mores are concerned. That they engaged in many promiscuous and questionable habits, just as other people of their day, may be deduced not only from Bible episodes but also from the specificity of the laws of the Torah which apply to sexual behavior. These laws cover many areas of sexual practices from the approved ones to acts and conditions still condemned by modern societies, such as sodomy and incest, rape, sexual abuse, bestiality, nymphomania, and homosexuality.

Here is the way the Mosaic law deals with two areas of perversion: "Thou shalt not lie with mankind as with womankind: it is abomination." *Lev. 18:22* "Neither shalt thou lie with any beast to defile thyself therewith; neither shall any woman stand before a beast to lie down thereto: it is confusion." *Lev. 18:23*

Apparently the Jews were not chosen to transmit God's will and laws to humankind and finally to give birth to Christianity for reasons of their moral superiority, for even their prophets were sometimes sexually corrupt, as the Lord himself charged: "I have seen also in the prophets of Jerusalem an horrible thing: they commit adultery . . ." *Jer. 23:14* The prophet Hosea married a whore, and Isaiah went about naked in Egypt and Ethiopia over a period of three years "for a sign and a wonder." *Hosea 1:2,3* and *Isaiah 20:3*

When sexual "immorality" was so prevalent among a nation's people that many passages of the Bible had to be devoted to its correction, it is a matter of curiosity that God should have selected them to be the moral models for all other members of the human race for all time to come. (Nations ranking high in morality are likely, on the whole, to be few.)

Sexual mores throughout the Bible are typically pagan in nature. The ancient tradition of gods and mortals engaging in sexual relations is a central theme which is introduced in Genesis: "And it came to pass, when men began to multiply on the face of the earth, and daughters were born unto them, That the sons of God saw the daughters of men that they were fair; and they took them wives of all which they chose. . . . There were giants in the earth in those days; and also after that, when the sons of God came in unto the daughters of men, and they bare children to them, the same became mighty men which were of old, men of renown." *Gen. 6:2–4*

In subsequent scriptures the part played by the supernatural in the pregnancies of Sarah, Hannah, and Elizabeth is rather specifically implied. And finally the union of God and maiden produced Jesus Christ, just as "human gods" were often born of such couplings in the mythological annals of Greece and Rome, Egypt, and other cultures whose gods were in the habit of consorting with human beings.

CHAPTER ELEVEN

The Apostles

In considering the works of the apostles told in Acts and the epistles, it should be remembered that nothing is claimed to have been written about Jesus's life until at least 20 years after he was supposed to have lived. Paul's epistles, generally asserted to have been the earliest documents, are usually attributed to the years from 50 to 70 A.D.

No one can do more than guess as to how the New Testament evolved. It has been suggested that the leaders of the new cult became exercised when one of its factions contemplated the compilation of such a book, and decided that they themselves would collect the various pamphlets, letters, and gospels that were already circulating about what Jesus was purported to have said and done and about how the disciples responded to his teaching and death, for an official Church record of their own. Finally, about 400 years after Jesus's birth, those who had been named bishops of the growing sect voted to decide what of the material would be designated as canonical. There were 318 of these bishops, every one infallible!

Much material was considered and many gospels were recommended. The book of Luke won acceptance by one vote. Without this piece of luck Christians would not have their Jesus in a manger, their shepherds watching flocks by night, or their heavenly hosts singing Glory to God in the highest. No creche! No one abiding in the fields! No swaddling clothes!

By such collection and voting, the New Testament might have come into existence, if the possibility of partial or complete fraud and forgery is denied, but the Roman sack of Jerusalem and destruction of the temple in 70 A.D., when the Jews were driven from the city, must have hindered research. Few converts were happy with the new book, and wrangling and dissension continued for a very long time. New translations and versions appear periodically.

The authorship of the books of *any* New Testament, no matter what version or edition, is open to argument. Whether the gospels were actually written by Matthew, Mark, Luke, and John cannot be proven, and there is no way to substantiate who wrote any of the epistles. For many Bible historians, the

New Testament is an anonymous book. No reference to it or to Jesus or to Christianity was found in the Dead Sea Scrolls.

⇒·◆·⇐

After Jesus's death, the disciples are left dangling. Admittedly men of undoc-umented intelligence and few convictions, for the most part, they had believed Jesus to be only the Messiah-Prince come to reestablish the Jewish kingdom, which all the prophets had predicted (as the embodiment of wish-ful thinking indulged in by subjugated peoples) and to shake off the yoke of Roman rule by causing the downfall of the priesthood, who found it expedi-ent to befriend those in power. Along the line of this belief, they ask Jesus just before the ascension (according to the book of Acts): "Lord, wilt thou at this time (when he returns) restore again the kingdom to Israel?" *Acts 1:6* This is what they had expected to happen—Jesus had failed to get his more grandiose mission of salvation across to them—and Jesus had led them to expect that he *would* come back very soon and gather up the Jewish saints, who would then occupy thrones in the new kingdom-to-be. The Bible does not make it clear just when the disciples realize that the kingdom of God preached by Jesus is a heavenly one. It is left to Paul, principally, to formu-late the theology of a mystical risen Christ as the savior-god of sinful mankind.

The first time that average persons read the accounts in toto of the res-urrection and ascension of Jesus, no matter what other reaction they may have, they are bound to feel astonishment at the conflict of details and the meagerness of enthusiasm and importance attached to both in the scriptures. The lack of immediate plans to capitalize on these events probably can be explained in several ways, but there is none of the "shouting from the house-tops" that might have been anticipated, especially if the purpose of their occurrence was to aid in proving the Messiahship and divinity of Jesus. And as for the ascension, it is significant in part in three ways: (1.) its secrecy (2.) the contradictory and almost flippant manner in which it is described in two of the gospels and in Acts and its total exclusion from mention in the remain-ing two gospels (3.) the *subsequent* failure by New Testament writers to give it anything more than the most fleeting "by your leave."

Of course, the resurrection and the ascension were the natural result of Jesus's origin. While human gods often have another god for a father or mother, such gods don't die without rising again; and once having risen, they usually get back up to Mt. Olympus in some fashion. These things happened to pagan gods all the time, and the Jews were always in contact with pagans, whether as conquerors or conquered or because Palestine was on a trade route. These pagan traditions made the miraculous circumstances of Jesus's life seem *less* than miraculous to both Jews and Gentiles of that day. People who lived at the time with which the Bible is concerned either believed that such things were possible or that magicians could make miracles *seem* to happen. In Samaria a god who post-dated Jesus "rose from the dead" every third day. Jesus and John the Baptist were both suspected of being Elijah back from the blue (who incidentally had ascended into heaven in a flaming chariot), and Herod, that "fox" as Jesus called him, feared that Jesus was John the Baptist risen from the recent dead. Elijah's second coming was expected to precede the Messiah.

Perhaps the mundane nature of the resurrection and the ascension was one of the reasons that very little was made of them, but to get to the bottom of the issue, one must examine the behavior of the *apostles* after both the resurrection and the ascension. Such a review would be relatively easy, if the accounts concerning their conduct as given in the Bible were consistent. Far from it.

In the first place, details of both the resurrection and the ascension themselves are as contradictory and muddled as any botched-up historical record ever could be. So it follows that the reactions of the disciples will prove to be equally as confused, and diligence on the part of the reader will only add to the chaos.

If one is willing to concede that Jesus did rise from the dead and did ascend alive into heaven, putting aside all the discrepancies that surround the several descriptions of both events found in the scriptures, the next question that surfaces in relation to the activities of the disciples is: how long a period elapsed between both events and why did the disciples wait 50 days before telling the public about either one? From here on the reader is on his own. The Bible won't settle any inquiry about these topics, nor, what's more, any question concerning how the risen *Jesus* occupied *himself.*

The book of Matthew is strangely brief about the whole business. The word "strangely" is apropos here, for the author of Matthew is not above a little invention of his own if it will make a prophecy fit. On the other hand, this author has yet to dispose of the saints who rose out of their graves at the time of the crucifixion and may not feel up to dealing with any more zombies. He has Jesus meet just once with the doubting disciples, on resurrection day at a mountain in Galilee. If readers decide to stop there, they will know nothing of the ascension, as the book of Matthew has not a word to say about it. Could be an oversight on the part of the author, who does, however, include the sequel to the story of the guards at the tomb (which he alone introduced). They are bribed by the chief priests to say that the disciples stole the body (right in front of their eyes and after they had sealed the tomb).

In the book of Mark, everything happens in one day. After Jesus rises from the dead, he walks with two disciples on a country road. Afterward, he meets with all the disciples while they are at meat (they don't miss a meal), and talks to them. At the end of his speech: "he was received up into heaven and sat on the right hand of God." *Mark 16:19* And they went and preached everywhere. Amen. Incidentally, they don't believe until they see him, but *ever since* doubt has been a ticket to hell.

The book of Luke also has everything happen within a day or two. The disciples refuse to believe several women, but Jesus meets two followers on the road to Emmaus on resurrection day and eats with them after carrying on a long conversation. As they recognize him, he vanishes. He then appears to the 11 in Jerusalem, who are terrified. He eats with them, and after expounding on the scriptures, he tells them to stay in Jerusalem until they receive power from on high. They then all go to Bethany, and he is carried up into heaven. Bethany is about a day's walk away.

The account in John is very indefinite time-wise. The evening of the day Jesus has walked out of the tomb, he enters (through the closed doors) the room where the disciples are hiding out and breathes the Holy Ghost on them, although Thomas misses out by being absent. Eight days later Jesus walks through the doors again and satisfies Thomas's doubts by letting him put his hand in the wounds. Later Jesus shows himself again to seven of the 11 who are fishing at the Sea of Tiberias. He builds a fire and cooks fish for all of them on the shore. Conversation follows. If Jesus ascends into heaven, the author of the book of John doesn't consider it worth mentioning. He leaves Jesus on the beach.

The impression left by the gospels is that, if the ascension took place at all, it occurred shortly after the resurrection, anywhere from the same day to something like within two weeks. During the time that Jesus is appearing and disappearing, the disciples seem to be either hiding out or going about business as usual, eating, walking, and fishing together (none has had a remunerative occupation for months, and they long ago abandoned their families). Seven weeks will elapse before the first sermon is preached, but no plans of any kind are being laid.

It is obvious from their varied reactions, that they have not for one minute believed deeply that Jesus would ever be seen again, once he was laid in the tomb, for they are both terrified and skeptical when he shows himself to them. They prefer to protect their own skins to keeping watch at the grave prepared to welcome him back to the realm of the living. There is little to admire about their behavior, and the reader can't help but feel that Jesus would be better served by his faithful women followers. The unreliability of the disciples must have been a big disappointment for him, considering that they had been in his confidence for many months and must now be relied upon to carry on his ministry. Although the disciples are portrayed later as men of courage and are rumored to have suffered martyrdom, it certainly takes a while for them to start playing hero, and readers actually find themselves feeling sorry for God (Jesus). Lazarus had met with more enthusiasm.

In desperation, now, to get at the truth, the Bible reader turns to the Acts of the Apostles. Unfortunately, this book is destined to come across as the least believable of all the New Testament books aside from The Revelation, for the reason that it contradicts the gospels and other parts of the Bible and draws the line at no rumor or tale no matter how unlikely or unfounded by history.

Acts hits the reader first with the claim that Jesus spent 40 days on earth after the resurrection, before he ascended into the clouds as the disciples watched. Two men in white (assumed to be angels) have been added to the scene to tell the apostles that Jesus will return in the same way he left. The Jesus of Acts spends these 40 days speaking to the disciples of things pertaining to the kingdom of God. He also commands them to wait in Jerusalem to be baptized of the Holy Ghost, although Jesus himself had already breathed it upon them after he rose from the dead, according to one account: "And when he had said this, he breathed on them, and saith unto them, Receive ye the Holy Ghost." *John 20:22*

The four gospels of Matthew, Mark, Luke, and John and the book of Acts were chosen by vote to be the inspired word of God, when the Bible was put together. One can only wonder at what other different locations the *rejected* gospels placed the ascension and how many different numbers of days they allowed Jesus to wander around or sit around waiting for takeoff time. Paul later writes that Jesus saw 500 persons at once in this interim, but the author of Acts makes no mention of this event, which would seem to be rather significant history, and 500 persons is about 480 more than any of the gospels includes in the number of spectators who would seem to have a head-start on the road to belief that leads to eternal life in Paradise. One also cannot help but wonder, to identify just one of many puzzling thoughts that arise, what Jesus *wore* after the resurrection, since the grave clothes were left in the tomb: "Then arose Peter, and ran unto the sepulchre; and stooping down, he beheld the linen clothes laid by themselves." *Luke 24:12* Of course, no details of Jesus's lifestyle for a period of perhaps 40 days are described. If the disciples, at least, saw him for 40 days, or even for an hour, why are such specifics never recorded but Jesus's exact words spoken during his ministry are supposedly remembered by them and set down at great length? Curiosity is permitted in some areas, it would seem, but considered trivial in others.

If 40 days elapsed between the resurrection and the ascension and they were spent by Jesus and the disciples in conversation, that would help to explain why it takes 50 days for the Holy Ghost to show up again and pave the way for a belated announcement to be made to the public concerning the fact that Jesus had lived up to his promise to rise again and go to heaven bodily to prepare a place for everyone willing to believe he was the Jewish Messiah and Savior of the World.

If the book of Acts is not correct about the 40-day hiatus, then the behavior of the disciples from the resurrection up to the Day of Pentecost comes into question again. They do accomplish one thing, although for what purpose, since they seem to exhibit none in any area, is not explained—they cast lots to determine who will replace Judas. Here the book of Acts *again* tells a different story, this time about the death of Judas, than is told elsewhere. This election constitutes the total positive action taken by the disciples for a period of 50 days.

When all is said and done, there is one inescapable conclusion, and this is that the disciples do not react to the resurrection, and after that to the ascension, in the way one would expect them to react. They are relatively unimpressed. They don't tell anyone, aren't tempted to tell anyone. Nobody gloats to the scribes and Pharisees. Nobody tells Jesus's mother. Nobody says, "Wow!" Everybody is matter-of-fact. Nobody celebrates. Nobody says, "I told you so!" and apparently they don't believe that Jesus told *them* so ahead of time. They don't assemble a crowd for the ascension. And if they now are convinced that what Jesus said about his second coming is true and that it will happen soon, why aren't they wasting no time in trying to save all the Jews (at least) from hell? Especially since Jesus has already given them the power to forgive sins? Don't they have *any* friends, family, or loved ones that they would like to see get to heaven?

The contradictory treatment of the resurrection and ascension in the scriptures, the details of which one would justifiably expect to be in 100 percent agreement, and the extraordinary behavior of the disciples and followers of Jesus at the time both events occur naturally give rise to skepticism on the part of anyone who reads the New Testament. And if such varying and unexplainable accounts are given of two happenings which everyone is required to believe or risk damnation, and which are supposed to represent the epitome of supernatural miraculous truth, doubt arises over the reportorial skills of the recorders of all the legends behind Christian dogma. The contradictory stories about the virgin birth and the crucifixion, to say nothing about the conflicting details of other events in the life of Jesus, have put an earlier burden upon the credulity of the scripture examiner. It is now even heavier.

Various factors may have influenced the inertia of the disciples. Their questioning of Jesus may have indicated that they expected him to set up his kingdom soon and they wanted to remain the inner *clique* that would form his inner *circle*, either in heaven or on earth. Or if they *were* in Jerusalem awaiting the Holy Ghost, what had happened to the Holy Ghost that Jesus had breathed upon them the first time they had met with him after the resurrection? Since they had already missed the opportunity to win converts by advertising the resurrection and the ascension, one would have hoped they might feel a moral obligation to atone for that and get right down to the business of alerting people to the imminent danger of burning in hell.

One logical reason for keeping mum, however, may have been that the disciples and followers were lying low out of fear for their lives. They weren't ready to be martyrs quite yet. Another possible reason for inaction is that the resurrection and ascension did not take place at all, and the disciples, with their leader dead (in whom they had not had total confidence and whose mission they had not really understood), believe all their dreams are shattered, and they are trying to pick up the pieces.

If, as is a possibility, they had been deliberately duped, they may be just now aware of the role they have played and fear reprisals. It may not have been intended that Jesus actually be put to death, or it may have been that his demise was faked. After all, death from crucifixion usually required many hours or even several days, and Jesus's legs were not broken to cause suffocation: "And Pilate marvelled if he were already dead." *Mark 15:44*

If there was a plot, Jesus himself may have been used, a theory that still finds credence, or he may have been an instigator of the plot. Whether or not the disciples were in on such a scheme, it would not be the first time in Jewish history that Messiahs had tried to foist themselves upon an expectant fatherland. The disciples might have stolen the body from the tomb, as the guards were bribed to say in the book of Matthew, but if that were true, it is strange that they did not try to capitalize upon the resurrection.

None of these theories is new, for the reason that they are possibilities which intrude upon the consciousness of anyone reading the New Testament. But to give the disciples their due, they may have just been weighed down by the realization that, because of the secrecy which had surrounded both the resurrection and the ascension, it could be exceedingly difficult to prove that a plot had not been carried out, whether it had or not.

Although 2,000 years later both events seem readily acceptable as "gospel," at the time they are supposed to have occurred belief in them depended upon the testimony of the disciples and a few women, none of whom was an unbiased witness. That was not enough, not when Messiahs were a dime a dozen. The book of Acts tells of two who had recently been put to death as pretenders, just as Jesus had. *Acts 5:36,37* One of these unfortunates had 400 followers, 280 more than Jesus could claim.

It is believed that some of the epistles *antedate* the first written records of the life of Jesus to appear in the Bible—the gospels—and none of those epistles was penned until from 20 to 30 years after God came to earth as an infant Jew, was "hanged on a tree," rose from the dead, and floated up into the sky to sit on his own right hand. For half a century or more that legend wasn't important enough to record. No disciple so much as kept a diary. Jesus didn't tell anyone to put down as a spiritual guide anything he said, but years later it became possible to quote him word for word. By that time any disciples yet alive had to be very old and at ages when memory often fails. (*Most* Bible scholars date the gospels in the *2nd* century.)

Surely at the time Jesus lived, some, at least of the educated people, could write. It was not a new art. And the disciples, even if illiterate themselves (though Matthew was a publican), must have had some friends who would kindly agree to write down as a favor a description of the wonders the disciples had seen and heard, in the interests of posterity. It isn't every day that God acts to save or damn humankind in the confines of an area smaller than the State of Maryland. Such events as the resurrection and ascension of God himself even seem significant enough to be remembered by several persons in exactly the same way. But why, the Bible reader has to ask, was the record left to chance? And for so long?

The gospels repeatedly tell of the crowds who listen to Jesus and watch him cast out devils, heal the sick, raise people from the dead, change water to wine, and serve meals to several thousand hungry souls with a few loaves and fishes. Yet at the first gathering of his followers after the ascension as described in Acts, exactly 120 persons are present, including the disciples and Jesus's relatives.

Whether these are the only *brave* future Christians of the day or whether this represented the total number who had been convinced by a vast display of magic and by the eloquence of Jesus is not explained. The scriptural passages telling of this meeting include the first definite mention of Jesus's family in connection with the resurrection and ascension. Apparently they had not been granted the thrill of being present at either, or of seeing Jesus during the time intervening. The exclusion of his family is always suggested by biblical biographical material about Jesus, which is so meager that the reader is forced to draw his own conclusions, one of them being that Jesus and his family had little feeling for each other. Some have claimed that Jesus's brother James becomes a disciple, but the Bible does not say so at the time Jesus chooses them. (Jesus's brothers dislike him.)

But Jesus's mother and "the women" (!) are finally named as part of the group that gathers after the ascension, if the reader has decided that the truth lies in the book of Acts, that the authors of Mark and Luke are wrong, and that the authors of Matthew and John chose to cut their stories short. They can't *all* be honored as reliable sources, and the reader must settle for one of the five, or for none at all. To continue with the story of the apostles, the reader must turn to the book of Acts, which, with the typical biblical challenge to consistency, is said to be the work of Luke.

——⟫·◇·⟪——

What it finally takes to get the apostles off their rockers is another of those remarkable legends of Christianity that would be dismissed as the worst kind of nonsense and superstition, if they appeared anywhere but in the Bible. It has been said if Jack and the Beanstalk graced the pages of the Bible, everyone would plant beans in the backyard. (In fact, giants do join the other fairytale creatures depicted frequently in the Word of God. They were the sons of Anak, King Og of the Bashan giants who had an iron bed over 16 feet long, and Goliath. For fear of giants, the Israelites hesitated to invade the Promised Land and were forced to wander 40 years to appease the Lord's wrath, which had been aroused because of their cowardice, not because of their superstition.)

This legend begins with the Day of Pentecost, which means the 50th day and is celebrated by Christendom the seventh Sunday after Easter: "And when the day of Pentecost was fully come, they were all with one accord in one place." (The scene had to be set.) *Acts 2:1* Whether before that day the disciples and followers of Jesus, and even Jesus himself, had intended to establish a new religion is doubtful, since the idea prevailed of Jesus's almost immediate return, and there wouldn't be time. But now something happens, not for the first time in the scriptures but with a similar rather startling effect.

Suddenly there is the sound of rushing wind, and cloven tongues of fire descend upon all at the gathering and sit upon their heads, causing them to speak in tongues and be filled with the Holy Ghost (a return engagement to at least ten of the disciples). This sudden ability to speak other languages, besides making years of study unnecessary, arrives at a time when: "There were dwelling at Jerusalem Jews, devout men, out of every nation under heaven." *Acts 2:5* (Women readers of the Bible must keep pinching themselves to remind themselves that they exist.)

Word of this strange tongue-wagging gets about, and many Jews from all over the world, as well as some of the local variety perhaps not quite so urbane, show amazement and newly-aroused fear when Peter preaches the first apostolic sermon and opportunely warns that this Pentecostal occurrence is a sign of the very last days, which are now at hand. Impressionable souls among them want to know what they can do to save themselves, and Peter and John begin to preach that there is only a short time to repent and be baptized in the name of the prophesied Savior, whom the Jews have just killed, and thereby receive the Holy Ghost, who is having a busy day.

Quoting the prophet Joel, Peter says that the time has come when there shall be signs in the heaven and earth—blood and fire and vapour of smoke: "The sun shall be turned into darkness, and the moon into *blood*, before that great and notable day of the Lord come." *Acts 2:20* These unwelcome predictions had been voiced in as many words by all the prophets, and Peter is making use of them to raise the hackles of fear, probably in all sincerity as he recalls Jesus's promises of impending horrors for an expiring universe.

Peter still thinks of salvation as being for only the Jews (it's going to take a complicated vision to convince him otherwise, although he's been listening to Jesus for many months), and he puts it all in a nutshell: "The God of *our fathers* raised up Jesus, whom ye slew and hanged on a tree. Him hath God exalted . . . for to give repentance to *Israel*, and forgiveness of sins." *Acts 5:30,31* Fear of punishment for sins is introduced as a way to gain converts, and the idea that the murdered Savior is the way to salvation is stressed, along with the coming-soon return of Jesus. These ideas will now begin to replace the Judaic concepts of Zion and a Messiah as being just what the prophets ordered.

⇒·◆·⇐

Several properly frightened converts begin to live together in a group, and the apostles insist that they sell their land and possessions and give every last penny to the apostles, allegedly to be distributed among all according to need, but complaints arise about the way this is done. Christians today oppose Communism, not realizing that the early members of their faith may have been among the first of the breed: "As many as were possessors of lands or houses sold them, and brought the prices of things that were sold and laid them at the apostles' feet." *Acts 4:31–37*

This is all followed by an incredible story of avarice and cruelty on the part of Peter that would add to the appeal of any volume about the devil. (The same could be said of many actions born of religious zeal.) A man and his wife, not wishing to be completely destitute, withhold a small amount of money. When Peter finds out, he frightens them both to death by accusing them of sinning against the Holy Ghost, then throws their bodies into a common hole. "And great fear came upon all the church, and upon as many as heard these things." *Acts 5:1–11* Fear seems to play a rather large part in the early words and deeds of the apostles.

The disciples are bound to need money, as they have been living off the populace at Jesus's instructions ever since they became disciples, purposely providing nothing towards expenses: "Provide neither gold, nor silver, nor brass in your purses, nor scrip for your journey, neither two coats, neither shoes, nor yet staves." *Matt. 10:9,10* But *now* the apostles are beginning to sound like modern evangelists who accumulate untold wealth through donations, helped along immeasurably by the medium of television.

⟩·◊·⟨

The father of Christian theology now arrives flat on his face. Peter and John have been carrying much of the load, preaching, performing miracles on Solomon's Porch, and incurring the anger of the high priest and the Sadducees (who do not believe in resurrection of the body). They have performed so many healings that people are being brought from neighboring cities to have devils cast out and diseases cured. They have been imprisoned and released by angels, and by preaching and teaching daily they have made several thousand converts (aided by many signs and wonders and finding it unnecessary to stress the ascension at all). They and the other apostles have been so busy that Stephen has to be appointed to take care of administrative details. After a long oration, he is stoned to death, and Saul appears for the first time, in the role of persecutor, although he has been snatching converts from their homes and delivering them up to the authorities for some time.

Paul (Saul) suddenly begins to spread the story that he has been literally and dramatically called to be the new spokesman for the developing cult. Many persons still claim to get a "call," but not quite in the startling manner in which Paul received his, probably because their contemporaries would take it all with a grain of salt (might even suggest a visit to the local "shrink"), Jesus's audible voice not having issued from heaven since Bible days. (Even then God's voice was sometimes mistaken for a roll of thunder.) Fabulous biblical occurrences, believed in days when the earth was "flat" and the sun moved up and down, for some reason make just as much sense today as they did when superstition served for science.

When Paul is stricken, in whatever manner, on the road to Damascus, he experiences an instant change of heart, but he remains a zealot and a very persuasive one. Undergoing a debilitating brush with death that leaves one temporarily blinded and with a ringing in the ears *might* make a changed person out of a superstitious victim. The real miracle of Paul's dedication to the cause of Christianity is his total comprehension of every angle of Christian theology, which he proceeds to divulge to all concerned. There is no dogmatical quagmire in which he does not find himself mired, and frequently to preserve the dogma, he has to become very dogmatic.

⟩·◊·⟨

Paul, up to the time of his conversion, believed that Jesus was just another impostor but that he also represented a real threat to Judaism, which Paul, as a Pharisee, was bound to defend. The greatest task which he and the apostles now face is to convince the Jews that nothing advocated by Jesus is a threat to the religion of Moses and the prophets, even though Jesus may have been somewhat more than the awaited Messiah. (Messiah here is used in the narrower sense of the word.)

⟱⟰

The Bible, with its usual maddening inattention to what might be adjudged relevant details (not actually regrettable, since details that do appear are frequently contradictory) doesn't tell the reader whether Paul had ever heard Jesus preach or even seen him. One would infer that he had, since Jesus was speaking to "multitudes" about the degeneracy of the Pharisees, and Paul was a dyed-in-the-wool Pharisee living in Jerusalem at the time, but Paul speaks only of a mystical encounter taking place. Perhaps Jesus wasn't as famous a speaker as the gospels imply (after all, Judas had to identify him in the Garden of Gethsemane). Even if he hasn't heard Jesus teach, Paul somehow manages, in spite of a golden opportunity passed up, to acquire an immediate grasp of every word Jesus ever uttered and exactly what implication it had. And by combining garrulity with obfuscation, argumentation with apparent logic, and theory with twisted fact, Paul makes it possible for the religion that came to be called Christianity (first at Antioch) to say anything that any sect or pulpit wants it to say. Which may be the reason that Paul is quoted by both more often than Jesus is.

Paul himself says that he learned all the mystery, which is one of his favorite words, by revelation, nothing from man. *Gal. 1:12 When* these lengthy revelations take place is *really* a mystery, for right after he reaches Damascus and is baptized (at the Lord's directions): "Straightway he preached Christ in the synagogues, that he is the Son of God." *Acts 9:20*

Actually, it will surprise no reader of the Bible to discover that Paul's activities from the minute he finds himself lying prone in the dust are up for grabs. The book of Acts can be depended upon for the usual variations from other scripture dealing with the same events, but Paul also contradicts himself. Acts says that Paul's companions on the road heard Jesus's voice, but Paul says they "heard not." *Acts 9:7* and *Acts 22:9* The part about "falling to the earth" would not have been traumatic, probably, since people of that day, at the slightest excuse, rent their garments or tore them off and covered themselves with dust or ashes; and the blinding light could certainly have been a bolt of lightning; but the voice of Jesus, if it had been heard by anyone besides Paul, would have been at least persuasive.

So persuasive, in fact, that one would imagine the exact content would be engraved upon the memory. Not so in Paul's case, or perhaps the story underwent embellishment as he retold it. *His* first version agrees with the *third-party* other account told first, which has Jesus identifying himself and then instructing Paul to proceed to Damascus where "it shall be told thee what thou must do." *Acts 9:6* and *Acts 22:10* When Paul tells about his experience all over again while defending himself to King Agrippa, Jesus has become somewhat more loquacious: "I am Jesus whom thou persecutest. But rise, and stand upon thy feet: for I have appeared unto thee for this purpose, to make thee a minister and a witness both of these things which thou hast seen, and of those things in the which I will appear unto thee; Delivering thee from the people, and from the Gentiles, unto whom now I send thee. To open their eyes, and to turn them from darkness to light, and from the power of Satan unto God, that they may receive forgiveness of sins, and inheritance among them which are sanctified by faith that is in me." *Acts 26:15–18* After coming to grips with this syntax, King Agrippa feels that Paul has gone mad.

The scriptures do agree that Paul went on to Damascus, where a man named Ananias has also been contacted by the Lord (in the matter-of-fact way the Bible often has of transmitting supernatural messages) and told to heal Paul's blindness and tell Paul to be baptized and receive the Holy Ghost and get about the business of saving souls. From this point on Paul and his biographer in Acts should have collaborated. He starts preaching right away in Damascus—or he doesn't. He goes immediately to Arabia and then back to Damascus—or he doesn't. He escapes from Damascus in a basket over a wall—or he doesn't. He goes to Jerusalem within a short period of time—or he doesn't. He waits three years to go to Jerusalem—or he doesn't. He wins the approval of the disciples—or he doesn't. He spends 15 days with Peter—or he doesn't. He sees only two apostles in Jerusalem—or he doesn't. He gets an introduction to the apostles in Jerusalem from Barnabas—or he doesn't.

⇒·◇·⇐

Paul is a mystic, not a narrator, and in this capacity he seems to receive impetus from his contacts with the oriental-flavored philosophies of the Mediterranean countries. According to Webster's New World Dictionary, a mystic is one who professes to undergo mystical experiences by means of which he intuitively comprehends truths beyond human understanding. Such truths are "mysteries," and Paul knows the meaning of the word and the advantages accruing to anyone who claims to be among the few to whom they have been "revealed." He brings the word "mystery" into his discourses at least 20 times, and throughout all his oral and written essays runs the implication that the ways of God are "past finding out": "How that by revelation he made known unto me the mystery; as I wrote afore in few words, whereby, when ye read, ye may understand my knowledge in the mystery of Christ." *Eph. 3:3,4* And: ". . . the mystery of God, and of the Father, and of Christ." *Col. 2:2* And: "Great is the mystery of godliness." *I Tim. 3:16*

If Paul ever knew or believed in a Jesus in the flesh who lived for over 30 years in the Holy Land, the reader of the Pauline epistles (the authorship of all 13 of which is disputed) will not get that impression. Paul's Jesus has become a spatial, formless, visionary "Christ" or "Lord Jesus Christ," who can "dwell" in people and comprise their very essence. Paul's ideology advocates a personal transcendence that few can visualize. If his "Christ Our Lord" ever dwelt on earth, it was for only a brief visit such as pagan gods indulged in, for to Paul "Jesus Christ" is a pervading, mysterious spirit who yet suffered a sacrificial death and played the part of a risen redeemer.

There is so much talk of the "spirit" in Paul's works that it is literally impossible to find more than a page or two which contains no reference to it. Sometimes it is interchangeable with the Holy Ghost, which also has innumerable functions and idiosyncrasies. "There is one body and one Spirit, even as ye are called in one hope of your calling; One Lord, one faith, one baptism, One God and Father of all, who is above all, and through all, and in you all." *Eph. 4:4–6* This is the mystic Great Spirit dwelling in everyone, which bears witness to the influence of the diffuse mythology of Paul's time. The supernatural is always there: "The Spirit itself beareth witness with our spirit, that we are the children of God." *Romans 8:16* And: "If we live in the Spirit, let us also walk in the Spirit." *Gal. 5:25*

He speaks of the Church as the enigmatic "Body of Christ," with which those in the "mind of Christ" can be united: "But we have the mind of Christ." *I Cor. 2:16* And: ". . . for the edifying of the body of Christ: Till we all come in the unity of the faith . . . But speaking the truth in love, may grow up into him in all things, which is the head, even Christ." *Eph. 4:13,15* "We are one body in Christ." *Romans 12:5*

The mythical struggle between Winter and Summer and Darkness and Light embodied in the Sun gods and gods of the Underworld have helped to shape Paul's metaphors and concepts: "For ye were sometimes darkness, but now are light in the Lord: walk as children of light . . . And have no fellowship with the unfruitful works of darkness, but rather reprove them . . . Christ shall give thee light." *Eph. 5:8,11,14* Paul warns: "Our God is a consuming fire." *Hebrews 12:29* And the words of John the Baptist come to mind: "He shall baptize you with the Holy Ghost and with fire." *Luke 3:16* (All this is in line with the theory that all religions are sun-worship.)

Whether or not Paul is responsible, the resulting mystique of intricate

Christian theology becomes one of many mystical components, including a resurrected savior as a mediator and a conglomeration of imaginary angels, devils, spirits, and ghosts. They carry the reader far from Jesus the "man" to wander in a supernatural maze. If the epistles were written long before the gospels, as is generally argued, Jesus may have lived only in the imagination in the form of another pagan-manufactured god, around whom a cult had grown up and who was substantiated into a human being by the gospel writers. And Paul himself, a figure who, if he ever existed, seemed to move in a phantom world of cosmic concepts, may have inadvertently hinted at such an incarnation. Paul's sudden appearance with all the answers is really quite phenomenal; and why was he needed to fill a role as large as he does when there were already eleven men available, as well as a group of women, who had been actual *companions* of Jesus and should have understood his message better than a Johnny-come-lately? The disciples had even had experience in missionary work. So why Paul? To preach to the Gentiles? After all, Peter has a dream that sets him straight on the Gentiles. (The claim has of course been made that some, and possibly all, of Paul's epistles are forgeries, and that Paul himself was invented as the author, but as always, such claims are speculation.)

In connection with the mysteries in which he finds so much fascination, Paul likes to dwell upon the all-pervading wisdom of the Christian God: "We speak the wisdom of God in a mystery, even the hidden wisdom which God ordained before the world unto our glory." *I Cor. 2:7* And: "That now unto the principalities and powers in heavenly places might be known by the church the manifold wisdom of God." *Eph. 3:10* The apostles and Christendom have much admiration for God's wisdom, but any show of intelligence in the laity is regarded as another of those many stumbling blocks on the pathway to "righteousness" (another pet word of Paul's): "We are fools for Christ's sake." *I Cor. 4:10* And: "That your faith should not stand in the wisdom of men, but in the power of God." *I Cor. 2:5* For fear that humankind might make use of its innate (God-given?) mental capacity to try to understand the supernatural (pagan?) "mysteries," Paul doesn't mince words (although he is a master at mincing when he wishes to be mysterious): "But avoid foolish questions." *Titus 3:9*

Clergy and priesthood owe much of their power and prestige to the willingness of many persons to concede that certain others have a special insight into the "mysteries" of religion acquired by revelation. No proof of revelation is required and Paul found it just that easy. He does agree to impart a bit of this inside information to others if they are not too intelligent or inquiring, in his own good time. But often when he tries to explain some complexity of the faith, he simply creates a more mystifying situation, to the understanding of which no one is permitted to apply the ability to think. By improvising mysteries which seem incomprehensible to all who have not been asked to share a little of God's wisdom, and aided by that master of fantastic imagery St. John the Divine and St. John's Revelation, Paul should have earned the gratitude of every member of the ecclesiastical arm of the Church. And theologians, too, ought to include Paul and John in their prayers acknowledging blessings bestowed. There are such metaphysical heights to explore and such occult depths to penetrate! And, after all, if mystery be present, can ignorance be absent in the ranks of the laity, that Church-advocated ignorance so opposed to the Old Testament Proverbs, which are almost entirely devoted to the praise of wisdom?

Among the mysteries that remain veiled and which the apostles, like Jesus, either were unable to solve or chose not to, are several that should loom as quite important to a Bible student, even one willing to settle for a minimum of information. The apostles are under the impression, for instance, which Jesus left with them, that he was coming back to earth within a very short time and gather up all the elect for his kingdom. The apostles believe it will happen at least during their lifetime, but the scheduled time remained, and still does, an unsolved mystery. The fact that they actually are convinced that the time is at hand makes it all the more convincing a scare tactic for them to use, and they do: "The end of all things is at hand." *I Peter 4:7* "The time is short." *I Cor. 7:29* "The coming of the Lord draweth nigh." *James 5:8* "For yet a little while, and he that shall come will come, and will not tarry." *Hebrews 10:37* John is even more specific: "Little children, it is the last time." *I John 2:18* All this will have a familiar ring to anyone who has heard several sermons.

Another mystery skirted by the apostles, just as it was by Jesus, is the nature of heaven and its future occupants, but believers apparently are satisfied with any eternal home that doesn't smack of existence in hell. When they are challenged to provide some information about the life-everlasting in Paradise so enticingly promised, the apostles come up with what is known as a dearth. John's Revelation makes of what was already a mystery a total enigma which theologians can only pretend to fathom after centuries of trying. It does give the dimensions of the New Jerusalem as a cube.

Paul writes of heaven as that Jerusalem: "But ye are come unto Mt. Sion, and unto the city of the living God, the heavenly Jerusalem, and to an innumerable company of angels, to the general assembly and church of the first-born, which are written in heaven, and to God the Judge of all, and to the spirits of just men made perfect." *Hebrews 12:22,23* Sounds deadly. Although Paul offers an even more beclouded picture of heaven on other occasions, he doesn't hesitate to sound the watchword of Christianity: "Set your affection on things above, not on things on earth." *Col. 3:2* According to the epistles, God is not happy with his creation The World and even more unhappy with his creation Humankind. Both are full of wickedness, and the only way the world can be improved is for people to ignore it and change themselves completely, and concentrate on future heavens, constantly striving to figure out what the stern ruler of those celestial regions demands of his flawed subjects on earth. Paul writes: "Mortify therefore your members which are upon the earth; fornication, uncleanness, inordinate affection, evil concupiscence, and covetousness, which is idolatry . . . But now ye also put off all these; anger, wrath, malice, blasphemy, filthy communication out of your mouth. Lie not one to another, seeing that ye have put off the old man with his deeds; and have put on the new man." *Col. 3:5,8–10* (For once Paul isn't picking on the women.) And: "That ye may stand perfect and complete in all the will of God." *Col. 4:12* (Got it!)

Many Christians have responded to the apostles' denunciation of the world by withdrawing partly or completely from it in anticipation of even an undefined heavenly one. The fact that many angels left their "first estate," thus making the creation of hell necessary as a place where they could be put into chains and darkness after Satan is finally overcome, would seem to suggest a heaven where intrigue and dissatisfaction have played a large part. And it will have the aura of an earthly courtroom for an extended period of time, for the Bible says variously that Jesus and Moses will judge, that the disciples will judge the tribes of Israel, and that the angels will also judge, while Paul claims that the saints will judge the angels. *I Cor. 6:3* When this mixed-up juristic procedure is resolved, humanity's billions, from infants to the senile, will at last be in their proper eternal location, and the saved can begin to enjoy all those untold delights in Paradise. But will they be happier there than the angels were, as they "meet the Lord in the air"?

And even joyfully ensconced in heaven, what will their form be? This question put to Paul by contemporaries who forget his warning about "foolish inquiries," elicits an evasive: "It is sown a natural body; it is raised a spiritual body . . . And as we have borne the image of the earthy, we shall also bear the image of the heavenly. Now this I say, brethren, that flesh and blood cannot inherit the kingdom of God . . . Behold, I shew you a mystery; we shall not all sleep, but we shall all be changed." *I Cor. 15:44–51* Case closed. And Jesus would return, before they all died.

The book of the Acts of the Apostles has a misleading title. All but seven chapters are devoted to Paul, who is a self-proclaimed apostle at best and one who was not readily accepted by the disciples, if one happens to turn to the right scripture: "And when Saul was come to Jerusalem, he assayed to join himself to the disciples: but they were all afraid of him, and believed not that he was a disciple." *Acts 9:26*

Some of the activities of Peter, James, John, and Philip are related in Acts, but most of the New Testament, exclusive of the gospels, concerns Paul, and he is indispensable to Christian theology. Whatever is still lacking can be ladled out of that witches' brew Revelation, a blend of dictation and prophecy "which must shortly come to pass" and delivered to John by an angel while John was "in the spirit."

━━▷◆◁━━

Before Paul announces his rather sudden recruitment by Jesus, the sermons and deeds of the disciples seem to be aimed at the tardy goal of convincing their fellow Jews that hell awaits all who do not believe that a god came to earth to save them from himself. The disciples are finally pretty sure of this themselves and also of the urgency involved, since they recall Jesus's claim of an early second coming. It is possible, of course, that they see an opportunity to seize power from the Jewish priesthood by capitalizing on a Savior and a promise of life eternal in the kingdom of God. Ambition cannot be ruled out when one reads that new converts were required to sell all their property and give the proceeds to the disciples.

As they all go about exhorting and haranguing, they work the same miracles that Jesus performed (and apparently that a good many fakers performed, too, according to a story of sorcery told in Acts 8). The ease with which many Bible characters are able to confound the populace somewhat diminishes the significance of Jesus's miraculous demonstrations. The book of Acts records many wondrous deeds and signs on the part of Paul, as well as those credited to the disciples.

Peter raises Dorcas from the dead, and Paul does the same for a young man who falls from a window during one of Paul's long-winded and notoriously dull sermons, but how earth-shaking does that make Jesus's resurrection look? Paul heals a cripple. *Acts 14:10* He drives out an unclean spirit from a soothsayer. *Acts 16:18* (It is hard to tell the sorcerer from the real thing, as any Jew of Bible times would probably have testified.)

Paul is in a trance; he sees visions. Jesus talks to him again two or three times, and the Holy Ghost won't be outdone, sending Paul off in all directions. Paul lays hands on some Ephesians who have been baptized the wrong way, and they speak with tongues and prophesy. *Acts 19:6* "And God wrought special miracles by the hands of Paul: So that from his body were brought unto the sick handkerchiefs or aprons, and the diseases departed from them, and the evil spirits went out of them." *Acts 19:11,12* Magic props up religion for the gullible.

Paul heals a man of palsy, and Philip performs miracles in Samaria. "For unclean spirits, crying with loud voice, came out of many, . . . and many taken with palsies, and that were lame, were healed." *Acts 8:7* It occurs to almost anyone reading all this that a lot of time could be saved, and a lot of suffering, if people didn't get all these conditions in the first place.

Paul lays hands upon people who then receive the Holy Ghost. Forgetting about "doing unto others," Paul also strikes a miscreant blind. The bite of a deadly snake, however, doesn't even make Paul's arm swell.

⇒◆⇐

All the apostles teach that the promise of salvation is to the Jews, and Paul starts out in the same key: "God raised unto *Israel* a Saviour, Jesus." *Acts 13:23* But soon it becomes apparent that they are meeting much opposition from the Jews, who are reluctant to accept a substitute for the religion of Moses and whose gullibility has been worn thin by a bombardment of pretenders and hocus-pocus peddlers and cultists, so the fertile field of the Gentiles appears on the horizon as a logical place to send in the horses. Jesus had stressed his own mission as being Jew-oriented and had placed relatively little emphasis on missionary work among the Gentiles; as a result it takes indignation on Paul's part to turn him to the Gentiles, although he maintains at various times that saving Gentiles has been his special assignment from the start. (It still remains that he began his preaching among the Jews in the synagogues and continues to preach in Jerusalem when he is not sojourning in Greece, Rome, Macedonia, and parts of Asia Minor outside Palestine.)

Paul has harrowing experiences with Jewish and Roman authorities, and there are occasions where his Roman citizenship saves the tent-maker from the wrath of both Jews and Jewish-Christians, as well as Roman officials. Paul's break with the Jews comes at Corinth: "Paul was pressed in the spirit, and testified to the Jews that Jesus was Christ. And when they opposed themselves, and blasphemed, he shook his raiment, and said unto them, Your blood be upon your own heads; I am clean: from henceforth I will go unto the Gentiles." *Acts 18:5,6* (So there!)

On the other hand, Peter has to have a complicated vision (the usual biblical ploy) to convince him that the uncircumcised are not too unclean to be included in the covenant of everlasting life in heaven. Jesus had not been able to get this across to Peter in person over a period of three years, because Jesus, for the most part, had the same prejudices. Peter tells Cornelius what he learned from the housetop vision: "Ye know how that it is an unlawful thing for a man that is a Jew to keep company, or come unto one of another nation; but God hath shewed me that I should not call any man common or unclean." *Acts 10:28* (Just the women.)

Peter never does remain totally happy about the inclusion of the Gentiles, and he and Barnabas eventually have a disagreement about it with Paul—that is, whether it is necessary for Gentiles to be circumcised. Paul, himself, won't go the last mile: God will render "glory, honour, and peace, to every man that worketh good, to the *Jew* first, and *also* to the Gentile." *Romans 2:10* And just to make sure there is no misunderstanding, he poses a question: "What advantage then hath the Jew? Much every way: chiefly, because that unto them were committed the oracles of God." *Romans 3:1,2* Paul's talk of oracles testifies to his familiarity with myth religions.

⟫·◈·⟪

The great popular appeal of Christianity, wisely stressed by the apostles, is surely the promise of everlasting life, available to all, in a paradise—an idea not original with the new faith. The religion of the Persians, who permitted the Jews to return to Jerusalem from Babylonia in 537 B.C., was founded by Zarathustra and embraced a belief in life-eternal after resurrection. Other pagan religions also held out hope for a celestial reward, and Islam's heaven is much more specific than Christianity's.

The apostles proceed to label Christ's resurrection as the victory over death for everyone, and Christ's promise of life-everlasting as the new covenant from God replacing the Old Testament covenant given to Abraham, which had prevailed under the Mosaic law and was supposed to endure forever. Death is humankind's most-feared enemy; to be saved from it is something for which the instinct of self-preservation makes the human heart yearn, and to achieve reprieve from it much of humanity is ready to follow any saint or impostor, no questions asked. When people can be convinced that there are only two alternatives and that one of those is everlasting torment, they are going to choose the other. The apostles use good psychology in achieving motivation by combining guilt, fear, and hopeful anticipation.

⟫·◈·⟪

The Holy Ghost is very big in the theology portfolio of the several apostles whose oral and written pronouncements are revealed to the New Testament reader. These evangelists are in the enviable position of not having to define anything—God, heaven, the soul, hell, angels, devils, the spirit, grace, the "mysteries," and least of all the Holy Ghost; in short the apostles enjoy the same immunity from demands for definition and proof that the Church enjoys today. The introduction of mysticism into budding Church dogma by the apostles, especially Paul and John, created an impression of an esoteric theology beyond the comprehension of the laity and produced a religious system as filled with superstitious imagery as that of some pagan mythologies. Terms that evince vague and visionary concepts carry within themselves a snobbish condemnation of requests for explanation, and they also are surrounded with an aura of privileged revelation and intellectualism that precludes naive demands for a *simplified* version of human relationship to whatever, if any, deity may happen to exist.

Myths, like fairy tales, are the antithesis of truth, but those connected with any adopted religion are granted a built-in confirmation by its adherents. As for the Holy Ghost, the many different interpretations of it to be found in the thoughts and prose of the apostles make of it a figment of the supernatural that is as improbable as it is impenetrable. It falls upon people, dwells in them, is carried in their hands, sends the apostles on journeys, causes earthquakes, and makes people talk in tongues and prophesy. It has the gift of speech in any number of languages and is pictured as the antagonist of Satan. When it appears in Samaria, a sorcerer who tries to buy the power to bestow it is reprimanded by Peter in one of his "holier than thou" chidings. *Acts 8:18–24* Twelve Ephesian *men*, who were baptized "unto" John the Baptist, have to be re-baptized to receive it (although it arrived on schedule when John baptized Jesus). *Acts 19:1–7*

—◦◦◦—

The struggle between God (or the Holy Ghost) and Satan is still going on, according to the apostles, who take advantage of every opportunity to warn the faithful against this fallen angel. Paul tells King Agrippa that Jesus included, in lengthy instructions to him at the time of his conversion, the information that Paul was to turn people from the power of Satan to God. *Acts 26:18*

Later he says that God will bruise Satan shortly, but apparently not very effectively, for Satan "hinders" Paul from making a planned journey: "Wherefore we would have come unto you, even I Paul, once and again; but Satan hindered us." *I Thess. 2:18* Satan is not only powerful, but tricky, in Paul's estimation, for Paul warns that Satan transforms himself into an angel of light. *II Cor. 11:14*

Peter is equally emphatic: "Your adversary the devil . . . walketh about." *I Peter 5:8* He evidently takes the book of Job as his authority for this pastime of Lucifer: "And the Lord said unto Satan, Whence comest thou? Then Satan answered the Lord, and said, From going to and fro in the earth, and from walking up and down in it." *Job 1:7*

—◦◦◦—

Life as the apostles see it must be lived as though tomorrow is the day of

doom for all sinners: "So that ye come behind in no gift waiting for the coming of our Lord Jesus Christ." *I Cor. 1:7* They insist that Jesus fulfilled all the
prophecies (in which the Jews placed total confidence) from the time of
Moses and that belief in him as the anticipated Prince and Savior and
Imperial Avenger is imperative for gaining life-eternal in heaven with God
and Christ and the angels. Worldly pleasures must be foregone in order to
avoid everlasting punishment in the next and the terrifying judgment of a
vengeful God: "And great fear came upon all the Church." Some converts
worry that they may die before the day of the second coming, but they are
assured by Paul that they won't be forgotten: "The trumpet shall sound, and
the dead shall be raised." *I Cor. 15:52* In the meantime the saints are miserable: "Even we ourselves groan within ourselves, waiting for the adoption, to
wit, the redemption of our body." *Romans 8:23* But Paul sets an example of
masochism: "Most gladly therefore will I rather glory in my infirmities, that
the power of Christ may rest upon me." *II Cor. 12:9*

Paul makes up his *mind* that his *body* is "vile," but then he points out:
"Know ye not that your bodies are the members of Christ?" *I Cor. 6:15* And,
addressing the males of the species, Paul, whose ego could not have survived
had fate ordained him to be a member of the opposite sex, points out a way
in which their appearance is special: "He (the man) is the image and glory of
God." *I Cor. 11:7*

⟹◆⟸

Paul has been called a "quibbler," and not without reason. There is no point
of theology or dogma too complex or insignificant for him to tackle, and he
has to be given credit for his temerity. After overcoming the long-standing
antipathy of any ardent Pharisee for a Gentile and opening the new faith to
the "unclean," he then has to try to resolve the contradictions between the
Mosaic law and the new "righteousness" that comes through grace by means
of belief. Salvation through the law and salvation through faith comprise a
conflict to which he is forced to address himself by the prodding of his fellow Jews. Of course, the other apostles find themselves in the same squeeze.
It all becomes very involved, and conclusions reached aren't always compatible with other scripture. Inevitably the apostles even contradict themselves.

⟹◆⟸

Paul's tremendous ego, although at times he is self-deprecating, enables him
to make authoritative statements about every aspect of what he deems fitting
behavior for everyone. His lists of sins are usually led off by those of sexual
misconduct. He assures all who will listen that he has been chosen by God to
spread the Word and recommends that everyone emulate him. The other

apostles are not modest, but Paul is the New Testament Moses handing down his own brand of law.

As sometimes happens to Paul, his didacticism is the brush he uses to paint himself into a corner. One of the most challenging theological questions to which the apostles, and especially Paul, have to address themselves is whether blame should accompany behavior that has been initiated by the Supreme Being. They have no apologies when God is charged with unfairness, and Paul, in a now-famous "potter and clay" assertion (borrowed from *Isaiah 64:8*) does little to resolve the matter to the satisfaction of anyone who labors under the conviction that humans should not be held responsible for actions other than those they themselves initiate. The classic example of God's interference in the behavior of persons who are then called to account and punished for it is the Old Testament story of how God "hardened" Pharaoh's heart. (Thus God's power could be displayed in the ensuing plagues, the slaughter of Egyptian first-born, and the overwhelming of the pursuing Pharaoh and his charioteers.) *Ex. 4–15*

Paul, when this atrocity is thrown up to him, angrily acknowledges the seeming injustice, admits that God causes people to act in various ways, but flatly declares that God can do as he pleases and it does not behoove man to question his ways. The *thinking* behind this incident with Pharaoh was not unique. It resided in the typical biblical premise that truth can be revealed only by "wonders and signs." God does not believe that "the truth will out" but must make a childish display of miracles, revelations, and prophecy-fulfillments. He has no confidence that his truth will stand on its own merits, and Paul agrees with him that the end justifies the means.

Paul and the other apostles find themselves in a position whose difficulty must be appreciated by the sensitive Bible reader. The implacable Punisher and prejudiced Slave Master of the Old Testament, interested only in the Jews, must now be white-washed and made into the likeness of the self-sacrificing, forgiving, loving Father-of-all-mankind of the New Testament. But for any moral leader to condone, in the pages of the Word of God —the Christian Bible—the concept that wrong-doers are punished *justifiably* by a deity responsible for their sins violates the sense of decency of the most depraved heathen. Even at the risk of sounding "lame," Paul might have been expected to claim that the "heart-hardening" stories were a result of misunderstanding, that God didn't actually act in such a diabolical way and never would. Instead: "Whom he will he hardeneth." *Romans 9:18* Obviously the point of view represented in this scripture is indicative of Paul's sense of justice. After all, he is ready to accept, without remarking on God's unfairness, a certain woman as a convert "whose heart the Lord opened." *Acts 16:14*

———◦◦◦———

The biblical attitude toward sex is that it is unclean, but all varieties of it are mentioned in the scriptures, and apparently it is very much in vogue at the time. The apostles, with much more emphasis than Jesus devoted to the subject, which was relatively slight, assign the greatest praise to those men who refrain from sexual activity entirely, and widows and divorcees are encouraged to remain in a state of self-denial.

The apostles are so sure that the bus will be leaving for heaven shortly that they are not concerned about the "multiplying" God orders in the Old Testament. They take to heart the Lord's promise to eunuchs that they would be chosen for special reward in the kingdom of God. *Isaiah 56:4,5* Paul becomes celibate, but not satisfied with total abstention for himself, he encourages converts to imitate him: "It is good . . . if they abide even as I." *I Cor. 7:8* "For I would that all men were even as I myself." *I Cor. 7:7* And: "It is good for a man not to touch a woman." *I Cor. 7:1*

Paul does concede, however, that marriage is better than fornication, a type of sexual misconduct, which, among others, brings out the righteousness in Paul that makes him unbearable most of the time. In the Revelation of St. John, those who are first with God are "they which were not defiled with women: for they are virgins." *Rev. 14:4,5*

⟫⟩◈⟨⟪

Hand in hand with this attitude toward women revealed to St. John goes *Paul's* antipathy towards them. The scriptures may not have a word for male chauvinism, but Paul is the personification of it. First he gets the pecking order straightened out: "The head of every man is Christ; and the head of the woman is the man; and the head of Christ is God." *I Cor. 11:3*

Fortunately for Paul's self-esteem he was born a male. In every letter to his flock, he devotes several paragraphs to putting women in their place and keeping them there. Like the Church today, he is not above making use of their diligence, as long as they don't aspire to positions of equality with men: "Let your women keep silence in the churches: for it is not permitted unto them to speak; for they are commanded to be under obedience." *I Cor. 14:34* "And if they will learn anything, let them ask their husbands at home: for it is a shame for women to speak in the church." *I Cor. 14:35* (Paul has quite a list of shameful things.) Women are one of his favorite targets, as lesbians, adulteresses, harlots, young widows who remarry, idle tattlers, and busybodies. He doesn't like their vanity and adornment, but they can win his approval (if it matters a darn bit to them) by bringing up children (of celibate parents?), lodging strangers, relieving the afflicted, diligently following every good work, and washing the saints' feet. (Paul is one of the saints.) After getting Adam off the hook by saying Eve was the transgressor, he suffers "not a woman to teach, nor to usurp authority over the man." *I Tim. 2:12* He's right, since women are "silly, laden with sins." *II Tim. 3:6* Will they be allowed to speak in heaven, or will they be anointing men's feet, as Martha's sister washed Jesus's, drying them with her hair, to his gratification? *John 12:3–8*

≡>·◆·<≡

A careful reading of Acts and the epistles will reveal that there was much dissension in the early Church and a good deal of jockeying for power. Paul quarrels with both Peter and Barnabas, and he mentions others who have incurred his displeasure, forgetting to "bless them which persecute you; bless, and curse not." *Romans 12:14* He speaks of two fellow workers "whom I have delivered unto Satan, that they may learn not to blaspheme." *I Tim. 1:20* And he also writes of Alexander the coppersmith who "did me much evil: the Lord reward him according to his works." *II Tim. 4:14* His tongue's in one cheek, and he won't turn the other one.

Filled with the Holy Ghost (which still seems to leave room for a good bit of hostility and intolerance), he addresses himself to a sorcerer who opposes him and Barnabas: "O full of all subtlety and all mischief, thou child of the devil, thou enemy of all righteousness, wilt thou not cease to pervert the right ways of the Lord?" Then, sounding more full of hatred than of the Holy Ghost, he gets carried away: "And now, behold, the hand of the Lord is upon thee, and thou shalt be blind, not seeing the sun for a season. And immediately there fell on him a mist and a darkness; and he went about seeking some to lead him by the hand." (Some non-Christians, surely.) *Acts 13:10–11* A deputy standing nearby, whom Paul and Barnabas are trying to impress and convert is "astonished at the doctrine of the Lord." *Acts 13:12*

In another astonishing recital of the swift display of such "doctrine," Herod is making an oration before the people of Tyre and Sidon, who start to treat him as a "god": "And immediately the angel of the Lord smote him, because he gave not God the glory: and he was eaten of worms, and gave up the ghost. But the word of God grew and multiplied." *Acts 12:20–24* The plausibility of an episode is not a requirement for its inclusion in the book of Acts, but it is certainly not unlikely that the biblical God would make short shrift of any potentates who tried to move into his territory. Adam and Eve had their wrists slapped in the Garden of Eden.

Such imperfections appearing in kings and tetrarchs of the day would seem to conflict with the preaching of the apostles demanding unquestioning submission to governmental officials, who are "the ministers of God to thee for good." *Romans 13:4* Paul states his premise: "For there is no power but of God: the powers that be are ordained of God. Whosoever therefore resisteth the power, resisteth the ordinance of God." *Romans 13:1–2* Not content with this blanket approval of all rulers and elected politicians, the apostles go on to caution against rebellion by slaves and servants, and children are instructed to obey their parents without question. *I Peter 2:18* and *Titus 3:1* Such arbitrary teaching is indefensible.

People who don't kowtow to officials of the State and who dare to criticize the government are called all kinds of names by the apostles who write the New Testament epistles. Peter gives these orders: "Submit yourselves to every ordinance of man . . . whether it be to the king, as supreme; Or unto governors . . . For so is the will of God . . . Fear God. Honour the king. Servants, be subject to your masters with all fear." *I Peter 2:13–18* He then proceeds to label all those underlings "presumptuous" enough to "speak evil of dignities." He calls them natural brute beasts, spots, blemishes, and cursed children. *II Peter 2*

—————

Differences among some apostles arose, naturally, over such questions as keeping the Sabbath, need for circumcision, and what foods might be eaten. Since such details are very much a part of the Mosaic law, Jews and Gentiles were bound to disagree heatedly about them, but any hope that the Church could rise above them and all other trivial considerations remained unrealized. And what is revelation to Paul is anathema to Peter. One would expect the message would be the same to both, but Paul says that: "When Peter was come to Antioch, I withstood him to the face." *Gal. 2:11* A picture of ecclesiastical quarreling over dogma is not exactly what one expects from the apostles, *or* from the Holy Book.

—————

James gets himself out on as many limbs as Paul. In one place he writes: "For he shall have judgment without mercy." *James 2:13* And in the next few lines he claims: "The wisdom that is from above is full of mercy." The apostles always have both hands behind their backs—in one is the God of love and mercy, and in the other a God of revenge and cruelty. They can hold out either one at will.

—————

James is also strong on the effectiveness of prayer backed up by faith. He uses one example: "Elias (Elijah) was a man subject to like passions as we are, and he prayed earnestly that it might not rain (on his parade?): and it rained not on the earth by the space of three years and six months." *James 5:17* (During this famine, the Jews were driven to eat their own children, a diet the Lord frequently threatens them with through the Old Testament prophets.)

This story makes a nervous believer out of anyone who reads James's assertions that "The effectual fervent prayer of a righteous man availeth much." *James 5:16* The passions that he mentions, common to earth-bound humankind, are execrable to the apostles but have proved to be rather useful in the preservation of the human race.

⟾◈⟾

Advice is given by all the apostles to avoid the company of all unbelievers, but they don't go so far as to tell wives and husbands to separate if one or the other is not convinced: "If there come any unto you, and bring not this doctrine, receive him not into your house, neither bid him God speed." *II John 1:10* Paul feels the same: "From such withdraw thyself." *I Tim. 6:5* (This is Christian brotherhood!)

⟾◈⟾

Only one epistle is credited to James in the New Testament, but in it he gives some instructions that have resulted in untold misery and still cause needless suffering and death: "Is any sick among you? let him call for the elders of the church; and let them pray over him, anointing him with oil in the name of the Lord: And the prayer of faith shall save the sick." *James 5:14,15* The members of various sects founded on these verses and relying upon James's authority choose to ignore the unreliability of another of his assertions: "For the coming of the Lord draweth nigh." *James 5:8*

Use of holy oils for healing is one of the many pagan practices adopted by Christianity.

⟾◈⟾

In an elaboration on the potter-and-clay theory, which obviously denies humankind self-will, Paul goes so far as to suggest (and probably revel in) the idea that the select are already chosen from birth and that it is useless to struggle against predestination: "For whom he did foreknow, he also did predestinate to be conformed to the image of his Son, that he might be the firstborn among many brethren. Moreover whom he did predestinate, them he also called: and whom he called, them he also justified: and whom he justified, them he also glorified." *Romans 8:29,30*

Paul continues in the same vein: "Israel hath not obtained that which he seeketh for; but the election hath obtained it, and the rest were blinded, (According as it is written, God hath given them the spirit of slumber, eyes that they should not see, and ears that they should not hear;) unto this day." *Romans 11:7,8*

To the Ephesians Paul is emphatic about it: "According as he hath chosen us in him before the foundation of the world, that we should be holy and without blame before him in love: Having predestinated us unto the adoption of children by Jesus Christ to himself, according to the good pleasure of his will." *Eph. 1:4,5* He congratulates the select of the Thessalonians that they are not among those whom God has chosen to assign to hell: ". . . God shall send them strong delusion, that they should believe a lie: That they all might be damned who believed not the truth . . . But we are bound to give thanks alway to God for you, brethren beloved of the Lord, because God hath from the beginning chosen you to salvation." *II Thess. 2:11–13* Possibly Paul has had a prior peek at the perfect population of Paradise.

Bible verses which speak of predestination are numerous: "And as many as were ordained to eternal life believed." *Acts 13:48* And: "He is the mediator of the new testament, that by means of death . . . they which are called might receive the promise of eternal inheritance." *Hebrews 9:15* And: "The Lord knoweth how to deliver the godly out of temptations, and to reserve the unjust unto the day of judgment to be punished." *II Peter 2:9* And Revelation describes a book of life which contains the names of the saved, "from the foundation of the world." *Rev. 17:8*

If any Supreme Being is to be accorded respect and admiration, let alone love, any hint of partiality or deviousness regarding the delegation of people to either a place of eternal punishment or a place of eternal reward would seem to present serious problems. But the apostles reinforce the implications that many have been ordained since the foundation of the world to share heaven with God, that God is in the habit of opening and closing hearts, that he deludes unsuspecting victims, that he "blinds" people so that they cannot see the truth, and that he deliberately denies others the capability of understanding the plan for salvation.

Actually, the theme of the entire Bible is God's partiality for the Jews. They start out being his Chosen People, and salvation for the Gentiles is a second-thought deal in the New Testament. Promises are made, prophecies are fulfilled, Jesus's entire life and purpose are preordained. Predestination may be a *necessary* part of belief in an all-powerful omniscient deity.

And Paul is absolutely right that God can do as he pleases; plus it follows that God *should* and *does* do as he pleases. Where Paul and the other apostles then have to be wrong is in their incongruous belief that humankind is *ever* in control. And that old nagging philosophical puzzle demands solving again—why didn't God make everything perfect? Or is this the best of all possible worlds? If not, why did God create Satan, as Zeus fashioned Pandora, to bring evil into the world, since the ability to see into and mold the future must have permitted God to know what the result would be? Paul says it all: "There is no power but of God." *Romans 13:1*

The apostles of the New Testament books which follow the four gospels are evangelists, and they are fanatical, competitive evangelists. Each has his own doctrine and great intolerance for the doctrines of the others. The doctrine of Paul won out with the Church and the Bible-makers. To disagree with him was blasphemy that earned his undying enmity. He claimed to have had special revelations that made him privy to mysteries too intricate for people to understand, and he forbade them to try. Jesus spoke to him directly from heaven. Such lines of communication didn't even require a switchboard in Bible times. Visions and trances often provided the setting, and Paul, Peter, and John all experienced them. Paul had the most, but John topped him for length, with The Revelation.

The apostles must try to build a bridge between the covenant of Abraham and the new covenant of everlasting life and convince their fellow Jews that adherence to the Mosaic law is no longer all that the Lord asks of them. Ever since Jesus was made into the Savior (however that came about), belief in him had become imperative for salvation from eternal punishment. All who did not believe that Jesus had fulfilled the prophecies of Judaism were headed for hell, according to the apostle-evangelists. The many arguments that arose over this switch from the "law" to "faith" occupy most of the apostles' time, when they are not performing the miracles required of most biblical characters. Much conflicting dogma is the result, as, e.g., James says that faith without works is useless (*James 2:17*), and Paul says only faith is needed (*Eph. 2:8,9*). Obvious contradiction doesn't make the antagonists any less positive.

Whenever they refer to Jesus, they usually seem to be speaking of some stranger whom they call Christ. It is hard to believe that three of them, at least, once shared many months of close association with a man called Jesus, so busy are they with building a theology around him. All the epistles sound like instruction books for converts, and the apostles themselves could be television evangelists.

Although mystery-understanders supposedly on the "inside" of everything, they are as ignorant and superstitious as any of their peers. Just like Jesus, they are adept at casting out unclean spirits; they can heal with handkerchiefs; they can speak in tongues; they carry the Holy Ghost in their hands; and they can raise people from the dead. The only way they can attract audiences is by performing deeds as miraculous as those being accomplished by sorcerers and magicians of the day, with whom they have to compete. The book of Acts demonstrates the predicament of the apostles (in the

248 Born Again Skeptic's Guide To The Bible

miracle department) with a story characterized by the hyperbole usually found in Acts. This is a tale of a demon that refuses to be evicted by a sorcerer who uses the name of Jesus, as Paul does. "And the evil spirit answered and said, Jesus I know, and Paul I know; but who are ye?" *Acts 19:15* The demon-possessed victim drives the exorcists away, because they are *false* exorcists. This is the brand of black magic and "miracle-working" that was common 2,000 years ago and which the apostles practiced in competition with Satan's con-artists.

Self-righteous persecution can usually be justified by religious zealots. The apostles were the first Christian "book-burners." "Many of them also which used curious arts brought their books together, and burned them before all men." *Acts 19:19* Their censorship extends to the question of free speech. Paul is an oppressor by any standards: "For there are many . . . whose mouths must be stopped." *Titus 1:10,11* He warns Timothy to avoid "oppositions of science." *I Tim. 6:20* To make sure that science doesn't make any inroads, he orders people to bury their intellects: "If any man among you seemeth to be wise in this world, let him become a fool." *I Cor. 3:18* His superstitious condemnation even extended to witchcraft. *Gal. 5:20*

The apostles are skilled at instilling fear. Even John who loves to speak of love and address his readers as "Little Children" describes a vision (The Revelation) so full of horrors and unnatural indignities that only a person with sadistic tendencies could remember it well enough to record it. If John is not the real author, it is sad that his name has been maligned. And it is too bad that the apostles are quite ready to make enemies and consign them to Satan, just as they paint a vivid hell for all who don't conform to their philosophy.

Perhaps they are all as miserable as Paul, who longs to be delivered from his vile body. Since misery will be the lot in the next life of all who find pleasure in *this* world, James may be justified in warning a class of society whom Jesus also berated: "Go to now, ye rich men, weep and howl for your miseries that shall come upon you." *James 5:1* The general attitude of all the apostles toward enjoyment afforded by the world God created echoes in James's instructions to everyone dwelling therein: "Be afflicted and mourn, and weep: let your laughter be turned to mourning, and your joy to heaviness." *James 4:9* Next to that, anything sounds like heaven.

Not only is life to be spent in gloom, according to the teachings of the apostles, but it is to be endured as a sterile, fearful, and selfish experience. It is a fleeting period to be devoted exclusively to saving one's soul and waiting for the time of transportation to the ethereal place where that soul may forevermore gaze upon Jesus.

If the world had followed Paul's directions for living on this side of the grave, the human race would have stopped reproducing itself—stopped doing anything but sit in church and sanctify itself in "righteousness." As the Hebrew Essenes retired from the streets of the Holy Land to live a barren hermit-like existence in the desert, for fear of unconsciously breaking one of the myriad laws of their religion and thus endangering their relationship with the Lord, so is humankind admonished by the apostles to hold itself apart from worldly pursuits and even from the company of any contemporaries who might cause it to fall by the wayside.

To the apostles the highest delight is to suffer affliction, the greatest glory to bear misfortune with joy, in the belief that misery is the result of personal favoritism on the part of the Lord, whose chastisement leads to a delicious after-life. Their few positive admonishments are to give to the poor (not devise a social program to alleviate poverty), make generous contributions to the church, and obey rulers, husbands, and slave masters. Long lists of "don'ts," however, usually led off by warnings about sexual aberrations, are impressed repeatedly upon the "elect."

There is no encouragement from any apostle to achieve noble goals that might benefit humankind, to acquire knowledge for the advancement of science, or to strive for any accomplishments in the arts which might enrich the life of their fellow beings; no encouragement to work in social fields to relieve human suffering. There is no praise or promise of reward for the physician, professor, scientist, engineer, public servant such as policeman and fireman, laborer, nurse, benefactor, mathematician, inventor, artist, writer, or welfare worker. The dedication required for such careers is dedication that belongs to the contemplation of God and the redemption of one's own miserable soul.

The epistles and sermons of the apostles teem with instructions for the proper behavior to insure salvation, instructions so intricate and ambiguous and so bewilderingly worded that hours may be spent in studying them to determine every nuance of meaning, as certain rabbis study the Holy Books of the Jews. But the sermons and epistles contain no suggestions or permission for the use of personal God-given mind and talents. Knowledge gained by education is to be shunned.

———⟫•◈•⟪———

How much authority the Bible reader wishes to accord the apostles might be determined by how much confidence one has in their infallibility as it is demonstrated in the scriptures. In spite of their claim that all mysteries have been revealed to them, along with all the "wisdom" of God, and that they have been designated to speak for God, when it becomes apparent that they know nothing of the universe and still believe the earth to be flat, one can't help but question. "And after these things I saw four angels standing on the four corners of the earth . . ." John wrote these words in The Revelation 7:1 (It took over 1400 more years to discover America.)

———⟫◦⟪———

While in the business of wondering, the reader may wish to ponder why the apostles found it almost impossible to believe that Jesus was the Son of God. It was not until the Last Supper that the disciples made up their minds, and even after Jesus had risen from the dead and visited the disciples *twice*, Thomas had to place his hands in the very wounds of the crucified Christ before he would believe in the resurrection which Jesus had foretold.

And what about Paul, that theologian unequalled? He was, after all, a resident of the Holy Land, Jerusalem in fact, at the time when Jesus was performing miracles right and left, rising from the dead, and defying the laws of gravity to return to the celestial abode (clad in heaven knows what). Yet Paul admits he put no stock in any of it before his dusty conversion, which left his companions strangely unaffected and after which he dedicated his life to setting everybody else straight.

Centuries later, however, people are not permitted to be skeptical when subjected to unverified reports of events that were unbelievable to those supposedly on the scene. When they on whose very streets and in whose very company the gospel story took place could not find it in their hearts to believe, is it reasonable to demand total acceptance by those not so privileged? What *new* evidence has been produced beyond that experienced by the disciples (which came close to being insufficient for them)?

They were *astonished* and *afraid* after the resurrection, did not even recognize Jesus, and were unimpressed by the ascension. In fact, *their* faith wouldn't have moved a child's sand pile, let alone a mountain, or the stone from the tomb of the teacher who had told them he was God. If tongues of fire hadn't descended on their heads (not even singeing their hair), the likelihood is that the disciples would have gone back to counting their catch at the Sea of Tiberias and been heard of no more.

———⟫◦⟪———

An unfortunate resemblance between the blood-thirsty law-giver of the Old Testament (Moses) and the father of Christian theology of the New Testament (Paul) must be admitted by even the most avid Bible-defender. Each was a self-righteous, deliberate murderer, both directly and indirectly. Moses slew an Egyptian who was mistreating a fellow Israelite and went on to direct, with the approval of the Lord, the annihilation of thousands who happened to get in his way on the march to Canaan. Paul voluntarily took part in the stoning of the martyr Stephen and delivered fellow-Jews up to persecution and imprisonment. Even after his conversion, he remained a heartless fanatic in his new intolerant cause.

These two great biblical moralists could not qualify to teach in any school system today, even if they managed to elude the death penalty which many of their followers now advocate. It cannot be denied that the No. 1 theologian of the Christian religion was a man who could find pleasure in throwing lethal stones at a fellow human being with the intent of inflicting excruciating pain and suffering and finally a bloody death (at the hands of a mob who would tolerate no difference of opinion about their god). As a member of that lynching crew, Paul displays the intolerance that colors his behavior in the missionary field. Peter is equally harsh and uncompromising, and special visions from heaven that try to soften both him and Paul are only partially successful. They remain unbending in their condemnation of all who do not adopt their creed, presaging the future attitude of the Church.

Re-examination of Peter's biblical career shows vast need for humanization of his brand of evangelical zeal, for in the true sense of the label, Peter was also a murderer. The revolting account of how he deliberately frightened two converts to death for withholding a few pennies from the communist Christian community will live on in Acts 5:1–10. Taken from this scripture, here are the words of the disciple to whom Jesus gave the keys of the kingdom—accusing words addressed to the widow who came to inquire about her beloved husband: "Behold, the feet of them which have buried thy husband are at the door and shall carry *thee* out!" This beautiful Bible story continues: "Then she fell down straightway *at his* (Peter's) *feet*, and yielded up the ghost: and the young men came in, and *found her dead*, and carrying her forth, buried her by her husband." (Christian young men!)

Two pitiful victims murdered and tossed summarily into a hole in the ground because of the avarice and self-righteous depravity of the first "Vicar of Christ"! Standards for judging morality, peculiar to the Bible, permit throughout its pages such criminals as Moses, Peter, and Paul to be held up as models for human behavior. The God of the Bible deliberately chose these three to be the teachers and purveyors of the Word, to be his representatives on earth—those brutes by any standards of decency:

This Moses who struck down an Egyptian and fled to the Midianites for protection from the law and who was to show his appreciation at a later date by slaughtering that same tribe. This Moses at whose orders thousands of other natives were slain and who spared neither children nor defenseless women.

This Paul who presided at the stoning of a saint and who dragged entire families from their homes to prison because they believed in the Christ who later was to reward him by choosing him to preach to the Gentiles. This Paul who did not hesitate later on to curse people and strike them blind.

This Peter who worshipped money so greedily that he would not even draw the line at using fear of the Holy Ghost (Jesus's idea of a Comforter) to cause people's hearts to stop beating. This Peter who lopped off Malchus's ear. *John 18:10*

What perverted moral precepts will prevail on the Christian Judgment Day? Present-day censorship demands that crime not be depicted as a "paying" thing, but the murderous rogues of the Bible are honored as law-givers and made into saints—to the surprise of no one who reflects on the savage God of hell and of the Old Testament and on Jesus's own words: "He that hath no sword, let him sell his garment and buy one." *Luke 22:36* And on the words of his parable: "Those mine enemies which would not that I should reign over them, bring hither, and slay them before me." *Luke 19:27*

Who can marvel that the history of the Christian Church has been a bloody one? And Paul and Peter, instead of telling everyone else how to save the immortal soul, perhaps should have been concerned with their own, for according to St. John: "No murderer hath eternal life abiding in him." *I John 3:15* St. Paul may after all be spared the embarrassment of meeting his victim St. Stephen at the portals of Paradise.

⇒•◇•⇐

Lovers of freedom, beware! The epistles lie forever in wait as a potential tool for authoritarian tyrants to forbid, in the name of God, all protest and redress for citizen, laborer, wife, and child. The apostles are emphatic: *Romans 13; Eph. 5:22–24* and *6:1–5; Col. 3:18–22; Titus 2:9,10* and *3:1; I Tim. 6:1; I Peter 2:18* and *3:1–6*

The word "obey" is the watchword of the epistles (as it is of many of Jesus's parables). Christ obeys God, the man obeys Christ, the wife obeys the husband, the child obeys the parent, the servant (slave) obeys the master, and the citizen obeys the authorities—unquestioningly, for such is the order of God. The oppressor is free to go to the Bible for divine sanction of any cruelty perpetrated against the person lower on the biblical totem pole than the oppressor. It has been done on a horrendous scale, and it can be done again at any time.

The Bible permits no recourse for the oppressed, and it was historically the tool used to prevent any uprising of the weak against the strong, who employed scripture as cruelty's ally. The harshness of some words of the apostles should be emphasized to alert every individual who prizes freedom and personal dignity and insists upon the right to secure and defend both. Consider Paul's admonitions to the Romans. Speaking of rulers and the "higher powers," he says to fear them, for the ruler is the "minister of God" who "beareth not the sword in vain, for he is the revenger to execute wrath upon him that doeth evil." *Romans 13:4* Peter agrees: "Submit yourselves to every ordinance of man for the Lord's sake." *I Peter 2:13*

Paul is adamant about preserving the class system: "Servants, be obedient to them that are your masters according to the flesh, with fear and trembling." *Eph. 6:5* And: "Let as many servants as are under the yoke count their own masters worthy of all honor." *I Tim. 6:1*

Although self-effacing submission of wives to husbands is a Christian condition clearly required by Paul, Peter reinforces its necessity by stressing that women must be in subjection to their own husbands as "Sara obeyed Abraham, calling him lord." *I Peter 3:6*

The Bill of Rights of the American Constitution is completely nullified by the Christian Bible.

There is no escaping the fact that the Bible is a racist book, and that racism is promoted by the apostles and practiced by Jesus. The Jews were commanded by the Lord to annihilate the Gentiles, and they carried on those wars with holy gusto under divine direction. Jesus made it clear that his mission was to the Jews, and Jews will sit at his table in heaven. Finally, when the apostles were preaching and writing to the new Christians, they set the stage for continued enmity between Jew and Gentile and for antipathy among various sects by teaching that congregations should separate themselves from all who held a different doctrine from their own. As a result of all this, every kind of bigot may embrace the Bible and burn the Cross.

CHAPTER TWELVE

The
Prophets

Just what is a Bible prophet? Thomas Paine in *Age of Reason* says that the word "prophet" meant "poet" in the days in which it is believed parts of the Bible were written. It is bound to have that interpretation at times in the scriptures, and "prophesying" must in many cases indicate singing or reciting poetry, because it is often done in groups with the aid of musical instruments such as harps and psalteries. Such "prophesying" was common in many pagan societies.

But biblical prophets also *predict* in the accepted sense of the word. They forecast doom and interpret dreams. Some of them dress untidily and walk around with unkempt hair and beard or even naked. They claim to have direct communication with God, usually in dreams and visions. They sometimes travel about in large groups but often dwell as hermits and may even be fed by birds.

Some of them can perform miracles, make iron float, and raise people from the dead, and Elijah doesn't even have to die before disappearing into the firmament in a flaming chariot. They can live in a whale's belly, part the waters of the Jordan, and make a little food go a long way without Hamburger Helper. They read strange handwriting on the wall and are cast into cages of wild beasts without peril to themselves.

They dare to reprimand rulers and give them dark messages and instructions from God. They are political and take sides. Books of the Bible are attributed to them, some of which read like poetry, with meter and cadence and phrasing. Elaborate allegories, flamboyant description, horrible predictions, and unrestrainedly ornate and vulgar language are characteristic of these books, which tell of visions and which portray episodes and periods of Jewish history and the coinciding behavior of the Lord, finally forecasting the establishment of Zion and the destruction of the Gentiles. Many of these predictions are so involved and obscure that they can be made to mean almost anything, and they are often couched in such enigmatic wording that Christianity has been "proved" on controversial interpretation of them. It is unlikely, however, that anything is foretold beyond the hoped-for re-establishment of an independent Jewish nation under a new Redeemer Prince of the House of David, with the seat of government at Jerusalem and the Old Testament Lord having dominion over Zion and Gentiles alike. For that Messiah, or Prince of Peace, Judaism still waits.

Much of the content of the books attributed to the prophets is pernicious and reeks with violence and lewd descriptions. Some passages, it is true, reveal touches of majestic poetic beauty, but the books on the whole must seem to any reader to have been spawned by religious and patriotic fanaticism of the most extreme variety. Some of the psalms are examples of prophecy set to poetry.

Prophets considered themselves servants of God, or at least wanted others to consider them as such, and in all their utterings lies the implication that they are his spokesmen. Whether they are charlatans seeking political influence or whether they are convinced that they are truly divinely-inspired, is unimportant. It was the custom of that day for anyone embarking upon a mission to consult soothsayers, seers, witches, necromancers, and prophets, with the twin purpose of determining the probable outcome of the venture and of gaining approval of the gods for it. The Greeks and Romans had special shrines for consultation with their deities. Very often constellations were used in divination, sometimes the entrails of animals.

Holy advisers have been esteemed in most rulers' retinues, and evangelists and other dynamic personalities have put on the robe of righteousness and walked the streets of many countries. In Bible days they called some of these reformers "prophets." They were the religious leaders, the divinely-inspired spokesmen of God.

Consultation with prophets or religious "insiders" had its advantages. Blame for failure of an enterprise would have to be shouldered at least partly by the supernatural, and it was a matter of prestige to put oneself under the guidance of heaven, as well as a matter of prudence, in view of the distrust displayed by the populace in anyone who failed to call for help from the gods in matters of state. Public prayer and church attendance is still practiced by all political figures in Christendom, and association with leading ecclesiastical personages is sought regularly by the ruling powers. Praying for divine guidance, as it is piously referred to, takes a public official off the hook occasionally, but alliance of Church and State during biblical days and throughout history has led to abominable discrimination and persecution. When the authority of the state becomes the manifesto of the gods, dissenting citizens have no choice but to yield.

There are always fanatics, religious and otherwise, who claim to have knowledge of the occult and the unique ability to see into the future. If their predictions, a percentage of which would by the laws of chance prove to be accurate, are laid by them directly at the door of the Lord, who would dare to gainsay such claims in a time of history when credulity admitted of a deity who could talk person to person with favored articulate mouthpieces?

<hr />

Moses, first and most esteemed of the Old Testament prophets, starts his career under a cloud as a fugitive from Egyptian authorities who seek him as a murderer. He then narrowly escapes being a victim himself when God tries to kill him in a hotel. *Ex. 4:24* This is his second close call with death, the first rescue having occurred when Pharaoh's daughter plucked him from the bulrushes and reared him at the royal court of Egypt. Moses says that he lived to be 120 years of age, 40 of which are spent in a desert wilderness, and he compiles a heroic list of accomplishments, starting with becoming the Jewish Abraham Lincoln during his 80th year.

The most astonishing achievement attributed to him and the one which proves the greatest boon to posterity is his authorship of the Pentateuch, at the beginning of which, with a flick of his Bic, he lays to rest for all time every nagging question of how the world began and of how the human race came into existence right by the Euphrates river, which also happened to be the cradle of the Jews. He knows all about the Garden of Eden and the two trees and how humankind became sinful and separated itself from God (although Moses himself remains very close). With his facts about the Creation he confounds science and makes speculation a waste of time and enemy of faith. Moses is privilege to the way it was from the very beginning of time (in the Middle East) although he feels no obligation to document the source of his information. And nobody knows when he lived, when he died, or where he is buried. Nevertheless—"In the beginning . . ."

When Moses can take a minute off from Bible-writing, he has several other demanding roles to fill, such as leading the Jews out of enslavement in Egypt, guiding them morally and physically through 40 years of wandering, serving as commander-in-chief of their armed forces en route to the Palestine wars of acquisition, and receiving and enforcing the Mosaic law of Judaism, the minute recording of which occupies much of the five books. Since Moses became privy to these intricate religious and civil rules of conduct, or at least a great portion of them, while he and God held two summit talks on Mt. Sinai each lasting 40 days (during which time he had nothing so much as a nibble of manna to eat) Moses comes across as either a fantastic scribbler or a reporter with total recall.

Moses doesn't explain what writing tools he employed, although he does give a vivid insight as to the method of inscribing used by the Lord, who delivered the Ten Commandments to Moses permanently engraved with the divine finger on two tablets of stone (which Moses then had to carry down the mountain in a state of near-starvation). Those tablets no longer exist, and neither do any papyrus rolls, animal skins, or clay tablets painstakingly "penned" by Moses.

Allowing him time off from directing the killing of babies and mothers, the violating of virgins, and the leaving of no one breathing, all the while dividing up the spoil with God, his achievement as author of these books is a staggering one. The translated King James version of those works comprises approximately 175,000 words, and even without the sentence structure used in languages today, Moses's manuscripts would have represented not only a prodigious physical accomplishment but an almost insurmountable logistical one for his aides—how transport all those brief cases?

Moses, by use of the third person, makes it possible to describe himself: "Now the man Moses was very meek, above all the men which were upon the face of the earth." *Num. 12:3* Meekness prevents most meek persons from calling themselves meek, but Moses is not the ordinary, run-of-the-mill Memoir writer, for he is able to include in his autobiography information about his God-foretold death, such as where it occurred and the place of burial: "And he (the Lord?) buried him in a valley in the land of Moab, over against Bethpeor: but no man knoweth of his sepulchre unto this day." *Deut. 34:6* The mourning period, according to Moses, was 30 days, after which the Israelites accepted Joshua, the son of Nun, as his successor.

Apparently Moses is already on the other side of Judgment Day and safely ensconced in heaven, as he appears with Jesus at the Transfiguration. And his place in history remains unchallenged, for he himself claims in that one-of-a-kind autobiographical trip down Memory Lane: "And there arose not a prophet since in Israel like unto Moses, whom the Lord knew face to face." *Deut. 34:10*

Tongue-in-cheek must eventually be abandoned in any consideration of Moses as the actual author of the Pentateuch. Scholars generally agree that these books could not have been written until hundreds of years after Moses is supposed to have lived, but even if the Moses-inscribed manuscripts could be viewed under glass, there would still be lacking any *authority* for their content other than "Moses (or the Bible) tells me so." Many religions are handed down from on high to some privileged intermediary. Moses was that spokesman for Judaism, and Jesus finished the job for Christianity.

<hr/>

Samuel, a prophet who also serves as a Judge of the Israelites during the period before the kingdoms, is given by his mother to be reared in the temple. Although the people desire a king, the Lord tells Samuel (direct communication between the Lord and the Jews is an everyday occurrence in the Old Testament) to warn them that their future rulers will prove to be oppressive. God's foresight will not prevent him from choosing reprobates to govern his Chosen People, however, and he instructs Samuel to find and anoint the first king—Saul. When, in time, Saul becomes worldly and lax in fulfilling his obligations to the task-master in the sky, Samuel, a strict moralist who insists that everyone worship constantly, warns Saul to shape up.

After Saul shows mercy to King Ahaz of the Amalekites, he is in great disfavor with God, finally loses his reason, and is replaced by David, as prophesied by Samuel. Properly terrified of divine wrath (the heritage of all who came under the dominion of the Jewish God), Saul prevails upon the Witch of Endor to call up Samuel's ghost, who predicts Saul's death. (Such attestation to the power of witches in the Word of God, coupled with the command of the Mosaic law not to suffer a witch to live, was to lead to the "legal" murder of unfortunate women, throughout the centuries, suspected of having the "evil eye" later described by Jesus as sinful. *Mark 7:22*) Samuel's return from the dead is not treated in these passages of scripture as being especially miraculous, for the reason that to return from the dead by a prophet or religious leader was already accepted as a possibility among the superstitious Jews, who had borrowed the idea of resurrection from pagan cultures.

Although David came to be idolized as a Savior of the Jews from the Philistines, the prophet Nathan tries to keep him in line morally, upbraids him, and foretells the death of his child by Bathsheba (another instance of the biblical tradition of visiting the sins of the fathers upon the children and making the innocent suffer for the guilty, a tradition which was to find its flowering in the death of a sinless God to redeem sinful humanity).

Nathan is a political prophet, aligning himself with David against Adonijah and plotting with Bathsheba to place Solomon upon the throne as David's successor.

Elijah the Tishbite is the champion of Jehovah at the time of the reign of King Ahab and Queen Jezebel, when Israel was reverting to Baal-worship. Filled with righteous indignation, he engages in several contests with the prophets of Baal, annihilating as many as 450 at a time. Dedicated to the service of the Lord, he, like all the prophets, preaches violence as the weapon to be employed in the struggle against non-conformity. This theory—that murder can improve the lot of humankind—is the crux of the Crucifixion 900 years later.

A wild, rough man who wanders the countryside, appearing unexpected-ly to pronounce ominous words of warning to backsliders, he calls down a three-and-a-half-year famine, making it necessary that he himself be fed by ravens as he hides out on the shores of a brook. A widow befriends him, and he sustains all their lives by causing oil and meal to multiply. When her son becomes ill and dies, Elijah convinces her that he is a "man of God" by bring-ing the child back to life. After predicting the deaths of King Ahab and Queen Jezebel, Elijah divides the waters of the Jordan with his mantle, and while he is carrying on a mountain-top conversation with his successor Elisha, a whirlwind carries him off to heaven in a fiery chariot.

Elisha comes close to out-distancing Elijah in the miracle marathon. An ill-tempered child-hater, he curses 42 children for teasing him about his bald head, and the Lord sends bears to devour them. (Fortunately, not all of the Bible is illustrated!) He aids and abets Jehu, a captain in the army of Israel who is in favor with God because of his murderous ways, and finally has Jehu anointed king of Israel after the death of Ahab.

Jehu, one of the fiends in which the Old Testament abounds, follows God's orders by killing the 70 children of Ahab and putting their heads into baskets at the city's gates, after which he murders Ahab's 42 grandchildren who live in Judah. Prior to this bloody orgy, he has had Jezebel thrown from a window so that he can ride over her body in a chariot. All of this wins Elisha's admiration.

Elisha's miracles are similar to Elijah's. He also divides the Jordan, sweetens the waters of Jericho, turns water to blood, makes it possible for a barren woman (his hostess) to have a child, brings that child back from the dead, makes a little oil fill many bottles, turns a kettle of poison into harm-less food, stretches a small amount of bread and corn to feed 100 persons, heals a leper, makes iron float, strikes a host of Syrians blind, and later restores their sight. Even after his death, the miraculous powers of Elisha go on, as a body cast into Elisha's sepulchre is restored to life when it touches his bones.

Anyone who reads the accounts of the Old Testament prophets finds nothing fresh or astounding in most of the deeds of Jesus that are supposed to make him a unique miracle-worker. What with the wonders performed by these prophets and those within the powers of pagan gods, there was "noth-ing new under the sun." And the equivalents of the prophets were pagan shrines presided over by priestesses.

After the Jewish nation had divided into two warring parts, Israel in the north and Judah in the south, each with its own ruler, the individual monarchs usually had their own prophets, who were sometimes rivals. This division took place about 925 B.C., and after that each king or queen would seek the advice and *favorable* prophecies of its own fortune-tellers. A story of such jockeying is told in the 22nd chapter of I Kings. Prophets consulted in this anecdote number in the hundreds.

Amos, Hosea, and Isaiah were all prophets of the 8th century B.C., and Amos is considered the first of the prophets to write. He tries to save the northern kingdom from God's revenge and with Hosea predicts its overthrow by Assyria if the people do not mend their ways. He has several visions of God which portray God's intentions toward sinful Israel. All to no avail, for the northern 10 tribes are finally conquered by Assyria and absorbed into their culture. The Jewish remnant remaining (there is always a remnant) is Judah.

The book of Isaiah is considered by Bible scholars to have been written by at least two different persons because of a disagreement in style and for certain historical reasons. The Isaiah of the greater part of the book is in constant touch with the Lord through visions and dreams. As the Lord's mouthpiece, a role he, like the other prophets, assigns to himself, he stresses the magnificence of the Hebrew Lord and warns of the judgment awaiting the Gentiles, which he deals with country by country. He calls the Jews to account with bitter words of humiliation but looks forward to the reunion of Israel and Judah, unless the Jews fail to reform, in which event the Lord will visit upon them terrible punishment: "If ye be willing and obedient, ye shall eat the good of the land: But if ye refuse and rebel, ye shall be devoured with the sword: for the mouth of the Lord hath spoken it." *Isaiah 1:19,20*

Words from this book have been used many times to prove that the prophet Isaiah foretold the coming of Jesus, but the *authors* of this book seem to yearn only for the reunion of Israel and Judah under an earthly David and a heavenly Jehovah: "Therefore the redeemed of the Lord shall return, and come with singing unto Zion; and everlasting joy shall be upon their head." *Isaiah 51:11*

The prophet Jonah has feet of clay but an equanimity that serves him well when he finds himself inside the belly of a whale. He is sent by God to warn Nineveh of impending destruction coming their way from the Lord, who has a weakness for destroying whole cities but usually doesn't favor them with a notice. For some reason Jonah is reluctant to go on this mission and tries to hide out from God on a Gentile ship.

When God sends a storm that threatens the ship, the sailors have to throw Jonah overboard, and the famous whale story begins. Although the whale's stomach may be upset, Jonah is not and spends his time offering up various long-winded prayers, not necessarily for deliverance.

When Nineveh heeds God's warnings, finally delivered by a late-arriving Jonah, and is spared, Jonah sulks. Prophets like to have their prophecies come true, especially if they are dire ones.

<hr>

Jeremiah, who has influence during the reign of four kings, as did Isaiah, appears at an unhappy age of Jewish history, at the time of the conquest of Judah by the Chaldean king Nebuchadnezzar, who carries its prominent citizens into captivity in Babylon and plunders the temple at Jerusalem, a conquest which is to last for 70 years. Jeremiah at the court of King Zedekiah, in the last days when Judah formed an alliance with Egypt to resist the Chaldeans, becomes a very controversial figure. Urging the Jews to submit to the enemy, he understandably is accused of being a spy and traitor and is the target of King Jehoiakim, who, along with Zedekiah and the other two last kings of Judah, ruled by *permission* of Nebuchadnezzar. When Judah refuses to continue to pay tribute to the Chaldeans and Jeremiah opposes this revolt, Jeremiah is thrown into a pit and rescued by a black male slave.

Jeremiah also forbids the Jews to take refuge in Egypt, although many of them do, Jeremiah's argument being that the coming captivity in Babylonia is a just punishment sent by God upon the Jews for their wickedness and should be willingly accepted. Jeremiah's benevolent treatment later by the captors and permission granted him to remain in Jerusalem, if he pleases, would seem to indicate that there may indeed have been a conspiracy between him and the invaders.

His reliability as a prophet is certainly in question when one considers his reassurance to Zedekiah that the king would die in peace. That prophecy came true only if Zedekiah later was able to find peace after his sons were slain in his presence just before his eyes were put out.

<hr>

The prophet Ezekiel, whose visions and trances could confound the most gifted interpreter, fortunately serves as his own. He is carried into captivity in Babylon, and during the years spent there under good treatment he tries to keep his countrymen on the straight and narrow, condemning the worship of alien gods and predicting a new day to come for Israel. His heritage as a priest's son serves him well.

The last eight chapters of the book of Ezekiel are needed by the prophet to describe just one vision. It contains detailed measurements and elaborate instructions for rebuilding the temple and controlling the populace when the Jews are finally allowed to return to Jerusalem and Judea. Ezekiel has a pen that drips with lascivious prose and carnal metaphors. No Bible student who calls these writings sacred could feel free to censor the product of any other author. Reportedly cleaned up in the translation from the original Hebrew, the original may just be imagined. Ezekiel, in a parable told in chapter 23, not only employs a metaphor of two whores but puts the tasteless words of the 49 verses into the mouth of the Lord.

One of the prophecies handed down to this prophet from the Lord (according to Ezekiel) which still awaits fulfillment or might even be labelled false concerns Egypt: "I will make the land of Egypt utterly waste and desolate . . . No foot of man shall pass through it, neither shall it be inhabited forty years." *Ez. 29:10,11*

⇒•◆•⇐

When it comes to dreams, the prophet Daniel finishes ahead in a very crowded biblical field. If the account of every dream, vision, and trance were to be removed from the Bible, the remaining volume would be surprisingly thin. And if one long meaningless vision filled chock-a-block with baffling imagery outweighs a large number of equally nonsensical dreams, then Daniel must relinquish the crown and allow it to grace the furrowed brow of St. John the Divine in recognition of The Revelation. After messages to seven churches have been revealed in its opening passages, this final book of the New Testament becomes prophetical, but, as with most biblical prophecies, no two persons could possibly come up with the same interpretation of it. Since St. John himself claims that all the predictions contained in it are short-termed, and considering that 2,000 years have gone by since John's fantastic experience with the supernatural, one may judge for oneself how much significance need be attached to The Revelation.

A dream is a dream is a dream, and the same may be said of a vision. Modern psychology calls the ones in which imaginary things are seen and imaginary voices are heard "hallucinations," and they are not considered a source of truth. Because nobody learns anything through personal contact during a vision or a dream, not even if it could be proved that neither was a fabrication, there can be no authority attached to any revelation or message said to have been received in such a manner. And there is always the possibility that prophecies may have opportunely been interpreted to coincide with events which have already taken place, that events are made to occur or claimed to have occurred to fit prophecies, that some prophecies are purposely phrased in ways that may be variously interpreted, or that the prophecy's fulfillment may have been the result of a lucky guess. The probability of fraud is in direct ratio to the degree of motivation that inspires the "prophet."

The unlimited gullibility of the people of Bible days encouraged Bible prophets to go into fantastic flights of fancy, and superstition endowed the likes of Isaiah with permission to proclaim dreams and visions to be a means of direct communication with the Almighty, as often as they were experienced. Such "communication" could never be verified and should have no meaning except to those whose confidence encounters no barrier by a lack of evidence.

The problem of authority and documentation is further complicated by the fact that it is not known with certainty the author of even one book in the Bible. The book of Daniel, for instance, is generally admitted to have been written at least 400 years after the period of time with which it deals. What possible authenticity can any of it have, since it is represented in the Bible as having issued from the pen of none other than Daniel and the real author does not choose to identify himself?

Daniel is supposed to be an upright Jewish prince carried off to Babylon when a youth. The book that bears his name is as full of fantasy as any collection of fairy tales written for the enjoyment of children. Lions' dens! Fiery furnaces! The righteousness of Daniel and his companions prevails over all of them, as the young men absorb the advanced culture of the Chaldeans but refuse to compromise their allegiance to the Hebrew Lord.

Now, Daniel cannot only interpret dreams, a capability that commands much deference in the scriptures, but he can, with God's help, tell the dreamer the contents and meaning of a dream forgotten by the dreamer himself. Such a service Daniel performs for King Belshazzar, who does not consider it a unique one, however, since he has already ordered all the wise men of Babylon put to death for not being able to accomplish it.

Daniel's own visions become so complicated that God has to send Gabriel to interpret them for Daniel, once even at mealtime. Finally, Daniel is able to read the famous handwriting on the wall predicting the downfall of Belshazzar for not being humble, but when he writes that Belshazzar was slain that very night, he slips up in a rather important way, for history shows that Belshazzar died in a peaceful way a bit later, in 561 B.C.

The last passages of the book of Daniel concern themselves with the "last days" often dwelt upon in the scriptures, and there is much talk of chariots and horsemen and ships and kings and the prince Michael (the angel

Michael?) and specific numbers of days, until even Daniel has to admit (as he did concerning an earlier vision) that "I heard, but I understood not." *Dan. 12:8* And his appeal for an explanation to a "man clothed in linen, which was upon the waters of the river" is met with a command: "Go thy way, Daniel: for the words are *closed up* and sealed till the time of the end." *Dan. 12:9* Today, however, there are theologians who can interpret these visions of Daniel's. Unfortunately Daniel died before he got to meet them.

The other books of the prophets are all built around the same themes. Hosea's instructions from the Lord are, admittedly, a bit unusual: "And the Lord said to Hosea, Go, take unto thee a wife of whoredoms and children of whoredoms: for the land hath committed great whoredom, departing from the Lord." *Hosea 1:2* (If the sexual mores of biblical days can be judged by the number of times references are made to prostitutes and whores, they do not earn a very high rating.)

The books of Hosea and the remaining prophets contain the same burning words of condemnation, the same insane ravings, the same bloody metaphors, and the same repulsive accounts of visions found in the writings of all the prophets. The reader cannot but be aghast at their inclusion in a collection of books labelled the Word of God.

Reeling from the horrors of other parts of the Bible, readers must now ask their sensibilities to recover from such passages as: "Their flesh shall consume away while they stand upon their feet, and their eyes shall consume away in their holes, and their tongue shall consume away in their mouth." *Zech. 14:12* And: "There shall the fire devour thee; the sword shall cut thee off, it shall eat thee up like the cankerworm. . . ." *Nahum 3:15* And: "Their bows also shall dash the young men to pieces; and they shall have no pity on the fruit of the womb; their eye shall not spare children." *Isaiah 13:18* And: "They shall eat every man the flesh of his own arm." *Isaiah 9:20* Such is the nature of the prophecies of the prophets.

After the Persian king Cyrus, whom many Jews regarded as the long-awaited Messiah Deliverer, permits the Jews to return to Palestine in 538 B.C. and rebuild the temple at Jerusalem, the prophets Haggai and Zechariah appear on the scene to encourage the people in the task of restoring the Holy City to its former magnificence. They foretell the glory that is to come and the fate of all Gentiles who do not accept the Jewish Lord. Zechariah is another of the prophets who are subject to architectural visions containing dimensions. He has a direct line of communication to the great Architect in the sky.

———⟫·◆·⟪———

The small country of Palestine in biblical times must have been overrun with prophets. Mention is made many times of great numbers of them and of "sons of the prophets" travelling about in groups. There is a confrontation between *450* prophets of Baal under Jezebel's protection and Elijah, on one occasion, and Jezebel has at least *400* more in her court. *I Kings 18* Just before that, Obadiah hides *100* prophets of the Lord in a cave. *I Kings 18:4* After all, prophets didn't have to work.

As Saul is en route to be anointed king: "Behold a company of prophets met him; and the Spirit of God came upon him, and he prophesied among them." *I Sam. 10:10* These prophets were "coming down from the high place with a psaltery, and a tabret, and a pipe, and a harp . . ." as Samuel had predicted. *I Sam. 10:5* Apparently these prophets are *per*formers rather than *re*formers.

A company of prophets accompanied by Samuel is seen "prophesying" by Saul's messengers, so the Spirit of the Lord comes upon the messengers and *they* prophesy. A second and a third group of messengers do the same. Then Saul also prophesies after the "Spirit of the Lord" comes upon him. He even strips naked and prophesies before Samuel, lying down naked all day and night. "Wherefore they say, Is Saul also among the prophets?" *I Sam. 19:20–24* That's as far as the Bible goes with that episode, which takes place while Saul is pursuing David, and it's probably just as well.

But David also prophesies: "Moreover, David and the captains of the host separated to the service of the sons of Asaph, and of Heman, and of Jeduthun, who should prophesy with harps, with psalteries, and with cymbals." *I Chron. 25:1* After all, David did play the harp and is supposed to have written most of the Psalms, although at least one concerns the Babylonian captivity: "By the rivers of Babylon, there we sat down, yea, we wept, when we remembered Zion. We hanged our harps upon the willows in the midst thereof. For there they that carried us away captive required of us a song . . . O daughter of Babylon, who art to be destroyed; happy shall he be, that rewardeth thee as thou hast served us. Happy shall he be, that taketh and dasheth thy little ones against the stones." *Psalm 137* Even a harp accompaniment couldn't enhance such lyrics, and the attention of the laity is seldom called to them.

———⟫·◆·⟪———

The Lord tolerates no one who uses divination, no "observer of times," no enchanter, no witch, no charmer, no wizard, no seer, and no "consulter with familiar spirits": "For all that do these things are an abomination unto the

Lord." *Deut. 18:11,12 Prophets* win approval as long as the Lord chooses them and they aren't *false*.

Of false prophets there are many, to no one's surprise. Even the New Testament has its deceivers: "For such are false apostles." *II Cor. 11:13* Moses deals with them handily: "If there arise among you a prophet . . . spake unto thee, saying, Let us go after other gods, which thou hast not known . . . Thou shalt not hearken unto the words of that prophet . . . for the Lord your God proveth you, to know whether ye love the Lord." *Deut. 13:1–3* The God of Moses is very insecure and is constantly embarking upon testing programs in order to reassure himself, and with good reason, for the Israelites were frequently falling by the wayside.

Some prophets are false through no fault of their own. In a story of treachery that makes the Lord despicable beyond belief, he is depicted as the instigator of a plot to bring about the death in battle of King Ahab: "And the Lord said, Who shall persuade Ahab, that he may go up and fall at Ramoth-gilead? . . . And there came forth a spirit, and stood before the Lord, and said, I will persuade him . . . I will go forth, and I will be a lying spirit in the mouth of all his prophets. And he (the Lord) said, Thou shalt persuade him, and prevail also: go forth and do so." *I Kings 22:20–23* (How can anyone ever "trust in God"?)

But the poor prophets—for them it's Catch 22, for the justice meted out to them is right in line with typical biblical justice: "The prophets prophesy lies in my name . . . By sword and famine shall those prophets be consumed." *Jer. 14:14–15* And: "If the prophet be deceived . . . I the Lord have deceived that prophet, and I will stretch out my hand . . . and will destroy him." *Ez. 14:9* Again: "Mine hand shall be upon the prophets that divine lies." *Ez. 13:9*

The prophet Jeremiah also has heard the Lord complain: "From the prophet even unto the priest every one dealeth falsely." *Jer. 8:10* But how are the people to distinguish between true and false prophets? Moses relays, from the mouth of the Lord, a test that can be used successfully, however tardily: "When a prophet speaketh in the name of the Lord, if the thing follow not, nor come to pass, that is the thing which the Lord hath not spoken, but the prophet hath spoken it presumptuously." *Deut. 18:22* And: "Even that prophet shall die." *Deut. 18:20* It behooves the prophet not to get his signals crossed, although it might conceivably at times require quite a few years to determine whether a prophet was on the up-and-up. Not surprising, too, that biblical prophecies come in all shapes and sizes of ambiguity.

⟹◆⟸

Prophets are accused of having other failings besides deceitfulness, as God speaks through Isaiah: "The priest and the prophet have erred in strong

268 <i>Born Again Skeptic's Guide To The Bible</i>

drink . . . they err in vision, they stumble in judgment." *Isaiah 28:7* And he also unburdens himself to Jeremiah: "For both prophet and priest are pro-fane . . . I have seen also in the prophets of Jerusalem an horrible thing; they commit adultery, and walk in lies." *Jer. 23:11,14* It's just possible that God had spotted Isaiah strolling about in the altogether for three years. *Isaiah 20:3* Or he may have heard gossip about Isaiah and a member of the opposite sex: "And I went unto the prophetess; and she conceived, and bare a son." *Isaiah 8:3*

⇒•◆•⇐

Not only are the prophets less than perfect in their behavior; they are no bet-ter informed about the nature of the universe than the average man on the street of their day. Credited by Jesus and Christendom with an ability to foresee events as many as 1,000 or more years in the future, they, like Jesus himself, have no inkling that the world will be found to be a sphere that revolves and moves in a yearly path around the sun, that the sun does not go "up and down," and that the moon emits no light of its own.

Describing the Day of the Lord, a favorite theme of the prophets, Isaiah warns Babylon: "The *moon* shall not cause her light to shine." *Isaiah 13:10* (Incidentally he predicts that from that time Babylon "shall never be inhab-ited, neither shall it be dwelt in from generation to generation; neither shall the Arabian pitch tent there, . . . But wild beasts of the desert shall lie there." *Isaiah 13:20,21* Wishful thinking repeatedly expressed by the prophets is that Gentile nations will all eventually be desolate.)

The prophet Habakkuk refers to Joshua's claim of a miracle without so much as a snicker: "The sun and moon stood still in their habitation." *Hab. 3:11* And the prophecies of The Revelation include: "And (Satan) shall go out to deceive the nations which are in the four *quarters* of the earth." *Rev. 20:8* St. John's prophetic vision, accompanied by instruction to record it for a warning to all people, reveals to him in vivid symbolism all that will take place at the end of the world ("things which must shortly come to pass" *Rev. 1:1*) but no hint of discoveries that will intervene, such as the existence of the continents of North and South America and the Arctic and Antarctic, elec-tricity, telegraph, radio, telephone, television, atomic energy, and a thousand other wonders of the *future*, the field in which the prophets, as well as Jesus, are experts, according to the Bible.

⇒•◆•⇐

Yes, there are prophetesses. A few token ones are spoken of in the scriptures of both Testaments, and one is even a heroine. Deborah, also a Judge of Israel, helps Barak in a battle to free Israel from the hands of the king of

Canaan, then composes a song about the victory. *Judges 4,5* And in the New Testament there is this reference: "And the same man had four daughters, virgins, which did prophesy." *Acts 21:9* Virgins are easily identified as such in the pages of the Bible.

⟫•◇•⟪

Prophets are often called Sons of Man in the Bible. Jesus calls himself both a prophet and the Son of Man. *Luke 12:10 Luke 13:33*

⟫•◇•⟪

Jesus calls John the Baptist a prophet, even says that John is Elijah returned to earth, but John denies it and corrects Jesus: "I am the Voice of one crying in the Wilderness." *Matt. 11:14 John 1:21* This is an expression straight out of Isaiah: "The voice of him that crieth in the Wilderness. Prepare ye the way of the Lord." *Isaiah 40:3* Jesus needs to prove that John is Elijah because of a prophecy from Malachi: "Behold, I will send you Elijah the prophet before the coming of the great and dreadful day of the Lord." *Mal. 4:5*

⟫•◇•⟪

Throughout the Bible and in some of Jesus's preaching and that of the apostles much condemnation is expressed for those who have "killed the prophets." Jesus even goes so far as to say, with what seems to be a great show of justice maligned: "The blood of all the prophets, which was shed from the foundation of the world, may be required of this generation. Verily I say unto you it shall be required of this generation." *Luke 11:50* Here again is encountered the biblical principle of human sacrifice of the innocent to make reparation.

⟫•◇•⟪

Paul rebukes his congregations for being too eager to put their piety on display: "How is it then, brethren? When ye come together, everyone of you hath a psalm, hath a doctrine, hath a tongue, hath a revelation, hath an interpretation." (He might have been chiding the Church today in the interest of ecumenism.) He cautions them to show a little restraint: "Let the prophets speak two or three . . . If anything be revealed to another that sitteth by, let the first hold his peace. For ye may all prophesy one by one . . . And the spirits of the prophets are subject to the prophets. For God is not the author of confusion, but of peace, as in all churches of the saints." *I Cor. 14:29–33* Everybody wanted to get into the act, but these chatterers are all men. Women don't speak in Paul's churches. They can't make sense.

⟫•◇•⟪

What a testimony to ignorance and superstition is this incredible book The Bible! Because it is proclaimed to be the infallible revealed word of the Lord of the Universe, no segment of it may be held up to scorn, even though that segment can be shown to have its roots in irrational attempts to penetrate the unknown. The pagan practice of consulting gods and forecasting by means of divination cannot be (anymore than can exorcism) derided by present-day Judaism and Christianity, for the Lord himself endorsed it. Ezekiel tells of a specific command: "Again he (the Lord) said unto me: Prophesy upon these bones . . . So I prophesied as I was commanded: and as I prophesied, there was a noise, and behold a shaking, and the bones came together . . . Then he said unto me, Prophesy unto the wind . . ." *Ez. 37:4–9*

Because the Jews placed much confidence in what their prophets foretold, or were traditionally *supposed* to have foretold, about a Messiah, and because they were constantly on the watch for him, Jesus was compelled, either in fact or in the New Testament role assigned to him, to pattern his activities after the prophecies and, at the same time, call attention to the similarities between himself and the subject of those prophecies. Thus the prophecies were made use of, either by Jesus himself, or by the cult which grew up around him (or around an invented Christ) to win acceptance of him by the Jews as the one who fulfilled those predictions.

There were untold numbers of such prophecies, and it would be difficult for any personality to conform to all of them, and even then they would have to be opportunely interpreted. In truth, various Jewish Messiah impostors *have* had followers for periods of time both before and after Jesus is presumed to have lived.

These prophecies are continually being dragged out in the scriptures of the New Testament, often by Jesus himself, to imply that they fit Jesus; however, sometimes they present difficulties of conformity, and these difficulties are no doubt one of the reasons for the rejection of Jesus by the Jews.

When John the Baptist denied being Elijah returned from the dead, the prophecy in Malachi remained unfulfilled and Jesus could not be the Messiah who was to usher in the "Day of the Lord." Yet Jesus had claimed that John was that resurrected prophet. Jesus makes several statements that suggest he recognizes the dilemma in which he finds himself throughout his ministry. Following his healing of "great multitudes," he "charged them that they should not make him known: That it might be fulfilled which was spoken by Esaias (Isaiah) the prophet, saying, Behold my servant, whom I have chosen; my beloved, in whom my soul is well pleased . . . He shall not strive, nor cry; *neither shall any man hear his voice in the streets." Matt. 12:15–19* Again he finds himself pressed: "Nevertheless I must walk today, and tomorrow, and the day following: for it cannot be that a prophet perish out of Jerusalem." *Luke 13:23*

The content of some prophecies has been misrepresented, whether or not intentionally, to make it useful in establishing a prophetical basis for Christianity. The classic example is found in Isaiah 7 and 8 and concerns the true meaning of the scriptural prophecy: "Behold, a virgin shall conceive, and bear a son, and shall call his name Immanuel." Isaiah is obviously not referring to Jesus, if and when the passage is put into context and its background explained as part of an incident that Isaiah is relating and in which he had a role as messenger to royalty.

Syria and Israel form an alliance to move against King Ahaz of Judah, and God sends Isaiah to reassure Ahaz and give the king a sign that Syria and Israel shall not prevail and shall be forsaken of both their kings. The sign, at first refused by Ahaz, is the above passage about the virgin. To make the sign come true, Isaiah then visits a virgin prophetess who bears the prophesied child. This shabby story has been seized upon to apply to Jesus. Incidentally, Ahaz was soundly defeated.

The book of Isaiah also contains other prophecies which Christian theologians choose to stress to verify the divinity of Jesus. Whether the rantings found in at least part of this book are the actual product of a fanatic by the name of Isaiah is meaningless unless one is willing to accept the premise that he is speaking for God. His tale of being chosen to do so by having a live coal applied to his lips in the inevitable vision is without verification, as necessarily are all such dreamy revelations, and there remains the question of what, besides his own reported assertion that he has a direct line to God, should cause one to reject the possibility that he is just another self-appointed spokesman for a deity that exists in his imagination. Or that he is actually a later scripture-forger (or two).

Isaiah's dependability comes under fire when one considers that he was wrong in another of his predictions. He wrongly pronounces King Hezekiah to be on his death-bed, then has to turn medicine-man with a lump of figs when he fails to foresee that God will change his mind and give the king 15 more years. (Because the old-time Jews wouldn't even believe God, Isaiah gives a sign by causing the king's sun-dial shadow to go backward ten degrees, a sign that was not without its drawbacks, since from then on Hezekiah's sun-dial couldn't have been too reliable. With the seriousness always assigned to every minute passage of scripture, some sect has probably been founded on the assumption that application of a fig-pack will cure terminal illnesses. Stranger conclusions have been drawn from Bible anecdotes.)

Isaiah's rapturous forecast of the reunion of Israel and Judah at the end of civil war between them didn't come about, and the northern kingdom was gradually assimilated by its conqueror Assyria. This reunion, the subsequent establishment of Zion at the expense of the Gentiles, and the recognition of the Jewish Lord as divine ruler of the whole world, are the sum total of Isaiah's predictions. And Bible passages forecasting a prince and savior would seem far more likely to apply to the time when the Jewish nation would once more be united and supreme (which the prophets hoped would be soon) than to a date from 400 to 800 years in the future.

Further scripture from Isaiah, as well as from the other books of the prophets, has been pounced upon as "proof" that Jesus had been the subject of prophecy. The following is another pulpit favorite: "For unto us a child is born, unto us a son is given: and the government shall be upon his shoulder: and his name shall be called Wonderful, Counsellor, The mighty God, The everlasting Father, the Prince of Peace." Here is another example of biblical passages being taken out of context. The probability that this verse refers only to a future king of a restored Jewish nation is substantiated by the very next verse: "Of the increase of his government and peace there shall be no end, upon the throne of David, and upon his kingdom, to order it, and to establish it with judgment and with justice from henceforth even for ever." *Isaiah 9:6,7*

The succeeding chapter deals with the continuing struggle involving Syria, Israel, and Judah, thus reinforcing the implied timetable of this prediction. And another consideration regarding the gist of verses 6 and 7 is that Jesus denied any connection with government and deliberately separated his ministry from civil authority. Isaiah further identifies the ruler-to-come in chapter 11: "And there shall come forth a rod out of the stem of Jesse . . . And the spirit of the Lord shall rest upon him, the spirit of wisdom and understanding, the spirit of counsel and might, the spirit of knowledge . . . And it shall come to pass in that day, that the Lord shall set his hand again the second time to recover the remnant of his people, which shall be left, from Assyria, and from Egypt, and from Pathros, and from Cush, and from Elam, and from Shinar, and from Hamath and from the islands of the sea. And he shall set up an ensign for the nations."

From all this it must be concluded that Isaiah is referring to a time hoped-for in the near future. In chapters that follow he predicts the fall of other nations and other cities when Zion shall be triumphant. They all expand his opening forecast: "Zion shall be redeemed with judgment, and her converts with righteousness, And the destruction of the transgressors, and of the sinners shall be together, and they that forsake the Lord shall be consumed." *Isaiah 1:27,28*

When Isaiah and the other prophets speak of the child of a virgin (except in Isaiah 7 where the virgin is a specific prophetess), they may well be indicating a prince or king of the mother-country Zion. Nations in the Bible are often spoken of as virgins or even whores: "The virgin, the daughter of Zion, hath despised thee." *Isaiah 37:22* Jeremiah uses the same metaphor: "For the virgin daughter (Jerusalem) is broken." *Jer. 14:17* And: "Again I will build thee, and thou shalt be built, O virgin of Israel." *Jer. 31:4* Jeremiah also refers to the king of Zion that Isaiah describes: "Is not the Lord in Zion? is not her king in her?" *Jer. 8:19*

With impunity Christianity has appropriated all the prophecies that predict a redeemer or prince born of a virgin to prove that Jesus was that prophesied king, whereas from the above scripture it is obvious that the Hebrew prophets were more than likely looking forward to a descendant of David as the child of Israel (the virgin). This explains all the talk of the "king" or "prince" who is going to re-establish the kingdom of Israel and bring the Gentiles under the domination of the Hebrew Lord. The Prophet Micah records words of the Lord that bear out the above theory: "Be in pain, and labour to bring forth, O daughter of Zion . . ." *Micah 4:10* A few verses later, the "ruler of Israel" is to come out of Bethlehem when "she which travaileth hath brought forth." *Micah 5:2,3* The succeeding verses describe how the new king will restore the glory of Israel.

Anyone examining these old prophecies and comparing them to Jesus's words and the writings of the New Testament must assume that there was collusion on the part of unknowns to make Jesus fit the prophecies (or the other way around) or that there was attempt on Jesus's part to shape himself to the prophecies, either because he actually did fit some of them, or out of a conscious effort to establish himself as the long-awaited Messiah of the Jews. To accept the premise that Jesus was prophesied as the Savior of the World in the Old Testament, one would have to give the prophesies much more scope than they seem to warrant in the light of the probability of what the prophets were hoping for, which was the pre-eminence of the Jewish nation.

It is clear from the content of the books of the prophets that the prophets themselves were super-patriots, whose concern was the welfare and longevity of Israel as a nation and her power position in relation to the Gentiles. They were not starry-eyed idealists who wanted to save the whole world from sin, and it does not seem likely that they would overlook the present problems of their nation and envision a time when God himself would come down to earth in human form to carry out some unlikely scheme, the purpose of which was to make it possible for Jew and Gentile alike to share a heavenly home. Indeed, the impression to be gleaned from the ravings of the prophets is that an integrated Paradise would be the last thing they would even tolerate. After all, their very laws forbade even any contact with Gentiles. No, their prophesied Redeemer would naturally fit their personal prejudices and aspirations. They were no different from the patriots of other nations.

———◆———

The books of the prophets all sound very much alike, and actually they all sing the same tune: The Jews have sinned, chiefly by worshipping idols, and a wrathful Jehovah will punish them, or is punishing them, for these "transgressions" by allowing them to be conquered by other nations. When they have completed atonement for this wickedness, they will be allowed to rebuild Jerusalem and re-establish the Jewish nation. This Zion will have a wonderful person, a Messiah redeemer, for a king, who will be raised up by the Lord. At this time great tribulation will be visited upon the Gentiles, who have persecuted the Jews in the past, and there will be a "new" earth ruled over by Jews under their God.

These prophets do not claim that their new king will be the Son of God in fact, but only that he will be of the line of David: "For the children of Israel shall abide many days without a king, and without a prince. . . . afterward shall the children of Israel return, and seek the Lord their God, and David their king." *Hosea 3:4,5* One reason that the Jews did not accept Jesus as their Messiah hundreds of years after the prophecies may have been that the Jewish nation had not been reunited or freed. They were not looking for a heavenly kingdom, just hoping for one of their own here on earth.

Old Testament prophecies have different connotations when they are quoted in the New Testament. The Day of the Lord seems to mean the time of the liberation of the Jews, in the Old Testament, but in the New it seems to indicate Jesus's second coming. Salvation of the Jews seems to refer in the Old Testament to the liberation of the Jews from the Gentile conquerors and the readmission of the Jews into the Lord's good graces. Salvation in the New Testament is forgiveness of sin and eternal life in heaven. The earthly kingdom of the Jews of the Old Testament becomes the kingdom of God in the New. The savior of the Old Testament is the anticipated new king of the House of David who will reign over Zion. The Savior of the New Testament is not just this prophesied Messiah but a divine Redeemer from sin who reunites God and humankind. The avenging *Yahweh* will punish the *Gentiles*. The Christian *Father* is also an avenger, but upon the *unbeliever*, and he is actually not very different from *Yahweh* in the sense that he still promises to show favoritism to Jews: "But glory, honour, and peace . . . to the Jew first, and also to the Gentile." *Romans 2:10*

———◆———

If such wild-eyed, dirty, half-dressed maniacs as the biblical prophets were to walk the streets today with such ranting and raving at the tips of their tongues and pens as are found in the passages of the Bible concerning them, orders for their psychiatric examinations would follow complaints from the public about their possible excessive use of drugs and alcohol. A few might be able to find some recognition as purveyors of oriental wisdom, but for the most part evangelists today in the Western World are well-dressed, refined, well-to-do orators who by their personalities and efficient organizations and exposure through the media are able to attract vast audiences more than willing to confer upon them, as the Bible does upon the prophets, confidence in their assumed role as special oracles of the Divine.

These several modern-day social reformers and messengers of God, in the tradition of their prophet role-models, still tell people how God wants them to behave, what will happen to them if they don't conform to those rules, and just how imminent and fearful is the *Christian* Day of the Lord. Although some of them profess to have healing powers, few lay claim to having parted the waters of a river or raised anyone from the dead. If they have elaborate dreams and visions, most of them do not submit tales of their trances to the credulity of the public, although Mahomet and Joseph Smith played Joan of Arc with remarkable success in her capacity for hearing "voices."

<hr />

Volumes have been written to prove the divinity of Jesus by the Old Testament prophecies, but surely the final argument must come down to what the Jews themselves believe. The prophets and the prophecies are, after all, theirs; the Messiah their heritage. What better authority for judging whether Jesus fulfilled those promises than the Jews themselves?

Their answer has been an emphatic denial that Jesus was the anointed one who would be identified by the prophet Elias (Elijah). Although Jesus said that John the Baptist had proclaimed him the Messiah and that John was Elias, John actually expressed doubt that Jesus was the Messiah, and John also vehemently refused to be exploited by Jesus. When asked point-blank if he himself was Elias (returned from the dead) John replied, "I am not." *Luke 7:19,20 John 1:20,21*

The ultimate conclusion is inevitable. Either Jesus was not the Messiah he claimed to be, or he was not powerful enough to convince the Chosen People that he was the prophesied redeemer. A less than omnipotent God.

The Way We Were

How memory cuts away the years,
And how clean the
picture comes.
—Jean Starr Untermeyer

The Way We Were

Would you believe 12 pounds? That was my weight when I was born at home near the railroad tracks in Sumner, Iowa, on January 12, 1915. I had two older brothers and was subsequently to acquire a sister and another brother, twenty years younger than my oldest sibling. My father and mother had grown up on farms near Sumner, Iowa, a small town in the Iowa cornbelt, but neither was enamoured of the backbreaking rural life of the turn of the century and had become "town folks" with all possible speed.

Shortly after my arrival, they moved into a new two-story house in Sumner, where I spent my first 13 years. Many of our relatives on both sides lived either in Sumner, on neighboring farms, or in nearby towns. My grandparents and "my uncles and my cousins and my aunts" enriched my life to such a degree that today I am an advocate of the family gatherings and relationships that were popular when I was growing up but that seem to have become the victim of a busier time.

We didn't wonder "who we were." We were a certain person's child, So-and-so's grandchild, somebody's niece, one of the Hurmences. We *belonged* to a wide circle of love, and we were important to a lot of people. After church on many Sundays we all met at my grandparents' homes for a big dinner, but the largest meeting of the clan was probably on the maternal side. The four generations, led by my "grape" grandmother (a little German woman who still talked broken English) merged into one life-system. We children became conscious of the inevitable progression from infancy to old age, and we saw that there was love and respect possible for all. The ties were very visible, but they did not preclude a sense of self. Narcissism hadn't yet become a way of life.

The Hurmence family owned the Sumner Telephone Company and the local power plant until my father became fearful of electrical accidents and gave up the power business. We owned the first long-distance lines in our area and operated the West Union and New Hampton exchanges. Ice storms were a cause of great anxiety. Although one of my father's brothers was in charge of maintenance, responsibility was shared.

After school, when I had enough courage, I would climb the flight of stairs to the switchboard area and my father's office to ask for a dime, which he would like to pretend for a while was too outrageous a sum for a child of the 1920's to request. I always came away with the money, and I finally realized, much later in life, that I could have been the recipient of many more favors, if I had realized sooner that an old softie was in hiding behind the occasional outbursts of temper that usually sent me to Mother with my requests.

Like other pioneers, my folks had homesteaded in North Dakota, along with two of my Dad's brothers and a sister. This venture was instigated by my Grandfather Hurmence, whose untimely death was all that prevented him from becoming one of the wealthiest men in our part of Iowa, thanks to a bold recognition of the many opportunities open to entrepreneurs in this land of promise, and thanks, too, to children who adored him and agreed to help carry out his ideas. He built small cabins in adjoining corners of three quarter-sections, and my mother and oldest brother lived out the required time in one, while an uncle and aunt waited out blizzards and a prairie fire in the other two. My father had to remain in Iowa, and it was a long year of separation for my parents, broken only by the few times Dad could make the trip from Sumner to New Salem.

On one of my grandfather's visits to the homesteaders, Mother complained about a low door frame which made it necessary to duck one's head upon entering and leaving the cabin. Remarking that such inconveniences helped to build character, Grandfather chided, "Humble yourself a little, just humble yourself." Waving his philosophy like a flag, he made his exit, soundly banging his head on what was to have been Mother's humility-builder. I don't know which would be missed the more by those to whom families are meaningful—the sense of family itself or the priceless family jokes. In my own family today, one or two phrases connected with familiar situations bring on hilarious shrieks. Oh, yes, and there are the home movies. Everyone has to be present at the showing to defend some article of apparel or some derided nervous mannerism. ("You've had that on the last three years. Don't you own another shirt?" "Oh, oh, there go those eyebrows again.")

My life in Sumner up to the eighth grade was filled with such happiness as only a small town could afford a child. School was easy for me, and teachers seldom assigned homework, so at 4:15 I was free during school months to do pretty much as I pleased. And weekends and summer vacation were anticipated with the realization that few restrictions would be imposed. The younger generation of our neighborhood, and often from other parts of town, appeared as if led by some pied piper, to gather in groups and gangs ready for what our parents must have assumed would be harmless activities.

An invisible magnet always attracted at least five or six of us, usually many more.

Often some of the gang were my cousins who lived on the street behind us. I was a tomboy, as girls who didn't play with dolls were called in those days (with a resigned shake of the head). Numbers made a wide variety of recreation possible, and we called upon our inventive genius to create any equipment we needed. We made our baseballs by wrapping string around black walnuts, and of course we fashioned our own kites—which, incidentally, hardly ever flew, even after yards of tail-strips had been either added or subtracted.

Many summer Saturdays young people from all parts of town gradually assembled at the Lutheran Church, which had a broad paved entrance leading to a wide flight of about 20 steps. This area served as our stadium. Roller skating was the spectator sport here, and younger kids looked on with secret admiration for the skill exhibited by older experts in fancy whirls and figures. Whistling "Barney Google," with his "goo-goo-googely eyes," some show-offs performed on two-wheel skates. We wore our elusive skate keys around our necks, as we skated on Sumner's sidewalks, but we also liked to roll hoops with a T-shaped "pusher" made of laths. The skate key was a summertime indispensable, second only to an old salt shaker for green-apple addicts. Mothers warned their children who feasted on this forbidden fruit that cholera morbus could be expected to strike them down in the bloom of youth, if they persisted in abusing their stomachs in this way, but to my knowledge this impending disaster, like the ever-hovering end-of-the-world, failed to materialize. Then, as now, preachers and evangelists kept everyone at differing degrees of "ready," and many a night I hopped out of bed to get down on my knees, thinking better of my earlier cheating—saying the "Now I lay me's" without assuming a kneeling position. God watched even the littlest of sinners who didn't show the proper submission. I certainly didn't *love* God—I was scared to death of him, even though I didn't worry much about sinning.

People of the area liked to mingle. Wednesday nights were band concert nights, and the stores were open. Everybody strolled the two blocks of "downtown" exchanging greetings, or sat in cars which had been, with foresight, parked there earlier in the day. Band concert night was an especial treat for farm families, and crop conditions and the progress of the kitchen garden were cause for either cheerful or gloomy conversations. If corn wasn't "knee-high by the Fourth of July," this was an alarming departure from the norm. A farmer was apt to be judged, however, more by the checkerboard straightness of his corn rows than by the production of his fields. An independent breed, Iowa farmers, persuaded by the government to take some acres out of corn cultivation, resorted to planting the hills a little closer together, thereby growing the same amount of corn as before, if not more. Who can blame them?

While our parents renewed acquaintances on these Wednesday nights and while the local musicians played bravely away to much appreciative horn-honking, we children picked up our own friends. I was always given at least a dime, which led to an agonizing decision—shall it be a sack of popcorn and a candy bar, popcorn and a bottle of pop, two candy bars? Oh Henry bars were *out*. They cost 10 cents all by themselves.

Often we were given ticket money for a movie at the opera house, and that was usually augmented by a nickel for popcorn. If you were a friend of the popcorn machine attendant, you could persuade her to pour on a little extra butter. Mary Pickford or Hoot Gibson on the screen competed apparently all unknowingly with the background music provided by a local pianist. How the movie house came to be called the opera house is a real puzzler, since opera, in the accepted sense at least, was the last form of public entertainment that would ever reach Sumner, and there seemed little need to provide a place for it.

Vaudeville did come occasionally to the opera house, and it was also the setting for declamation contests or for local talent shows. Whistling was a skill displayed by some performers, a skill genteel enough to admit of participation by respected women of the community. Nobody laughed! The "readings" might be humorous or very dramatic, and there were one or two teachers in town who trained would-be "readers" in effective technique. I remember one unusually moving performance about a victim of a miscarriage of justice that made such an impression on me that I still oppose capital punishment unconditionally.

High school plays and operettas were well-attended by townspeople, who were likely to be generous with uncritical applause. There was town loyalty for its own.

Once a year the Chautauqua came to town. That took care of the culture. But there were also other less elevating tent shows. In spite of these occasional glimpses of the world outside, Sumner was as provincial as the somewhat limited means of communication of the times necessitated. Automobiles were just coming into broader use, and the main road into town, known as "the pike," was merely gravelled. The Chicago Northwestern railroad, which ran through the middle of town, was the most dependable link to places of any distance.

As a result of this "isolation," Sumner citizens sponsored many community functions and celebrations. The city park on the banks of the Little Wapsipinicon was often the setting. Sumner has not abandoned this tradition. On a recent visit I attended a city-wide talent show, with a "hometown boy" m.c., that was anything but "corny." It may be a longing for identification with a compatible group that has given the small town nostalgic appeal and led to the popularity of communes and cults, in recent years.

Sumner's park was also the scene of individual group activities and picnics. The long tables provided under the trees would be lined up end to end to hold the fried chicken, potato salads, apple pies, and watermelons that were the picnic staples before diets took all the fun out of eating. Family reunions of prodigious size were the order of the day, and the automobile was making it possible for family members to come from longer distances to attend them.

As a child, I gloried in the prevailing culture. That is not to make a significant comment on its social implications, pro or con, or on the worth of the various roles played out in that culture. I leave all such evaluation to the psychologists.

I have played up the part that the city park played in all our lives, but for everyday usage as a play arena for children, nothing was a substitute for the vacant lots that for some reason nobody ever seemed to want to build on. Our games of tag were significant for their complete lack of discrimination between the sexes. Girls and boys had equal qualifications for Pump Pump Pull Away and Skunk Hole and Red Rover. Actually, recreation enjoyed by youngsters in those days may have been marked by less conscious competition between the sexes than is common today, perhaps owing to the fact that attention was seldom called to it. Such attention is needed to bring about better social conditions, but it does have an unavoidable tendency to polarize, at least for a time.

Woman's liberation had not yet become an issue in Sumner. Women, men, and children played their traditional roles with no realization that any other order could ever be proposed. Women were guardians of the home and children, and any remaining energy went into club and church work. Men were the providers and the important persons who accomplished things. At family gatherings, women prepared the food and looked after the children, while the men sat on the porch smoking cigars, waiting to be called to be first at the table. Women and children ate last. I resented that setup, but I haven't seen a lot of change. (Men still thank the Lord for meals prepared by women.)

My brothers had first chance at the car, even after I could drive. From childhood on they lived under relaxed rules and were forgiven most mischief because "boys will be boys." It was impossible for a girl born in 1915 and living in a German community not to realize that she didn't rate quite as high as the boys. Women and girls could seldom rise above second place, even if they "tried harder."

My mother always kept our home neat and clean, but unless it was her turn to entertain the Ladies Aid or Missionary Society, we children had the run of the place. We built endless tents, jumped on beds when she changed the sheets, roller-skated (as learners) in the upstairs hall, slid down the stairs on rugs, built trains with chairs, and mixed up sticky kettles of flour-and-water paste. After supper (we ate our dinner at noon) and Sunday afternoons we played games of Flinch, Parcheesi, and Touring, accompanied by much arguing about rules. With no television, and radio just a-borning, we were obligated to provide our own entertainment. When we got our first radio set (antiseptically called a Radiodyne) we used to huddle around it and take turns listening on the crackling earphones to KDKA. Family friends had to be called in to share the amazement. Radio reception was to improve rapidly, however.

Most people had Victrola phonographs, but we had an Edison *graphophone* in a cabinet with a hinged top. You could listen to "The Pirates of Penzance," but first you had to feel like winding up the "talking machine," as purists still called it. We all took lessons on musical instruments, and naturally that included the piano, since every living room had to have one to hold the family portraits. Mother had learned to play on their family organ, and our family "sings" gave me a legitimate excuse to yield to the urge I felt to break into impromptu rendition of all the popular sheet music of the '20's, as well as the oldies from *The Golden Book of Favorite Songs*. It's not true that you can be anything you want to be. To be a singer, you need to be able to do more than carry a tune. But with Mother at the piano, I worked off some of my frustration. "Beautiful Ohio" was my favorite, but at the end of our concert, Mother obliged with the lyricless "Trip to Niagara."

My father preferred to sit out the song-fests reading one of the books that meant so much to him. Formal education stopped for him with a high school diploma, as it did for most of his contemporaries, but throughout his life his remarkable ingestion of "book learning," coupled with a gift for remembering the contents of a printed page, resulted in a comprehension on his part of many areas of human experience and an encyclopedic memory bank of significant facts and trivia that made him a formidable opponent in the arguments he loved to invoke. His concentration when he was reading was so intense that surrounding bedlam would go completely unnoticed.

One of our favorite indoor pastimes was playing caroms with cues on a board at table height, around which our feet made not so much as a single print on our Wilton rugs. It was impossible to wear out a Wilton, except at the seams. It is a tribute to my mother's sense of priorities that, at a time when a woman might be judged by the perfection of her housekeeping, she imposed so few rules about what we children were permitted to do within her domain. At times she did have a maid to help with the housework. In Sumner we called them hired girls, another of those matter-of-fact appellations that were employed with unfeeling disregard for the sensibilities of others. All the Archie Bunker slang designations for people in other categories from one's own were acceptable usage. (Hired girls were apt to be farm girls who wanted to live in town.)

Community attitudes were cruel and uncompromising. Church membership didn't make people more humane. Woe to the child with no father and the tart who dyed her hair. Eyes must be lowered by women and children as they passed the saloon. But such condemnation was not peculiar to the early 1900's. The self-righteous pass judgment in every time period, handily aided by the Bible.

Human derelicts and unfortunates were not always hidden in institutions, as they are today. Most of them were kept at home, and, although objects of sincere pity, they were shunned by all who didn't like to be reminded that "there, but for the grace of God, go I." (Religionists have never been ashamed to proclaim that their deity shows favoritism.) There was at least one demented creature I was warned to avoid.

It was also a time of dread if gypsies stopped off in Sumner. A myth was commonly believed that they stole, not only everything that wasn't nailed down, but helpless kiddies, as well. Mothers actually corralled their little ones behind locked doors, until these poor, maligned wanderers bowed to the Unwelcome sign and travelled on to similar receptions elsewhere.

We children had our own private terrors. My chief one was the local Catholic Church. Dark hints circulated among Protestants of mysterious rites that went on inside. The few Catholic children I knew were objects of disguised scrutiny on my part to detect any strange characteristic that might have been the mark of their religion. What I expected to find I have no idea. Unless it might have been a "C" branded on the forehead.

There was talk of the Ku Klux Klan, and we youngsters were properly apprehensive, although I doubt any of us knew what the Klan was. The fear that kept popping up and seemed the most likely to materialize was the repeated prediction that the end of the world was upon us. Some timorous fundamentalists were always awaiting it, either on hilltops or in caves. Actually, there could have been no immediate cause for alarm, since the event was momentarily expected, and the Bible says it will come as a thief in the night. So, the thing to do is expect it, and not worry, just as there is no reason to look for the Messiah until Elijah appears, very likely in his same departure chariot, to announce him.

This brings me to the large part the Methodist Church played in my youth. My parents were church members and supporters, with both their time and money, but they were not devout, and religion was not a part of our home life. Our social life, however, was geared to the Church, and we children often accompanied our parents to church suppers, activities, and parties, besides the regular church services on Sunday. What fun to creep around the empty pews and aisles, the study, and the choir loft and classrooms, while the grown-ups were busy in the basement! It was scary, too, as if some disembodied presence with flowing hair was watching from some mysterious throne in the sky. Zap! and it might be the end.

Once a week it was Sunday School and church and Epworth League at night. I liked the hymn singing but detested the sermons and prayers, during which I amused myself by imitating the preacher's gestures with a knotted handkerchief draped over my fingers, or by creating rubbings from the embossed titles of the hymn books. If my sister and I caught each other's eye, we broke into smothered giggles, which lasted until Mother caught *our* eye.

I took communion. Why not? Everybody else did, and I like grape juice. Besides, all those processions to the altar rail meant a shorter sermon and less strain on my ears, which were attuned to catch the first notes of the doxology, followed by the benediction, as pleasant to the ears as any audible reprieve. Not waiting for the preacher's handshake, I was free to dash for home and the Swiss steak simmering on the back burner. Home was only a block away, just far enough for the sanctification, so faithfully acquired, to rub off. I was left with a wonderful feeling of a different sort—one of relief. God was taken care of for another week.

Sumner Hurmences were Methodists, but the ancestral Heermans, Hermanse, Heermance family were Dutch Protestants (Dutch Reformed Church) who settled in Rhinebeck Province, Dutchess County, New York. My early ancestors had slaves, although it is not generally realized that slavery was very common in New York in pre-Revolutionary days. Of course the Bible did not denounce slavery—quite the opposite. So there was no reason the Church and slavery could not flourish side by side. The Roosevelt clan arrived at about the same time as the other Dutch settlers, along with the Vanderbilts. Some of these immigrants got rich.

Mother's people were German Protestants. They attended the Evangelical Church in town or the Union Evangelical Church in the country. My paternal grandmother was an independent, outspoken member of the Norman family. Her father and mother came to the United States from England, and she was haughty English to the core. The story is told that she refused for a time to move into the new farm home Grandfather built north of Sumner, but I don't vouch for its accuracy. This farm was a show-place with imported furniture. The barn, a source of pride to any farmer in a dairy country, was purported to have been an absolute marvel for its size and modern features, but both house and outbuildings have been destroyed by fire.

Grandfather Hurmence died before I was born, and my grandmother lived in town while I was growing up. When the family gathered there, I ran for the stereoptican viewer. I've been around the world in three-dimensional slides many times.

Our church had to have pledge-nights, at which the business men of the congregation would announce in front of everyone just how much their pocketbooks and gratitude for blessings received would permit them to give back to the Almighty. The Methodist Church didn't stress tithing, and I heard some indignant remarks from my father about those whose publicly announced intentions were not matched by actual fulfillment of the pledge. No doubt the heavenly bookkeeping system made due note of all such malingering. It was never clear to me whether bricks in the celestial mansions were subject to removal or promptly mortared in.

On Children's Day and at Christmas, in our church, the mothers were producers of a pageant with the children as performers, and this situation sometimes led to injured feelings among parents who felt not enough recognition had been given to the unique talents of their offspring and, not surprisingly, among the fledgling artists themselves, some of whom aspired to do more than just "brighten a corner." Most of the little budding saints, however, had to be persuaded against their will to don the improvised robes and assorted halos, wings, and crowns that biblical pageantry demanded. There were always a few whose juvenile charm and sprinkling of ability earned for them spots on the program for reciting the seasonally resurrected " 'Twas the Night Before Christmas" or rendering the novelty song with the delightfully-surprising ending: "When Apples Grow on the Lilac Tree."

When the Christmas program finally ended, the Methodist Santa Claus ho! ho! ho!ed his way out of a crepe paper fireplace and began his task of calling out the names of all young members of our congregation. When you heard your name in its proper place in the alphabet, you either bounded or sidled up to St. Nick to accept a sack containing candy and nuts and a beautiful orange. This was probably the only Santa Claus you were likely to see that year, and he was a little intimidating. In fact, he looked a lot like God.

Some indulgent parents arranged ahead of time for a doll or some especially attractive toy to be attached to the huge Christmas tree for presentation to their child, but gift-opening time at our house was Christmas morning. Still, Christmas Eve with our fellow Methodists was a tradition. The Church, if not religion, was a way of life for us.

Methodism purposely avoided any trappings that could be construed as smacking of anything but the plainest Protestantism. Church decor was positively spartan. There were no crosses, no religious pictures, no gold candle-sticks, no chancel accessories except for a golden-oak pulpit, and no velvet runners, and the preacher wore a suit exactly like those worn by laymen. The Lord had to make it on his own; there were no tender traps. No pipe organ lifted one to spiritual heights. The only deliberate aesthetic touch was in the stained glass windows that shed a soft light over the sanctuary, which was not without an uncluttered charm of its own.

I was very fond of our minister's wife, and she apparently took a liking to me. Having no children of her own, she seemed to enjoy my occasional vis-its and insisted on giving me free, destined to be fruitless, lessons on the 'cello. I can't believe I played a solo in church, as it is hard to imagine any-one with less musical promise than I showed.

My parents became quite friendly with this dedicated pair, and one sum-mer they joined us and another minister's family from a neighboring town on a camping trip to Mammoth Cave and Lincoln's birthplace in Kentucky. The temerity with which this venture was undertaken can be appreciated by con-sidering the unpredictable behavior of the products of the infant auto indus-try upon which we had to depend for our transportation. Although the Model T was a general favorite, we owned a Willys touring car. Rumors of wheels detaching themselves and of motors that balked at hills did not shake our confidence, and after all with two clergymen in the party—what better insurance? Each family had its own tent, and we all wore khaki knickers, shirts, and hats. Staying together on the highways was not unfeasible at 35 miles an hour. This trip was a treat for my father, who was a victim of Lincolnmania, but he paid dearly for it. Our tent, which attached to the car, had to be pitched every night in some park. When it rained, the "curtains" had to be put on the car. They had isinglass inserts. These first cars had no heaters, and I remember a winter trip of some distance when my brother and sister and I had to lie on the floor of the back seat under a fur robe to keep from freezing.

Bleak Iowa winters happened to saint and sinner alike. It seems now that we had snow all winter long, and my lower lip was usually cracked and bleed-ing during those cold months. Mother made a point of warning us not to put a wet tongue on cold metal, so I did that one day while standing in front of a railing before going into the meat market to buy 25-cents worth of round steak for supper. I left all the skin of my tongue on the railing, but that beat standing there till spring.

When the snow began to fall, farmers replaced the wheels on their wag-ons with sled runners. These wagons were horse-drawn, and the jingle of bells on the harnesses rang out in the crisp air, especially on Saturdays when trips to town were necessary to obtain supplies. Abandoning our own slides and ice skates, we of the younger generation put these excursions to our own use. It was time to "hop bob-sleds." Trotting along with the wagon, we jumped onto the runner frame, clinging for dear life to the high side boards. Hours of bumming such rides could be enjoyed by employing the shuttle system. Some drivers refused to cooperate, probably with our safety in mind.

Whether our parents were aware of the danger involved in many of our activities is a moot question. Once we left the house, we were more or less on our own, and a minimum of anxiety was shown about how we chose to amuse ourselves. We all learned to swim in a muddy hole of the creek that ran through the park. There were no lifeguards, but those who couldn't swim wore canvas water-wings. It seems to me now that we did risk injury on the bag swing. In fact, the one spanking I remember getting at the hands of my mother was after falling from the swing platform. I imagine there was a good deal of relief reaction rather than anger, in the punishment. The bag swing was usually harmless fun, but the platform was high, and your timing had to be perfect so that you jumped on the gunny sack bag just as it reached you after being swung towards you by playmates on the ground.

I looked forward to the weekends and summer vacations when The Sheik came home from Upper Iowa University. My oldest brother was handsome in the Valentino tradition of the day, a member of the "flaming youth" set, and "yes, he was collegiate." He was popular with the flappers, who were really charming with bobbed or pinned-up hair, spit curls, and short skirts. Some of them were truly beautiful, our family album shows. Beauty shops were starting to give permanents with machines, but the most requested hair style at the beauty salons, and the one which did not risk being regarded as tawdry, was the marcel, which demanded a special iron and a good bit of skill on the part of the operator.

There was no public library in Sumner then, but people had books, and I chose those that suited my taste. Fairy stories were big, and teachers read The Bobbsey Twins series out loud a chapter at a time before starting class work. Many books had a religious theme, probably in the belief that no opportunity must be lost to get in a lick for the Lord. Almost everything written for children stressed moral ideas or exemplary behavior. I gravitated to Little Women, Girl of the Limberlost, and Pollyanna. Anne of Green Gables hung right in there with The Five Little Peppers. What role models they all provided!

It doesn't help my prestige any to admit that for a time at least my first choice in literature was Elsie Dinsmore, a book I found at my grandmother's. Elsie's grim life, characterized by a tyrannical father who demanded instant obedience and inflicted cruel punishment held a horrible fascination for me. Several times during the summer I would walk up to Grandma's to read this book. In preparation for this afternoon of singular delight I repaired first to the rhubarb patch, where I chose the thin, tender green stalks and peeled them. Grabbing a shaker of coarse salt from the kitchen, I headed upstairs to jump onto the softest of the four feather beds. Snuggling there with my sadistic book, my "pie plant," and my salt was "paradise enow.'"

I used to wonder why anyone would live on a farm, and I guess I still do. There wasn't anything about them I liked. At times I would "go out to the country" to help my aunts at threshing season. I was good help, but I dreaded going into the dirt cellars where the foods that needed cooling were kept. Of course, we all drank out of the same dipper and bucket. The well water was refreshing, but keeping the bucket filled was only part of the kitchen work. Hearty meals to satisfy voracious appetites had to be prepared for the threshing crew. Nobody had heard of calories. And if you've never had wheat chaff in your clothing against a sweaty body, you haven't itched. Those were the days of the "backhouse" and the oil lamp. Lamp wicks had to be trimmed just right, but when you got up at 4 A.M., you weren't too interested in reading late at night.

A couple of summers our family went to North Dakota with one of my uncles and his family to harvest a wheat crop on land near Cooperstown. We all lived in an old shack of a house, just like "poor white trash," but we kids had a barrel of fun rigging up telephones in the barn and sliding down the barn roof. We would make a fire pit outdoors out of rocks and heat pails of water as if preparing for a birth in the family. We wore coveralls and straw hats, and we learned to walk bare-footed in stubble and take lemonade to the men and hired hands working in the field. We made paper cigarettes filled with flour, which were great for puffing out smoke but could have been lethal, if we had inhaled.

We played a game intended to clean up our language. Our mothers gave each of us a cotton bag full of beans. Every time one of us said, "gosh" or "darn" or "heck," the culprit was under orders to atone by giving a dried bean to each of those who overheard. The two older boys of us cousins treated the whole idea with contempt, and, perching out of reach, would make the very air blue with the forbidden epithets, much to the helpless indignation of the small fry. It was another victory for Satan.

The grown-ups were fearful of hail storms and wheat rust, and it was a relief when the time came for the big Avery tractor to pull the three binders around the section that held our crop. Before the threshing crew arrived, the bundles had to be shocked, however, and it dawned on me just how much effort it took to put bread on the table.

This whole project, which included planting the wheat in the spring, was prompted by the high prices that obtained in the grain market after World

War I. When these settled down, the project was abandoned. But all these tastes of rural life created in me something less than an affinity for my heritage. Farm life involved interminable hard work under unpleasant conditions and sans the conveniences beginning to be enjoyed in town, such as electricity and the telephone, and others not particularly new, such as plumbing. Under certain conditions, too, country roads became almost impassable. But the drawback that impressed me the most was the restrictive nature of farm life. At four in the afternoon it was time to head for home. The "chores" could not be put off. Cows had to be milked and stock and fowl fed and watered. True, families with a dearth of sons old enough to be of use were likely to have other help, unfailingly referred to as the "hired man," but *someone* had to be there.

Life on an Iowa farm in the 1920's surely had rewards that were not apparent to me. Certainly relatives of mine who lived in the country seemed happy enough, and fortunately there are many who feel that way. I'm sure that rural electrification was one of the "blessings," possibly the greatest, that enabled the rewards to continue to eclipse the drawbacks for those who like it "down on the farm," and oddly enough my husband was to be a pioneer in the rural electrification program.

When I think back on my old-fashioned small-town childhood, I realize that throughout all those years I was almost a completely free spirit. Even though I was expected to conform in some basic ways, such as in church attendance and scholastic achievement, there was a freedom from supervision not possible today, accompanied by a freedom of movement, a freedom of association, and even a freedom of thought.

Children were appreciated and enjoyed, but a relatively small amount of pressure to achieve was exerted. We were not the sole apple of our parents' eyes and not expected to be their only reason for living, or if we were, our parents were careful not to place that onus upon us. Family togetherness was not forced or planned but occurred as a natural condition of the moment. Parents gave freely of their time when necessary, but family affairs were geared to the adults and did not revolve around the offspring. We children were encouraged to initiate our own amusement and pursue our own interests. Whether purposely, or because it was their nature, my own parents adopted a laissez faire attitude towards our minds that left us leeway to form opinions of our own. In religion, as well as in other areas of life, we were free to find answers for ourselves with a minimum of guidance.

Of these freedoms, the one I appreciated most as a child was the freedom to move about at will, which the comparative innocence of the times made possible. Very few boundaries were drawn, as long as we adhered to a time schedule and touched home base when it was expected of us. Not only were we permitted to wander willy nilly within the confines of Sumner, itself, but parental approval extended to rural areas at the edge of town. With our friends we searched the woods for hazel nuts and jack-in-the-pulpits and hiked along the railroad tracks to pick the cowslips growing in the marshes which gave that dainty wildflower its plebian name.

These rural excursions gave us an appreciation of the change of seasons that is most noticeable in the midwest. Although I personally could not face the horrors of the Christian Easter, I participated with enthusiasm in a more palatable celebration of the advent of spring that, like Hallowe'en, Christmas, and Easter, had a pagan origin. We called it May Day. Unfortunately, it doesn't seem to have survived the passage of the years.

Dancing around the May pole was going out of fashion, but we greeted the first day of May by observing a custom that was unmatched for sheer beauty and that was free of the deception involved in Santa Claus and the Easter Bunny. For days we had spent hours making May baskets out of boxes and cardboard cones by decorating them with crepe paper fringe and tissue paper and filling them with popcorn and candy. Wildflowers picked at the last minute added to their appeal, and after dark we delivered them to our schoolmates' doors, calling out, "May basket for Betty," or whoever it might be, and hiding behind the shrubbery waiting to be found and chased. The first of May is still with us, but whatever became of May Day? It deserved a better fate.

The Sumner Telephone Company was sold in 1924, but my father stayed on as manager three more years and then accepted a position with the new owners, which required us to move to Newton for one year and then to Elkhart, Indiana, where I attended a high school that was a part of that state's superior educational system. Elkhart was the home, at that time, of the New York Central shops, a large band instrument industry, and Miles Laboratories. The latter was to hit upon a bonanza in later years with a product called Alka Seltzer.

Our residence in Elkhart was a large, three-story house on the St. Joe River, and the time was just before the Depression and one of prosperity for our family. We found a neighborhood Methodist Church, and I not only continued my church attendance but became very active in Epworth League. One summer I spent a week at a Methodist Young People's camp, where we congregated for prayers and singing, participated in social events, and took part in the sort of superficial Bible study that is approved by the ecclesiastical arm of the Church for reasons that became clear to me when I delved deeper into the scriptures on my own initiative.

It cannot be denied that I was for a large part of my formative years consistently exposed to religion and that not once was I given a hint that the

Christian religion was anything but established Truth. I was not attuned to it, but it meant so little to me in anything but a social way, that I was not motivated to question or examine it. So mechanical and so second-nature had it become for me that, without any compunction at all, I would have been willing to swear (on a stack of them) that Bibles were the revealed word of God and that, although everything might not be right with the world, the Christian God was incontestably "in his heaven."

By the time I was in high school, I was just as familiar with the Bible as were most of my friends, and I doubt that most teenagers could have identified the gospels with the New Testament then, just as I doubt that most of them could today.

Actually, we were not called "teenagers" in my day, and the implied stigma also was missing, along with any expectation that at the end of our 12th year we would become any more fractious than we had proved to be in the past. Automatically putting people into categories and burdening them with all which those categories often imply can't help but encourage them to strive to fit the mold. Just as when children realize that they are expected to grow up to be Christians, most of them will, having seen their parents follow the same pattern. Few ever get around to asking why. They unconsciously obey Paul's admonition to "avoid foolish questions."

The Depression finally caught up with us, and my father accepted a position with a telephone company headquartered in Lubbock, Texas, at that time a windy, sand-blown West Texas caprock town of 20,000. It was the jumping-off place, as far as I was concerned, and I was as depressed as the economy. But the move to Lubbock proved to entail a benefit that hadn't occurred to my provincial mind. Lubbock was the site of a new college— Texas Tech, which has since become Texas Tech University, and which, contrary to its name, has always had a strong liberal arts tradition.

Living in a college town at a time when tuition throughout the country was low, meant that my brother, sister, and I could all acquire a higher education simultaneously, in spite of the state of our family finances. Eventually, four of us were to claim Texas Tech as our alma mater.

As a journalism major, I was a reporter on the staff of *The Toreador*, Tech's campus newspaper, and this training led to my employment in the college publicity office after I received my degree in June of 1935. Mid-way of the year I spent doing publicity work, I began dating a mechanical engineering senior, who was working his way through college. As a student assistant in the engineering school, he earned $35 a month. After his graduation in the spring of 1936, he was hired by Douglas Aircraft in Los Angeles, California. His salary was $90 a month, and we decided that was plenty on which to begin a married life. I travelled west by train.

The City of Angels seemed to us a veritable Eden. There was no smog then, only beauty of every kind, embodied in the sparkling Pacific, clean wide beaches, abundant foliage and flowers, beautiful mansions, persistent sunshine, and everywhere majestic palm trees. We decided it would be exciting to be married in fabulous Hollywood, so behind Paramount Studio at the home of a retired minister who married couples for a fee, we promised to spend our lives together.

We rented a little stucco house in Santa Monica but soon moved to a "court," which was just a row of attached apartments. They were all over Los Angeles. Our rent was $30. We were smitten with a unit that rented for $35, but $5 bought a week's groceries.

Eleven months after we were married, our daughter was born in Dr. Welby's hospital. She reigned as queen of our Santa Monica abode, and although Shirley Temple lived only 20 blocks away, Shirley didn't have a prayer. We did go to see her in the Christmas parade down Hollywood Boulevard. All in white fur, dimpled hand waving, and curls bouncing, she may have inspired the expression "living doll" that December night of 1936.

I was very domestic, playing my 1930's housewife role to the hilt. I did the laundry on a rub board, made a pie from a pumpkin, and cooked such big meals for my husband that he finally found enough courage to point out that he was putting on weight. We were "tippy-toein'" constantly to keep from hurting each other's feelings. Forced to live on a strict budget, we managed a double feature on bank night with a 9-cent malt on the way home.

But we didn't need money to enjoy ourselves in Southern California. We went for numerous drives around Beverly Hills and the San Fernando Valley, always hoping to catch a glimpse of movie stars outside their grand homes, for Hollywood was enjoying its heyday, and we were fans. Once I did see Lionel Barrymore driving an open yellow convertible and wearing a *beret*. For the most part we had to be satisfied with the footprints and handprints at Grauman's Chinese or driving past the premieres and the Garden of Allah.

One night we parked at the beach and peered over the fence at Marion Davies's Ocean House swimming pool spanned by a Venetian bridge. We didn't worry about guards, but people didn't have the fears they have now. Irving Thalberg and Norma Shearer, and Cary Grant, too, lived in houses farther down the beach. One night Marion and William Randolph Hearst hosted a circus party with a huge tent set up on the tennis courts at Ocean House. We could see it, flags waving, from the highway that led to Malibu.

The enchantment of California at last failed to compensate us for the low wages most Californians were willing to accept in return for the privilege of basking in a near-perfect climate, and we made plans to return to Texas in a second-hand Chevrolet coupe. Desert, mountains, flat tire, and crying baby made the trip memorable.

After a short time working for Reed Roller Bit in Houston, my husband applied for the position of city manager at Spur, Texas, and subsequently became the youngest such official in the state at 25. Spur was a typically friendly, wind-scarred little West Texas town, about 70 miles from Lubbock, off the caprock. There were dust storms and blue northers, but there were also out-going people ready to welcome newcomers. My neighbor was a typical Texas pioneer woman in her seventies. Nearly every day she would ask me if I had "boiled something." She didn't mean water or potatoes. She meant dried beans or greens, which she simmered with salt pork. Taking pity on the dumb Yankee wife, she would give me some of this West Texas specialty, and with cornbread we had a Texas treat.

From her I became aware of another facet of Texas hospitality, which is that you don't return empty dishes or containers. You put food in them first.

Texas people are friendlier more quickly. The stranger clerk calls her female customer "Honey," and friends advise each other that it's cold enough to wear a sleeve. "Y'all" is always plural, and it's the handiest of designations. They've used "Miz" for years. It's Texas for "Mrs."

As a city manager, my husband had to be a jack-of-all-trades: an engineer to run the municipal power plant and maintain streets and facilities, an official to assist in governmental functions. Housewives called him to repair refrigerators and stoves, but he also put in a new sewer system and butane gas plant.

Spur was a ranch headquarters for the South Plains area of West Texas. These ranches included the huge spreads of the Swenson, 4–6, and Pitchfork brands. The surrounding country where cattle didn't run was used to grow cotton and maize, wherever mesquite had been cleared.

We made frequent visits to Lubbock, Perryton, and Plainview to visit relatives and friends. In 1940 we made a wise decision and bought a corner lot in Spur for $125. With an FHA loan we built our first house, for $3200.

Our first son was born in a Lubbock hospital in 1940. He and his sister made a cute pair. I dressed them up every afternoon and went somewhere to show them off. It took a long time to do the housework in those days, but Spur women found time for elaborate showers and bridge parties. Baby sitters were eager to work for 25-cents for an afternoon or evening.

After eight years in Spur, my husband became superintendent of the electric power department in Lubbock, and we built our second home there. We were sad to leave our Spur friends, but we keep in touch with some of them. Our second son had arrived in 1944, so our family now numbered five. My sister and family soon moved to Lubbock, and both sets of our parents lived there, making family gatherings and outings possible.

We liked Lubbock, except for the dust storms and windy days that resulted in a climate often unpredictable and sometimes unpleasant. A couple of times the sky turned totally black; people coming out of theaters thought the end of the world had arrived. Tumbleweeds and garbage-can covers and debris of every kind would go flying. But Lubbock could also be the scene of winter storms and floods. Yes, in spite of the flat terrain we did have a flood, owing to the inadequacy of the storm sewers to carry off the water from a nine-inch rain accompanying a tornado that struck nearby. Violent weather is not unusual in West Texas, but much of the time the air is dry and agreeable, and even summer nights are cool.

In 1950, my husband accepted a position as manager of a rural electric generation and transmission co-operative being organized in Central Missouri, with headquarters at Jefferson City, a position he was to fill for 25 years. This entailed leaving our family and friends, but it was a return to the midwest for me.

Topographically Jefferson City is the opposite of Lubbock and the South Plains. Situated in the Ozark foothills, it could be described in our younger son's words to his grandmother: "Everywhere you look, there's no flat place." The hills, trees, and streams, and the Missouri river bluffs make it a picturesque "Storybook" place to live. For a quarter century, we found there both personal satisfaction and rewarding relationships.

Our children were always good students and won several honors both in high school and college. All three have degrees from the University of Missouri. They now have their own homes, and the three families, containing our eight grandchildren, enrich our lives.

Upon retirement, my husband received much recognition for his pioneer work in rural electrification. We now live at the beautiful Lake of the Ozarks in mid-Missouri, 40 miles from the state capital. I have been recuperating from illness the last several years.

The
Book
of
Ruth

By Ruth Hurmence Green

The *Book Of Ruth* is the posthumous collection of the writings of Ruth Hurmence Green, originally made possible by contributions to the Ruth Green Memorial Fund. The original volume was dedicated to Ruth's memory as "a loving friend and a courageous advocate of freethought and women's rights."

CONTENTS

The Book of Ruth

Preface

Ruth Hurmence Green "took her life," wrote *Capital Times* reporter Jacquelyn Mitchard in her tribute to author Ruth Green, "because she believed profoundly it was hers to take."

To lie helpless in a hospital bed, to exist from one plateau of pain to another, to be a burden dying by degrees was not Ruth's way. She was caring, she was independent, and when cancer returned for the fourth time, Ruth quietly and deliberately put her affairs in order, wrote her own obituary and ended her life at her Missouri home with an overdose of medication.

Ruth touched many lives with her thoughtful letters and with her book *The Born Again Skeptic's Guide to the Bible*. Readers appreciate that book's freshness, its intellectual impact, its gentle humor and the obvious analytical patience its writing involved. The final chapter, a warmly personal reminiscence of small town life in the America of the 1920's, enabled those who were never to meet Ruth to regard her as their friend.

A "half-hearted Methodist" most of her life, Ruth first read the bible cover-to-cover when convalescing from illness a few years ago. Her shock, she often said, was worse than the trauma caused by her illness. A skeptic, she soon became "mid-Missouri's resident atheist," campaigning ardently for an end to bible illiteracy and for absolute separation of church from state. She had changed from a church-every-Sunday housewife into a writer and activist who vowed "never to be seen in public with an unconcealed bible."

She starred in an educational film *A Second Look at Religion* and was a premiere columnist for the Madison, Wisconsin, monthly *The Feminist Connection*. She became a spokesperson for the Freedom From Religion Foundation, serving on its board of directors. She was its secretary at the time of her death.

My personal acquaintance with Ruth Green started in 1978 when syndicated columnist Roger Simon wrote a piece about the fledgling Freedom From Religion Foundation which was printed here and there in newspapers around the country including the *Kansas City Star*. Ruth wrote a memorable letter to the Foundation in response to that column, and in no time I felt as though we had always been friends. My family and I treasure memories of Ruth and of visits to her Lake of the Ozarks home where she and her husband Truman dispensed the world's warmest hospitality. Although I understand the timing of her death and applaud her act of self-determination, 66 years could never be enough for Ruth, who had such remarkable verve and ability and a most important message to disseminate.

"She was brilliant, sensitive, strong and always concerned about the happiness of those who touched her," said Sheila Thompson, a staff person for the Foundation. "I lost someone I loved and admired, and humankind lost some of its sanity and hope for a better world."

This book contains a sampling of Ruth's writing—articles, letters, verse, autobiography. Some of the pieces appeared as columns in *The Feminist Connection*; others, such as "Christian Family or Christian Fantasy," were unpublished letters to newspaper editors. Some of the shorter pieces, including "Excuse Me For Thinking," were letters to me. Ruth's stirring speech, given at the Unitarian Church in Columbia, Missouri, a few months before her death, is reprinted here, and the book concludes with the beautifully written "Memoir of an Iowa Childhood," completed by Ruth in June of 1981.

The Freedom From Religion Foundation is indeed privileged to share with you *The Book of Ruth*.

Anne Nicol Gaylor
President
Freedom From Religion Foundation
January, 1982

The Book of Ruth

Part I

Essays On Religion

Christian Family
Or Christian Fantasy?

The family today may be undergoing change, and it may be facing extinction. If, however, it depends for its existence on the enslavement of women, it deserves to perish. No institution should become an altar on which one segment of society must become the human sacrifice, and no institution is worthy of existence, if it is used to breed slaves to maintain it. Personally, I believe the family will survive on the basis of its inherent values, although perhaps in a somewhat altered pattern.

Those who claim that the Judeo-Christian deity put his stamp of approval on the family should be required to prove that he did. Let them go to the Word of God, the Bible, and prove that this deity invented by the Jews cares a hoot about either human life or the family. I'll show you that he doesn't.

There is no other book in which human life, all life in fact, is so cheap. The fiendish Lord of the Old Testament orders the Jews to kill, rape, and torture without pity entire nations, "infant and suckling, young man and virgin, and the man of gray hairs." *I Sam. 15:3* and *Deut. 32:25* If they do not obey, they feel the wrath of the Lord's vengeance themselves. His favorites dutifully massacre thousands, rip up pregnant women, and dash little ones against the stones, putting heads in baskets and mutilating their victims. This criminal of all time drowns the entire population of the world except for the family of a drunkard. He hardens Pharaoh's heart to make it possible to put all the firstborn of Egypt to the sword. He comes to earth incarnate in such a manner that all male children under two in a vast area must be killed, again with the edge of the sword. Tell me, if you can, that human life is sacred to the Lord.

Children are not a blessing in the Bible. They are a curse. Eve's punishment was borne by every woman who would follow her on earth: "I shall greatly multiply thy sorrow and thy conception; in sorrow shalt thou bring forth children." *Genesis 3:16* The Bible portrays the sexual act as dirty, even sinful. David, the great patriarchal ancestor of Jesus, sings: "I was shapen in iniquity; and in sin did my mother conceive me." *Psalms 51:5* Even Mary had to be purified after the birth of Jesus. *Luke 2:22*

The New Testament yields little support for the family as even a Christian priority. Jesus not only shows contempt for his own family, even refusing to speak to them on one occasion (*Matthew 12:46–49*), but demands that his followers abandon theirs, specifying that those who wish to be his disciples must "forsake all that he hath." *Luke 14:33* He makes it clear that all who have forsaken their families and houses shall "receive an hundredfold and shall inherit everlasting life." *Matthew 19:29* He says there will be commendation for eunuchs who have made themselves such "for the kingdom of heaven's sake." *Matthew 19:12* Isaiah says eunuchs will have a reward "better than of sons and daughters." *Isaiah 56:4,5* Because of these Bible promises, many chose to become celibate. Not very conducive to preservation of the family, is it?

Jesus warned women not to become pregnant. He says: "Woe unto them that are with child, and to them that give suck, in those days." *Luke 21:23* Those days are the ones at the time of his second coming, which many Christians now feel is imminent, and this warning by Jesus would seem to justify birth control and abortion. He also says the days are coming when women would wish they had never given birth. *Luke 23:29* Insensitive to woman's role in the Palestine of his day, he tells a parable about ten virgins who await one bridegroom and the five who are rejected. Does all this sound like support for women as wives and mothers and for the family?

Paul furthers the idea that sex is to be avoided. While he grudgingly permits marriage as a last resort for those who "burn," he says: "It is good for a man not to touch a woman. . . . Now, concerning virgins, it is good for a man so to be. Art thou loosed from a wife? Seek not a wife." *I Corinthians 7* He reiterates God's curse upon women that their husbands should rule over them, and he says that a woman has "not power over her own body, but the husband." He orders young women to shut themselves up at home, not even visiting their neighbors for fear they might gossip, and women are not permitted to speak in church or to teach in any fashion. Should they marry, they are to learn everything from their husbands. Widows are to house strangers and wash the saints' feet! Women who want to go back to the Bible had better read it. They should familiarize themselves with the Mosaic Law, which Jesus said he came to uphold by "every jot and tittle." *Matt. 5:18* Besides the ten commandments which they cherish, they will find orders for women to be stoned and burnt to death, enslaved, and "thrust through" with the sword. The ten commandments are part of the Mosaic Law. Can we ignore the rest of it?

Throughout the Bible, men who stay away from women are considered holy. God orders Hebrew men to "come not at your wives" when they are preparing to meet with him. *Ex. 19:15* The book of The Revelation says that the ones closest to the Lamb in the New Jerusalem will be 144,000 male virgins, "they which were not defiled with women." *Revelation 14:4*

Ethics put into the mouths of fictional gods by ancient tribesmen are not applicable to our society. Prayer to such gods will avail nothing. We must consider our problems and achieve rational solutions, unfettered by outdated behavior rules, which the gods refuse to alter. A nation on its knees is on its last legs, and that has been proved throughout history. The Bible has been used for centuries to persecute millions of human beings, and Christianity has decimated families as Jesus promised it would: "For I am come to set a man at variance against his father, and the daughter against her mother, and the daughter in law against her mother in law. And a man's foes shall be they of his own household." *Matthew 10:35–36* On Judgment Day families will be torn apart. Does anyone still presume to picture the Bible as pro-family and pro-life?

BOOK OF RUTH—CHAPTER 2

Suffer The Children To Suffer

"Happy shall he be, that taketh and dasheth thy little ones against the stones." *Psalms 137:9*

The Bible is fertile ground for all who might wish, for any reason, to employ extreme severity, if not actual abuse, in the treatment of children.

Adults who want to beat children find no reason to refrain from corporal punishment when they go to the scriptures, and they are even instructed to whip them mercilessly. One irate parent or guardian with a Bible is all it takes to inflict pain to the point of death upon an unruly or "stubborn" child:

"Withhold not correction from the child: for if thou beatest him with the rod, he shall not die. Thou shalt beat him with the rod, and shalt deliver his soul from hell." *Proverbs 23:13–14*

But, as history books and modern newspapers attest, many children have died, especially when the Bible-inspired beating was performed by the reader who turned to Proverbs 20:30: "The blueness of a wound cleanseth away evil: so do stripes the inward parts of the belly." An ungentle Dr. Spock of Proverbs is responsible for "Spare the rod and spoil the child."

"Honour thy father and thy mother: that thy days may be long upon the land," etc. (*Ex. 20:12*), was to be taken literally. Honor was to be bestowed, not because it had been earned, but to save the child's very life. Not only were smiting and cursing capital offenses when perpetrated against a parent, but should children be stubborn or espouse a "false doctrine," fathers and mothers were to stone them to death or run them through with a sword. At one time a "stubborn child" statute in Massachusetts evolved from this Mosaic law.

Because Jesus upheld the Mosaic Law by "every jot and tittle," saying that it would "never fail," and because the Bible is being advocated these days as the basis for legislation in our country, it is important to become familiar with all of this "Good Book." In the area of child abuse, there is much to learn.

At the very heart of Christianity itself is the pagan superstition that the gods must be appeased with the dearest and best, and ultimately the human sacrifice of the firstborn son. Such sacrifices are required by the Old Testament of the Bible and are played out in the person of Jesus as the Son who is killed to placate God.

Children as human sacrifices are not strangers to the Bible, possibly because the scriptures make it clear that they are necessary. Everyone who has ever been to Sunday School knows about the "beautiful Bible story" of Abraham and Isaac, in which the Lord orders a father to make a human sacrifice of his dearest son. Although God is satisfied this time simply with Abraham's willingness to slit Isaac's throat (*Gen. 22:1–14*), he makes Jephthah actually burn his daughter as an offering of thanks for victory in battle. *Judges 11:30–40*

Instances of kings and warriors using their children as human sacrifices horrify any sensitive Bible reader, and the mass slaughters of children by the Lord as he wreaks his vengeance on the heathen and the backsliders make one wonder how it is possible to carry a Bible without getting the blood of children on the hands. God's brimstone, flood-waters, plagues, famines, and pestilences take a grisly toll of the innocent, and when his vengeful famines continue so long that women boil their children for food, he still has to be persuaded to end them.

There is not one instance in the Bible wherein the Lord ever spares a child in the commission of all these atrocities and in the conquests which he directs and masterminds through his bloodthirsty servants, Moses and Joshua. The Lord's orders are always worded in such a way that the meaning is crystal clear: "Thou shalt save alive nothing that breatheth." *Deuteronomy 20:16* And "Slay both man and woman, infant and suckling." *I Samuel 15:3* On the few occasions when he *seemed* to spare children, they were female babies, and young girls who were still virgins, for the enjoyment of the priests and captains. *Numbers 31:18*

Children in the Bible are also made to "pass through the fire," a purification rite echoed in New Testament theology which finds Jesus baptizing with the Holy Ghost and with fire. And his own birth came about in such a way that all boy babies under two living in Bethlehem and all the coasts were put to the sword. Or so the Bible tells us.

But it becomes too heart-rending to proceed. Suffice it to notice only in passing: the two bears which God sends to tear 42 children to pieces for teasing a prophet; the innumerable times when children pay for the sins of the fathers; the heirs who are killed by their brothers and grandmothers to insure the throne; the lions who break the bones of children; and the times children are seduced and sold by their brothers, eaten by their parents, buried alive, raped, beheaded, enslaved, and abandoned. The sheer inhumanity of the Bible would make a hardened adult shudder, and yet this book is put into the hands of children who will find their counterparts victimized on page after page.

Young people may find it enlightening to discover the Bible's strange conception of parental love when they read that Job is wonderfully content to have his first set of children replaced by a second brood of seven sons and three daughters, after the original siblings were all crushed by God to test Job's loyalty. They may become alarmed at the words of Jesus which promise rewards for all who abandon their families:

"There is no man that hath left house, or brethren, or sisters, or father, or mother, or wife, or children, or lands, for my sake, and the gospel's, but he shall receive an hundredfold . . ." *Mark 10:29–30*

Anyone who is not yet convinced of the inhumanity of the Bible towards children should turn to the threats which are a great part of the 28th to 32nd chapters of Deuteronomy, which for their fierceness are not matched in any other literary volume, and to the books of the prophets, whose sadism comes from the mouth of the Lord.

From Deuteronomy and Jeremiah alone, one will be treated to such unfeeling intentions of God concerning the young as: "The sword without and the terror within, shall destroy . . . the suckling." *Deut. 32:25*

And "Their sons and daughters shall die by the famine." *Jer. 11:2*

And "I will dash them one against another, even the fathers and the sons together." *Jer. 13:14* And "I will bereave them of children." *Jer. 15:7*

And "I will cause them to eat the flesh of their sons and the flesh of their daughters." *Jer. 19:9*

And "Her daughters shall be burned with fire." *Jer. 49:2* And "Thou art my battle ax and my weapons of war, for with thee will I break in pieces old and young." *Jer. 51:20*

And "Their children also shall be dashed to pieces before their eyes." *Is. 13:16*

These children whom God is going to dash to pieces include infants: "Their infants shall be dashed to pieces, and their women with child shall be ripped up." *Hosea 13:16* And no illegitimate child has any hope of salvation, according to this same prophet, whose God told him that "I will not have mercy upon her children, for they are the children of whoredoms." *Hosea 2:4*

There is much more. One can only wonder how religious proselytisers can ban books from libraries under the auspices of protecting their children, while handing them that most fearsome and bloody of books, the Bible.

Book Of Ruth — Chapter 3

The Animal Kingdom Of God
Attention: Humane Society

The Creator is no friend to animals. They were fashioned in a vain attempt to provide a helpmate for Adam. It was the failure of this plan that made the creation of Eve necessary. As the story of original sin unfolds, it must be assumed that the Lord introduced death into the world when he made coats of animal skins for the human malefactors.

Every animal from higher to lower feeds upon other forms of life. Darwin's survival of the fittest is often determined by the ability to be more the diner than an item on the menu. Most insects and animals die agonizing deaths. Human beings are fed upon, weakened, and killed by organisms that cannot be detected by the naked eye, even though people today are not the victims of creatures of prey as often as they were in the perilous past. There are even a few scientists who believe that plants can feel, which only suggests more agony. No *benevolent* "being" could have designed nature.

The superstition known as religion has added to the distress of animals in cultures which demanded sacrifice to their deities. The best and often only acceptable sacrifice was the one involving the gift of the finest animals (or the first son).

The Bible pictures the shedding of blood as absolutely essential in many cases. Paul says, "Without shedding of blood is no remission." *Heb. 9:22* Blood had to be spilled to redeem human beings from their original sin. Old Testament sacrifices under the Mosaic law on the part of the Jews were usually carried out with animals, although human sacrifice was not unknown and was even demanded by the Lord on several occasions. The ritual of sacrifice, preserved in the Paschal Lamb of the Jewish Passover, culminated in the human sacrifice of Jesus Christ. Christianity in its derivation from the fearful need to appease vindictive gods is actually no nobler than the religions of savages who regularly and cruelly practiced human sacrifice. Christians are "washed in the blood of the Lamb." *Rev. 7:14* The blood of human beings and animals is the great purifying agent of the Bible. Finally, even God must bleed.

Ancient Egyptians were accustomed to stand in a pit and let the blood of sacrificed bulls pour over them. They believed themselves to be purified by this blood bath. The Bible prolongs this gruesome superstition.

When Jesus drove the money changers from the temple, these were merchants who sold doves for sacrifices in the temple, but Jesus does not condemn the sacrifices themselves. He says he came to uphold the Mosaic Law that demanded sacrifice, and after healing the sick, he instructs them to offer the sacrifices required by the Law. He never renounces the indiscriminate sacrificial slaughter of animals.

The treatment of animals in the Bible could hardly be more inhumane. Here are some prime examples:

1. Humankind is given dominion over all the animals. *Gen. 1:28*

2. The Lord places serpents under an everlasting curse "above all cattle, and above every beast of the field" and dooms them to enmity with humanity. *Gen. 3:14*

3. Abel's animal sacrifice finds favor with the Lord over Cain's offering of grain. *Gen. 4:5*

4. All the animals of the earth are drowned, except for a few of each species, in a heartless plan to eliminate *human* sin. The Lord then curses all animals with the dread of humankind, instructing Noah that "every moving thing that liveth shall be meat for you." He enlarges upon this antagonism between humans and animals by making sure that "whoso sheddeth man's blood by man shall his blood be shed," and he makes sure that there will be such bloodshed by decreeing that man's blood would be required at the "hand of every beast." *Gen. 7–9*

5. Animal sacrifice is part of the Mosaic Law and is demanded by the thousands throughout the scriptures to appease the Lord or as an expression of gratitude. The "sweet savor" of burning flesh is especially pleasing to the Old Testament deity. The firstborn belonged to the Lord. *Exodus 13:12,13*

6. After first "hardening" Pharaoh's heart to assure his refusal to "let my people go," the Lord visits upon Egypt several plagues and pestilences that torture and kill the same animals repeatedly. These plagues include lice, flies, boils, locusts, hail, fire, and disease. Victims included horses, asses, oxen, camels, and sheep. *Ex. 7–11*

7. The Lord kills all the firstborn of the cattle in Egypt on Passover night, by putting them to the sword. *Ex. 12:29*

8. Horses pulling Pharaoh's 600 chariots drown in the Red Sea. *Ex. 14:28*

9. When the Jews invade Canaan, they follow God's orders to leave alive "nothing that breatheth." In the siege of Jericho, for instance, they "utterly

destroyed all that was in the city, both man and woman, young and old, and ox, and sheep, and ass, with the edge of the sword." *Josh. 6:21*

10. To teach the Jews a lesson, God also destroys birds in a cruel display of temper, stacking up quail to a height of three feet to the distance of a day's journey in every direction from the Hebrew camp in the desert. *Numbers 11:31–33*

11. Samson kills a lion with his bare hands and tortures 300 foxes by tying them tail to tail and setting their tails on fire. He performs most of his feats when the spirit of the Lord is upon him. *Judges 14:6 and 15:4,5*

12. David houghs (hamstrings) 900 horses. *II Samuel 8:4*

13. Solomon offers up 120,000 sheep and 22,000 oxen to assure the sanctity of the temple at its dedication. The altars are incapable of handling all the blood. *I Kings 8:63,64*

14. The Lord permits Job's domestic animals to be destroyed in a loyalty test carried out by Satan. "The fire of God is fallen from heaven, and hath burned up the sheep." *Job 1:13–19*

15. Jesus casts devils into 2,000 pigs, who run frantically into a lake and are choked. *Luke 8*

It cannot be denied that at times the Lord displays a grisly form of kindness to animals, as a means of taking revenge upon various persons or groups who have aroused his wrath. He sends two she-bears to "tear" 42 children who are teasing a prophet *(II Kings 2:23)*, permits the lions in the den to break the bones of Daniel's accusers and those of their wives and children *(Daniel 6:24)*, lets dogs feast on Jezebel's body *(II Kings 9:35,36)*, and constantly threatens to send beasts to eat the flesh of his Chosen People. *Ezekiel 33:27*

Finally, in the days of judgment described in the Apocalypse, the fowl of the air are invited to feast on both animals and humankind: "And I saw an angel standing in the sun; and he cried with a loud voice, saying to all the fowls that fly in the midst of heaven, Come and gather yourselves together unto the supper of the great God; That ye may eat the flesh of kings, and the flesh of captains, and the flesh of mighty men, and the flesh of horses." *The Revelation 19:17,18*

Book Of Ruth—Chapter 4

Thou Fool!

My mother taught me not to call people names. Not nice, she said, not kind. I grew up to realize that epithets were a tool for intolerance. This conviction contributed to the revulsion I felt upon reading the New Testament and finding it a repository for the most insensitive name-calling I had ever encountered.

Sweet Jesus, the incarnate God of perfect love, exhibited a special talent for demeaning castigations. It took a thick skin and a complete lack of self-respect to spend an hour in his company. Should an honest question be asked or a difference of opinion voiced, one would be branded some kind of scoundrel, in the manner of those advocates who cannot call upon self-confidence and conviction based upon truth to defend their positions. One seldom finds Jesus in an extended passionless philosophical dialogue which allows the presentation and consideration of all aspects of a subject. He is much more likely to be indulging in invective.

Ye fools and blind! Serpents! Dogs, whited sepulchres, enemies. Faithless generation! Adulterous generation! Satan! Hypocrites, ye who work iniquity. Generation of vipers! Perverse generation! Thou blind Pharisee! Wicked and evil generation! Scathing and withering retorts often accompanied Jesus's derogatory descriptions of his adversaries and of anyone who was slow to comprehend his sometimes enigmatic ramblings.

As God, Jesus was required to pass harsh judgments, his apologists may maintain, with some justification. No room can be found for compassion when one is concerned with everlasting torture.

The role of judge, however, is reserved for the supernatural: "Judge not, that ye be not judged." *Matthew 7:1* Unfortunately, nobody communicated this command to the apostle-evangelists who wrote the epistles which occupy one-third of the New Testament. In the process of establishing the dogma of Christianity, Paul, Peter, James, Jude, and John (after devoting much space to the question of the need for manicuring the male sex organ) show no restraint in expressing the frustrations and resentment they felt towards all who rejected the divinity of their latter-day Jonas.

If your knee does not bow or your tongue proclaim Jesus Christ, here is a summary of how you are portrayed in the pages of the Good Book, courtesy of the Epistles:

You are weak, dead, slain by sin, unstable, sensual, and devilish. You changed the truth of God into a lie, your foolish heart was darkened, and you have pleasure in doing things outside the law. Despising the riches of God's goodness and forbearance and longsuffering, you are a natural brute beast, a spot, and a blemish, beguiling unstable souls. You are unwise, imprudent, perishing, slothful in business, carnal, and sold unto sin, given up to uncleanness through the lusts of your heart to dishonor your own body. Holding the truth in unrighteousness and not liking to retain God in your knowledge, you are asleep, entrapped, jealous, conceited, profane, and in error, and you have changed God's glory into an image made like to corruptible man and to birds and four-footed beasts and creeping things. Professing to be wise, you became a fool. Sin and no good thing dwell in you, and you worshipped and served the creature more than the Creator, for which reason God gave you over to a reprobate mind to do those things which are not convenient.

You do things of the flesh, have not the spirit of Christ, and are confounded by the weak things of the world. Not only that, you are uncharitable, vain, deaf, mighty, noble, ensnared, and double-minded, addicted to war, evil thoughts, greediness, and chambering, and cursed with drunkenness and a defiling tongue. You dare to exhibit a superfluity of naughtiness, although you have a conscience seared with a hot iron and are without excuse, receiving unto yourself the recompense of your error because you glorified God not as God. You obey wrath, unrighteousness, and indignation, and you are despiteful, proud, disobedient to your parents, without understanding and natural affection, unprofitable, miserable, and contentious. You are certainly a fornicator, and you may even be given up unto vile affections, changing natural use into that which is against nature, working that which is unseemly, and abusing yourself with mankind.

You probably glory in the flesh, burning in lust for one another, while some of you also defile yourself with mankind, fulfilling desires of flesh, being carnally minded pleasure lovers and servants of sin. Many of you are adulterers and adulteresses, whoremongers with diverse lusts, who creep into houses and lead captive silly women laden with sins, proving that you are concupiscent with dishonored bodies. It is obvious that you are cunning and wanton with eyes full of adultery and forsakers of the right way, accepting the wages of unrighteousness gone astray. Obedient to the law of sin and death, you are fallen cut-off branches, thinking only of yourself with dissimulation, and rendering railing for railing and evil for evil, while you deceive the hearts of the simple and experience inordinate affection.

Uncalled you are and killers of the just with a heart nourished on slaughter, puffed up by your fleshly mind, drunk with wine, and inventors of evil things. Implacable, unmerciful, inexcusable, and crooked, you are boasters and backbiters, haters of God, worshippers and servers of the devil, whisperers with deceitful tongues and poison lips given to filthy communication. You are unruly, unreasonable, and beguiling, walking disorderly with vainglory, malice, and clamor. Some of you may be teachers of the law, perjured persons with a shipwrecked conscience, persecutors, busybodies who subvert hearers with debate and profane and vain babblings, disobeyers of truth, and self-condemned judgers of others. Traitors who resist truth, you wax wanton against Christ, speaking lies in hypocrisy and drowning in destruction and perdition.

Loving rusty money and corrupt riches of cankered gold and silver, you are greedy of filthy lucre, supposing gain is godliness, whose God is your belly and whose glory is in your shame, minding earthly things such as philosophy and pleasure seeking, and speaking in words which man's wisdom teaches. Brought to naught by things that are, deceivers of self, puffed up one against another, you think that you know something, but you are slow bellies, anti-Christs, and sheep going astray. Enemies, transgressors, purloiners, deceivers, brawlers, reprobates, evildoers, liars, heretics, and evil beasts, you are subverted, sinful, iniquitous, ignorant, and infirm, with evil hearts, imagination, filthiness of flesh and spirit, and mouths full of bitterness and feigned words, because you cast off your first faith.

Infidels you are, scoffers and haters of God, linked with Belial, alienated from the life of God, giving heed to seducing spirits and doctrines of devils, never able to come to know truth, walkers in darkness, idol worshippers, deniers of Christ, and defilers of the temple of God. You confess not, tempt Christ, abide not in him, do not have God, teach false doctrines, have fellowship with devils. You corrupt the word of God, for you are God haters, idolators, and children of the devil. You are a natural man, walk as a man, and are the servants of men, or you may be a woman who practices witchcraft or wanders about from house to house. Without a doubt you are lawless and profane, unwise and perverse, idle and high-minded, given to vain jangling, foolish talking, corrupt communication, jesting, and guile.

Ever learning, doting about questions, you walk in vanity of mind, having darkened understanding, and lying in wait to deceive with cunning craftiness. You think yourself to be something when you are nothing, being desirous of vain glory, self-willed, proud, and presumptuous, when in truth you are barren and unfruitful, cursed children with moth-eaten garments, false prophets and false teachers living in error with the deceivableness of unrighteousness. Partakers of evil deeds, you are dogs returned to their vomit, washed pigs returning to wallow in the mire, servants of corruption, clouds and wells without water, anathema, offenders, destroyers, and adversaries. In filthiness, error, and evil conscience you blaspheme with an unbridled tongue, fight, and kill, behave uncomely, cause divisions, sedition, and strife. Children of wrath you are, dead in your trespasses and sins, backbiters, extortioners, defrauders given to madness and vain deceit, speaking things which you ought not.

With impenitent hearts you treasure up wrath, yield your body members as instruments of unrighteousness unto sin, bring forth fruit unto death, and with feet swift to shed blood you are manslayers and murderers of fathers and mothers. Deceived by sin, you are brother haters, strikers, brawlers, truce breakers, false accusers, promoting riot and fraud. Not God fearers and not Abraham's seed, you are worthy of death. Incontinent, fierce, and injurious, your end is destruction.

Yielding to infirmities of the flesh, your affection is on things of earth, you also yield your body members to be servants of uncleanness and iniquity, consenting not to wholesome works but establishing fellowship with unfruitful works of darkness and the princes of this world. Wise after the flesh, you ask foolish and unlearned questions and rail about oppositions of science, striving about words to no profit as unruly and vain talkers, envious, malicious, and hateful busybodies, abominable and defiled unbelievers and cursers. Believers in old wives' tales, you are turned unto fables and pollutions of the world, and under a mist of darkness you utter great swelling words of vanity. Addicted to folly, malignancy, hatred, variance, emulations, anger, envyings, dishonesty, and lasciviousness, you commend yourself, but in fact you are unrighteous and unlearned world lovers. Murdered, blind, and malicious, and non-lovers, you are despisers of those who are good.

Double-tongued and with itching ears, destitute of truth, you are tattlers with corrupt minds who trust in uncertain riches and evil surmisings. You are heady and unthankful with foolish hearts. Your throat is an open sepulchre given to disputings and bitterness. Conformed to this world, you do not believe in Judea and are requirers of signs. You are government despisers and power resisters, judges of anything, covenant breakers, and excusers. You cause offences and doubtful disputations, working uncleanness with greediness. With blindness of heart you embrace the wisdoms of this world and are one that planteth and watereth. Avengers, stumblers, harlots, and murmurers, you commit unlawful deeds, and in the sin of lust of eyes and of the flesh you create wantonness, for you are seducers. With sporting, revellings, and banquettings, you are unclean, uncomely, and pernicious. In pride of life and covetousness, you are self-destructive and damned.

You have crept in unawares, who were before of old ordained to the condemnation, turning the grace of God into lasciviousness, denying the only Lord God and the Lord Jesus Christ. Filthy dreamers who defile the flesh, despise dominions, and speak evil of dignities, you have gone in the way of Cain and run speedily after the error of Balaam for reward, perishing in the gainsaying of Core. You are spots in feasts of charity, feeding yourselves without fear, clouds carried about of winds, trees whose fruit withereth, without fruit, twice dead, plucked up by the roots. Raging waves of the sea are you, foaming out your own shame, wandering stars to whom is reserved the blackness of darkness forever. You have ungodly committed ungodly deeds. Ungodly sinners, you have spoken hard speeches against the Lord. You are complainers, walking after your own lusts and having men's persons in admiration because of advantage. Mockers you are, too, who separate yourselves, having not the spirit. You are in the fore with garments spotted by the flesh, and you have no life.

But you do have an accurate picture of Christian love!

BOOK OF RUTH—CHAPTER 5

The Religious Woman's Birthright

Traditionally throughout the world, it has been impressed upon women that subjecting themselves to men is the way to win the approval of man-made gods and that the more submissively they accept male dominance, the closer to sanctification they come. Until women are ready to admit that much of the oppression and discrimination they suffer is a heritage of religion, they will continue to sell their birthright for a mess of pottage.

When the Lord placed all the future sins of humankind at Eve's door, he set the stage for every kind of abuse of the female sex it is possible to imagine, and the chronicles of innumerable crimes against her person and dignity fill the pages of the Word of God. Since she introduced sin into the world, she is condemned to suffer agony at childbirth and to submit to her husband in all things.

The Bible moves right along from Eve to Sarah, who, as the wife of the father of the greatest nation on earth, has a pimp for a husband. By passing Sarah off as his sister instead of his spouse, Abraham has God's help in using blackmail to become wealthy. If critics think this is sordid, let them proceed to the night when Lot's virgin daughters bed down with daddy. After all, since Lot's late wife has turned into a pillar of salt for looking back to where her friends were burning to death, there was no other way for Lot to father heirs. Such is the morality of the Bible.

Sarah has a considerable amount of help from the Lord in giving birth to an heir for Abraham, although her gift of her maid for Abraham's needs has resulted in Ishmael. Still, Sarah is thrilled to get pregnant in her eighties, in typical biblical fashion: "And the Lord visited Sarah as he had said, and the Lord did unto Sarah as he had spoken. For Sarah conceived." *Gen. 21:1–2* The Bible student may make what he or she chooses out of that. Still, Jesus was God's only *begotten* son, or was he?

Sarah is mean, and Abraham is meaner, when she insists he send Ishmael and his mother off into the desert and he accommodates her. God has shown a similar regard for womanhood by incinerating all the female population of

Sodom and Gomorrah, even though the cities' sinful reputation had been earned by the homosexuality of their *male* population. Before this holocaust, Lot had offered his daughters to the Sodomites to protect two male angels, although the later behavior of his daughters toward their despicable parent doesn't indicate any resentment on their part. Women of the Bible have no pride.

Even before the mass slaughter of blameless women and children at Sodom and Gomorrah, the monotheistic deity of the Bible in his infinite mercy drowned all the women on the face of the earth, sparing only four who were as noble as an alcoholic Noah. And when that same deity handed down the Law to Moses, he was not satisfied with labeling the female sex unclean and worth many shekels less than the male sex, but he ordered that witches, prostitute daughters of priests, and girls not virgins on their wedding day be stoned or burned to death.

Every natural function unique to the female sex is deplored by the Mosaic law and becomes the means of labeling woman unclean for a considerable part of her lifetime, including the months she is engaged in reproducing the human race (with or without her consent and even when the process is put in motion by the Lord in the form of the Holy Ghost, as Jupiter came upon Danae in a golden cloud). And although the conception of Jesus is seen as "Immaculate" by the Roman Catholic Church, his birth defiled Mary: "And when the days of her *purification* according to the law of Moses were accomplished . . ." *Luke 2:22*

As if humiliation were not enough, the Lord decrees the hideous slaughter of *both* women and children, especially throughout the pages of the Old Testament. Women, when not actually butchered, are consigned to rape and concubinage by the biblical deity, sometimes in public view: "Their children also shall be dashed to pieces before their eyes; their houses shall be spoiled, and their women ravished." *Isaiah 13:16*

Episodes in which women suffer harsh penalties follow in each other's wake implacably in the scriptures. God's punishment for David's sexual misconduct fell, with typical Bible justice, upon the innocent: "Thus saith the Lord, I will take thy wives before thine eyes and give them unto thy neighbor, and he shall lie with thy *wives in the sight of the sun*." *II Samuel 12:11* After David's concubines are sexually abused by his son Absalom, David imprisons the *concubines* for life. Jezebel is thrown from a window, run over by a chariot, and eaten by dogs, because she is faithful to *her* religion.

On and on go the indignities and the inhumanity. Solomon has 700 wives and 300 concubines to keep him warmed up, and when David is old and in need of heat, a young virgin serves as a blanket. (The Mosaic Law actually includes rules for plural marriage: "If a man have two wives. . . .")

Deut. 21:15) Women who are victims of God's frequent famines are reduced to eating their own children, and God makes Jephthah sacrifice his young daughter as a burnt offering.

Then there is the concubine who is mistreated all night long so cruelly by a mob that she dies, and whose body is then cut up into 12 pieces. Each gruesome story becomes more horrifying than the last. The biblical Lord buries alive the wives and children of two princes who dare to challenge Moses. In an attempt to persuade God to end one of his awful plagues, a Jewish priest kills a Midianite princess by thrusting a javelin through her belly. *Numbers 25:8–13* Such behavior was common among the Old Testament characters: "All the women therein that were with child he ripped up." *II Kings 15:16*

It would be hard to find literature more degrading to women than the books of the Old Testament prophets. The use of metaphor enables the authors of these books to label nations hated by the Jews (and by God) as types of disreputable women. In the book of Nahum, Nineveh is portrayed as a shameless woman, whom the Lord addresses thus: "I will discover thy skirts upon thy face, and I will show the nations thy nakedness, and the kingdoms thy shame. And I will cast abominable filth upon thee." *Nahum 3:5–6* Jeremiah 51:33 records more of God's words: "The daughter of Babylon is like a threshing floor, it is time to thresh her." In the book of Lamentations, Jerusalem is referred to as a menstruous woman. And hardly anything more derogatory can be said about a place or a people than: "Behold, thy people in the midst of thee are women." *Nahum 3:13*

A lecherous Lord reveals his carnal appetites in a withering condemnation of Hebrew women transmitted to Isaiah and shamelessly recorded by that prophet in the Holy Bible: "Moreover the Lord saith, Because the daughters of Zion are haughty, and walk with stretched forth necks and wanton eyes, walking and mincing as they go, and making a tinkling with their feet: Therefore the Lord will smite with a scab the crown of the head of the daughters of Zion, and the Lord will discover their secret parts." *Isaiah 3:16,17* One gets the impression it won't be a new discovery on the Lord's part.

The Bible perceives the female as the sexual toy of the male: "And seest among the captives a beautiful woman, and hast a desire unto her, that thou wouldst have her to thy wife; Then thou shalt bring her home to thine house; ... and after that, thou shalt go in unto her, and be her husband, and she shall be thy wife. And it shall be, if thou have no delight in her, then thou shalt let her go whither she will." *Deut. 21:11–14* There were few places a used woman could go, since virginity was so highly regarded by men of the Bible that a woman who did not possess it at the proper time could be cruelly put to death. In fact, a timely angelic announcement to Joseph re Mary's pregnancy probably saved her from his revenge, in the form of execution under Jewish law.

Although delights afforded by the female body for men are stressed in some books such as Song of Solomon and Proverbs, the general attitude toward cohabitation expressed in the Holy Book is that it is a necessary evil, refraining from which is a mark of purity and piety, especially on the part of men.

BOOK OF RUTH—CHAPTER 6

Jesus And Women

Treatment of the female sex established in the Old Testament undergoes little improvement in the New Testament, which continues the biblical snarling at women. Since men and women are both defiled by the sex act, according to biblical doctrine, Jesus had to be born of a virgin, as were many pagan gods. This virgin Mary is expected to be deliriously happy at the prospect of being pregnant on her wedding day, never having slept with the groom. She is left with an assignation story about a ghost, which she is free to tell to as many persons as she thinks will believe her.

Jesus later denied that his mother was a virgin and that he was his own father in one of his three guises. In The Revelation he settles the whole question by claiming Joseph as his father: "I am the root and the offspring of David." *Revelation 22:16* Matthew and Luke both call Joseph a descendant of David.

Jesus is almost contemptuous of Mary. When she finally finds him in the temple after anxiously searching for him for three days, the 12-year-old Jesus rebukes her with the arrogant words: ". . . wist ye not that I must be about my Father's business?" *Luke 2:49*

At the marriage feast in Cana when his mother appeals to him, he replies to her in the following manner, before the guests: "Woman, what have I to do with thee?" *John 2:4* On a later occasion, when she tries to speak to him in the midst of a crowd, he ignores her, saying that his family consists of those who do the will of God and inferring that she doesn't. (So much for the vaunted Christian family.) Throughout the gospels Jesus has no interest in or concern for his mother, with the single exception that John alone says she was at the crucifixion and that Jesus, seeing her, puts her in the care of one of the disciples. Since Jesus supposedly knew exactly when he was going to die, this certainly was a last-minute, haphazard arrangement on his part.

Jesus did not reject the Mosaic Law. How could he, since as the God of the Old Testament which he claimed to be, he had been the law-giver through Moses? Jesus admired Moses and endorsed the Mosaic Law emphatically: "For had ye believed Moses, you would have believed me: for he wrote of me. But if ye believe not his writings, how shall ye believe my words?" *John 5:46–47* How, indeed?

And Jesus guaranteed that not one "tittle" of the law should fail. Logically, then, indecencies toward women permitted or commanded under the Mosaic Law are sanctioned by Jesus, including the practice of Onanism, which enslaved Hebrew women as the sexual partners of the brothers of their dead husbands, if the husbands died without leaving an heir.

Further heartlessness toward women under the law of Moses is exhibited graphically by Jesus in an episode related in Chapter 12 of Mark, wherein some Sadducees tell a story about a woman forced to become the sexual property of *seven* brothers. Whose will she be in heaven, the Sadducees ask? Without expressing even slight indignation at this violation of the bodies and dignity of womankind, Jesus says there will be no marriage in heaven, and besides, he continues, God is the god of the living, not the dead. Not only is the chattel of the seven brothers abandoned in death, but, contrary to the picture of an afterlife in heaven painted by Jesus on other occasions, so are all of humankind.

Jesus taught that a man may divorce his wife if she is unfaithful and that anyone who marries her will be an adulterer. He gives no woman permission to divorce her husband for any reason. And woe to pregnant women and nursing mothers at the end of the world, warns the Savior. *Matthew 24:19* (It would seem only fair to give women a nine-month warning.)

He seems to have an affinity for prostitutes, going so far as to forgive them as long as they "go and sin no more." Mary Magdalene, that wayward damsel whose past was sanitized after Jesus cast out exactly seven devils that had possession of her, seemed always to be in his company from then on. And not only Mary Magdalene, but a whole set of "groupies" followed Jesus and his disciples about: "And the twelve were with him, And certain women . . . which ministered unto him of their substance." *Luke 8:1–3* It is futile to search for any scriptural reprimand on the part of Jesus for the males who are partners-in-crime of the loose women he encounters.

Although Jesus's female friends and followers, including his hostesses, remain loyal to the end, in contrast with the cowardly disciples, who desert him to a man, women are not privileged to join in the meetings with him after the resurrection or to witness the ascension. Neither are his mother or sisters.

In fact, modern women who think Jesus showed high regard for their sex in their traditional capacities as wives and mothers, daughters and sisters, really ought to judge him by what he teaches: "If any man come to me, and hate not his . . . mother, and wife, and children . . . and sisters . . . he cannot be my disciple." *Luke 14:26* He elaborates on his theme to make it clear that he came to set members of families against each other and to encourage men to abandon their families. In this same theme of "I'm Number One," he criticizes Martha for busying herself about the house for him and his entourage (whom he has instructed to sponge off everyone for food and lodging) instead of listening to him expound about how to get into a heavenly mansion, in the kitchen of which she probably figures she is going to be stuck.

Jesus himself did not marry, he did not father children, and all those who followed his example were commended by him. Paul was to find this idea of celibacy for both sexes much to his liking, or so he pretended, although one of the apocryphal gospels spoke of a female secretary Thecla who was his steady companion. It is hard to believe that Christian women today, who ascribe to the theology of Paul, are actually cognizant of his contempt for their sex, although it has continued to be a thorn in the flesh of Church apologists, who are reduced to the old argument of "other folks, other strokes" and all that jazz.

Paul, the disciples, and all early Christians took Jesus at his word and believed that the second advent would take place before they died. To them replenishing the earth was useless, and it was imperative that all prepare their bodies for the heavenly home that was in the process of completion. Celibacy had always been regarded by the Jews as a means of self-purification. Moses had cautioned them in the wilderness to "come not at your wives." Thus Paul put much store by it: "It is better so to be" were his words following his own claim of his celibate state.

One is hard-pressed to think of a deprecating opinion that Paul does not entertain about women, although he was pleased to use women to support the Church, just as women today are satisfied to devote time and energy toward maintaining that institution, while the men hold the positions of power and glory. Let these women seek parity with men in the sectarian hierarchy, and they will soon suffer disillusionment or else agree with Paul that subjection is their ticket to salvation.

Paul gets off to a good start in his crusade to ensure that the female sex will harbor no delusions of grandeur in the ranks of the new *Brotherhood*, by calling many of them lesbians. *Romans 1:26* But he also condemns any other kind of sexual relationship. In the spirit of the Mosaic law, he furthers the idea that the act of love between a man and a woman is unclean, and he could hardly be more specific: "It is good for a man not to touch a woman . . . Art thou loosed from a wife? seek not a wife." *I Corinthians 7*

Married persons, claims Paul, care for worldly things while the unmarried are free to concentrate totally on spiritual things. He who has enough will power to remain a virgin "doeth well." Anyone who gives not a woman in marriage does better than one who does. A woman whose husband dies may marry again, but she will be happier if she doesn't. Forced to face up to the weakness of others, Paul finally does concede: "But if they cannot contain, let them marry, for it is better to marry than to burn." *I Cor. 7:9*

Paul does not fault his God for making this "burning" instinct a part of the makeup of the human race. He seems to feel that the method chosen by God for the reproduction of life on earth is not only vile but wicked, and to Paul marriage is just a barely-sanctioned way out for the weak and ungodly. Further, he found nothing in the teaching of Jesus to make him think otherwise. With its usual license, the Church has twisted the scriptures to make marriage a holy institution and even a sacrament, and today New Testament teaching on it is purposely obscured so that marriage and the family have become the Christian way of life.

Woman's place in the pecking order is defined by Paul, and the Church has made women love it. Female members of sects such as the Mormons resist every effort to elevate them to a position of equality, and many have been known to throw their pride to the winds and applaud evangelists who demand that wives permit their husbands to beat them. It is to woman's shame that Paul's line of command does not lead to open rebellion on her part, but his pomposity is not challenged: "A man . . . is the image and glory of God: but the woman is the glory of man. For the man is not of the woman; but the woman of the man. Neither was the man created for the woman; but the woman for the man." *I Cor. 11:7–9* "But I would have you know that the head of every man is Christ; and the head of the woman is the man; and the head of Christ is God." *I Cor. 11:3* So much for the Trinity, and one can see why Paul is the darling of the male-dominated Church.

In case any woman has a bit of pride left after all this, Paul humiliates her even further: "Let your women keep silence in the churches: for it is not permitted unto them to speak; but they are commanded to be under obedience, as also saith the law. And if they will learn anything, let them ask their husbands at home: for it is a shame for women to speak in the church." *I Cor. 14:34,35* How fortunate it is that at least one sex knows everything and is willing to educate the other.

But Paul isn't finished. He instructs Timothy: "Let your women learn in silence with all subjection. But I suffer not a woman to teach, nor to usurp authority over the man." *I Tim. 2:11,12* Can woman hope for more respect in heaven? The book of the Christian woman's faith gives her short shrift on earth.

Paul seems to have a special contempt for widows and carries on a veritable vendetta against them. The older ones win his approval if they are "well reported of for good works; if she have brought up children, if she have lodged strangers, if she have washed the saints' feet, if she have relieved the afflicted." *I Tim. 5:10* How nice for *Saint* Paul's feet.

He also wants these older unfortunate women to spend much time teaching the young women "to be sober, to love their husbands, to love their children, to be discreet, chaste, keepers at home, good, obedient to their own husbands." *Titus 2:4,5* Young widows fall abysmally short of Paul's standards, "for when they have begun to wax wanton against Christ, they will marry; having damnation, because they have cast off their first faith. And withal they learn to be idle, wandering about from house to house; and not only idle, but tattlers and also busybodies, speaking things which they ought not." *I Tim. 5:11–13* The behavior of widowers is left to their own discretion. Perhaps they seldom gossip or visit their neighbors.

Here are a few more gems from Paul, the former member of a lynch mob that stoned an innocent man to death and who continued his abominable behavior by striking people blind and cursing them and by engaging in petty quarrels with his fellow-workers in an effort to be the top banana in a new cult: "For the woman which hath an husband is bound by the law to her husband so long as he liveth." *Romans 7:2* It is impossible to imagine the misery and tragedy that still are born of this categorical precept from the lips of a man whose attitude towards marriage was one of disdain. And, again: "The wife hath not power over her own body, but the husband." *I Cor. 7:4* Again: "(I will therefore)…that women adorn themselves in modest apparel, with shamefacedness and sobriety; not with braided hair, or gold, or pearls, or costly array; but (which becometh women professing godliness) with good works." *I Tim. 2:9* Old women are warned not to drink too much wine.

Paul is the arch-enemy of womankind. His mouthings have through the centuries been employed to justify untold crimes perpetrated against her, to cast over her a pall of guilt for causing the mythical downfall of the human race, to make her a scapegoat for the misdeeds of men, to hold her in subjugation, and to deny her a sense of personal dignity and worth. And Paul, that preacher nonpareil who also warned slaves not to seek freedom but to please their masters in all things, and who exhorted citizens to be unquestioningly subject to principalities and powers, that very same Paul laid all his prejudices and acrimony toward women at the door of the imaginary supreme being who, according to the Bible, ordained their role to be one of subservience and perpetual atonement for Eve's "transgression."

The Bible is a book whose theme is sin, blame, and punishment. Woman is still all too willing to be branded the perpetrator, target, and victim that the scriptures make of her. She really hasn't "come a long way, Baby." And she will remain "on hold" until she frees herself from the restraints of religion, vaccinated by spirituality against the sickness of striving for self-realization.

For the Word of God is not erasable, and it does not waver in its mandate to womankind: "Wives, submit yourselves unto your own husbands, as unto the Lord. For the husband is the head of the wife . . . Therefore as the church is subject unto Christ, so let the wives be to their own husbands in every thing." *Eph. 5:22,24.*

BOOK OF RUTH—CHAPTER 7

Motherhood According To God: Eve Was Framed

"Cursed shall be the fruit of thy body." *Deut. 28:18*

"I will greatly multiply thy sorrow and thy conception; in sorrow shalt thou bring forth children." *Gen. 3:16* In the dear dead days beyond recall, when gods confronted human beings face to face, the Lord's curse upon Mother Eve forged the Judaic-Christian concept of motherhood. In short, the Bible makes motherhood the enduring bane of women, one of the first of hundreds of curses and threats against both sexes which issue from the lips of its vengeful anthropomorphic deity.

This scourge is Eve's punishment for supposedly wanting to eat of the tree of knowledge, and subsequently any intellectual outreach on the part of women was traditionally condemned by the Church as being contrary to orders of the Lord. Eve's disobedient act, performed before she knew the difference between right and wrong and aggravated by her generosity toward Adam, was considered such a frightful sin that all humanity was to bear it from the time of conception:

"I was shapen in iniquity, and in sin did my mother conceive me." *Psalms 51:5* (This is one of the few irrelevant scriptural passages, albeit ugly, which anti-choice advocates are wont to drag out, for lack of any direct biblical admonitions, to deny abortions to women. It is taken from a Psalm of David.)

To understand just how badly Eve was framed, it is necessary to go to Paul. Paul is the wellspring of Christian theology—that stone-thrower rewarded for his fanaticism by being made a saint, a saint with his own special propensity for cursing people and striking them blind. Paul says that sin was decreed so that Jesus might come and grant grace. Thus, Eve was *forced* to play the Pandora role of loosing sin upon the world. Mother Eve, you gave birth to Christianity. In sin did you conceive it.

Because of the curses of Genesis, relief from physical suffering was historically withheld from women in childbirth. Anesthesia, which was used first in dentistry, was not developed until the middle of the nineteenth century. (Antisepsis also had to wait until a few years later.) Queen Victoria is said to have been one of the first to brave the wrath of the Almighty by insisting on analgesics during her several childbirth ordeals.

Although motherhood may have been a curse, it was a vital function of Old Testament women, necessary to their very survival. Barrenness was sheer disaster for them. Its seemingly common occurrence among Bible women made way for all kinds of hanky panky with the Lord and the prophets, who are forced in several instances to remedy the situation, as the gods of mythology regularly copulated with women of earth to produce heroes and demigods.

The most important biblical example of such mythical couplings is of course what Thomas Jefferson derided as "the mystical generation of Jesus by the supreme being as his father in the womb of a virgin" which he compared to the generation of Minerva in the brain of Jupiter. (Jefferson was at one with the founding fathers in his contempt for Christianity.) This Christian dramatization of the beauty of motherhood, portrayed in hundreds of Madonna and Child paintings, is introduced in the Bible by a blunt, pregnant passage: "She was found with child of the Holy Ghost." *Matt. 1:18* Scripturally, Mary's pregnancy with Jesus was initiated much as that of Danae with Perseus, who was fathered by Zeus in the form of a shower of gold pouring through a window.

Among the Bible's barren women were Sarah, Rebekah, Rachel, Samson's mother, Hannah, Elisha's hostess, and Elizabeth. Strangely enough, the important issue of these divinely-induced pregnancies were male; the birth of only one specific female is recorded in the Bible, that of Dinah.

Should a Hebrew in Bible times die without producing an heir, his widow was required to accept his brother as a sexual partner, in hopes that an heir for the deceased could be produced. When Jesus is told about a woman who has been forced to wed seven brothers, he shrugs with his usual insensitivity to the status of women as male property under the Mosaic Law, which he said he came to uphold by every jot and tittle. He warned that heaven and earth would pass, but not one smallest part of that Law would fail. The Ten Commandments are only a few of the Mosaic behavior rules.

The Jewish patriarchal society demanded sons. Motherhood for its own sake is so hostage to necessity in the Bible that Lot's two virgin daughters deliberately become the means by which Lot acquires heirs, in one of the Bible's more prurient family scandals.

Jesus recognized this priority when he did ecstacize on one occasion with this tribute to giving birth: "A woman when she is in travail hath sorrow, because her hour is come: but as soon as she is delivered of the child, she remembereth no more the anguish, for joy that a *man* is born into the world." *John 16:21* (The Council of Churches has quite a challenge ahead of it when it sets out to eliminate sexism from the language of the Bible. It may bog down when it gets to Jesus.)

The measures to which Bible women would go to obtain offspring are crystallized in the sordid 30th chapter of Genesis, where Jacob's polygamy and her sister's fertility cause such jealousy that Rachel is willing to let her husband impregnate her maid (an everyday affair in the Bible) so that she can claim the child for her own by having Bilhah bear the child on her (Rachel's) lap. (This is the same kind of expediency exhibited by Rachel when she offers Jacob's sexual favors to Leah in exchange for a mess of mandrakes, a narcotic plant of Bible days, which one feels must have been readily available to the hallucinators of the scriptures.)

Understandable as it is that Old Testament women were desperate to have several children in order to assure their own status in the tribe, it is somewhat strange that they were not reluctant to subject a child to the contemporary barbaric social conditions of their day. Nothing could have been cheaper than human life in the Bible, and the prevalence of torture, exploitation, murder, and execution in biblical days made life a harrowing experience even for the Lord's favorites. Not only were brutal inter-family and intra-family treachery common, but ongoing enmity between tribes and nations meant that hideous wars and conquests went on unceasingly, with women and children often the spoil at the specific orders of God.

Thomas Paine asks the readers of his *Age of Reason* to consider the anguish of a Midianite mother who finds herself taken captive by Moses in the rape of Canaan at the Lord's behest, with her husband, brothers, and sons slain and her girl babies and virgin daughters divided up among the captains and the priests of the Lord. *Numbers 31* This is the Moses who is such a favorite of this bloodthirsty deity that, even though a murderer himself (of an Egyptian), he is chosen by God to deliver the several Decalogs, one version of which is now often posted in our public school classrooms in violation of the First Amendment of our Constitution.

For those who wish to promote the idea that motherhood is glorious in the Bible, it would be wise to be as discriminating as the clergy in quoting scripture. Such proselytizers would not want to read aloud about Hagar and Ishmael being sent into the desert alone by the Jewish ancestor of every Christian, Abraham.

They might not want to refer to God's habit of making women sterile to punish men. They would do well to avoid passages about "delicate women" eating their own children (*Deut. 28:56–57*), being oblivious to a threat to cut another mother's child in two, and apparently concurring with their spouses to use their children as human sacrifices or to make them "pass through the fire."

It would be unwise to quote scriptures about a grandmother who murders her grandchildren and mothers that thrust their children through for worshipping false gods or that permit their sons to be stoned for being stubborn and their daughters for not passing a virginity test. It might be shocking for listeners to hear about beating children black and blue to save them from the devil. All such deeds in the Bible are either participated in by the child's mother or performed with no protest from her, in strict obedience to the Lord's Law.

People who think the Bible is a book that praises motherhood and mothers might be astonished to learn that rules for slavery in the Good Book give a slave's wife and children to his master and allow all captive women and children to be made slaves. Two hundred thousand women and their sons and daughters were taken as slaves by the Israelites in one day. *II Chron. 28:8*

Some people might even be surprised to discover that the wisest man of the Bible, King Solomon, had 1,000 wives and concubines (and still found time to build the Temple), that the Lord forced the Israelites to *abandon* their foreign wives and mutual offspring, that he orders pregnant women ripped up and children dashed against the stones, sends two bears to tear 42 children to pieces, rewards a prophet who kills all the children of one family and puts their heads into baskets, gives sons and daughters to others, and that his many curses include the threat that "cursed shall be the fruit of thy body." *Deut. 28:18*

The truth is that it would be almost impossible to find a book in which mothers and children are held in more contempt or subjected to more atrocious brutality than they are repeatedly in the Bible, whose authors were true to the savagery of their time. Into the Lord's mouth they put such beastly orders as: "Slay utterly old and young, both maids, and little children and women: but come not near any man upon whom is the mark . . . fill the courts with the slain." *Ez. 9:6,7* And "Slay man and woman, infant and suckling." *I Sam. 15:3,7*

Biblical records of the conquests and invasions of Canaan included such scores as the entire population of Jericho and 12,000 men, women, and children of Ai by the Lord's commander-in-chief, Joshua, who outdid even Moses in his appetite for blood. *Josh. 8*

Mothers and children are frequently punished in the scriptures for their husbands' and fathers' guilt. David's child was stricken with a fatal illness because of his father's adultery. The wives and children of two guilty princes were buried alive, those of a thief were burned along with him. The families of those Babylonian men who plotted against Daniel were thrown with them into the den of lions, who "broke all their bones in pieces." *Daniel 6:24* Space does not permit further elaboration, but such instances of the innocent suffering for the guilty are in line with the curse of original sin and led finally to the crucifixion.

Jesus's blessing of the children, after he has ordered families abandoned by all who wish to follow him, rings a little false to any mother who reads the story of his refusal to heal a Gentile child because of its race, until the pitiful and persistent pleas of the child's mother move the more compassionate disciples to urge Jesus to comply.

Mothers horrified by this tale may conclude that anyone, human or divine, who is able to heal a sick child and refuses to do so is not worthy of respect, let alone worship. (Theology often came first with Jesus even over the most basic human feelings.) And how does the medical profession today feel about anyone capable of such heartlessness being labeled The Great Physician?

Since Jesus (by some miscarriage of justice called a Savior) says that he came with a diabolical plan for damning most of humankind, it is a devious deity who will require "multiplying" and make mothers his machines for manufacturing hell fodder. With the cards deliberately stacked against every newborn, who according to Bible teachings belongs to the devil at birth, conscientious Judeo-Christian women might very well see contraception and abortion as their moral obligation, and motherhood as a questionable state.

Jesus seems to concur in this attitude when he says: "Woe until them that are with child and to them that give suck in those days." *Matt. 24:19* Here he is speaking of his second advent, and he later predicts gloomily that a time will come when it will be said, "Blessed are the barren, and the wombs that never bare, and the paps which never gave suck." *Luke 23:29* Paul echoes this sentiment in his epistle to the Galatians, when he writes, "For it is written, Rejoice thou barren that bearest not . . ." *Gal. 4:27* When Jesus describes himself as a "thief," he warns that the elect will be snatched from their families at his second coming. Perhaps that is the situation which will make women wish they had never become mothers, a situation predicted by a torturer who glories in entrapment and surprise with a goal of accumulating as many victims for his boiling waves as he can picture wailing and gnashing their teeth.

In vain will the Bible reader search for compassion toward mothers in any part of the New Testament. Celibate Paul tells women that they can be saved from Eve's curse only by bearing children and devoting themselves to the family—which Paul sees as flourishing in spite of his recommendation that a man not even touch a woman. Each child thus becomes the mother's atonement for Eve's sin, the human sacrifice to which all Christian theology is inevitably and finally reduced.

Motherhood in the Bible is often achieved in a sordid way, as when Jacob impregnates his daughter-in-law after she disguises herself as a prostitute. In polygamous and incestuous marriages, vicious rivalry existed as to which wife or concubine could produce the most offspring.

Anyone who reads the gospels must wonder whether the indifferent attitude of Jesus toward his own mother is supposed to represent the ideal mother and son exchange of feelings. Yet motherhood is so idealized by the Church today—often to the point of denying women activity outside the home—that one would expect to find it glorified on almost every page of the Word of God. Au contraire, as the debonair opine. Not only are the functions which make it possible for a woman to reproduce considered unclean and associated with superstitious taboos under the Mosaic Law and not only is sexual union denounced as unholy and a sign of weakness in men, but the very act of giving birth requires purification of the mother. Childbirth must culminate in *sin* offerings. *Leviticus 12*

One would prefer to think that the birth of God himself would not defile his human mother, but the Bible reveals that Mary underwent 40 days of postpartum cleansing (it would have required 80 days had she produced a female). During this time, Jesus's mother was too contaminated to approach the sanctuary or touch any hallowed thing. A similar purification rite is still practiced by many Christians.

The ultimate insult to motherhood, however, can be found in the book of The Revelation, that cesspool of horrors and obscenity reserved for those who find their masochism still unsatisfied after having their finer sensibilities assaulted by the preceding 65 books of the Bible. When Jesus reveals this last message to John through an angel, he offends civilized readers with a salacious description of the dragon who waits for the woman to deliver the child. Standing before her, the dragon seeks to devour the child at the moment of birth. With its disgusting talk of whores and horned beasts, The Revelation cannot be expected to enhance any concept, and motherhood is no exception.

Those who profess to find motherhood enhanced in any part of the Bible will be sadly disillusioned, should they actually examine this Word of God. The only way one can pretend otherwise is by maintaining that the Bible doesn't mean what it says.

BOOK OF RUTH—CHAPTER 8

The Bible's 'Strong' Women

Whenever anyone dares to criticize the portrayal of women in the Bible, a protest is usually raised that the *strong* biblical members of the female sex have been ignored. The fact that some female Bible personalities overcame their repressive situation to attain positions of prominence is not denied by those of us who criticize the Bible and its concept of womankind as an appendage to the male to be used as he chooses. That a few highly intelligent and forceful women should emerge in male-dominated societies is not surprising, but their scarcity in the scriptures only goes to prove the rule of exception.

For every Huldah in the Bible (a "prophetess who dwelt in Jerusalem in the college" and who was on a pipeline to the Lord) and for every other prophetess, there were thousands of concubines, cringing wives, handmaidens, maidservants, slaves, "witches," prostitutes, and "whores" at the mercy of the chauvinistic male community. And for every "virtuous woman" who "eateth not the bread of idleness," there was a husband who lolled at the city gates, "When he sitteth among the elders of the land."

Behavior of Bible women as a whole must be viewed in the light of the patriarchal society of which they were a part. Although women of the Bible are for the most part understandably passive, verily there are some spunky, even sassy, ladies to be found in its pages.

Some Bible women were rebels at a time when rebellion was undertaken at the risk of the rebel, and such action went unpunished only when it worked to the benefit of a member of the male sex. But strong-minded women of the scriptures were driven by a variety of motives and character traits, and it does not follow per se that they were admirable persons, even though we may appreciate their temerity. It would be unfair to judge them by today's standards, were it not for the premise that the Bible is timeless in its ethical teachings.

Today, when the Bible is being dusted off and proposed as a viable substitute for our sans-god Constitution, it is imperative, for the preservation of the liberty that we have enjoyed under the principle of state-church separation, that we familiarize ourselves with the true content of this old record of superstitions and fables known as the Good Book. A perusal of the behavior and fate of women in the Bible is just one facet of the investigative process needed to counter the burgeoning wave of American religious fanaticism threatening to rival the hysteria which brought Iran to its present state.

It is in this area of religious extremism that we come to one of the strongest women of the Bible—Jezebel. Let us see how she was rewarded for dedication to her own brand of monotheism. This wicked witch of Phoenicia, a devotee of Baal, became the wife of King Ahab of Israel, who paid tribute to still other idols. Recognized as the power behind the throne, she tried to turn the Israelites to Baal worship. For being alarmingly successful, she was thrown from a window by two eunuchs, run over by a chariot and eaten down to an unidentifiable residue by ever-present Holy Land dogs. Poor Jezebel had the wrong religion, but she was certainly strong.

Now let us turn to Delilah of the big bad Philistines, whose well-known treacherous seduction role resulted in the death of several thousand of her own people when the Spirit of the Lord came upon her hirsute lover Samson and helped him pull down the temple.

The slaughter of thousands (old-hat stuff to Bible readers) brings to mind another scheming seductress, whose name sometimes graces women's circles in present-day churches . . . who else but Esther? Hiding her true identity in order to compete for a dethroned queen's crown, this virgin submitted to twelve months of saturation with "oil of myrrh and sweet odours" to assure that she would be pure enough to contend for King Ahasuerus's sexual favor and win out over many true daughters of the realm. She used her new position, attained in this degrading manner, to save her own people at the cost of the lives of 75,500 of her husband's subjects.

It is hard to match such strength, but some feminists might prefer that of Vashti, the dethroned queen, whose loss of the crown was punishment for her refusal to appear before a drunken crowd of gluttons at the command of her spouse. Such rebellion had to be further squelched by an edict that every man in all provinces of the kingdom must "bear rule in his own house." Not unsurprisingly, Queen Vashti quietly faded away, after her property was confiscated, to be heard from no more, her private liberation movement strangled at birth.

But wasn't Eve the first feminist? Didn't she defy the Lord himself in order to acquire knowledge from a piece of fruit? Alas, she had no way of knowing what the apostle Paul was to say about female intellectual aspirations in the New Testament—namely, that a woman must learn everything from her *husband* (providing this font of learning knew anything at all and was willing to let her in on it). Because *Eve* educated *Adam*, she was cursed, along with every member of the human race to come. By causing the "fall," however, she became in reality the mother of the Christian religion. So why hasn't Eve been canonized? Let's hear it for St. Eve! (Judas made it to sainthood, and he was no more important to Christianity than the first trangressor.)

Another strongly disobedient woman whose curiosity got the best of her is known in the Bible simply as "Lot's wife," but whether being turned into a pillar of salt is reward or punishment is brought into question when Jesus says that his followers are the salt of the earth. In any case, her demise made it necessary for her two virgin daughters to have such strength of character as to creep into bed with their inebriated father (described in the New Testament as "righteous Lot") for the purpose of providing him with heirs.

Let us move on to Rebekah, whose reputation as a strong woman is unchallenged. After all, she also has given her name to women's church circles, and didn't she produce twins after overcoming that biblical female ailment called barrenness? With the aid of the Lord, ever-ready in the gynecological department, Rebekah finally bore twin sons, of which she very much preferred the latter-born. So strong and determined was she on Jacob's behalf that she waited until her husband was blind and on his deathbed to trick him royally, with the result that her favorite (and co-conspirator) became the father of the twelve tribes of Israel, after the Lord decided to hate (forever) the rightful heir of Isaac. There's no denying that Rebekah played a large part in biblical history.

Miriam, a Bible prophetess, was the sister of that escaped murderer Moses (who broke two of his own Ten Commandments), and she indubitably had to be a strong woman to set up *her* hue and cry about his marrying a heathen woman and thus breaking Hebrew law. This slander of his chosen lawgiver upset the Lord no little; it was generally known that he reserved for himself the right to castigate Moses. Needing to come up with a punishment that would be especially repulsive, he made Miriam leprous for a period of seven days.

Much is heard of Deborah the warrior, and it will be enlightening to discover why she is such a heroine to Bible advocates. Not only a prophetess, but a sweet singer and a judge of Israel, she sounds like a woman worthy of unguarded admiration—until we examine the cause for which she earned renown. It seems the Canaanites were fighting to retrieve a part of their land that had been stolen from them by Joshua, whose bloodthirsty invasion of Canaan had included the levelling of Jericho and the totalling of its entire population of people and livestock. Deborah led the Israelite army in this later confrontation, spurring them on to slaughter over 10,000 of the enemy.

A Kenite woman by the name of Jael was destined to be the ultimate heroine of this battle, when she was so moved by her own super-patriotism that she invited the fleeing captain of the Canaanites into her tent, under the pretense that she would hide him. While he was sleeping, she pinned his head to the ground with a tent stake, thus qualifying for entry in the Biblical "strong woman" competition. (After splitting his head open, she proceeded to cut it off.)

That famous kinswoman Naomi was, with no effort on her part, a somewhat gentler type than Deborah and Jael, but she was strongly determined to find a partner for her daughter-in-law. She urged Ruth to make herself tempting and sneak into Boaz's granary for the purpose of crawling under his skirt.

The next strong woman seems to be Abigail, who went behind her husband's back to befriend David and present him with an enormous amount of food from her spouse's store. She then frightened her unsuspecting mate to death, and, what do you know, David had been waiting in the wings all the time. He knew a strong woman when he saw one.

And he really ought to have, because he already had a strong woman for a wife, of whom he was once so enamoured that he was willing to kill 200 Philistine men in order to buy her with their foreskins. Michal became a little too uppity for his taste, however, and the Lord made Michal barren for the rest of her days.

The "strong woman" title may have to go to Queen Athaliah: Anyone who will murder 69 of her 70 grandchildren to retain her throne, of a truth is strong in some respects.

The New Testament doesn't provide us with many specific women, but at least two or three of them could be thought of as strong on occasion. Mary finally asserted herself when she reprimanded 12-year-old Jesus in the temple after a frantic search necessitated by his failure to inform her of his plans. After rebukes, ostracism and rudeness, she eventually and with provocation forgot all about being a strong mother and left him to his own devices.

Mary Magdalene was strong enough to have housed seven devils in her body (exact location unknown), which was sure proof of the degree of earnestness she had devoted to her profession.

Here, then, are the strong women of the Bible. Whether today's woman wants to use them as models for herself and her daughters is left to her personal judgment. And whether she wishes the Bible to be the basis for the laws and customs under which women must function is also a decision she may be called upon to make. The time for that decision appears to be now.

Book Of Ruth—Chapter 9

Ten Biblical Threats To Your Freedom

1. There are many whose mouths must be stopped. *Titus 1:10–11*

2. Submit yourself to every ordinance of man for the Lord's sake. *I Peter 2:13*

3. Avoid oppositions of science. *I Tim. 6:20*

4. Many brought their books together and burned them. *Acts 19:19*

5. The powers that be are ordained of God. Whosoever resisteth the power shall receive to themselves damnation. *Romans 13:1–2*

6. Ye wives, be in subjection to your own husbands. *I Peter 3:1* The husband is the head of the wife. *Eph. 5:23* He (the husband) shall rule over thee. *Gen. 3:16*

7. Servants be obedient to them that are your masters, with fear and trembling. *Eph. 6:5*

8. Children, obey your parents in all things. *Col. 3:20*

9. Be content with your wages. *Luke 3:14*

10. Put them in mind to be subject to principalities and powers, to obey magistrates. *Titus 3:1*

BOOK OF RUTH—CHAPTER 10

Gideon Exposed!

Has anyone ever wondered what qualities of Gideon inspired the Gideon Bible Society to appropriate his name? The answer, to be found in Judges, chapters 6 through 9, is representative of Bible content which caused Thomas Paine to call the Holy Book "a history of wickedness."

Gideon was the typical God-approved hero of one of many brutal Old Testament war narratives. One of the inhumanly cruel leaders of the rapacious Hebrew invaders of Canaan ordered by the Lord to annihilate seven nations and "leave none breathing," Gideon was designated by the Christian God to be one of the many saviors of the Old Testament Jews. (The Lord weaves many a tangled web as he manipulates his Chosen People, thus necessitating their rescue from the hands of "enemies" he has allowed to conquer them whenever they falter in loyalty to him.)

After a fabulous series of angelic visits, meaningless sacrifices, and miraculous occurrences, coupled with the sly plotting of an egotistical but insecure Lord, Gideon caused *multitudes* (never were there so many multitudes as are to be found in the pages of the Bible) of Midianites and Amalekites to flee before only 300 "men of Israel." After slaughtering 120,000 "men who drew swords," Gideon triumphantly accepted the heads of two Midian princes. In the process of pleasing the Lord by doing away with 15,000 more idolworshippers, Gideon ordered his firstborn to slay two Midian kings. When the son declined out of fear (he was, after all, very young), Gideon executed them himself on his way to the performance of another satisfying chore. He had vowed to torture the men of Succoth and slay all the men of Penuel (because they had taunted him and refused to feed the Israelite army), and Gideon was a man of his word.

Finally, Gideon initiated a plan to reward the Lord for his assistance in the campaign, and ordered his men to give him the golden earrings of their victims, which he added to the booty he had personally torn from the bodies of the two kings and from the necks of their camels. All of this he melted down to make an ephod, which, alas, then became a "snare," turning Gideon and his house of 71 sons into Baal devotees. His son Abimelech grew up to be the killer of 69 of his half-brothers in Gideon's own domicile.

The Cruelest Bible Verses

How to decide which are the most distressing verses from the Bible? Which are the few that make me cringe the most? What do I use for a measuring stick? I wish the whole Bible could be made to drink the purity test of water and dust that is reserved for the wives of jealous husbands. Its belly would surely swell and its thigh rot. *Numbers 5:12–31*

When the Lord thy God hath delivered (a City) into thine hands, thou shalt smite every male thereof with the edge of the sword: but the women, and the little ones, and the cattle, even all the spoil thereof, shalt thou take unto thyself; and thou shalt eat the spoil of thine enemies, which the Lord thy God hath given thee. Thou shalt save nothing alive that breatheth; but thou shalt utterly destroy them. *Deut. 20:13,14* and *Deut. 20:16,17*

And seest among the captives a beautiful woman, and hast a desire unto her, that thou wouldest have her to thy wife; Then shalt thou bring her home to thine house, and she shall shave her head, and pare her nails; And she shall put the raiment of her captivity from off her, and shall remain in thine house, and bewail her father a full month: and after that thou shalt go in unto her, and be her husband, and she shall be thy wife. And it shall be, if thou have no delight in her, then thou shalt let her go whither she will. *Deut. 21:11–14*

If a man have a stubborn and rebellious son, which will not obey the voice of his father, or the voice of his mother, and that, when they have chastened him, will not hearken unto them: Then shall his father and his mother lay hold on him . . . and all the men of his city shall stone him with stones that he die. *Deut. 21:18–21*

Happy shall he be, that taketh and dasheth thy little ones against the stones. *Psalms 137:9*

Then they shall bring out the damsel to the door of her father's house, and the men of her city shall stone her with stones that she die. *Deut. 22:21*

And thou shalt eat the fruit of thine own body, the flesh of thy sons and of thy daughters which the Lord thy God hath given thee, in the siege and in the straitness. *Deut. 28:53*

Moreover all these curses shall come upon thee, because thou hearkenest not unto the voice of the Lord thy God to keep his commandments . . . And they shall be upon thee for a sign and for a wonder, and *upon thy seed forever.* (If you do not obey the Mosaic law) *Deut. 28:46*

Ye serpents, ye generation of vipers, how can ye escape the damnation of hell? *Matt. 23:33*

And the brother shall deliver up the brother to death, and the father the child: and the children shall rise up against their parents, and cause them to be put to death. *Matt. 10:21*

But whosoever shall deny me before men, him will I also deny before my Father . . . Think not that I am come to send peace on earth: I came not to send peace, but a sword. For I am come to set a man at variance against his father, and the daughter against her mother, and the daughter in law against her mother in law. And a man's foes shall be they of his own household. *Matt. 10:33–36*

Therefore, the Lord will strike with a scab the crown of the head of the daughters of Zion, and the Lord will discover their secret parts. *Isaiah 3:17*

Behold the day of the Lord cometh, cruel both with wrath and fierce anger, to lay the land desolate: and he shall destroy the sinners thereof out of it . . . Everyone that is found shall be thrust through; and everyone that is joined unto them shall fall by the sword. Their children also shall be dashed to pieces before their eyes; their houses shall be spoiled, and their wives ravished. *Isaiah 13:9,15,16*

It is good for a man not to touch a woman. *I Cor. 7:1*

There are many whose mouths must be stopped. *Titus 1:10,11*

Servants, be subject to your masters with all fear. *I Peter 2:18*

If there come any unto you, and bring not this doctrine, receive him not into your house, neither bid him God speed. *II John 1:10*

If any man among you seemeth to be wise in this world, let him become a fool. *I Cor. 3:18*

Be afflicted and mourn and weep; let your laughter be turned to mourning and your joy to heaviness. *James 4:9*

Submit yourselves to every ordinance of man for the Lord's sake. *I Peter 2:13*

They that resist (powers) shall receive to themselves damnation. *Romans 13:2*

Take every man his sword by his side, and go in and out from gate to gate throughout the camp, and slay every man his brother, and every man his companion, and every man his neighbor. *Ex. 32:27*

Therefore thus saith the Lord God: Woe to the bloody city. I will make the pile for fire great. Heap on wood, kindle the fire, consume the flesh, and spice it well, and let the bones be burned. *Ez. 24:9,10*

I will even appoint over you terror, consumption, and the burning ague, that shall consume the eyes, and cause sorrow of heart . . . I will also send wild beasts which shall rob you of your children. *Lev. 26:16–22*

Behold, I will corrupt your seed, and spread dung upon your faces, even the dung of your solemn feasts. *Malachi 2:3*

I will make mine arrows drunk with blood, and my sword shall devour flesh. *Deut. 32:42*

Verily, verily, I say unto you, Except ye eat the flesh of the Son of Man, and drink his blood, ye have no life in you. *John 6:53*

And the Lord said unto Moses, Take all the heads of the people, and hang them up before the Lord against the sun. *Numbers 25:4*

Slay man and woman, infant and suckling. *I Sam. 15:3*

And David commanded his young men, and they slew them and cut off their hands and their feet and hanged them up over the pool. *II Sam. 4:12*

And he said, Throw her down. So they threw her down: and some of her blood was sprinkled on the wall, and on the horses: and he trode her underfoot. And when he was come in, he did eat and drink and said, Go, see now this cursed woman . . . And they went to bury her: but they found no more of her than the skull, and the feet, and the palms of her hands. *II Kings 9:33–35*

And Moses said unto them, Have ye saved all the women alive? . . . Now therefore kill every male among the little ones, and kill every woman that hath known man by lying with him. But all the women children, that have not known a man by lying with him, keep alive for yourselves. *Numbers 31:15–18*

All the women therein that were with child he ripped up. *II Kings 15:16*

O Princes of the House of Israel, who pluck off their skin from off their bones: who also eat the flesh of my people, and flay their skin off them; and they break their bones and chop them in pieces, as for the pot, and as flesh within the caldron. *Micah 3:1–3*

Wherefore if thy hand or thy foot offend thee, cut them off . . . And if thine eye offend thee pluck it out. *Matt. 18:8,9*

And his lord was wroth, and delivered him to the tormentors, till he should pay all that was due unto him. So likewise shall my heavenly father do also unto you. *Matt. 18:34,35*

Thus were both the daughters of Lot with child by their father. *Genesis 19:36*

I have two daughters which have not known man; let me, I pray you, bring them out unto you, and do ye to them as is good in your eyes. *Genesis 19:8*

So the man took his concubine, and brought her forth unto them; and they knew her, and abused her all the night until the morning. *Judges 19:25*

And it came to pass, that at midnight the Lord smote all the firstborn in the land of Egypt, from the firstborn of Pharaoh that sat on his throne unto the firstborn of the captive in the dungeon; and all the firstborn of cattle. *Ex. 12:29*

The Lion is come up from his thicket, and the destroyer of the Gentiles is on his way. *Jer. 4:7*

The Book of Ruth

Part II

A Sampler

346

BOOK OF RUTH — CHAPTER 12

The Emperor's Visit

Recently a man came to the United States amidst one of the greatest shows of costly pageantry and magnificence and clothed in the most elaborate accoutrements possibly ever witnessed in this country. A man who:

1. Advocates the enslavement of all humanity to a king he claims to represent and thus total submission to himself.

2. Consigns to eternal torture all who resist this enslavement and all, including children, who have not undergone the ritual of baptism which signifies their subjugation.

3. Claims to be successor to a biblical first pope who frightened two converts to death and threw their bodies into the ground. *Acts of the Apostles, chapter 5*

4. Showed contempt for the United States Constitution by challenging the principle of state-church separation defined by the First Amendment.

5. Defines freedom as complete obedience to his doctrine.

6. Denounces the laws of the United States which permit divorce and birth control.

7. Denies women equal rights with men in his organization, which provides for no redress for any of its subjects.

8. Forbids the comforts of marriage and sexual fulfillment to thousands of his servants, who work for little monetary compensation.

9. Vehemently denies women autonomy over their bodies, turning them into victims of an accident of birth and making them breeding machines, and wants the U.S. Constitution amended to conform to his sexist theology. Values a woman's life second to that of an embryo which may be born deformed, insensate, or dead.

10. By his stand on procreation endangers the survival of the human race in its losing struggle with overpopulation and depletion of the earth's resources, admitting that "millions are starving."

11. Celebrates a human sacrifice.

12. Eats flesh and drinks blood, along with his devotees, in actual "teaching."

13. Encourages public homage that involves kneeling to him and kissing his ring.

14. Repeatedly carries a replica of an execution scene and continuously moves his hands in the shape of a torture symbol.

15. Continues to censor, in the name of his king, all books, television, movies, and products of the arts to 700 million persons and aspires to extend this censorship worldwide.

16. Is head of several theocracies which deny citizens equal rights and freedom of worship.

17. Is totalitarian ruler of an institution that has been responsible for the persecution, torture, and slaughter of millions of human beings.

18. Commands a hierarchy that for many centuries impeded science, education, and the healing arts and was responsible for the Dark Ages of Europe.

19. Is absolute monarch of a sect that, through alliances with heads of states, imposed serfdom upon Europe and Russia and class systems that brought on bloody revolutions.

20. Has as his goal to make the world bow down to him; and is heir of a long line of despots who engaged in crusades, inquisitions, massacres, and holy wars to achieve this aim for themselves.

21. By pronouncements and encyclicals tries to spread his philosophy and theology into every area of human activity.

22. Takes money from the poor to build costly edifices for the glorification of his king.

23. Makes no accounting of his wealth and is free from taxation, thus forcing others to support his proselytizing efforts to enslave them and to enable him to perpetuate his hierarchy.

24. Tolerates tension throughout the world today in the form of religious fanaticism that expresses itself in excessive patriotism, sexism, and racism.

25. Is granted a dangerous infallibility by millions in fields of behavior that involve the quality of human life, and even life itself.

26. Shows no remorse for the misery his autocracy has introduced into the world.

Was this man Idi Amin? Was he roundly denounced in his host country and ordered to confine his rituals to his own property and domain? Did the media demand that he submit to the type of questioning on issues that other heads of state have to undergo? Was he asked to defend his arbitrary views to a public that had been subjected to them?

No, it was the Roman Catholic pope, in full panoply, who was praised and officially greeted by the wife of the United States President and entertained at the White House, and who was treated with awestruck deference and privilege and granted unlimited access to our media, whose members competed in handling "His Holiness" with approbation very close to adoration. They assumed the right to proclaim from the public airwaves and the printed page that the citizens of the United States look *en masse* upon the pope as a benevolent autocrat and their personal friend, when it is entirely possible that a majority of them regard him as a would-be dictator who is bending every effort to increase his influence in America, even to the exploitation of our media.

The press, which bewails any encroachment upon its freedom to expose all sides of an issue, refused to fulfill its duty to present a true picture of the feeling engendered by the pope's visit, although the principle of freedom of speech was called upon in last-minute desperation to permit the pope to breach the wall of state-church separation on the Washington Mall.

The pope was unassailable, treated as an idol instead of a controversial figure. There was no fearless newsperson willing to defend the Constitution. And when the pope was mouthing "human rights" and "freedom" and "justice" and concern for the poor and the hungry no commentator pointed out: "Look! The emperor is wearing no clothes!"

BOOK OF RUTH—CHAPTER 13

Excuse Me For Thinking

We are always confronted with the accusation that women have not been creative. Well, no wonder. The attitude women have had to contend with is illustrated by this passage from the autobiography of Charlotte Bronte:

She writes to the poet-laureate of England for a little encouragement. Here is his reply after 10 weeks: "There is a danger of which I would, with all kindness and all earnestness, warn you. The day dreams in which you habitually indulge are likely to induce a distempered state of mind and, in proportion as all the ordinary uses of the world seem to you flat and unprofitable, you will be unfitted for them without becoming fitted for anything else. Literature cannot be the business of a woman's life, and it ought not to be. The more she is engaged in her proper duties, the less leisure she will have for it, even as an accomplishment and a recreation . . ."

Charlotte was so thrilled to get this put-down from him that she replies, in part: "I am afraid, sir, you think me very foolish . . . I am not altogether the idle, dreaming being it would seem to denote. My father is a clergyman of limited income, and I am the eldest of his children. He expended quite as much in my education as he could afford in justice to the rest. I thought it therefore my duty, when I left school, to become a governess. In that capacity I find enough to occupy my thoughts all day long, and my head and hands too, without having a moment's time for one dream of imagination. In the evenings, I confess, I do think, but I never trouble anyone else with my thoughts . . . Following my father's advice—who from my childhood has counselled me, just in the wise and friendly tone of your letter—I have endeavored . . . to observe all the duties a woman ought to fulfill . . . I don't always succeed, for sometimes when I'm teaching or sewing, I would rather be reading or writing; but I try to deny myself; and my father's approbation amply awarded me for the privation."

Here is her abject postscript: "I could not help writing, partly to let you know that your advice shall not be wasted, however sorrowfully and reluctantly it may at first be followed."

How much genius was stifled by male and social ostracism of any woman who did not comply with the domestic slavery demanded of them? A pitiful need to win the approbation of pious fathers was so desperate that women had to apologize for thinking. Here was the unique talent exhibited by Charlotte and Emily reduced to a trait to be suppressed and apologized for. Imagine all artistic creation being accomplished under a pall of guilt.

Her two older sisters showed writing ability, too, but died because of the rigors of the school for clergymen's daughters where their father permitted them to undergo exposure and cruel treatment terrible enough to cause their death in their teens.

This was life 140 years ago. But we still are told what woman's proper duties are. How much genius and talent are still buried under a pile of laundry?

BOOK OF RUTH—CHAPTER 14

Bible Justifies Slavery

(A letter printed in the *Kansas City Star*, March 17, 1980)

I'll be surprised if I am permitted to point out the irony of the black community of Kansas City relying upon the Christian churches to rescue it from economic distress. It is not considered wise to remind society that it was the Old and New Testaments of the Bible that were the authority for keeping humanity in serfdom for centuries and for legitimizing slavery in America, making a bloody civil war necessary to give slaves human rights under our Constitution.

A little history lesson is called for. Thomas Paine, who wrote *The Age of Reason* denouncing the Bible, exerted every effort to outlaw slavery in the new government, but he was overruled by the slaveholders. During the slave era, the Bible was opened at many different places to justify slavery. The Old Testament Mosaic Law contained specific rules about slaves and their treatment and gave permission to beat them as long as the beating was not fatal "for they are his (the owner's) money" (*Ex. 21:21*). The contention was also made that God had ordained slavery because of the behavior of Noah's son Ham (*Gen. 9*). Jesus said he came to uphold "every jot and tittle" of the Mosaic law. *Matt. 5:18*

Not once did Jesus denounce slavery as such. In fact, many of his parables dealt with slaves and masters, in which he upheld barbarous punishment on the part of the master toward any slave whose behavior was found to be wanting. Slaves in these parables are "justifiably" whipped and "delivered to the tormentors" (*Matt. 18:34*). And Jesus says the kingdom of heaven "is like unto" these parables. His teaching was that in the next world the "last would be first" and the role of master and slave would be reversed, but the meek and downtrodden were to wait it out.

It was the "infidel" Abraham Lincoln who freed the slaves from the South led by Christian Jefferson Davis, after the antislavery movement had been led by freethinkers, as it was the humanist movement that rescued the western world from the Dark Ages of the church.

Those who deny my contentions about the Bible should turn to the Epistles to see what Paul and Peter have to say about "servants" and masters. Here are only two examples: "Servants, be subject to your masters in all fear" (*I Peter 2:18*). "Servants, be obedient to them that are your masters . . . with fear and trembling" (*Ephesians 6:5*). There are many more instructions about slavery in the Christian Holy Book.

Ruth Green
Eldon, Mo.

Forsooth, Ruth!

Ruth was a widow, and she didn't want to be.
You can hardly blame her for that.
She asked herself, wouldn't it be just loverly
If I could find a rich old cat?

Mother-in-law Naomi had a trick up her sleeve.
Right on, said Ruth, I'll foller.
In just a short time they were ready to leave
In pursuit of the almighty dollar.

Old Boaz was busy harvesting his crops
When Ruth and Naomi laid the trap.
One night he hit the bottle a bit too hard
And went into the barn for a nap.

Before long Boaz was less than alert
And that's when they gave him the shaft—er,
Guess who sneaked in and crawled under his skirt?
Let's hope they lived happy ever after.

Virgin, Beware!

If somebody stands at the door and knocks
Be sure to call out, "Who is it?"
It could be the Holy Ghost waiting like a fox
To pay you a little visit.

The Answer

Your spouse is getting ready to leave you
You're in debt, you've embezzled from the boss
You're a victim of alcoholism
You've had to sell your stock at a loss.

You're handicapped, you're in a sanitarium
You're addicted to cigarettes and grass
You've been sentenced to a life term in prison
Your doctor's just found a solid mass.

You've gambled away your life's savings
You're an overweight compulsive over-eater
You're going through a middle-life crisis
And your husband has become a wife beater.

For all this there is a panacea
You might say it's the latest prescription
That's heard on every hand and from the pulpit
(You just give them your problem's description.)

You can't buy it in a jar or a bottle
But it's guaranteed to purge you of trouble—
It's a great big dose of Christ Jesus
I advise you to get it on the double.

If you're weary and if you're heavy-laden
With everything from failure to cancer
If you don't gag at swallowing bullshit
Then you'll find that Christ is the answer.

His Eye is on The Sparrow

Implacably watching, he sits on his throne giving heed,
Never blinking, just *noticing* all of his creatures in need.

Of the millions in agony, pleading their pain and duress,
Each victim he dutifully lists as "observed in distress."

No threat to the animals, fowl, or the fish does he slight,
Or that to the sparrow who, falling, is stricken in flight.

True, nothing avails all the wretches who suffer and cry
And the sparrow continues to plummet and fall from the sky.

Still, the fact of their anguish is duly recorded and noted
By that divine overseer to earthlings completely devoted.

And this species called human gets special attention, we know,
For the hairs of their heads are counted and numbered just so.

All That Praying

(This verse accompanied one of Ruth's letters to an editor who did not choose to print her letters.)

President Carter can't govern without it,
Pages in the papers attest to its worth.
Evangelists on the airwaves shout about it,
Chaplains see that Congress suffers no dearth.

Last night I decided that I would see
If all those prayers are actually heard.
So I wrote this letter and uttered a plea
That finally the editor would run one word.

National problems do not abate;
But if *this* appears it's fair to mention
That though the *biggies* do not rate,
Trivial things get prompt attention.

Christianity the Beautiful

Purification by fire and blood,
Inescapable predestination.
Crosses and altars and edges of swords,
Doom-assured preordination.

Piercing and eating of human flesh,
Destruction of flawed creation.
Potter and clay and hardened hearts,
Sly proving and mean temptation.

Ghosts and demons and exorcism,
Spirits and emanation.
Curses and threats and vengeful wrath,
Floods, quakes, and devastation.

Brimstone and napalm and boiling waves,
Diabolical anticipation
Of anguished weeping and gnashing of teeth
And futile recrimination.

Narrow paths and strait, strait gates,
Stingily-proffered salvation.
Strong delusion and crafty deceit,
Everlasting damnation!

It's Like Communication, Man, Y' Know?

Hey, man, y' know, it's like something is, y' know, beginning to get on my,
y' know, like nerves. It's like, y' know, everybody, but, everybody I mean,
keeps, y' know, saying, like "Y' know." Like it's all the time, man. Y' know
what I mean?

You Know Who

The Book Of Ruth

Part III

A Search
Of The
Scriptures

BOOK OF RUTH—CHAPTER 15

What I Found When I "Searched The Scriptures"

A lecture by Ruth Hurmence Green at the Unitarian Church, Columbia, Missouri November 16, 1980

This morning I'm going to tell you what I found when I joined that small group of masochists who regularly decide to muddle through the entire Bible, even if it kills them.

My text is taken from the 5th chapter of John, the 39th verse, wherein Jesus instructs someone who probably can't even read, to "search the scriptures."

Today when the Fundamentalists are once more insisting that the fundamentals of fundamentalism are fundamental to our being No. 1 on the Lord's totem pole, it's very brave of you to invite the "resident atheist" of mid-Missouri to share her thoughts with you. Did you know that this 65-year-old grandmother has become a threat? When I appear infrequently on talk shows, it is not unusual for listeners to be warned to turn off their sets, if they are thin-skinned. I assume that all of you have examined your epidermis and found it to be of sufficient density to permit you to listen to me. And as for those other listeners, as far as I know, none of them ever turns off the set. They pounce upon me, via the telephone, and accuse me of excerpting and of taking out of context. I always agree to stop, just as soon as the preachers do.

Some Christians accuse me of misappropriating the title of born again. They say you have to have a "religious experience" to be re-born. But I *have* had a religious experience. It began when I was a child reared in a small Iowa town by parents who were less than devout Methodists but who required their children to attend church and Sunday School and Epworth League regularly, and it ended when my reading of the entire Bible for myself started a train of thought. This led to my conviction that the natural is so awesome that we need not go beyond it and that there is no evidence in nature for gods with or without bodies, parts, or passions. A purposeless, non-discriminatory/amoral universe exists, and I am part of it and subject to its apparent laws. How all this came about I don't as yet know, and neither does anyone else, and I'm inclined to assign the same ignorance to the Bible writers. Today evolution of human intelligence has advanced us to the stage where most of us are too smart to invent new gods but are reluctant to give up the old ones. . . .

My text is taken from the words of Jesus to the Samaritan woman at the well, one of the rare times when Jesus addressed anyone who was not a pure Jew. Most of the time he adhered to the law whereby Jews did not associate with Gentiles except perhaps to do business with them. If a Jew married a Gentile, unless the Jew was Moses or Solomon of course, the Lord would reward anyone who thrust them through their bellies, or so my scripture search revealed. Almost the whole Bible is anti-Gentile. The most glowing prophecies, which Jesus said he came to fulfill, described the annihilation of the Gentiles on the Day of the Lord. "The lion is come up from his thicket and the destroyer of the Gentiles is on his way." *Jer. 4:7*

Today when I hear the Christian clergy encourage the laity to search the scriptures, I fear one of the Lord's many lying spirits has found a home. Secretly proselytizers must pray the Bible will continue to gather dust on the shelf so that *they* can continue to conspire with the media to expunge passages like: "O princes of the house of Israel, who pluck off their skin from off them and their flesh from off their bones, who also eat the flesh of my people and flay their skin from off them, and they break their bones and chop them in pieces, as for the pot and as flesh within the caldron." *Micah 3:1–3* God is speaking, and here is his description of the day of the Lord: "Everyone that is found shall be thrust through, and everyone that is joined unto them shall fall by the sword. Their children also shall be dashed to pieces before their eyes; their houses shall be spoiled, and their wives ravished." *Isaiah 13:15–16* The Lord could certainly use some help in promoting his big events.

There wasn't one page of this book that didn't offend me in some way. In fact, after a session of searching the scriptures, I always wanted to take a bath with Grandma's lye soap. And when I encountered the Bible's disdain for women, I very often almost pitched the good book across the room. I vowed never to be seen in public with an unconcealed Bible in my hands. Thomas Paine, the true savior of the world, denounced the Bible for me: "I sincerely detest it as I detest everything that is cruel."

But it wasn't only the cruelty and the unimaginable atrocities. If there is *obscenity*, you'll find it in this book. If there is *pornography*, you'll find it in the scriptures, and you won't even have to search. I don't advise opening the Bible aimlessly and reading aloud the first passage that meets the eye. You might violate a censorship law. Strict censorship would mean that the Bible would have to be sold from under the counter.

You can know just how much religion meant to me as a child when I tell you how I used to amuse myself in church by making rubbings from the covers of the song books, but I was a staunch little participant when it came time for hymn singing. Today I shudder at the awful content of some of those hymns, based as they were on the Christian precept that "without shedding of blood is no remission." "Let the water and the blood from thy wounded side which flowed be of sin the double cure, save from wrath and make me pure." Now I wonder why any god would have to die to save sinners from his own wrath. I was "washed in the blood of the lamb." There was a "fountain filled with blood," and I sang loud and clear about it. I had a good idea of how I rated with God every time I sang, along with the rest of the poor wretches in the congregation, "Would he devote that sacred head to such a worm as I?" We were all crawling on our bellies at the feet of a capricious fiend who might, as the *patriarchs* were in the habit of doing, put his feet upon the necks of his enemies at any time. And we were concurring with the pagans that sacred blood could purify, pagans who let the blood of sacred bulls pour over them.

I looked forward to "Communion Sundays." To me grape juice was grape juice was grape juice, and a wafer was a wafer was a wafer. We Methodists practiced the pagan cannibalism of eating the flesh and drinking the blood of a god, but we were nicer about it than the Catholics. Besides, on Communion Sundays the sermons were shorter and sometimes we got to the Doxology more quickly, that testimonial to the Platonic Trinity, which for several hundred years confounded the Church Fathers and divided the Roman Empire into at least 18 quarreling sects, none of whom knew what they were fighting about, and which schisms contributed to the decline and fall of this greatest of states. Rome had thrived for 1,000 years with pagan gods at the helm and expired after only 150 years under the Christian banner.

But what *did* I find when I finally searched the scriptures? In two words: Disillusionment and Release. The "blessed assurance" finally came over me that the Bible and its gods were the products of folk tales and invention all mixed up with a dash of history and seasoned with vast quantities of superstition, and at last I was able to "let a little sun shine in" to dispel the pollution of fear and guilt that befogs the mind of every indoctrinated person. I became the born again skeptic who rejected all gods.

I never thought of myself as a juvenile sinner, at least not a bad one, but I was one, according to the Bible. Paul says avoid foolish questions, and I had some. I never put them to anyone, so perhaps that lets me off the hook. It's hard to tell. One tiny sin even thought about can damn you forever, but I'm not sure at what age children can be excused from the flames, or is it the boiling waves? Jesus didn't seem to know whether hell was a furnace or a lake of fire, and there's very little talk of it in the Old Testament at all, and even less of Satan, who is very polite and nobody seems to be trying to chain him up again after his expulsion from the battlegrounds of heaven, where even the angels weren't happy. But Jesus turned down his generous offer of all the kingdoms of the world, and even after letting old Lucifer set him on a steeple and after camping out in the wilderness with him, Jesus never does reprove Satan for that scene in the Garden. After all these shenanigans, the Bible tells me that *Jesus* died to cause the death of *Satan*, but the Lord works in mischievous ways his blunders to perform and Satan still walks about winning most of our souls. I ask you, who is ahead in the mystic struggle between good and evil?

Apparently Satan is indestructible, even by an omnipotent god. He is always there to create that "superfluity of naughtiness" which James deplores but which comes as such a relief on the heels of Paul's righteousness, whenever we dare to "put our affections on things on the earth" and forget for a few refreshing minutes about being Paul's living sacrifices to God.

In all frankness, I'm very proud of the child that I was, because, you see, even then I thought the Bible was a book of fairy tales. I realize now it was the only way I could accept the hideous stories of the Flood, Abraham and Isaac, Jephthah's daughter, Samson pulling down the temple, the execution of the Hebrew babies by Pharaoh, the midnight slaughter of the Egyptians, and last but most repulsive to me on the biblical horror scale: the crucifixion, which has given us a heritage of and a landscape made ugly by that Christian torture symbol, the Cross. I'm sure they won't be satisfied until the bleeding victim is hanging on every one. I am not convinced that execution scenes inspire and uplift us.

Today Christian parents can purchase recordings, advertised as very realistic, of the infant death scenes in Egypt and the Holy Land as recreated by the industry, and they can buy Bibles in comic book form with every ghastly tale completely illustrated. And these people have the nerve to condemn TV violence. And, by the way, in time for Christmas buying, there is offered a replica of The Last Moment, a Jesus head in its final stages of agony. Christianity has a special propensity for making a silk purse of a sow's ear. It is this unique talent that has enabled the Church to peddle the Bible as the Good Book, this book in which human life is the cheapest commodity and human sacrifice the most valued abomination.

When I was growing up, we read Grimm's and Andersen's Fairy Tales avidly, and surely many of the stories told of cruel deeds, but these deeds were *condemned* not approved, and besides we knew it was all make believe. I remember the very day it finally registered with me that the Bible stories were supposed to be true and there actually was a Holy Land and a real human god who did miraculous things. I was stunned, and from that illuminating day on for much of my life, I always felt a distaste for religion. My distaste joined hands with my doubts.

It took me 300 pages to tell in my book what I found when I finally searched the scriptures, and it's very hard to condense all that. Let me begin by saying that I *didn't* find the Wonderful Words of Life, another one of the melodious descriptions of the biblical message I learned in the church. I expected to find a semblance of love, but what I found were vengeance and threats and curses. The word curse and its various forms appear 205 times in the Bible, and a curse isn't always called curse. The last word in the Old Testament is "curse," and I was so happy in the book of The Revelation to read that "there shall be no more curse." I felt that would truly be heavenly. I was so tired of curses like "The blood of your lives shall I require." This bloodthirsty god made sure that his appetite would be satiated by cursing humanity with the Bible and the Cross. The Bible, itself the ultimate curse, is an in-depth profile of the divine spleen.

Human beings start out under a curse and are forced to suffer from it all through their lives as punishment for original sin, but under divine justice they have still not made atonement but are now required to kill their redeemer, as if one sin will be wiped out by the commission of another. This second sin does not anger the Lord, however. He is happy if, now that his wicked children have tortured him to death, they will feast upon his body and call him a Savior. These reprobates he now considers attractive enough to spend eternity with him, as a reward for turning him into a human sacrifice to himself.

I kept waiting and waiting for human beings to do something admirable in the Bible. I read way through to Omega, and don't waste your time, folks. You're a stinker all the way through. But don't worry about it, because the Lord loves stinkers. It is the happy, successful people who use their minds to accomplish something that he hates.

I had always heard the words "free will" bandied about, but I never could see how God's will could prevail if human beings could do anything they wanted to do. And do you know I was right? I found out that God is the Malevolent Manipulator, the potter who fashions the clay to "honor or dishonor," as Paul and Isaiah agree. I was horrified to read how he hardened Pharaoh's heart, and then I read in the New Testament that as many as were ordained to eternal life believed. And there was more about strong delusion, and there was Jesus saying the way was deliberately obscured even from righteous people who want to know it and that his stories, which I call the terrible parables because they're usually about tormentors and slaves, could be understood by only the disciples. Honestly, now, have you ever known of a bigger bunch of clods than the disciples? After all, Luke tells us that they "understood none of these things." A friend of mine says Jesus was the Rodney Dangerfield of the Holy Land. He just couldn't get any respect from his family, his neighbors, John the Baptist, the disciples, or the Jews, not even from a fig tree, and I wondered if he was the first omnipotent god to come to earth and not be recognized.

But then I began to admire the disciples. You see, they were wonderful skeptics. They demanded evidence right up to the time tongues of fire landed on their heads, an event which reinforced my belief that any god who wanted to be a savior could reveal itself equally to all. I think a tongue of fire on the head would persuade me. How about you?

But I still didn't know what kind of monster was this god, until I saw that Jesus *deliberately* hid his light under a bushel. "Tell no one" was often his command.

Why, I asked myself, is the human race denied evidence about Christianity? Why is it a virtue to accept *any* religion without it, when it would seem the one area to require it, if the punishment for error is unforgivable? Even Abraham asked for evidence, and the Lord obliged him with a magic trick. The Old Testament Jews repeatedly exacted signs and wonders, and God even had to make a sundial shadow go backward. Why is it a *sin* for people to demand evidence about Christianity? Truth is not stashed in the F file under Faith, and no virtue should be attached to belief in what is stashed there.

Christians tell me that they have a higher destiny than the lower animals, because *Homo sapiens* can reason. But the Bible tells me that this gift of reason, which they call god-given, may be the match that lights the fires of hell for all who dare to use it, since whatever is not of faith is sin.

Next I came across all the predestination stuff and how the names of the saved are already written in the book of life from the foundation of the world. No preacher ever told me about that, and I certainly see why. And I began to wonder a little (actually a lot) about the Master Plan of the Great Designer, who does everything on impulse and whose every bungled procedure leads to the Cross. I was desperately trying to assign some purpose to the Almighty Architect. But in spite of all the How-Great-Thou-Art's, the devil kept popping up with these nagging questions. After losing out with Job, he'd been racking up victories all over the world and had moved on to me. I could see no motivation for the creation, Adam was an afterthought *gardener,* Eve had to be fashioned as his helpmate when the lower animals didn't fit the bill, and childbirth was declared a curse. Now there's a plan!

And the question that nagged me the most about the New Testament master plan is one which Christians ignore today but which bothered Paul. Since Jesus suddenly appeared with the gift of eternal life, what was the fate of all who lived before he came? Paul's notoriously big heart bleeds, but he concludes that the pre-Jesus Jews are denied eternal life. At the same time he doesn't assign them to hell, so we are left to assume that all human beings who existed for four million years before Christianity are mouldering forever in their graves.

The plan was for Jesus to come to earth 2,000 years ago with a pocketful of miracles and souls for the people who were then alive. After his return to heaven from Earth (it is about 12 septillion miles from Earth to the edge of our galaxy with 400 billion suns to dodge) he is going to build those mansions, come back before his generation dies out, finally put an end to the world which has been such a rotten disappointment, and deposit *most* of these souls in hell. No wonder heaven is only 12,000 furlongs wide, long, and high.

So much for the justice we are supposed to find in this book where we are told to look for behavior guidelines. Guidelines which go on to teach that it is ethical for the innocent to suffer for the guilty, and that morality is served when we let a blameless person pay for our misdeeds, as if expiation could ever be achieved in such a way. And how can the Bible teach responsibility when everything is preordained and predestined? Fay Wray in the hands of King Kong had more control over her fate than human beings at the mercy of the Bible deity.

And guess what further entrapment I discovered on his part?

Paul, that lyncher who never became less cruel and struck people blind as he set the example for elitist Christians in their dealings with nonbelievers, saying "From such withdraw thyselves" and "let every unbeliever be accursed," tells us that everyone was declared a sinner intentionally by the Lord so that Jesus could come with the gift of grace. Did humankind fall, then? Or were they pushed because Eve wanted to eat of the tree of knowledge?

Paul goes on to reveal (after all, he is the only one to whom the mystery has been exposed) that God *next* formulated the *Mosaic Law* in order to *increase* sin (disobedience to the law) so that *more* grace might be *needed*.

I simply could not absorb what I was being told. I decided that if, by god, we mean rascal, then the god of the Bible was the greatest god who had ever lived in the minds of human beings. And I took a second look at him as a Santa Claus. His gift of grace was given to all who believed, but only those ordained to eternal life *believed*. And the Jews were deliberately given the

"Spirit of Slumber" so that they could not see or know the truth. By this time I was completely bewildered. The Lord who established Judaism had now come up with a plan to damn all Judaists to hell!

And what about this eternal life business? Didn't God make Adam and Eve leave the garden because he feared they would eat the fruit of another tree and live forever? My head was spinning. And didn't this Lord say, "Beside me there is no Savior?" And don't the Jews believe in one-third of the Trinity, and doesn't any third equal the whole? And don't the gates of the New Jerusalem have inscribed over them the names of the 12 tribes of Israel? And aren't the ones closest to the Lamb during eternity going to be 144,000 male Jewish virgins? Help, theologians! Tell me how you turned the Chosen People into the Damned People?

I'm only kidding. The Bible told me how they did it. The Jews didn't recognize their Messiah, that's how. They didn't know he was supposed to be the Lord in human form. Now, really. It was obvious to me by this time that the Jews had created the Lord, instead of the other way around, as I had been taught. I was familiar with some mythology, and now I began to deprogram myself, and I saw that the Lord was just as fabulous as Zeus and Horus, and Jesus only one of many crucified saviors. I saw that gods come in very handy. They may explain the Unknown, and they might help you if you treat them right. And if you want to be important, how better than to make up a supreme being who names you his Chosen People and despises everyone else? If you want to control your people, how better than to put a thousand rules into a god's mouth and have him annihilate anyone who disobeys them? If you want to take other people's land, how better to justify it than to have your god tell you to do it and leave no one breathing? If you want to be sexist and racist, how better to condone it than by having a sexist, racist god not only approve it but order it? If you are typical of the times and inclined to be cruel, how better to burn, hang, drown, smite, mutilate, and torture than to have your god command you to do it and set the example himself? If you want to kill your neighbor, your friend, and members of your family, and thrust your children through when you're not beating them black and blue, what better way to get permission than from a god who is an amoral fiend himself? Poor God! We can't always choose our biographers.

To me the Bible seemed a book written by nobody knows whom in a barbaric age, solely about the Jews and their superstitions. Sometimes I wonder why the Jews don't renounce it as defamatory and that goes for both Testaments. A similar record of most ancient cultures would read much the same. But let me go back to the Messiah, who was supposed to save the Jews from the Gentiles and reestablish the Jewish kingdom.

It is absolutely ludicrous for Christianity to be telling the Jews that their

Messiah has come and turned out to be their Lord in person. Most of the time the Jews had no problem recognizing the Lord in the Old Testament, even when he wrestled with them and disguised himself as a pillar of cloud or smoke. This god didn't do anything but hover over the Jews for 4,000 years, and I'm supposed to believe they don't know him as Jesus? After all, the Bible made it clear to me that Jesus did not fulfill some of the important prophesies, such as the one that Elijah must first appear and anoint the Messiah. When confronted with this, Jesus said that John the Baptist was Elijah, but John said he was not. In fact, Jesus was never anointed, and for the Jews he was anything but a deliverer.

Personally, I felt that the angel Gabriel should be belled, not only to protect unwary women from him and his Holy Ghost partner in crime, but to warn everyone that this angel of the Lord is very careless of the truth. Not only did Jesus not save the Jews from their sins, but he never occupied David's throne or ruled over the House of Jacob for one hour.

Even many people who reject Christianity have been reluctant to criticize Jesus the person, and I fully expected to find the Sweet Jesus we hear about today on every side. And of course I used to warble about being in the garden with Jesus and "he walks with me and he talks with me."

Well, I was hard pressed to find any place in the gospels where Jesus walked with anyone or talked with anyone without castigating them and calling them names. "Blind guides! Fools! Whited Sepulchres! Faithless and perverse generation! Woman (for his mother)!" Jesus was sweet only when you agreed with him, and even then you had better pay attention. His usual discourse included one of his terrible parables, after which he abruptly departed.

Oh, how Jesus was served up to me in church! I heard only the nice things most of the time, and some of the questionable behavior and teachings once more became the silk purse, but the Jesus of the gospels was a stranger to me, and again, I see why. Recently the pope has accused people of tampering with the simplicity of the words of Jesus. He should be eternally grateful for the tampering that's been so carefully accomplished. Should the *gospel* Jesus ever be resurrected, the astonishment I felt would be widespread.

The other day I went into the store where I usually buy paint. I was greeted at the door by a sign: IF YOU OPEN YOUR HEART, JESUS WILL COME IN. They gave me a paint stirrer on which was their lettered conviction: Jesus is Lord. I wanted to ask them if they'd ever heard of the Crusades and the Inquisition and the Dark Ages, all of which could be laid at the door of Sweet Jesus? I wondered if they knew that his words had often led to some of the most reprehensible crimes against humanity and some of the most immoral personal behavior ever documented. And you can rest assured I was never told that he was an exorcist who talked to devils, that he believed certain maladies were caused by possession, that he healed with spit; that he knew nothing of the Universe and believed the earth to be flat, that he cursed a fig tree for not bearing out of season, that he had to be persuaded to heal a Gentile child because he said his message was only for the lost tribes of Israel, that he refused to wash his hands, that he damned three cities for not welcoming him, that he was rude to his mother and lied to his brothers and taught family abandonment, that he cast devils into 2,000 pigs who ran into a lake and were drowned, that he defended slavery and told how to beat servants, that he told people to hate their lives, to mutilate their bodies, to drink poison, handle snakes, and jabber nonsense, that he said he came with a sword to cause hatred and division. I was told only the same old tired parables, never the brutal ones. I wasn't told that he was superstitious and believed in the evil eye, and I was not aware that he loved to describe the sufferings of the damned and seemed always to be plotting to trap as many of them as he could. Sure, I knew all about the adulteress he defended, but it was never pointed out that he let the adulterer go or that he told a story about ten virgins awaiting one bridegroom and said woe to pregnant women and those who are suckling babies at the end of the world. Jesus is Lord and everything that supported that statement is what I was told.

Can you imagine how many sermons I listened to without realizing that Jesus convinced his followers that he was coming right back before his generation died out and that they were so sure of this that they made such statements as: "Now once in the end of the world hath he appeared." *Heb. 9:26* This was supposed to mean that the end of the world at that time would make it unnecessary for Christ to come again and again to forgive the sins of succeeding generations. As a child I was terrified about the End of the World. I didn't know the moon had to turn to blood first. Or that there would be swords and kings and horses. When I finally faced up to the fact that I could not admire in a deity what I condemned in human beings, I knew that I could not denounce Torquemada and Hitler and worship their Bible counterpart who knew that his salvation plan would be damnation for most people of the world. Didn't he say that many are called but few are chosen and that strait is the gate and narrow is the way and few there be that find it? Not only is he comfortable with this situation but so seem to be those who worship this divine sadist. We all know that Christians are the only happy people. The Christian business of making themselves happy is a 20 billion dollar one.

But it wasn't only the gods of the Bible that I found not to my taste. I searched the scriptures in vain for someone to serve as a role model for human beings who wished to lead exemplary lives. Let's see now. There was

Abraham, a pimp for his wife, and a blackmailer who would have been charged with abandonment and child abuse in today's society. Lot was next, a drunkard guilty of incest with his two virgin daughters, one of 19 cases of incest in the Bible (not counting the children of Adam and Eve). Then there was Noah, another drunkard, who curses his grandson for his son's behavior. I waded through the other family scandals till I got to David, and we all know about him, except I hadn't been told that he hated the lame and the blind, tortured captives, and hamstringed horses. Samson was another animal torturer; he tied 300 foxes together two by two and set their tails on fire. Solomon was so wise he had 1,000 wives and concubines. And Gideon! I wonder if the Gideons ever read about how he slaughtered and tortured thousands with the Lord's help. As far as getting acquainted with your hero or heroine goes, women who belong to Esther societies in their churches would be scandalized if they actually became familiar with this hard-hearted Hannah of the Persian court. And I certainly hoped my parents hadn't named me after Ruth, when I read about her sordid seduction scene with her kinsman. I finally happened upon one reputable person in the Old Testament. He was distinguished by his coat of many colors and his honorable and forgiving nature. Joseph, of course. He was one of the gems I sometimes speak of that can be found by wading through the muck of most of the Bible.

But my greatest revulsion towards those who were next to God's own heart has to be reserved for Peter. If I were the pope, I would not smile when I was addressed: "Thou art Peter." I was already familiar with Peter's cowardly behavior and Jesus's sometime contempt for him, but little did I know how low he could sink when it came to revenue and profit. I have pity for him if he was crucified either right-side-up or upside-down, but he never did have to answer for frightening two converts to death for withholding some money from the communist Christian church and throwing their bodies into the ground with nary a last rite or extreme unction. Speaking of murder, Moses was guilty, and Paul was an accessory. The Bible does not allow any murderer to enter the kingdom of heaven, but St. Peter even has the keys.

I don't know how the courts can make criminals swear upon the Bible, when this book is a chronicle of every kind of crime committed by the Lord and his favorites. If I were a defense lawyer, I would say, "Look, Judge, my client only did what so and so does in the Bible."

You know, as we get older, we are sometimes afflicted with palsy, an uncontrollable shaking of the head. Age hasn't yet given me this malady, but I read the Bible, and I've been shaking my head ever since. Even my husband is a victim. Sometimes, upon hearing the traditional propaganda about the Good Book, we can be seen shaking our heads at each other. As long as this forbidding tome is left to the clergy, they will make of it what they will. That is why I call it a behavior grab bag. It is possible to pull out justification for imposing your will on others, simply by calling your will God's will. I can even use the Bible to forbid you to jog, practice law, take a census, or sleep on a downy pillow.

History and current events prove my point. The divine tyrant of the Old Testament still has his feet on the necks of Judaists, Christians, and Moslems, and they refuse to shake him off. They have prostrated themselves before the imagination and superstitions of the long ago and choose to be enslaved to the morality of an age of ignorance and savagery. People have made an idol of the Bible. And they call all this freedom. Pardon me while I shake my head.

I didn't know whether to laugh or cry when I encountered the taboos and make believe of the Bible. By spending a few minutes with the Lord, I experienced medievalism again, with its myths and bugaboos of our fearful, groping ancestors . . . virgin births, angry gods, human and animal sacrifices, purification by fire and blood, angels, devils, spirits, souls, ghosts, crucified redeemers, heavens and hells, signs and wonders, resurrections. Incidentally, I found nine specific resurrections of the dead in the Bible, several ascensions, miracle workers by the number. I found that Jesus wasn't unique in any way that would make him divine, and as for the prophets, do guesses about the future make you messengers of a god? And anyone can have a revelation or be inspired at any opportune time.

I shudder when I hear people demand that we go back to the Bible. I have just one suggestion for them, that they read the Mosaic Law of the Old Testament and remember that Jesus said he came to uphold that law by every jot and tittle. Then let them read Paul and see how his theology nullifies our Bill of Rights, opposes science, forbids pleasure, discourages any accomplishment and personal pride, recommends that mouths must be stopped and books burned, that women submit to their husbands totally, and that men not even touch women.

While I was finally searching the scriptures, I had to keep pinching myself to be sure I existed. The Bible's language is so sexist that most of the time one is not conscious of the female sex, *and* most of the time that's probably just as well, since from Eve on, women are the culprits and the disposable property of the male population. The double standard waves over every page. Sex is sinful. Eunuchs and celibacy are praised as signs of holiness and purity. Several million monks and nuns testify to this recommendation.

I did become convinced that Eve should replace Mary as the heroine of Christianity. The Bible tells me that Eve was responsible for the fall of man. No fall—no need for a redeemer—no Christianity. Mother Eve, you gave birth to the new faith. In sin did you conceive it.

I am pleased as punch no longer to believe in a god who declares reason a sin, who will not choose many noble and great and wise things but has chosen the base things of the world, the foolish things, the weak things and the things which are not. A god who can choose his companions in eternity and prefers Jerry Falwell and Tammy Bakker over Albert Einstein and Marie Curie. I am no longer a fool for Christ's sake. And I have no more desire to be a sheep than to be a fool.

Skepticism is the way to knowledge, and that is why I am proud to be a skeptic.

The Book Of Ruth

Part IV

Memories

Book Of Ruth

Memories

Part of me wants to be ten again, sauntering barefoot down the alley behind our house, curling my insteps around the sharp rocks, wincing at the hot Iowa earth, sucking in my breath trying for the hundredth time to whistle a tune, thinking how grown-up I was becoming and how everything was right with the world. But another part of me knows that I wouldn't want to go back, and I ponder the strangeness of the certainty that I would reject any offer to make me that child again, with all the growing up and living to do over. Not for a minute would I seriously contemplate such an opportunity, even though mine has been in general what is called a good life, and even though the pleasant times outnumber the bad.

How many of us would say in honesty, "Let me live my life over again; let me have the same experiences once more?" Does this reluctance tell us that existence is not as appealing as it is perceived to be, that we see it, approaching its close, as, if not an ordeal, a sort of unpredictable gauntlet that we are forced to run by the bittersweet circumstance of being? Is life a boon, then, or a condition which few would choose, in full understanding of what it entails? Perhaps, after all, life as a gift is a myth, and we are destined to be so bewildered at our unsolicited and seemingly purposeless coming-about that we create gods to bestow prestige upon us.

Gift or imposition, my own life began January 12, 1915, in Sumner, Iowa. I was delivered by Dr. Whitmire in my parents' bedroom in a rented house not far from the Chicago Great Western tracks that wound through this typical midwest town of about 2500 in a northeastern area of the state. The doctor's handscales weighed me in at 12 pounds, the only time I was ever large for my age. "Ruthie" I was to be, although it was surely not any shyness of demeanor which dictated that I be addressed by the diminutive of my biblical name.

I was never a "Ruthie." More like a "Bossy," an epithet occasionally thrown at me by friends experiencing moments of high dudgeon brought on by some supercilious behavior on my part. To neighbors and relatives I was a "tomboy," a derogatory, tongue-clucking classification reserved for girls who took part in those challenging activities ordinarily assigned to boys. My mother gave up early on stimulating my maternal instincts, and my last

Christmas doll with its bisque features, natural hair and eyes that opened and closed, languished undisturbed in its crib, neatly tucked into the bedding my mother had stitched on her treadle machine. I preferred to dress my *kitten* in the clothes she had sewn for my doll. I don't know how my mother felt about all this; she didn't lay many guilt trips on me.

No doubt I was welcomed into our family. After the arrival of two boys, the traditional desire for male offspring has usually been satisfied, and, besides, I was never made to feel less important to my parents than my brothers. I have a dim memory of feeling occasional resentment when the boys were accorded certain privileges not granted my sister and me, but I seldom rebelled openly at the attitudes of the day. Had there been more sex discrimination in our family, a smoldering consciousness of its pervasion in our culture would have burst into a feminist activism on my part many years before it actually did.

My brothers did not treat my younger sister Marian and me as inferiors, and I can recall no disdain ever exhibited by them for our being female. Our family inter-relationship was always one of mutual consideration, kindness, and respect for one another. At one time I heard my father accuse my mother of always having been partial to the boys, but I personally had no reason to feel that she was.

My mother was not what is known as demonstrative, in any case. Overt displays of emotion were not her nature, and I seem to have inherited a reticence in that area to the extent that I often envy those who are capable of expressing deep feelings openly. On the other hand, my parents' equanimity contributed much to my own sense of security.

As a child I remember my mother breaking down only twice in my presence, and these were times of terror for me. Still, children of my day at least did not have to worry about becoming "products of a broken home." Divorce was not a threat or even a dreaded possibility, in the minds of children of the 20's. Not unheard of, certainly, but approximately on the same scale of likelihood as that of being struck by lightning. An occasional overheard parental argument, though it might even be intense, portended no change in the status quo. Extreme situations existed, of course, but on the whole, the surface of middle-class America's domestic inviolability remained serene.

I was a middle child. I don't know who chose the names of my older brothers Vaylard and Howard, but I thought they were not only unusual but elegant ones, well-suited to our distinguished surname, a perverted spelling of the Dutch "Heermance." (I have heard it said that the Dutch had a hankering for varying the spelling of their family names, and the examination of gravestones in a Dutch cemetery will verify this idiosyncrasy.)

Marian was only two years younger than I but the opposite in coloring.

Her blue eyes and light brown hair and my own hazel eyes and dark hair didn't preclude inquiries about the possibility of our being twins (fraternal, of course). My mother's propensity for sometimes dressing us alike no doubt prompted that assumption, and I came to understand why she chose to make two identical dresses. Far from being the skilled seamstress my mother was, I eventually teamed up with the tools of the trade to create several articles of clothing for my own offspring and grandchildren (with excruciating attention to every detail of the deceptively labelled easy-to-make patterns I was careful to choose). After agonizing over each gather and seam, I felt that I could have "run up" a duplicate with wonderful ease. In fact, it seemed a shame to waste my hard-won expertise, and I smoothed and folded those tissuey pattern pieces for storage with real regret.

My mother sometimes demonstrated her respect for the frugality of the times by making dresses for my sister and me out of discarded garments of her own, prompted more by her creative impulses than by any economic necessity. I was very open about it all and told a stranger admiring my mother's handiwork that "Mama got it out of the attic."

We built and moved into this handsome two-story frame house with "the attic" (actually a half story) in 1916. It was only two short blocks from Sumner's business district and across the street from two churches and in a direct line of any sanctified rays that might be emanating from them. The Evangelical church was ringed by large catalpa trees, while the U.B. (United Brethren) church "catty-cornered" from it was flush with the street. Our own church, the Methodist Episcopal, was one block closer to "town," and the Lutheran church, with a tall steeple surmounted by a large cross, was only a block away on the street behind us. Sunday mornings were easily identified, as the various bells competed with each other for the allegiance of the faithful.

And every noon and 6:00 P.M. were announced by the "halloo" of the town whistle (mounted on the water tower) that swelled and receded with infallible regularity. We adapted our schedules to Sumner's signals. No matter what transpired, the bells rang and the whistle blew. Life went dependably on, but occasionally the citizenry was reminded that the sequence of days could be terminated. Upon the demise of any member of the Lutheran church, its bell tower reverberated with a doleful peal for every year of the deceased's age. The cold hand of doom brought a "pause in the day's occupation" that served the dual purpose of honoring the departed and reminding fellow members of the congregation about the tenuous nature of existence and the wisdom of populating the pews the following Sunday.

My youngest brother was born when I was in the sixth grade, and I am speculating that I may have anticipated this latecomer to the family circuit with a bit more enthusiasm than my parents felt at the time. A latent maternal instinct proved to have been present in the tomboy all the time, and I took over some of the care of this towheaded charmer, becoming quite proprietary and fatuously parading him about in his new velvet suspension-type carriage, expectantly awaiting lavish words of praise from passers-by for his unique brand of infantile appeal. For several years I willingly assumed much responsibility for his care, and cheerfully responded to peremptory requests for graham crackers and cream, a favorite snack, but during his infancy I had an experience that brought home to me the transient quality of life that often intrudes upon a state of human satisfaction with the status quo.

One of my father's brothers and his family lived on First Street behind us, and I was fond of playing with my several cousins and visiting with my busy aunt. Another little boy was born into their home a few weeks after I welcomed my own new brother, and I became very attached to him and found time to take him for similar airings. Unbelievably, after a brief illness, this nine-month-old cousin became another of pneumonia's many victims of those years before penicillin. I can still see the relatives gathered around the tiny casket for prayers in the family living room before the funeral at the church and the burial in Union Mound cemetery. I was tearful and stupefied. For the first time I saw that it wasn't wise to allow yourself to be too happy— always keep your fingers crossed became my philosophy. I was unprepared for the precariousness of human existence. I had known about death, but now I had to relate to it.

It was my first encounter with the reality of my bedtime prayer—"if I should die before I wake." This ugly apprehension inflicted upon children had carried little significance for me up to now. Still, it was not so much myself I saw standing perilously at the gates of the Great Beyond as it was all the dear ones who made my world a delight. It was then I began to play the game that involved angry criticism of the Lord: IF I HAD CREATED THE WORLD. Does the saint live who has not blasphemed in this way?

My outlook on life was never quite the same, but soon the hurt scabbed over, and some of my playmates and I were even seen to be playing funeral.

Another game occasionally dramatized by my sister and me, and a neighbor girl about our age, spoke to our interest in the mystery of s-e-x, which we would have suffered torture rather than express to an adult. We knew little about having babies and often speculated on how the newcomer made its entrance into the world. Although pregnant women more or less secluded themselves, it was apparent to us and anyone with eyes just where the unborn spent nine months, but the birth process itself was pure imagination on our part. All we knew for sure was that the expectant mother went to bed mysteriously ill, and that somebody (a nurse or a doctor) soon brought in a baby, which she was inordinately pleased to see. Acting this out, we knew nothing, and at the same time we knew everything. Since then I've thought about our improvised deliveries. Whatever they lacked in reality, they made up for in drama.

⟹◆⟸

The Hurmence family owned the Sumner Telephone Company, and at one time the local power plant. The latter was sold after a near-fatal accident occurred that heightened my father's fears about the still somewhat novel dangers of high voltage electricity. One day an employee instinctively brushed aside a fallen "hot line" that promptly straightened him out like a board. Dazed, he managed to get to his feet, stunned not so much by the shock itself as by the realization that he had survived to tell how it felt to encounter 2400 volts of electricity.

My father told of his own skepticism, at the time the power plant was purchased, that a market could be developed for the newfangled washing machines and fans. The placing of the former out on trial, and the arrival of the next steamy Iowa summer (ideal for growing that famous Iowa corn) took care of his doubts.

Many welcome devices were appearing, to free women from the drudgery of housework in the early part of the 20th century. Irons heated on a wood stove, and foot-operated sewing machines began to give way to electrical appliances that presaged what was to come. Our own kitchen was a testimony to the widening gap between the old and the new. Against one wall was a kerosene cookstove, and opposite it sat an electric range. Bottled gas cookstoves were timidly accepted by overworked housewives, and the domestic chains of women who, unlike my mother, could not afford to hire "help," began to slacken slowly but inevitably. (There remained the mystery of why elaborately beruffled and beribboned gowns also began to go out of style about the time it became easier to wash and iron them.)

At one time the Hurmence Telephone Company operated exchanges at New Hampton, Hawkeye, and West Union, Iowa, and long distance lines between several small towns in the area. The telephone lines themselves, while not involving the lethal threat of power lines, gave my father and uncle much concern in the icy Iowa winters. Mother's younger sisters at times were employed as "hello girls" at the switchboards. The telephone operator, often addressed over the wire by her first name, was regarded as a confidante and source of information and general assistance by the community, especially in times of emergency. A cot was provided close to the switchboard for the night operator.

Most telephones were hung on the wall, but many of the handsome burnished-brass table and desk phones were fated to be indiscriminately destroyed when newer equipment replaced them. Today they are sought by collectors.

The Hurmence Telephone Company office was on the second floor of a building in Sumner's business district and was reached by a dark staircase and landing. Sweeping these stairs was a weekly task assigned to my brother. (It paid a not inconsiderable 25 cents.) On the few occasions when he was otherwise occupied, I was allowed to take over this Saturday morning chore. Painfully responsible and determined to outshine my sibling, I began by liberally sprinkling the red sweeping compound over the steps, after which I wielded the broom industriously, making sure to remove all the debris from the corrugated rubber mats. My perfectionism required that no offending dust particle escape the special brush provided to dislodge grime from the corners.

This entire painstaking performance was an inescapable manifestation of my scrub-the-sidewalk Dutch heritage. From the time I could straighten the rug or strain to adjust a picture, I insisted upon, and applied myself to maintaining, spotless orderliness in all my surroundings. The need for absolute pristine organization at all times has tyrannized me mercilessly throughout my life and even today dictates that every drawer and cupboard be in a state of uncompromising neatness. From this curse of insistence upon torturous tidiness there is no escape, and my tombstone will surely read, "She died on a freshly-made bed." My family knows that I live in horror that an offensive piece of satin lining will protrude impudently from my coffin for all eternity, as fit punishment for the agony my loved ones have had to suffer because of my obsession with order and cleanliness. (Should I be reduced to ashes, may my remains be distributed evenly upon the winds.)

Because my father could be vehement and somewhat sarcastic at times, I was in awe and probably unjustified apprehension of what I perceived as an easily triggered display of temper. Consequently, I usually took my requests to my mother, expecting her to relay them to him for consideration, should they require parental deliberation. At times, however, I would brave the stairs and the formidable air of his private office to ask for a dime!

Joking with some business acquaintance or friend who happened to be with him at the time, he would not fail to bestow upon me what he hinted was a considerable sum for a child of the 20's to be asking. (Dimes were bonuses that required agonizing decisions of how they should be squandered. Not once did I ever purchase an Oh Henry, the only candy bar priced as ridiculously high as 10 cents.) My "sweet teeth," an expression adapted by my small nephew to describe his uncontrollable craving for certain carbohydrates, were an inherited craving. Candy in some form was usually to be found either on the person or within easy reach of my mother and maternal grandmothers, but no guilt had to be attached to such indulgence in the days before it was determined that sugar was a sinister deterrent to long life. (My grandmothers lived into their nineties, and my mother died at the age of 88.)

In these days when almost every food that human beings enjoy is declared to be hazardous if not sinful, we of the older generations recall philosophically the dire warnings from authorities that tomatoes caused cancer in the digestive tract and that food cooked in aluminum ware should be ingested only by would-be suicides.

<hr />

Sumner was a delightful place in which to grow up in the 20's. Sumner was small. Sumner had trees. Sumner had a creek. Sumner had a park. Sumner's environs were graced by a few wooded sections. Sumner had a change of seasons that allowed for every kind of activity in the recreation repertoire of the young. But best of all, Sumner was safe. Parents were able to give their children freedom to move about with little supervision, a license made possible by the comparative innocence of the times and the character of small town midwest life. We youngsters were free to wander at will within the city limits and even a reasonable distance beyond, as long as we appeared for meals and "punched the clock" on schedule.

When I think back on my delicious childhood, I realize that throughout those amiable years I was nearly a completely free spirit. Though I was expected to conform in some areas such as scholastic achievement, the prevailing permissiveness translated for me into an autonomy not only of movement, but of association, and even of thought. This independence was a prerequisite to the creativity that we as children were compelled to exhibit in shaping the pattern of our leisure hours.

Addiction to as yet nonexistent television fare did not threaten that inventiveness, and we made use of it to devise our own recreation and often the equipment needed as well. Our baseballs were black walnuts laboriously wrapped in string, our slingshots were made of forked sticks and strips of innertube. Our kites, fashioned of brown wrapping paper, ranged from a simple diamond shape slightly bowed, to the more complex box type. These latter inanimate harbingers of spring seldom rewarded their creators by soaring bravely on the wind. Should a few specimens rise falteringly for an exhilarating moment or two, they usually took sudden dives calling for agonized decisions about the need for more or fewer strips of tail. The undaunted determination displayed by boys and girls racing to and fro to lift their handiwork into the clouds would have launched a thousand ships.

Each change of season was celebrated with its own rites. Some unseen but dependable dictator decreed that on certain days of the year kites should fly, tops spin, mumbledypeg knives flip, ball bats and racquets swing, and marbles and croquet balls roll. Robots that we were, we cooperated.

School days ended at 4:15, and from then on I was unencumbered with chores or rarely-assigned homework. Weekends and summer vacations were anticipated with the realization that few restrictions would be imposed upon my carefree hours. The younger generation of our neighborhood, frequently augmented by participants who wandered over from other parts of town, appeared as if led by a resurrected Pied Piper, to gather in groups poised for what our parents must have assumed would be harmless fun. At times these activities took place after dark, when games of Run Sheep Run sparked occasional complaints from the growers of backyard gardens, for whose product we had the inexcusable disdain often held by young people for the concerns of their elders.

On many summer Saturdays, youths of all ages congregated at the Lutheran church, but not for spiritual purposes. Providence had provided a fortuitous entrance to this house of the Lord—a large concrete area fronting on a wide flight of steps leading into the sanctuary. Voila! A stadium! This setup was an open invitation to communal roller skating, and to my knowledge we were never asked by authorities to refrain from disturbing the peace that passeth understanding or from using the area to indulge in the pursuit of worldly pleasure.

Less skilled performers looked on with open admiration for the fancy whirls and figures executed by a few experts with the heady gusto commonly demonstrated by those who receive the unrestrained adulation of their peers. Stark envy understandably composed a large part of that adulation, for several of the objects of it were able to dazzle their public on skates which boasted only two wheels. Most of us didn't even know where to obtain such skates, which we regarded as on a par with the rarely encountered unicycles.

Sumner was just beginning to pave its streets, but sidewalks were wide and plentiful, and they were indispensable to our lifestyle. After all, you could skate on them, roll a hoop on them, or ride a bike on them. Or walk on them with stilts. Or skip rope on them. Or stub your toe on them. Or spin tops on them. Or play jacks or hopscotch on them, meet a friend on them, wheel a baby carriage on them, or go home on them. Trees have won the kudos of poets, but who has been moved to pen an ode to the prosaic sidewalk? We aren't sure who can make a tree, but it surely takes human know-how to make a sidewalk. Sadly, today sidewalks have given way in importance to the thoroughfare, that busy pathway of the automobile, and one may look in vain for them in some housing developments. In such unconscious ways we deprive our children.

We didn't have spending money or allowances, but few of our pastimes required funding. There was no admission charge for the ice skating rink or the swimming pool, both of which were opportunely and unofficially located in the Little Wapsipinicon, the "crick" which wound along the outskirts of Sumner, and which also provided a dam where, unbeknownst to our parents, we could perch precariously with our eyes on a bobbing cork, and try to snare unwary bullheads. But the Little Wapsi served a more important function. Blocks of ice cut from it during the winter preserved the food of Sumner residents throughout the year. When the temperature reached the 90's, the sight of the horse-drawn ice wagon at the end of the street attracted a swarm of sweaty youngsters begging for a chunk of frozen water temptingly garnished with sawdust. Squeamishness about the source of this natural coolant, however, was not allowed to interfere with the enjoyment of iced lemonade by people who lived in houses not yet introduced to air conditioning. I doubt if it was generally known that freezing does not kill germs. Besides, one must not ask too much of human prudence.

⋙⬥⬤⬦⋘

We were beginning to see, on Sumner's streets, the last of the horse as a means of locomotion. In the way the electric refrigerator was gradually replacing the back porch icebox with its demanding drip pan and insatiable appetite for the frozen substance of the Little Wapsi, so the new chariots on wheels were about to put Old Maud out to pasture for good.

Far from being hailed as the latest of the proliferating wonders that were to prove a boon to civilization, the Model T had been generally looked upon as a risky innovation doomed to a short life span. Few predicted the size of the impact that Mr. Ford's contribution would have on the American lifestyle; indeed, at first the automobile was little more than a toy for the more adventurous spirits of the community.

True, a certain amount of derring-do was involved in operating these mechanical steeds. Those who had learned to harness, coax, and control the live variety now found that a certain mastery was also necessary to coerce and manipulate this new tool of the devil. To first retard the spark on the steering column just so, then to move gingerly to a crouched position between the headlights and apply oneself to turning the crank in such a considered way as to avoid kickback and a possible broken arm, and finally to plunge behind the wheel and frantically nurse the belching, hiccoughing patient back to health by means of choke and throttle—all this incurred a commitment to progress of which any red-blooded citizen might be proud. (Should a particular engine prove annoyingly reluctant to catch hold, it might even be necessary to resort to giving the cranky vehicle an encouraging push, or even, in desperation, to jacking up a back wheel preparatory to attacking the crankshaft with renewed determination, if not unflagging zeal.)

Pride of ownership, and an ill-concealed self-congratulatory feeling of satisfaction at having tamed the latest monster to be foisted upon humankind, both combined to lessen the annoyance engendered by such attendant inconveniences as road conditions that lagged behind the new mechanization, nonnegotiable inclines, and precariously-attached wheels that occasionally disengaged and rolled lazily and dishearteningly into the ditch.

Although most people had a Model T, my parents were owners of a Willys Knight "touring car." Ironically, these early horseless carriages were in no conceivable sense suitable for touring, or indeed for any venturing out whatsoever in extreme temperatures unless one was indisputably in a state of grace, as they were completely open to the weather and equipped with only detachable curtains bearing isinglass inserts. On one bleak midwinter trip from North Dakota back to Iowa, we children huddled on the floor under a heavy lap robe, a standard seasonal accessory for automobiles at a time when concern for mechanical performance left little room for any concession to human comfort, such as a heating system. Still, it wasn't long before our family was able to purchase a Buick brougham which even sported a vase for flowers, a furbelow seldom utilized and soon to be regarded by the industry as a refinement incompatible with the indispensable automotive requirements of the bourgeoisie.

The paving of Sumner streets was a natural consequence of the advent of the new means of transportation, but hard-surfacing of the "pike" into Sumner from Fayette on the east and Tripoli on the west had to wait a bit. Up to then a gravelled road like the pike represented the epitome of highway excellence. Farmers traditionally faced with the dirt and ruts of rural byways looked upon the pike as their personal yellow brick road.

Twenty-five or thirty miles an hour being necessarily just about top "tin lizzie" speed, unfamiliar driving hazards and mishaps such as detached wheels did not cause many injuries or fatalities. Besides, the chassis of a vintage car was so high off the ground that my mother on one hurried afternoon backed all unknowingly over my little brother, who proceeded to toddle off with only an accusatory trace of axle grease on his romper, leaving my mother in somewhat of a state.

No doubt the housewives of Sumner felt a highly personalized enthusiasm at the prospect of seeing asphalt applied to the city streets, but it was also an exciting time for young people. We were fascinated by the massive rollers maneuvering with elephantine grace at the behest of the operators (one of whom was to become a human sacrifice to Sumner's decision to conform to the rapidly changing 20th century) as they ponderously sculpted the new symmetry that provided our little town with an unfamiliar cosmopolitan physiognomy.

With an increasing number of various makes of vehicles moving briskly along the spanking new pavements and lined up at the curbs downtown, truly a transformation had been accomplished. We children could scarcely remember the old dusty avenues and were quick to make use of these inviting surfaces for our own activities, which the still comparatively light traffic flow seldom impeded.

Gradually, as automotive improvements emerged, the "tin can" image generated by the Model T faded. But problems of maintenance not related to the care of the old horse and buggy remained, and chief among them had to do with a further vulnerability of the four wheels. Unfortunately, tires on these wheels were fitted with inner tubes that insisted on deflating whenever a rock or sharp object penetrated the casing to a sufficient depth. At times, when a piece of tubing worked its way unnoticed through a hole or weak place in the outer covering, the resulting explosion, which had a shattering ability of its own for announcing the presence of an emergency, came to be christened (among other less polite epithets) a "blowout."

"Flats" of any kind inevitably tested the degree of dedication of all and sundry aficionados of the new conveyances, who, to effect a repair, had first to apply a "boot" patch to the casing with special cement, and next, not yet having proved their mettle, were bound to proceed to the punctured inner-tube, in need of a bandaid of its own.

How small the world was becoming with the prospect of a car in every garage and improvised shed! What enticing vistas unfolded! How suddenly nearer and dearer seemed distant friends and loved ones! How quickly within reach became the purple mountain majesties and fruited plains! The many discomforts and drawbacks of the "touring" car as a temporary home away from home counted for naught. America was turning into a nation of neophyte explorers. Comfortable hearths were unhesitatingly, even eagerly, abandoned for the open, if not always hospitable, road leading to those formerly only dreamed-of sites having to do with American history and folklore, places reachable in the past only by those who could afford, financially and healthwise, to brave the unpleasantries of the railroad and steamboat.

Ramshackle filling stations had begun to mar the landscape, and all of them did not feel obligated to provide "necessary" comforts. Families with children, especially, withheld purchase of gas and oil until they had been assured that, yes, there was a restroom.

My father saw the broadening horizons as a wonderful way of satisfying his abiding curiosity concerning history and the exploits of the genus Homo sapiens, a curiosity which for him had reached full flower in a field of interest labelled Lincolnmania. All of this came together one summer when we made plans with two other families to walk vicariously where little Abe may have played on the woodland paths, and gaze worshipfully upon the log cabin where he had purportedly been born.

We children were also to get our first taste of the South, a part of our country as foreign to me as if it lay beyond the farthest seas instead of within a few hundred miles of our back door. I didn't exactly expect to see slaves. After all, I did know that they had been freed by our hero Mr. Lincoln at the instigation of the North (luckily *my* habitat) but Stephen Foster's nostalgic lyrics had engraved on my consciousness such a picture of plantations, Ole massas, loyal blacks, and kinky-headed "pickaninnies," that I had to struggle to overcome my preconceived image of "Dixieland, Dixieland."

This was a camping trip with all the accoutrements of what is commonly identified as camping in its purest form. Our companions were family friends—two ministers and their wives and the young daughter of one of the couples. The total of amateur campers and the equipment necessary to preserve life and afford comfort made it a miracle that we required only three cars for our brave safari to the other side of the Mason-Dixon Line. Days of sight-seeing and totting up an agreed-upon amount of mutual mileage inevitably led to nightfall, when we put up our tents in public parks or, through the importunings of our clergymen, in handy churchyards, with access to all outdoor conveniences. Who can say that a terrifying storm one night that threatened to set our entire caravan down in a neighboring state, was not quelled by "faith the size of a mustard seed" in the makeup of one of our proprietors of the pulpit?

True to the spirit of the adventure upon which we were embarked, we all wore newly-purchased khaki knickers or trousers, shirts, and hats. Our itinerary included parts of Indiana, Kentucky, and Tennessee. After paying proper tribute at Lincoln's cabin and visiting the Old Kentucky Home, we came upon the Old Oaken Bucket, which only an appalling dearth of material could have made the inspiration for a song. Poor Mr. Foster was truly reduced to scraping the bottom of the barrel, if not the bucket.

We found that Mammoth Cave had been left to speak for itself. Its primeval gloominess was not yet defiled by refinements such as electric lights, and squeezing through and climbing over its dank formations was scarcely made easier by the need to carry a lantern and offer a hand to anyone in difficulty. Not far from here, in yet another underground chamber, Floyd Collins was to languish, pinned by a rock in such a way as to defy all rescue attempts, and finally dying a death which turned him into the hero of a ballad destined to appeal to the hyperbolic sentimentality of post-Victorian America.

By the same childish provincialism that shaped my stereotyped view of the Deep South, Texas to me meant ranches and cowboys; the East was populated with pilgrim types and bounded by Plymouth Rock and the Statue of Liberty, with New York City somewhere in between, and the West was wild, with a desert, some mountains called the Rockies, and a fabulous place known as Hollywood. Happily, the automobile was to expand all such imaginary concepts for the proud citizens of America the Beautiful.

The new ease of getting about had a further salutary effect upon one custom of the day that was already popular with old and young. Families, far from being in danger of dissolution and of vanishing from the cultural scene, demonstrated a sturdy cohesiveness that expressed itself in annual "family reunions" attended by nuclear units from far and wide to celebrate a common patriarchal heritage. These genealogical orgies could now reach even greater proportions, and in Sumner, at least, they were sometimes of such a size that the Municipal Park was called into service as the meeting ground.

<hr>

It was not only families who made use of Sumner's park. Community organizations of all descriptions and sizes found it the ideal retreat for numerous picnics and outdoor events, where the entertainment might have been justly accused of being secondary to the bill of fare. Long tables were lined up under the trees to dispense the fried chicken, potato salad, baked beans, watermelon, and devil's food cake that contributed to the general joie de vivre before calories took all the fun out of eating. When women spent hours in sweltering kitchens preparing an excess of the kind of foods that were lauded as guaranteed to "make the mouth water" and "stick to the ribs," they had no fear that when serving time came they would be treated like criminals guilty of conspiring to emasculate their "victims' " will power and of being responsible for causing them to break the commandments of their various diets.

Because baby-sitting had not yet been recognized as a profession, and grandmothers were not always available for supervising small fry, the younger generation were often included in these outings. Upon arrival and without urging, youngsters predictably abandoned their elders in order to take advantage of the opportunity to frolic with friends, wade in the creek, and play on the slides and swings.

In fact, we children often accompanied our own parents to informal parties and social functions with the understanding that we would not interfere with the parlor games that usually comprised the wholesome entertainment of Sumner's Episcopal Methodists. The family of the 20's was a somewhat contradictory unit. Indissoluble and closely-knit, to be sure, but not necessarily committed to a stifling oneness that precluded the two parts, siblings and parents, from being attentive to their own interests and goals. No father felt a compunction to be a pal to Junior, and few mothers wished to be regarded as their growing daughter's best friend.

Right or wrong, there was a natural "distance" between the two generations that bode well for parental authoritarianism but did little to encourage an interchange of confidences and opinions. We did not doubt our parents' concern for our welfare or their dedication to our future as successful, fulfilled human beings; but we also were not given to feel that we were their sole reason for living or that their personal satisfactions of the moment were 100% dependent on our own.

My father and mother both came from the large families that were the order of their day, and several of their brothers and sisters lived either in Sumner, or, on my mother's side at least, on nearby farms. I had great affection for those two clans of sturdy midwestern stock, made up of a satisfying number of my "uncles and my cousins and my aunts," but I simply took them for "granite," assuming that a generous supply of available relatives was the natural heritage of all children.

Like many Sumner residents, my paternal grandparents had retired, after years of farm life, to live in town, but my Grandma Hurmence had been a widow as long as I could remember and resided alone in a large frame house only two blocks from us. For some reason, however, I spent more time at the home of my maternal grandparents, who had also moved from a farm into Sumner. My small dumpling of a "grape" grandmother lived with these grandparents long enough for me to remember her usage of such quaint phrases (born of her German background) as "Make the light out." Her accent, which we called "Dutchy," was also characteristic at times of the speech of some of my other German relatives.

Mother's parents were both of German extraction, but my father's mother was haughty English to the core. His Dutch paternal ancestry, added to this English blood, and my German genealogy, made me a European mixture, but I couldn't have cared less about my ancestry. In time, however, I did become aware of the fact that I was a "damn Yankee," a holdover designation from the bitterness generated by the Civil War, which had left an enduring if unspoken rift between the North and South 50 years after the fact. Surely with no conscious malice but with cruel insensitivity, we thought it great fun to pantomime a song about a Civil War figure: "John Brown's (arms make a rocking motion instead of the word 'baby') had a (here a cough to indicate the word 'cold') upon his (here the singer pointed to the chest in lieu of saying the word), and they (circular motion on the upper body in place of the word 'rubbed') him with camphorated oil." All this, of course, was a parody of the odious: "John Brown's body lies a 'mouldering in the grave." And occasionally one could still hear how "We'll hang Jeff Davis to a sour apple tree." I didn't know anything about John Brown and nothing at all about Jeff Davis or what war was the inspiration for "We're tenting tonight on the old campground" and "Just before the battle, Mother," which we rendered at school (with heartrending pathos) from "The Golden Book of Favorite Songs."

Reverberations of the North-South Saga still echoed faintly in the land, and a holier-than-thou undercurrent of scorn prevailed among us damn Yankees for any culture that had practiced slavery; however, I don't recall any blacks in Sumner. Dark talk of the Ku Klux Klan and the burning of crosses reached the youth of our town and held the usual fascination that mysterious terrors had for us as long as we felt safe and protected.

Another of these intoxicating fears was reserved for the gypsies who occasionally made brief stops in Sumner. Mothers actually corralled their offspring behind closed doors to assure that their tots would not be kidnap victims of these scruffy maligned visitors, who soon bowed to their reputation and moved on with expectations of similar receptions in other timorous communities. It mattered not that no case of child stealing by any real live Romany Roamers was generally known to have been documented. Religion is not the only area in which legend and fact need not be synonymous.

The community fear of intruders did not extend to occasional stop-overs by the "tramps" who rode the freight trains that passed through Sumner regularly and noisily. Odd jobs and a free meal were offered without hesitation at our back door, and I assume the same hospitality prevailed throughout the neighborhoods within easy walking distance of the rails. I detected no air of the "romance of the open road" among these derelicts. They were simply another part of the culture which flaunted "poor farms" and insane asylums, for which euphemisms of a kinder nature had not yet been devised.

Because I was privileged to function in a multiple family situation, I had no problems with my identity and wasted little time wondering who I was. I was indubitably someone's child, someone's grandchild, niece, or cousin. To my Grandma Messerer, for instance, I was "Clara's girl," and I was happy to be thus classified. Having an intimate interrelationship with the several generations of my own family, I learned to respect the distinctive roles of each in the family human.

One reason I was often at the home of my maternal grandparents was that Mother's family was nothing if not gregarious, and many Sundays we all chose to gather there after church for a limited family reunion of our own that usually numbered in the twenties. The pattern of those Sunday afternoons could have been chiseled in stone. The women repaired to the kitchen to complete the food preparation and care for the infants, while the male members of the assembly gravitated either to the front porch and the porch swing, with their cigars (at least, my father smoked and could provide tender loving care for a stub indefinitely) or to the side yard to pitch horseshoes, awaiting the call to be first at the table. Their conversation usually dealt with the odd behavior of Uncle Sam or the perilous state of the crops.

The children old enough to escape the apron strings of solicitous mothers ran outdoors to find their own amusement, the older ones shepherding the younger, all the while trying to remember that we were still wearing our Sunday clothes. After the men had eaten their fill, the biblical "women and children" finally sat down to what was left. Not that there was a scarcity of good plain Iowa cooking, but for some obscure reason my favorite piece of chicken was the neck.

By the time the cleanup tasks were completed, it was not long till four o'clock, and time for the farm families to leave for home and the "chores," as the hired man frequently had Sunday off. Before this exodus, however, persistent efforts were made to line up everyone for snapshots that today, mounted in dusty albums, preserved all of us forever as we were at one moment in history, smiling for posterity in my grandparents' front yard. There I am with my sister, in the organdy dresses our mother had made for us, flanked by a gaggle of cousins who believed, as did we, that there would be endless carefree Sundays to meet and play together at "Grandma's."

Grandma Messerer was a stoic, with old-fashioned virtues and deep religious convictions, a kindly native of Germany who had seen years of the hard work that went along in those days with life on an Iowa farm in Bremer County, one of the richest agricultural and dairy areas of the state. I was always comfortable around her, but my grandfather was completely oblivious to his numerous grandchildren. Not once did I say a word to him, and he reciprocated in kind. Never having seen him laugh or enjoy himself, I pictured him, probably unfairly, as an awful grouch. Many of those elderly Germans around Sumner seemed rather grim to me, but for most of them, life had been real and life had been earnest, and a bit of humorlessness was excusable at a stage when they had a right to expect a better deal than old age often affords.

Today I wonder whether my grandmother was consistently ecstatic at the ongoing prospect of her progeny descending upon her *en masse*, overrunning the premises inside and out, and leaving her to cope with the aftermath. Earlier, she had accepted the responsibility of rearing an older cousin of mine, whose mother had died in childbirth. I had not known my mother's sister Alice, but I knew that her death had been a family tragedy, and for me at least she always came to mind at the strains of the chauvinistic tribute (another Golden Book Favorite) to: "Sweet Alice, Ben Bolt, Sweet Alice, whose hair was so brown. She wept with delight when you gave her a smile, and she trembled with fear at your frown." Personally, I felt the shrinking Alice of the song was better off dead, and I was convinced that had my Aunt Alice been anything like my liberated mother, that song would have been dreadfully out of date. I believe her death was a continuing sorrow to my grandmother, whose other children, however, were to live to old age.

Family gatherings at my paternal grandmother's were neither as large nor as frequent as those at my mother's parents. Grandma Hurmence was what is known as a "character," and I regret that I did not cultivate her more than I did. My failure to do so is admittedly rather odd, as I was usually intrigued by interesting grownups. I was also addicted to the unattractive habit of monitoring adult conversations whenever I could get away with it. Then again, children are not always known for taking advantage of opportunities which prove to be fleeting. At times I did call upon this white-haired matriarch and beg (successfully) to be allowed to help with the housework. I knew she was a generous employer where her grandchildren were concerned and that she paid well above the maximum attainable from sources unmoved by family ties. I could always use pocket money in those days when the penny candy counters had a "wondrous attraction for me" and when jawbreakers could be relied upon for 15 minutes of enjoyment in return for one copper cent, which may have been the sweetest bargain in history.

From what I have learned about this grandmother, she would probably have been an articulate feminist today. Strong-willed, independent, outspoken to the point of tactlessness, she is rumored to have refused for a time to move into the imposing new farm home my grandfather had built. Her residence in Sumner, although attractive enough from the street, was an architectural oddity on the inside. It was the only single family dwelling in my experience to feature a dining room larger than any other room in the house and to be cursed with a tortuous spiral staircase as the only access to the second floor bedrooms and bath.

For a time, one of my cousins lived here with my grandmother. She was a charming brunette with shingled hair and an infectious giggle, and when she and my handsome oldest brother laughed and joked together, I looked on enthralled. I longed to be just like them.

My sense of family was strong, but I also had a sense of belonging to the community. No doubt, my parents' regular participation in community activities was responsible for my conviction that these activities were intended to include me. Sumner was a town that put emphasis upon the social needs of its citizens. The calendar could be relied upon to provide occasions for parades and celebrations, but Sumner was also on the Lyceum and Chautauqua circuits. Culture and "improvement" were mobile in the 20's. Travelling tent shows stopped over regularly, too, as well as vaudeville troupes that performed at the Opera House. "Opera House" may have been one of the prime misnomers of all time, as opera in the accepted sense was the last form of entertainment that would ever reach Sumner.

The fact that children were allowed to fill up the front rows at any and all of the above forms of amusement convinces me that the content of the material could be trusted to stay within the strict decency limits of small-town America. Sex was reserved for the Bible.

Local talent enjoyed a wonderful exposure in Sumner in the days before radio and television provided an effortless source of entertainment. With no knobs to turn to bring instant diversion (and what has since come to be known as escapism), a variety of community functions offered gifted and not-so-gifted individuals occasions for fulfilling themselves in an artistic way. A beautiful voice, an instrumental dexterity, a flare for magic, a gift for drama, all guaranteed their possessors invitations to contribute to the success of events sponsored by a variety of organizations. These opportunities were of a frequency that spoke well for the civic-mindedness, patriotism, and conviviality of Sumner's citizens.

One talent which enjoyed much appreciation has since "gone with the wind" so to speak—believe it or not, a proficiency for whistling. This was an art reserved for women who could maintain their poise, with their lips puckered up, long enough to imitate bird calls (in a manner which usually improved on nature) and to embellish familiar melodies with enough practiced trills and thrush-like chirrups to have astonished even the songwriters themselves, had they been privileged to be in the ranks of the admiring listeners. The admiration was genuine; besides, it would have been judged impolite to be other than appreciative of the expertise of someone who might be closely or even remotely related to the person sitting next to you.

My own admiration for these performers, who have few imitators today, was a natural result of persistent and fruitless efforts on my part to accomplish more than a pathetic sort of incompetence in the whistling department, and I envied anyone who was able to make a flute out of lips and tongue. Not until much later did I feel curiosity for the appeal that acknowledgment of oneself as a "whistler" held for even prominent matrons of the community, but it probably had something to do with the scope of the average woman's access to self-expression in those days being more or less limited to "feminine" pursuits. Whistling was no doubt perceived as being "feminine," by default. *Men* were certainly never identified as whistlers in any but a casual sense, unless they happened to be artists who painted their mothers in rocking chairs (where female parents were to be seen only with babies in their arms or at a time of life when rockers claim many of both sexes).

Attendance at public school functions often furnished another form of community relaxation, attracting even those who were not obligated to show loyalty to participating relatives and friends. Sports were not yet perceived as the ultimate medium for student achievement, and in Sumner, on the academic level at least, getting a ball across a line or through a hoop had less drawing appeal than the various plays, operettas, band concerts, and oratorical contests staged by young aspirants.

These presentations were held in the separate new gymnasium provided for pupils in the elementary and high school grades, which were located on two different levels in the building next door. The only time grade school children invaded the marble halls of the upper-class students was to attend music class and an occasional assembly and to use the assembly hall as a lunchroom, along with all those who from choice or necessity brought their lunch from home.

On the rare days when my mother was not at home to feed us at noon (and this was always our main meal—dinner) she packed my lunch in a paper sack, a repast which could be counted on to contain an orange with the rind symmetrically scored to make it easy to peel). For me it was great fun to experience the novelty of eating with the "country kids," who were unable to go home at noon, and who were obligated to provide for all their own transportation from the farm, if they wished to continue their education in town. There were no consolidated schools, and, not only was there no *forced* busing, there was no busing of any kind.

True to custom, parents usually took their children along with them to school activities open to the public. I was an enthusiastic member of the audience. Applause for all the performers was predictably hearty, and I revelled in the chance to add to it, with prolonged periods of clapping until my palms tingled. It's likely that not all of the histrionic art was closely geared to juvenile minds. I remember one or two dramatic situations in those theatricals when my ignorance about the birds and the bees led me to wonder in my own mind why the husband of the drama felt surprised to find his wife pregnant, as I did have an idea that father and mother had something to do with babies. Even though I have become somewhat more sophisticated since then, I still tend to register astonishment when I am asked to accept such male innocence, as I have noticed that the calendar is a common concern between most husbands and wives in childbearing years.

I was captivated by the comic and dramatic renditions at the high school declamation contests, but I much preferred the dramatic variety, because of the manner in which the "declaimers" outdid themselves to lift the audience to heights of emotion seldom experienced in the humdrum of daily existence. One could actually take lessons in how best to deliver these "readings," and it was usually obvious who had been taught an effective technique and who had decided to rely upon instinct and endowment. I think it had something to do with intensity. And gestures. I'm sure it did.

The Opera House saw a lot of me. It was the home of Mary Pickford, Tom Mix, and Douglas Fairbanks, and I knew them well. They flickered and jerked about, larger than life, and spoke not a line that could be heard, but I sensed what they were projecting from their exaggerated silent-movie expressions and manifestations of emotion, and I scarcely had to wait for the titles to be imposed upon the screen to know how the sentimental plot was progressing. Melodrama these plots surely were, but they must have suited the trend of the times or else simply satisfied a war-weary nation's hunger for a return to the naiveté of the past.

I was also keyed into the mood of the action on-screen by the nature of the piano accompaniment originating at one side of the stage. Dusty sequels with "thundering herds" of cattle and horses were a large part of the script of the silents, and the mood-setter at the ivories had to be equal to the demand that the keys move as nimbly as the galloping hooves. Light-hearted scales and arpeggios further assured us that love scenes were joyous, and there was plenty of instrumental mood indigo for the approach of the villain or the intrusion of the seamier side of life. It is my opinion that every "moving picture" must have arrived at the hands of the exhibitor with detailed instructions for the theater's musician. More ostentatious movie houses may have employed orchestras or organists, but one reliable and versatile pianist, able to enrich the triumphs of Hollywood on what was surely less than a Steinway, sufficed for Sumner.

Piano-playing was considered another of those purely "feminine" accomplishments and was safely on the list of respectable outside-the-home employment for women that included teaching, typing, clerking, waitressing, switch-boarding, and hair styling. It was also all right to be an author. An occasional strong-minded member of the female sex ventured into the areas of business ownership, and a few notorious ones tried outlawry, but the goal of most women was to be "ladylike." Mothers were of the opinion that for their daughters' future happiness it was necessary to convince them that "ladylike" was next to "godlike." If the word "ladylike" is no longer heard in the land, it will not be mourned by all of us who grew up under its tyranny. No squelch quite equalled that of being admonished that one was coming up short in the feminine dignity competition. That just wouldn't be ladylike.

Most women in my mother's circle of friends devoted their excess energies and mental capabilities to club work and volunteerism, both of which were very big in Sumner. Church and charity work served as outlets for any female aspirations to seek a fulfillment of sorts outside the domesticity which was the preoccupation of over one-half of the national citizenry. Although women were enfranchised at last, I don't recall overhearing a single note of concern on their part for anything to do with politics or their own treatment under the law. I knew that some of them had been members of the Women's Christian Temperance Union, but suffragettes? I doubt it. Feminists who had struggled to win the vote for their sisters had overstepped the bounds of ladylikeism after all, and it took a while for the new mantle of citizenship-awareness to settle upon the shoulders of "ladies" who resisted a re-definement of their roles.

My mother, for instance, was a self-assured young matron with a nice sense of humor and a quick mind—a conscientious wife and mother—but she kept within the limits of tradition, and her outreach never extended beyond membership in Missionary Societies, the Ladies Aid, sewing circles, and "culture" clubs, although she did work as a telephone operator early in her marriage. Just how many Marie Curies have drowned their minds in the dishwater and the babies' bathwater will never be known.

Of course, it took the greater part of most days to do the housework then, but some women had "hired girls"—farm girls for the most part who wanted to live in town. I usually made friends with any help which we employed. I liked to do housework, but part of my sociability was a result of my yen for picking the brains of any adult who would show an inclination to tolerate me.

My favorite of the several domestics who worked for us at intervals happened to be the target of gossip, of which I heard rumors, but, like most children, I made no moral judgments, and apparently my mother was willing to compromise her principles, in the cause of a spick-and-span house and some assistance in the kitchen. I used to help this congenial young woman clean the sweet corn. In those days, sweet corn always had at least one large green worm, very much alive, at the top, just as a common expectation, in the days before pesticides, was to find a smaller genus of creepy crawlers in most fruit. It was wise to pay attention to the location of the next bite when partaking of the "apple a day" that guaranteed to make pariahs of the medical profession.

This particular "hired girl" was no dumbbell, and she was kind. She had a saying reserved for moments of out-of-the-ordinary occurrences that I assured her did not represent the best of grammar. When she would observe that "strange sights happen on Hallowe'en," I would insist that *sights* couldn't *happen*. Since then, I'm not quite so sure they can't.

I remember one housemaid who worked for us after we had moved to Indiana and I was in high school, who did not meet my housekeeping standards. In my book, it was downright sacrilege to dust *around* objects on pieces of furniture, and such was the degree of my perfectionism that I would surreptitiously follow this slacker around and do the job up right. My mother, and most other homemakers (fortunately for their sanity) were satisfied to admit that perfectionism in domestic janitoring could never be achieved, and they were the happier for it, in a world where dirt is a large part of the environment and where the force of gravity assures that dust will accumulate relentlessly and indiscriminately on all surfaces. And accumulate. And accumulate.

In a vain effort to convince myself that a thick layer of dust is as easy to remove as a thin one, I have told myself that few obituaries record that the deceased enjoyed a fine reputation for being a superior dust and grime remover.

We used to sing a little ditty that defined the contemporary woman's routine. It described the days of the week, and the activities assigned to each one, in the following way: "Today is Monday, today is Monday—Monday wa-a-sh," etc. On Mondays my mother obeyed the rhyme and did the laundry. She was lucky enough to have an electric washing machine in the basement. Into this she would cut up a bar of Fels Naphtha soap. White clothes had to proceed to the boiler, to be stirred with a stick. It's possible all that steam kept my mother's complexion lovely—or it could have been the jar of Pond's Vanishing Cream on her dresser.

I knew the cream was there, because, whenever we were angry at her for some curtailment of our fun, my sister and I would take everything off this dresser and hide it in my parents' large closet. She never mentioned these retaliatory incidents but simply returned all articles to their proper place. (And that was even before Dr. Spock told parents how to deal with their children's tantrums.)

⇒•◇•⇐

Saturday nights were inescapably bath nights for us children. A change of underwear could then be made on Sunday mornings. Winter meant long underwear, which I dreaded because it was scratchy and tight when first put on, and it was hard to pull stockings over it. During the week it gradually loosened, and at the ankle it became so stretched out that the excess had to be folded over in a pleat and the stockings painstakingly worked over it. By the end of the day, the underwear was riding up and the stockings falling down, a miserable situation that worsened from bath night to bath night.

We children slept on a screened porch upstairs in the summertime. When the moon shone and the stars winked, it was almost like camping out in the treetops, but when a midwest storm made the branches sway as the lightning cracked and Thor threw his hammer close by, I ran to my parents' bed.

We always kissed our parents goodnight, and I liked to watch my mother get ready for bed as she gracefully braided her hair into one plait. No one seemed to care if we fell asleep on the couch downstairs, but it was agony to have to undress in a sleepy state.

Wednesday nights in the summertime were occasions for area residents to enjoy a contrived amalgamation of business and pleasure in downtown Sumner. Merchants kept their stores open, the streets were brightly lit, and the Sumner band, made up of volunteers seated on the porch overhanging the city hall, played a rousing concert to much appreciative whistling and to enthusiastic horn-blowing issuing from parked cars. Many of these vehicles had been positioned with some foresight earlier in the day along the two blocks that made up Sumner's business district, with a view of providing a home base for residents arriving later in the evening. The purpose was to mingle with friends and the farm folk who had driven in to shop and exchange pleasantries with those fortunate enough (as I saw it) to live in town. To me there was a vast chasm separating the two ways of life, and I must admit to feeling superior to all whom I believed were by some trick of fate destined to endure living in the country.

It did not occur to me that, fortunately for all of us who enjoyed eating, many people had *chosen* this existence and would not trade places with me for any reason. Today there is a great nostalgia for the wide open spaces and the peace of rural surroundings—a general yearning to get "back to the soil," but I was oblivious to any such thinking and remained convinced that I was one of the lucky and privileged members of the human race who lived in a municipality (but who were also a much smaller part of the population than they are today, when mechanization has greatly reduced the farm population).

These mid-week nights were typical of the relaxed times that prevailed when I was a child, but the band music was lively enough. I became convinced then that no band offering will stir up a crowd like one of Mr. Sousa's contributions to patriotic fervor. After all, bands were invented for marches and vice versa, and as long as there remains a *Stars and Stripes Forever* to reinforce the *Star Spangled Banner*, passionate feelings for our native land need never fade.

Sumner's band also played for the Fourth of July parade. I knew that the Fourth was a patriotic holiday, but I wasn't as moved by the spirit of our founders as by an anticipation of a full day of festivities. People felt no embarrassment at overt displays of national pride, but I believe most holidays were seen chiefly as opportunities for the communal gatherings which seemed to attract Iowans in the 20's.

The money I was given for fireworks went mostly for the thin inch-long mini-crackers considered safe for children to light and toss hastily into the air, but my father had found an ingenious way to insure our safety even further. He made each of us a holder by drilling a short tunnel in the bottom of an 8-inch-long toy tenpin; all that was required was for us to insert the firecracker into the cavity and then light it with a piece of smoldering punk. In that way, we could allow it to explode "in our hands" with little if any risk.

I also saw to it that I had a large supply of "nigger chasers." (In Sumner all the since-discredited racial slurs and slang were accepted practice—e.g., the junk man was referred to as the "sheeny," and our country's black people made no public protest at being spoken of as "niggers"; but most of it was more habit than bigotry. I detected no social consciousness about any of the belittling designations that were commonly used to identify certain ethnic groups.) "Nigger chasers" were nickel-size disks wrapped in red tissue paper and they were sure to provide almost as much enjoyment for the money as penny jawbreakers. When we rubbed these "coins" on the sidewalk, sparks danced out on all sides with a delightful crackling sound. The remainder of my Fourth of July budget was spent on sparklers and Roman candles, a glorious means of closing a long day of celebrating our nation's independence.

This day of high excitement (second only to Christmas in importance for me) literally began with the appearance of "the dawn's early light" of our national anthem. Neighborhood children were eager to get about the business of paying loud tribute to our country's freedom from tyranny by initiating the popping and banging of gunpowder reserved for this historic day when extreme emotion demanded an extreme outlet. (Later in life we moved to Texas, where I was horrified to see firework stands going up at the approach of Christmas; I was reluctant to reconcile the season with what seemed a completely alien way of observing it. Since that time, Yuletide fireworks seem to be catching on in other areas of the country; ye olde American enterprise is seldom found wanting whenever some new gimmick promises to prove lucrative.)

After applauding a mid-morning parade of floats down First Street, while artfully dodging firecrackers randomly tossed into the crowd, we either accompanied our parents to a picnic at the park or drove with them to spend the rest of the day in the country at a celebration planned by the Union Evangelical church, which claimed some of our relatives as members. After a program of local talent calling attention to the occasion, picnic baskets were brought out, and our parents having at least satisfied their craving for casual conversation with friends and acquaintances, we returned to town to run about our backyard like human fireflies waving our sparklers in the humid Iowa night. As we aimed Roman candles over the neighbors' barn, we were bound to reflect upon the short life of all fireworks and the realization that even the Fourth of July was doomed to go out in a blaze of glory.

July 4th was only one of many summer days awaiting our pleasure, and when young people gathered outdoors, we often organized games of Skunk Hole, Pump Pump Pull Away, Red Rover, and croquet. There was little sex discrimination. Girls were as eligible for these games as boys, and most of the activities were available to both sexes, as they took place on vacant lots where nobody ever seemed to want to build anything. Several families owned croquet sets, but these were not always left at the ready. Tripping over an unsuspected wicket was an unpleasant experience with varying degrees of serious consequences.

When we met in my cousins' yard on Main Street under a huge tree, we took turns on the bag swing. This was the only such swing I ever saw, but I'm sure there must have been many more, as feed sacks were in good supply, and there was no shortage of straw for stuffing them. Hanging offensively from a tree branch, this great lump probably would not comprise an appealing piece of modern playground equipment, but our particular eyesore also had a high platform to go along with it. When your turn came, you stood bravely at the edge of the launch pad waiting for someone on the ground to propel the heavy bag in your direction. At this point, a reliable sense of timing was a good attribute to have, to assure that you leaped to straddle the bag at exactly the right time. A consciousness of the danger involved added its spice to this precarious sport.

Although the only time I was spanked by my mother was after I had fallen from this platform, other seasonal perils seemed to engage her concern to a greater degree. We were repeatedly warned not to wade in creeks on "dog days" and not to eat green apples, the latter for fear of being struck down in our prime by a dread malady called "cholera morbus." The thinking behind the dog days alarm was that, in midsummer, dogs were extraordinarily susceptible to rabies. Affected animals supposedly would immediately run to water, where the foam around their mouths would wash off, to float downstream and lodge in any cut or scratch on the body of a wader. Lockjaw would inevitably develop, and before you would even know you had been the same as bitten by a mad dog, you would die a hideous death.

The possibility of any of this happening was probably about a million to one, and as far as I know no Sumner child ever suffered more than a stomach cramp from eating a green form of the forbidden fruit. Personally, I continued to carry a salt shaker about with me at green apple time, and it was as much a part of my summer uniform as the skate key I wore around my neck.

I have since become philosophical about fears that through the years I have seen attach themselves to almost every human enjoyment. They seem to require a pre-knowledge of what is a source of pleasure, after which they immediately take the form of a warning not to indulge in it.

Many of our pastimes when I was young contained an element of risk, and it is not surprising that the idea of guardian angels should prevail among all who contemplate the precarious circumstances which accompany the business of growing up. Children are often oblivious to life- and limb-threatening conditions and even seem to "tempt fate" with little regard for the consequences. It is typical of youth that harm to their own persons is usually a remote if not nonexistent possibility, as for instance when my uncle and aunt were building their new two-story frame house and my cousins and I dared each other to leap back and forth across the stairwell opening located in the attic. Missed footing meant a plunge to the concrete floor of the basement, but our ethereal guardians were vigilant, and we lived to keep them on the alert for future chilling escapades. As this house neared completion, my obligation to pester adults even put me into conversational rapport with the roofers, and I also was driven to climb the scaffolding inside the Evangelical church when it was being redecorated, to chat with the painters. My particular celestial protectors felt right at home in this latter location, and the workmen didn't seem to mind my intrusion. I have always found their breed to be very kind to curious small fry.

The Old Swimming Hole at the edge of Sumner's park was not exactly the safest place in the world. No lifeguards were on duty, and no ropes divided the waters. An unspoken acceptance by accomplished swimmers of a responsibility for the welfare and instruction of those who had not yet overcome the density of the human body to stay afloat in a muddy creek was one of the reasons that tragedy was kept at bay. Personally, I wore a device called water wings until I could navigate on my own. A canvas band across the chest connected two inflated protrusions rising behind each shoulder and provided buoyancy as long as I remained on my back, and I did learn to swim in this way. Actually, I had less dread of drowning than I had for the bloodsuckers that attached themselves to any skin surface which was not covered by our one-piece bathing suits. These slimy little black parasites could reach the table in short order, and it paid to interrupt the banquet before they gorged themselves too heavily.

I looked forward every summer to the week when my two cousins from Minneapolis came on the train to visit us. These boys were the same age as my sister and I. The older one was a leader—one of his favorite pastimes, in which we participated for some inexplicable reason, was to go to the park and "drown out gophers." We staggered to and from the creek carrying buckets of water, in the hope that some sodden pasture rodent would eventually scramble to daylight to face its tormentors. I was secretly relieved that we seldom found any gophers at home. None of us was consciously cruel to animals, and I had the softest heart imaginable where they were concerned, so I have to leave our behavior to the child psychologists.

Often on summer nights we assembled in the backyard to view the northern lights, a phenomenon frequently visible in Iowa. When I learned to say "Aurora Borealis," I was not only proud but convinced that it was one of the most beautiful word combinations that could be imagined. I liked it better than cholera morbus, which up to that time had been my favorite tongue twister. I had no problem spelling either one. Spelling bees at school were just made for me. What a wonderful opportunity to feel superior!

In a few areas, however, I had to be satisfied to be outshone. One of these was sewing, and by the time it was taught to girls in the seventh grade, it was certainly time for me to be humbled. But it was also not too bright of me to choose to make a yellow crepe nightgown with a *square* neck faced with lavender ribbon. Our teacher in this class was pennywise in the extreme and required us to save our basting threads, as if our spools did not contain what must have been close to a mile of filament for holding material together temporarily.

Some girls knew how to use a thimble, but it took me many years to learn that. I doubt if I ever wore that gown, but at least sewing class helped to show me that I wasn't destined to prevail in every area.

Another department in which I was easily bested was art. I could just barely draw a circle with a compass, and a similar lack of expertise showed up at Palmer Method time, when we were taught to use the whole arm for writing, rather than just the fingers. Personally, I have never known anyone who used the Palmer Method.

I faced up to my shortcomings bravely. I simply assuaged my ego by concluding that skills such as sewing, art and handwriting were of minor importance.

Iowa summers wore on to fall, and inevitably to Iowa winters. Stocking caps and sleds and cracked lips and long underwear and frozen towers of cream on milk bottles—these were winter. And fat snowmen with sticks for arms and pieces of coal from the coal bin for eyes.

Nothing else was ever as black and insidious as a coal bin. Ours was a dungeon-like cubicle off the furnace room. Like the ark, it had one small window, for the chute that brought in the coal from the delivery truck. Our furnace turned this inky product of millions of years of decomposition into a season's comfort by making steam for our radiators, which performed a second function of drying the soggy mittens, gloves, and scarves that we were required to leave in the entrance hall, along with our galoshes, before we were allowed onto our Wilton rugs. Not that it was possible to wear out a Wilton rug, except at the seams.

Every winter night my father had to "bank" the furnace, and this process kept us warm, until morning sent him back to release this benevolent tyrant from its smoldering apathy and set it to roaring and fulminating once more. It took a strong arm to play caretaker to our furnace, but on snowy evenings when the radiators made happy talk while the wind howled outside, we felt wonderfully snug and protected, and if the fireplace happened to be adding its own staccato accompaniment, shivers, not of cold but of sheer physical bliss, came over me. Then my mother might go to the piano, and we would gather around her and sing from the Golden Book and the church hymnal and a well-worn stack of sheet music. What my own singing voice lacked in quality, I made up for in volume, because singing with my mother at the piano was one of my very favorite things to do.

I could carry a tune, and I did it enthusiastically, helping to make the selections, and never tiring of "Drink to Me Only with Thine Eyes," "Believe Me If All Those Endearing Young Charms," and "The Little Brown Church in the Vale." Then I begged for "Beautiful Ohio," best-loved of them all, and Mother would wind it all up with "A Trip to Niagara."

My father did not take part in these sessions but preferred to go on adding to his total of ingested books. I do believe the house could have burned down around him and he would not have noticed until the pages began to scorch, but we never had to maintain silence for my dad. His concentration was impervious to interruption.

I have a mixed picture of my father, but I think the one of him with a book is my most treasured. He felt privileged to have even a high school education, but all he really needed to learn in school was an ability to read and write. From then on, he had the tool to turn his mind into a storehouse of knowledge that scholars would envy. He was to lose much of his hearing in his old age, but I was happy that his eyesight remained unimpaired and his mind free of any trace of senility.

He was a man who could be scathingly sarcastic and vociferously furious, but he was also a parent who would seat his children on the kitchen counter and shine their shoes for Sunday School and then read the funny papers to them after church. He was basically very sentimental, a trait that came to full flower when he compiled the Hurmence family history not long before he died at the age of 80, and that he felt I should be happy to edit because, after all, my college major had been journalism. Although women are generally credited with a greater capacity for tenderness and nurturing than men, I'm not sure this assumption is valid. The female role through the years has called for a great display of feminine "sweetness," but sympathy and concern for loved ones are more than likely merely human qualities, and their assignment exclusively to one sex may be just another tragic result of sexism through the centuries.

Confined indoors as we often were in winter months, we played endless games of Flinch and Parcheesi, built trains with the dining-room chairs, and mixed up sticky kettles of flour and water paste for long-forgotten crafts. When I say that I learned to rollerskate in our upstairs hall, I may give the wrong impression about the appearance of our home. Permissiveness prevailed in most areas but I recall two instances when recriminatory scenes resulted from what were merely accidents. We children somehow managed to break two sections of our Tiffany table lamp on one occasion, and on another we broke the end of a rocker from a chair by letting it become caught under the radiator. On the other hand, we were allowed to jump unrestrained on the beds while my mother changed the sheets. Finally, we would settle down on the bottom one, that may have been fresh off the line to save ironing, and let her make the bed on top of us. We also spent many hours sliding bumpily down the waxed staircase on our stomachs with a throw rug as our *truly* Flexible Flyer. Another of our favorite indoor pastimes was "shooting" caroms at a board set up on a table in the living room. We used pool cues and developed such a considerable skill at caroming wooden rings into corner pockets that my oldest brother would display great agony when he missed an easy shot, falling back in distress and crying, "Anguish in the heart!" Here again, as we moved about the board, our Wiltons never attested to the punishment they took from our Oxfords and buttoned shoes.

Unfortunately, I did not inherit my mother's easy ability to keep her standards of housekeeping in line with her standards of homemaking. Under the obligation of doing so in my own home, I was to find it difficult to make the compromises necessary to insure that my own compulsions not override the pleasures of other members of the family. Priorities are often at war with one's drives. In those of us to whom a crooked picture or rumpled rug are a source of pain, much envy is felt for those who are able to make peace with reality. After I was married, my mother used to say that when my sister and I came to visit, Ruth always ran for a dust cloth while Marian went directly to the telephone.

Like many middle-class homes in Sumner when I was young, ours had a sun porch, screened on three sides, opening directly off our living room. Why it was known as a sun porch I have no idea. Anyone who wanted to sit outside in the sun, while risking speculation on the part of associates as to his or her sanity, was welcome to do so (although patios and barbecue pits were not yet a part of the culture), but sun porches had roofs to keep the sun off. Summertime in the Midwest usually found people seeking *surcease* from the pitiless rays of the only star earthlings have ever seen with the naked eye, making copious use of electric fans (oscillating kind preferred), and still managing to stay free of wonder about why provision for home cooling continued to lag miserably behind development of devices for keeping the human body comfortable in winter. I suppose it was because you could actually die from the cold, but only *felt* that you were expiring from the heat.

In a day not far removed from a time when it was regarded as sinful to expose more than a minimum of the body to public view, sun worship and the ritual of acquiring a tan awaited more liberal attitudes toward human sexuality. Puritanical mores borrowed from the Bible discouraged any but the most conventional concessions to soaring temperatures even in the matter of *casual* dress. No member of either sex wore shorts or revealing clothing for purposes of relaxation, and the masochism of Sumner's church members who would regularly, on the Day of Rest, don their Sunday best (calling for women's corsets and men's high stiff collars) and subject themselves in a steamy House of the Lord to the castigations of an equally-perspiring clergyman passeth understanding.

The asceticism of Christianity that made pleasure in this world a pitfall for enjoyment of it in the next, may have accounted for the Lord's slowness in providing for the invention of air conditioning and the ensuing comfort of his devotees, at whatever temple they chose to pay their respects, especially on days when the thermometer and relative humidity conspired to test the caliber of a saint. If suffering is redemptive, as the Good Book proclaims, the ninety-degree weather in a house of God during the 20's did its share to assure staunch churchgoers a measure of well-earned advancement along the narrow path to salvation. I doubt, however, that air-cooling of sanctuaries resulted in a great increase of attendance at church services. Removing the sacrificial ingredient dispels the miasma of self-righteousness that emanates from the wearisome nature of most religious worship and that is flaunted in the faces of all those who refuse to be the "living sacrifices" to their god demanded by that Master Masochist Paul as he gloried in his infirmities and "vile body."

My personal recollection of Sunday morning at church in mid-summer, before mechanical air conditioning diminished the atonement quality, is one of positioning myself next to someone displaying a willingness to defy Paul, as well as a tireless determination to stir up the humid air, already heavy with solemnity, by means of one of the cardboard fans supplied by various advertisers for the use of the congregation, and kept in the hymnal rack on the back of the bench in front of each penitent. It was a sneaky way for me to capitalize on the industry of others.

When I say that attending church services involves masochism, and that participation in worship rituals is a source of boredom, I am reflecting not only my own attitude as a child but the ongoing attitude of most adults. (A recent TV survey, for instance, revealed that the answer to a question about the dullest place in which to find oneself was "in church.") Church was just supposed to be good for us; it wasn't obligated to entertain us. The pastor's regular feeble attempts to instill a little cheer with a small joke or anecdote remotely related to the text was usually only briefly successful, and I'm not sure the Lord approved. He isn't known for his sense of humor.

My own parents were Methodists but hardly devout. When I was a child, the church was a social unit as much as a religious one, and in that sense it played a large part in our lives. We had no religion in the home except for certain Methodist rules, such as no liquor and no "euchre" playing cards (because they were used by gamblers, as if dominoes were not). There was also some feeling about what was proper in the area of Sunday behavior, but nothing very restrictive came out of it.

The new church building, that my father as a member of the board had helped to bring into existence, opened its doors for our family to attend worship services every Sunday morning and evening. We youngsters also attended Sunday School and when a bit older Epworth League, both of which I enjoyed as opportunities to take part in the activities planned for young people. I was the passive Christian child with no serious doubts, and probably would have been willing to swear on a stack of Bibles that God was in his heaven and all was right with the world. Secretly, I felt it was all much ado about nothing, as I had no sense of being a sinner, and, if my behavior mattered all that much to this bearded old man in the sky, he could simply make me conform, and why didn't he just do that with everyone and be done with it. My only fears were for the end of the world and they were real ones, for some cult or other was always anticipating it from some remote cave or hilltop. As for myself, I wasn't ready for the screeching halt of everything that was just beginning for me. I wanted to postpone my trip to some vague

Paradise as much as my fellow Methodists did.

The chilling Sunday School stories of the Flood (although it was told to us as sort of just another tale about animals, which the literary world seems to regard as the prime topic for children's literature), Isaac as a human sacrifice (which the church somehow conceives of as another of its "beautiful Bible stories"), and the midnight massacre of the Egyptians, were mercifully as unreal to me as the fairy stories I liked to read. Mr. Andersen and the brothers Grimm had certainly created some grim sequences, but we were conscious of the fact that these fantasies were just that and presented no threat to us in any form. It followed that I regarded all these awful Bible stories as fairy tales too, and the Holy Land was as fabulous to me as the Land of Oz, and Jesus as mythical as Ali Baba. *Only* as figments of the imagination did I accept them, although I was willing to go along with this game that everyone seemed to be playing.

What a shock it was to realize finally that what I was hearing was supposed to be true! Whales actually *swallowed* people who sat around with seaweed on their heads, waiting to be coughed up! Tooth fairies weren't real, but angels *were!* People *could* come up out of their graves (although I had seen one or two corpses, and they appeared irreversibly immobile to me)! As far as God went, however, he was still as mysterious as ever, and he had nothing to do with me.

The church as a place to have fun, however, had very much to do with me, and if conviviality were the *essence* of religions, what a different world it would be! Our church was in many ways essentially a club of sorts with several purposes, one of which (and surely the most meaningful to me) was, as I have said, purely social. There were various kinds of laity get-togethers, but one of my favorites was built around occasional chicken pie suppers. Once again several of the "ladies," that thankless mainstay of the church from the time Paul is said to have written his epistles, spent the day in the church kitchen preparing the food for what was probably a money-making project of one of their benevolent organizations. My mother and the others didn't seem to mind doing this volunteer work, though the attraction of it surely had more to do with the camaraderie it generated than with the charm of the facilities at their disposal, as anyone will know who has experienced the stark sterility of a church kitchen. Charm is not a word that comes to mind when one is conjuring up a mental image of the less spiritual side of denominational machinery. The power of prayer is seldom brought to bear to enhance the underpinning of the temple.

An air of busy gaiety prevailed among these handmaidens of the Lord as they occupied themselves at the huge kitchen range or set the long tables in the large basement assembly room that also served as Sunday School rooms for the younger children when partitions were in place, and the reason that I can say this is that some of us whose mothers were demonstrating their stewardship on that particular day were allowed to join them after school. I can't remember being a bit of help, but a few of us would race around between the tables, prowl the back halls and stairs, and creep about the auditorium and choir loft, even the study, moving on to the classrooms situated at the back of the building and on the balcony, where the folding doors could be opened to provide more seating space for the congregation on special occasions.

The Methodist god was not concerned with petty rules which might have isolated him from his subjects, and this habitat of his on earth held no areas too sacrosanct for us to frequent in the most matter-of-fact kind of way, although I cannot deny a certain consciousness of "presence" that was reinforced when the hollow echoes of our raised voices bounced back from the bare plastered walls of the deserted rooms and corridors. Sumner Methodists were also not obsessed with what is called "holiness," and with "sacred" and "hallowed" objects and places. Mystery and things of the spirit enjoyed only a minimum of emphasis among them, and it was considered desirable to stay as far away as possible from anything that smacked of Catholicism. There was no pipe organ, no velvet hangings or runners, no gold crosses. Our minister was indistinguishable from the layman, wore no garb affected by the clergy, and delivered sermons from behind a simple golden oak pulpit. Other than the stained glass windows, our church had no tender traps. The Lord had to make it on his own, and woe to his mortal representative whose message from on high ran into overtime.

When the afternoon had worn on, and it was time to partake of the "church supper" that was now ready to be served, and as the men and other members of the congregation began to gather after leaving their places of business or employment, we joined our parents at the table and afterwards watched the entertainment and games that sometimes followed the cleanup chores.

<hr />

Some form of nourishment is still considered an essential adjunct to many social gatherings having nothing to do with religion, and then as now the problem of refreshment at such events was often solved by what was accurately described as the potluck supper. Besides being an expedient way to share responsibility for catering to one of society's customs, the potluck supper was in the past one more opportunity for women to display culinary superiority, if they so chose, although many uninspired macaroni and spaghetti casseroles and unimaginative jello salads and desserts could also remain anonymous if one wished. As a true child of my mother, I had no confidence in the cooking accomplishments of any other contributor, and as the lines formed before a great conglomeration of "pots," I was not about to rely upon luck and had already queried my mother about what *she* had brought. With the finickiness of the well-fed child, I was convinced that only food from our kitchen and prepared by *ma mère* was fit to eat.

I was relieved if she had furnished some entrée, but I was especially gratified if she had taken the time to fix my favorite gastronomic delight—deviled eggs. Whenever I was obligated to furnish a "covered dish" for a party, I invariably volunteered to bring the deviled eggs, and that added up to somewhat of an imposition at home, as just the act of *peeling* boiled eggs was a frustrating experience in days when our eggs were always farm fresh. My mother could have been forgiven if her reaction had been upon occasion, "Not deviled eggs again!" but my concern for her reaction was out-weighed by my personal food addiction, one that has not abated through the years.

My mother was what was known as a "good plain cook." It suited me that she didn't serve foods like liver and kidneys and brains and headcheese, all items I considered beneath my fastidious tastes. We were seldom treated to "gourmet" concoctions, but the delectable accomplishments of a good plain cook should never be subjected to comparison with the pompous chefery that goes under the title of "gourmet" and calls imperiously for wines, exotic spices, and unnatural combinations of elusive ingredients. No one brought up on good plain cooking can ever be seduced by any dish with a French title.

Grocery shopping was effortless in the "olden days." My mother would go to our telephone and call McAloon's Market. She then proceeded to read the grocery list aloud, and within an hour or two our order arrived at the back door. Once a month she stopped by to pay the bill, and I managed to go along, because at that time we children were given a sack of candy from the management. Of course, occasionally my mother did the shopping herself.

McAloon's didn't sell meat, so we had to buy it at the meat market. In Iowa, we ate meat and potatoes and gravy. If you fried the steak or the porkchops, you made pan gravy by adding flour to the drippings and letting it brown. When you added the milk, it made a delicious hissing sound that was better than a dinner bell.

We *always* had dessert, even though it might be just canned fruit. When it was apple pie, I was ecstatic, but when the cream pie turned out to be lemon under all that meringue, my heart sank.

Seldom did I eat anything between meals in the presence of my mother without being warned that "you'll ruin your supper" or without being told, "Don't eat that while it's hot." (The latter instruction was reserved for times when I was tempted with freshly baked cookies or cake.) Fussy eaters or children who left food on their plates were reminded about the "starving Armenians," whom we were to regard ourselves as so thankful not to be that we would gobble up every crumb. Just how that would ease the hunger pangs of the mysterious Armenians was not imparted to us.

True to the insistence of women to turn every holiday and "day of rest" into an opportunity to work extra hours in the kitchen turning out special feasts, Sunday noon was the time of the week when we could expect the best our table had to offer. Before we left for church, my mother would put the Swiss steak on a slow burner, and although I acquired a basic knowledge about cooking from watching how things were done at home (and incidentally getting all the tiresome chores such as cleaning the celery and de-stemming the strawberries), I have not been able to duplicate that particular delicacy. A completely toothless diner could have enjoyed the original after it had simmered deliciously on our electric range waiting for us to sit down to "Sunday dinner" following church services. It was then we profited from the arduous patience exhibited earlier in the day by my mother, as she pounded flour and seasonings into a thick piece of round steak with the edge of an old saucer (steak for which I had probably paid 25 cents on a trip to the butcher shop for her).

When my sister and I became a bit older, we were sometimes expected to "start supper," if Mother was delayed at one of her club meetings, by cutting up the leftover boiled potatoes and starting to fry them in a skillet. But I did not do much cooking or baking on my own, being satisfied to be an onlooker at such times as Saturday morning, which, in those days of strictly-scheduled housework, was unfailingly bake day.

Hearty was what meals were supposed to be, with no thought given to calories or cholesterol, and somehow many of those heedless diners managed to live into their eighties and nineties. Some people were fat, some people were thin and some were in between, much as they are today. Second helpings were refused by guests at the risk of giving insult to their hostesses, who made up for any earlier short-comings with even richer desserts. No matter what calamities might pertain in other areas of life, the pleasure of eating was allowed to be undiminished.

Of the many remembered church suppers, one variety was actually served in the sanctuary. It was called the Last Supper, a reenactment of that sexist love feast, described in the gospels. We called it communion, and there was nothing final about it, as, unlike its biblical counterpart, even the female sex was permitted to partake of it the first Sunday of every month. Like the sheep of the scriptures, the congregation filed docilely down the aisles to the railing around the altar, where we sank to our knees right there in front of everybody, and were served the stingiest little wafer and swallow of grape juice that ever earned the title of "supper." The pastor could have poisoned every one of us without encountering any protest, and without any apology on his part, as all he was required to say was, "This do in remembrance of me."

You may believe that I didn't know what this ritual was all about, but with the child's love of pageantry, I wanted to be a part of the solemn parade, and, in the realization that no one else seemed to feel like a fool, I tried not to. Besides, on communion days the sermon had to be shortened, and any procedure that had that effect won instant approval from me.

Although sermons, responsive readings, prayers, and hymns rarely produced an atmosphere of hilarity, I was often taken with the giggles during church services, especially if I caught my sister's eye. These giggles had to be stifled in response to penetrating glares from our mother, and we went back to making rubbings from our hymnals. When that became tiresome, we wrapped our handkerchiefs around our hands with the knot at the middle finger and proceeded to duplicate the minister's gestures. Not really very nice, and now that it's a bit too late, I'm hopeful that our childless pastor did not notice or take offense.

To me he was nice enough, but I had a special liking for his wife, who in turn seemed to have a liking for me. She insisted on giving me 'cello lessons, and I have a faint recollection (the mind has a way of blanking out painful memories) of playing some sort of solo in church. I must explain that when I was a child, no parents worthy of the name would fail to provide musical instruction for their offspring, without any regard for the presence or absence of inclination or ability in the makeup of the potential pupil. Girls were usually assigned to the piano, as every home already had one in the living room to hold the family portraits. My older brothers produced quite a few squeaks from their saxophones and clarinets and solicitously did some of their practicing seated on the basement stairs.

My transition from piano to violin to 'cello surely was a testimony to determination on my mother's part to turn me into a musician of sorts. Few persons demonstrated less talent and enthusiasm than I exhibited at my weekly sessions with teachers who must have seen the futility of it all but were willing to do their part to the tune of thirty cents for a half hour of nearly wasted instruction. I did acquire a minimum skill making it possible for me to play the electronic organs manufactured today, lauded as demanding only the dexterity of a baby.

I took most of my piano lessons from what was cruelly and pityingly designated in those days as an "old maid," another of the many stereotypes then indigenous to the culture of small-town America. I'm sure this self-contained woman, who lived with her parents, knew that I had not exactly developed any fingertip calluses at the keyboard between lessons, but she bowed gracefully to fate and was satisfied with minimum success in my case. My Saturday morning interludes at her home evidently interrupted the weekly baking duties, as warm spicy smells were always wafted pianowards by means of a swinging door to the kitchen. (Ours was obviously only one of many homes that observed the traditional domestic schedule, whose rigidity was none the less real for all its obscure source.)

A typical orgy of baking went on at my Grandma Messerer's on those Saturdays, and was responsible for the week's gooseberry and raspberry pies, in season (with rich crusts made of lard), and for those saucer-size sugar cookies and their molasses twins that reposed in a hinged tin in the pantry. Although my first stop upon coming in the back door at Grandma's was unfailingly the cookie box on the pantry shelf, not once in all those childhood years did I find this container less than half-full. I was just as brazen and proprietary on Grandma's garden paths, where I helped myself to rosy strawberries that were ineptly guarded by a scarecrow, pods of young peas resembling rowed-up little green pearls, and crisp carrots in every shade of orange.

Our family was one of the few that didn't boast a garden of sorts. A few thorny and neglected blackberry bushes behind the garage, three or four apple trees shading the back yard, and a sparse phalanx of asparagus spears marching around the clothesline poles provided the total of our personal homegrown produce. But most gardens were large and plentiful, and visits to aunts in the country invariably included an evaluating tour of "the garden" by the ladies, with a view of checking on the progress of the flowers and vegetables. The state of victory over the elements and bugs was duly commented upon, and oh's and ah's of admiration were duly balanced with understanding clucks of sympathy that may have been generated, at least partly, by visions of sweltering canning days to come.

Our next-door neighbors on both sides were older couples with large and flourishing gardens that put us to shame. The surname of one of these couples even seemed to rub it in; it was, ironically enough—Garden. The head of the house on the other side always planted potatoes, and because pesticides were not yet in use, he could be seen regularly as Mr. Patience himself, with brush in hand, implacably sweeping potato bugs from the plants into a receptacle. I tried not to dwell on the fate of these cute little ladybugs, who had been presented to me in nursery rhymes as being capable of experiencing concern for the fate of their children at home. I wished that they could "fly away home."

I seldom exchanged so much as a greeting with these elderly neighbors, not because any of us was particularly unfriendly, but because, in my childhood, this age group seldom interested themselves in children who were not kin, and children in turn had little interest in them. To tell the truth, I was no doubt like my contemporaries in my conviction that most "old people" existed to frustrate the younger generation and complain about their activities. I couldn't picture them as ever having been as I, and my usual goal was to avoid any contact with them, unless they happened to be related to me.

Coldly ignoring our perennial lemonade and popcorn stands, most of Sumner's elderly population, for instance, had no problem resisting the importunings of miniature sales persons, whose wares were, after all, seldom priced over a nickel. To this day I find it impossible to say no to pleading little faces with something to sell, all because of these lemonade-stand experiences and my own memories of being briskly turned away many times with my jars of salve and True Grit newspapers, etc., and finding myself (or so it seemed), rejected. How many incubating careers in all areas have had their oxygen cut off by confrontation with unfeeling grown-ups? Or is early failure simply an introduction to the "real world," serving to weed out the incompetents?

⇒◦◇◦⇐

In 1920 my parents homesteaded in North Dakota, along with my dad's brothers and a sister, an adventure instigated by my Grandfather Hurmence, who was always alert for some new enterprise that might prove lucrative. This patriarch was the incarnation of the American spirit that inspired the opening of new frontiers and "getting there firstest with the mostest." He was also an adored father, and when he died unexpectedly at the age of 59, his children were bereft.

It was his idea to build cabins on adjoining corners of four quarter-sections near New Salem, which individual members of the family would occupy for the time required to get title. My mother and three-year-old oldest brother lived in one, my father's sisters in two others, and an uncle, charged with caring for the women, in a fourth. Tales of 45-below-zero blizzards, lignite which they cut and burned for fuel, and a menacing prairie fire, became part of the family homesteading legendry, but as usual there was also humor in some of the stories, such as the one about my grandfather's comeuppance. It seems that on one of his checkup visits to the homesteaders, Mother complained about a door frame being so low that it was necessary to duck one's head upon entering or leaving the cabin. Pompously reminding one and all that such inconveniences help to build character, Grandfather chided, "humble yourself a little, just humble yourself." Waving his philosophy like a flag, he made his exit, soundly banging his head on what was to have been

Mother's humility builder. This incident did serve to humble my grandfather a bit, but my mother felt only amusement, as she had warm feelings for him. (Several years later, my father sold his quarter section for $3.00 an acre.)

My father's affinity for North Dakota as a land of opportunity led to a later venture in which he and two of his brothers obtained some acreage near Cooperstown to grow wheat, in an attempt to take advantage of the high grain prices resulting from World War I. During the summer we spent several weeks in an old frame house on this property while harvesting and threshing those crops. Today my mother strikes me as having been a resourceful person with a pioneer spirit of her own, to have agreed to my father's various financial escapades that required her to be subjected to primitive and even hazardous conditions, but at that time I felt nothing but appreciation for the opportunity to rough it on the North Dakota prairies. My cousins and two of my siblings and I dressed in coveralls and became so used to going barefoot that we could walk across a field of stubble sans shoes as we helped our mothers carry refreshments to the men in the field.

With our background, it's not surprising that we youngsters rigged up a telephone system in the sagging barn, and we had other ways of entertaining ourselves. Long vertical boards on this barn's roof made it possible for us to slide down and land on an adjoining shed, a pastime that finally aroused parental alarm at the worn state of the material covering our posteriors. Rather than abandon our celestial incline, we tied gunny sacks around our middles. Meanwhile, we had gotten into the habit of expressing our enthusiasms and disappointments in somewhat uncultured language, and this usage gradually became so pronounced, that our mothers hit upon a scheme to encourage a refinement of our speech. We were each given a bag of dried beans with the understanding that we were to forfeit one to every playmate who overheard us using an offending gosh, darn or heck! A dearth of beans in one's sack boded ill. Our two older brothers, closely allied cousins that they were, proceeded to perch on the barn roof and make the very air blue with the verboten expletives, daring us to try to collect the fines. We younger siblings ran to "tell" and indignantly demand justice, but it proved to be another victory for Satan.

We had a wagon wheel merry-go-round where we sat in the sun, wearing our straw hats and smoking our own brand of cigarets—rolled-up papers containing flour that we puffed out in powdery clouds and that, fortunately for the state of our lungs, we knew better than to inhale. By some obscure thinking on our part, hours would pass as we piled up stones to make an outdoor fireplace, and brought cans of water to a boil as if a birth was pending. When threshing days came, the big Avery tractor arrived to pull four binders to cut the grain and tie it in bundles, which then had to be shocked and threshed. Through all this, I came to realize how much effort was needed to put bread on America's tables.

This was not to be my only experience with threshing times and crews. Once or twice I helped out during the harvest season, at the family farm where one of my mother's brothers now lived. My aunt would probably have appreciated almost any kind of domestic help in satisfying the voracious appetites of a threshing crew, but I think I was very likely not the worst she could have obtained. I was a diligent worker, but my one reluctance surfaced when it was necessary to bring the dairy products up from the "fruit cellar" that substituted for mechanical cooling devices before the days of rural electrification. I had visions of rats and snakes and undefined terrors, but I must admit all such imagined loathings came to naught and were never imparted to my elders. Sometimes it takes more courage to admit to cowardice than to appear brave.

Kerosene stoves and lamps were still standard farm appliances, and indoor plumbing was still as far beyond the horizon as the privy was beyond the back door. The oil lamps had to be cared for by washing the chimneys and trimming the wicks, but when one arose at 4 a.m., one was not very eager to burn the oil at midnight or even very long past sundown. The "backhouse" swarmed with flies in the summer and was so uninvitingly cold in winter that most beds concealed a chamber pot for emergency use. And, although printed toilet paper is supposed to be a novelty, old Montgomery Ward catalogs served as the original and could be read at leisure, simply by leaving the door ajar a crack or two.

Farmers helped each other by becoming members of threshing crews which travelled from farm to farm at harvest time. Whether the threshing machine was jointly owned or rented, I can't say, but it was a hellish contraption that spouted chaff in all directions, and anyone who hasn't accumulated wheat chaff on a sweaty body in an Iowa summer simply hasn't itched.

These personal experiences only contributed to my ongoing dislike of anything that had to do with rural life, and the loneliness, the lack of running water, the cow lot with its mud and pungent manure, the chicken coop with hysterical hens dashing about at the slightest fright, the ducks who pecked each other to death, the grunting and squealing of the pigs as they were "slopped"—all this, coupled with the embarrassingly overt sexual behavior of the various farm animals—blinded me to the splendor of the "amber waves of grain" and the checkered corn fields with their palsied tassels shaking and nodding in the breeze. "Knee high by the Fourth of July" was the measurement expected of Iowa corn in those days, a goal made possible by the black Iowa loam that was no doubt only one of the "things of beauty which were a joy forever" to midwest farm folk. But, as far as I was concerned, these folk were welcome to the whole shebang, and I am still not much of a lover of nature, having discovered that under its deceptive allure there is usually a large supply of "chaff" waiting to descend upon the unsuspecting devotee, in the form of mosquitoes and chiggers, poison ivy and sumac, sunburn and allergies, ticks and flies, rashes and welts, frostbite and stomach cramps, and . . . . Suffice it to say that Mother Nature seems to have a "real mean streak."

Still, nature and I did not always strive together. I'm not sure it could be called communing, but I often hiked down the railroad tracks, or hunted for hazelnuts and jack-in-the-pulpits in the woods. Possibly protected by a natural immunity at the time, I was spared any bouts with poisons from plants and insects, and the only snakes I saw were of the innocuous garter variety, although in our china cabinet at home was a rattle from the extremity of some long-deceased reptile, which could have been an Iowa rattler. I have since heard that rattlesnake hunts are held in some areas along the Little Wapsi, but I knew of none at the time.

I like to walk, and fortunately so, as no one chauffered me anywhere. I'm not sure just when my mother learned to drive, although there was some story that she gave herself her beginner's lessons on our piece of North Dakota's unencumbered plains. I usually went about town on my own power anyway, and that is why it was such a great thrill to be presented my first bicycle on my tenth birthday. No queen's carriage ever appeared as dazzling to its owner. We were not showered with presents in those days, and some of them per se stood out. Only one gift ever disappointed me—a Bible I received one Christmas and that I waited for almost 50 years to read, or even to open, except to write my name on the flyleaf. I still have it—an elegant black leather book with the traditional grainy finish sensitive to the touch. Its pages are edged in scarlet and as thin as tissue paper, and its type is so dainty that it is ironic to discover it capable of recording the barbarous texts of the Good Book. After I finally familiarized myself with this unwelcome offering from my parents, which had pristinely outlasted my ennui and lack of curiosity, I wondered how it was possible to handle Bibles without getting blood on the hands. I vowed I would never be seen carrying one in public.

<hr />

Sumner was almost completely flat and thus well-suited to bicycles and rollerskates. There was a slight rise between our house and town, but for the most part, it was hard to find even a hilly place to go sledding in winter. And I can't remember ever doing that in Sumner. Winter, however, brought us a method of travelling over the snow that is no longer available to most children today. We called it "hopping bobsleds."

As soon as the streets and farm roads became snow-packed, farmers substituted runners for the wheels on their wagons, and on Saturdays a stream of such vehicles began to glide down First Street toward the business district. Sleigh bells on the horses' bridles rang out on the biting air as we stood on the curbs awaiting an opportunity to jump onto the runners of a wagon belonging to an agreeable driver, cling to the side, and ride bumpily but briskly for several blocks, then catch a similar ride back. This shuttle system worked for hours, even though some farmers, no doubt with our safety in mind, refused us access to their conveyances. Such refusals simply necessitated a slight delay until the next driver came along, who could be expected to be more cooperative. This seasonal custom, like many of our recreational pastimes, held the element of danger that seasoned a measure of our fun.

Hayrides on an Iowa winter night were not unheard of and attracted unsuspecting young people who had not yet experienced such consequences as frostbite and chilblains, the latter a stubborn inflammatory condition that can cause unbearable itching for weeks. Before I realized that I had "weak ankles," I went ice skating a few times on the frozen creek that wound through the open pasture area bordering Sumner on the south. (Skating on a rink has no relationship to the exotic experience of skating along a winding ribbon of ice in an open field.) The younger generation did keep a wide place on this glassy concourse clean-swept and bonfire-lit as our own personal rink, but it was all too bitterly cold for me and my weak ankles (and my apparently even weaker constitution), and I left ice skating to a heartier breed.

I was not quite as prudent when it came to another hazard presented by northern Iowa winters. I can't say I wasn't warned not to put my tongue on metal while out in zero degree temperatures, but one day while leaning over a metal railing outside the butcher shop and gazing in the window, some compulsion toward self-destruction found my tongue solidly glued to a relentless length of black iron. I was now reduced to standing there until spring or painfully parting with the skin (?) of my tongue. I found out it isn't necessary to be a physicist to appreciate some of nature's laws.

Our home had a tiled entrance that my mother must have counted among her material blessings, especially in winter. Its single steam radiator was not large enough, however, to accommodate all the soggy mittens and gloves that of necessity overflowed onto the heating surfaces in the living room, there to send up miniature clouds of steam of their own. These emissions no doubt added to the moisture that sometimes accumulated on the window panes as frosty white canvases for young artists.

Indoors we seldom felt threatened by the cold, as comforting intermittent knockings and tappings issuing from the radiators assured us that the insatiable monster in the basement was temporarily at least, well-satisfied with its feedings and was roaring in appreciation. A modicum of courage was required, I must admit, to entrust oneself to unreliable motors, and venture out onto outlying dirt roads between drifts that might be as high as your conveyance, but our family did not undertake that risk very often. We didn't make many trips outside of Sumner at any time of the year. Shopping expeditions to Waterloo, 45 miles away, were momentous undertakings, much anticipated by me as an opportunity to eat in a cafeteria and maybe even buy a coat with a fur collar. My mother had a stylish beaver hat with a matching muff when I was about four years old, and I posed with her for one of those everlasting black and white snapshots that I found when I had to go through her "things" after her death at the age of 89. In this picture I was wearing an oversized crocheted stocking cap, and I had a furry white muff of my own that hung from my neck; my mother's coat with a beaver collar fell to her ankles. My mother had a sense of style, which she bequeathed to my sister. You either have that, or you don't. It has nothing to do with being "well-dressed." That her chic, added to a certain refinement and affability, made her sought out by other women was evident to me even as a child. The senility of her last years was a degradation that her children found hard to accept. Senility means that its victims have become strangers, strangers with few of the qualities that endeared them to their families and friends, who must now play out a ghastly charade doing its best to wipe out the beautiful memories of a happier time. And to be robbed of one's dignity when one has become helpless and frail is the final dehumanization. It is very likely the fear of this humiliation, more than any dread of death, that wipes the smiles from the faces of the aged.

Growing old, of course, was not going to happen to me, just as I was never going to die but be the first person outside of the Bible to be immortal. If I could just hold off the end of the world, I was prepared to go on forever, and my current, thoroughly nice setup was going to continue ad infinitum. Winter would follow summer, and both would find me still riding my bike and hopping bobsleds. And my parents and siblings wouldn't change either.

I haven't seen a bobsled in many a day, at least not the kind we had in Sumner, nor any other sleighs such as some individuals owned—e.g., the daughter of one of the town's oldest and wealthiest families. This liberated woman could be seen on occasion at the reins of her own handsome horse-drawn equipage on Sumner's streets. She spent little time in her hometown and was probably looked on askance by its citizens, but I looked on her in awe and admiration. She wore heavy makeup, hennaed her hair, and I believe she even smoked cigarettes, but, more important, she owned a tent show that included Sumner on its circuit. That there were such worldly women was a revelation to me and that she should be a local product was even more mind-boggling, in spite of the fact that members of the female sex who owned their businesses were not unknown to Sumner. It's possible that she was not as much of a rarity as I imagined her, but she was definitely not anything like most of the women I knew.

It was the sociability of my mother and her friends, their genuine liking for each other, and their pleasure in each other's company that strike me today. They brought their handwork to meetings, where they often played pen and pencil games to much merriment and give-and-take, and they took snapshots standing in semicircles with their hands on each other's shoulders. They belonged to the Eastern Star and kept its secrets. (My own mother departed for lodge meetings with an air of mystery that I accepted as outside of my claim on her, and I still have no idea what the Eastern Star is all about.) They shared recipes and cheerfully put on Children's Day programs and Christmas pageants at the church.

The Christmas pageant called of course for yards of sheets, fabricated gossamer wings, and shepherds' crooks not readily available around Sumner, as well as more or less enthusiastic participation by the youth of the congregation. A certain amount of jealousy pertained, among the roster of those either willing or compelled by their parents to take part, as to who would play the leads, and it's quite possible that it also extended to the ranks of the mothers producing the program. I had no illusions about who would play Mary. It was inevitably some little blond beauty with an abundance of sweetness. Although my coloring was more appropriate, I fell short in both the beauty and saccharin departments and was well-satisfied to be an angel on a stepladder poised to act as undesignated prompter, insufferably impatient with all those who could not memorize or spell as well as I could with the greatest of ease. I wonder if anyone really liked me.

My favorite song in the Christmas pageants was always "We Three Kings of Orient Are," and it was certainly more glamorous for a boy to be a king than to be Joseph or a knucklehead shepherd. Especially Joseph, who was required to be as insignificant on stage as he is in the Bible. Realism did not dictate the necessity for a live baby Jesus or living and breathing sheep, and no decision had to be made about camels, all of which simplified things for the mothers in charge.

After the pageant, everyone was relieved to return to the nineteenth century. Some child recited "A Visit from St. Nicholas," and then appropriately enough, the Methodist Santa Claus "ho-ho-ho'ed" his way from a chimney prop and emerged, to begin distributing sacks of candy, nuts and fruit (usually an orange). But not to just anyone. Santa had a hearty voice, and he used it to call the name of each Methodist child. One by one, bashful or not, Dick and Jane trooped up to the huge Christmas tree and accepted their bounty. (Of course, there were extra sacks, so that no visitor was left out—our Methodists were kindhearted, lovely people.) I always thought Santa looked a lot like God.

The tree lights (thanks to Edison the atheist) sparkled in a choir loft, and a few doting parents would arrange for a doll or teddy bear to be placed on the tree for Santa, in a state of feigned surprise, to find and deliver in person while the congregation looked on. I didn't mind that the tree contained no present for me. I knew that our presents from Santa would be under our own tree Christmas morning. Toys were not given throughout the year, and it was important to find your heart's desires on that day. I finally caught on to Santa; I noticed that his handwriting was exactly like my mother's.

Many children were terrified of Santa Claus, and fortunately for timid youngsters every street corner did not hold one. I can understand their timidity. I was just as frightened of circus clowns and magicians. I noticed that they sometimes made fools of the public, and I had a horror of being one of their victims. I remember the shock I felt at one of the Chautauqua programs when a speaker, about whom I (in my seat at the front where the children always sat) had been whispering disparaging remarks, announced that he could read lips. I don't know his purpose in saying that, and it's doubtful that he had paid any attention to a little girl confiding in a friend, but he ruined my evening.

—————⟫•◈•⟪—————

Children's Day was less solemn and less biblical than the Christmas spectacle. Any kind of talent was welcome. A child or youth who could recite, sing, or play a musical instrument with any degree of expertise could be imposed upon captive audiences, whose appreciation was conditioned by the closeness of the individual's relationship to the members of the cast, as well as by the touted appeal of precocity.

One performance by a young neighbor of ours made a lasting impression on all who witnessed it. Roddy had a child's problem pronouncing his l's and r's, and by some unkind coincidence was chosen to sing "Wind of the Western Sea." The lyrics of this lullaby unfortunately contained a surfeit of the offending consonants, but Roddy braved it out and achieved an especially unique rendition that emerged, hilariously, as: "Bwow, Bwow, bweathe and bwow, wind of the western sea, Whiwhe my wittewun, whiwhe my pwittiwun sweeps." I hope Woddy outgrew his minor speech impairment and harbored no resentment towards the several in the audience who struggled to stifle their titters, and failed.

The agonies of young thespians are many and deep. I recall one searing experience of my own, as a young participant in a children's stage show of some kind sponsored by the Chautauqua on its annual visit to Sumner. Somehow my mother was late bringing my costume to the van, where we were dressing to leave for the tent that served as the Chautauqua auditorium for the week it quartered in Sumner. After my sobs brought solicitation and reassurances from the personnel in charge, my mother arrived to find me in a state of collapse. Somehow I managed to recover in time to make it possible for the show to go on. Part of my suffering came from my compulsion always to be on time and always to fulfill any commitment I had made. Being tardy for school was unthinkable, surpassed only by being absent. I was a strict taskmaster where my personal integrity was concerned, even as a child. I wasn't totally obnoxious.

I was sure that my oldest brother didn't find me obnoxious at all, and I found no fault in him—it was a hopeless case of hero worship. And why not? In the days of Valentino and movies laid in Araby, he was not called the Sheik for nothing. With lightly pomaded black hair and the whitest of teeth (and tall and thin in his striped blazer), he brought an air of excitement home with him on his weekends and vacations away from Upper Iowa University. I basked in his vitality. I hovered. I longed to serve. I begged to press his pants. The 25¢ he gave me to do it was never a factor.

This brother was a "flaming youth," and yes, he was collegiate. It was not unusual for him to be called on the carpet by my father soon after his arrival, but he quickly rebounded from all perfunctory reprimands and became my big brother home from college. His girlfriends were the "flappers" with their short-skirted, long-waisted dresses, their bobbed hair and spit curls—all simply and completely adorable. Some still had soft long hair done up in buns; some had marcels; some had the new permanent waves, and they all did the new dance, the Charleston.

My semi-religious parents made some show of disapproving of dancing and other such unrighteous indulgence, and this oldest brother always claimed that he had to break the ice for the rest of us. He played his saxophone in a little band, and I could hardly wait to memorize the words of all the sheet music he brought home. I kept trying to "do the Charleston," but one leg rebelled, and some long-forgotten observer, out to get a laugh, remarked that this was my "Methodist leg." Barbed remarks do not go over the heads of children. They leave their residue of pain. My sister and I used to reminisce. She would say, "Do you remember when . . . ?" And often we recalled different shared events in our lives. But I have always had recurring memories of personal hurts. One petty instance of insensitivity not really worth a minute's notice still takes me back to an afternoon when I was walk-ing home from school. I was blowing up a balloon, and as I passed a woman standing on a porch, the balloon suddenly exploded in my face. For whatev-er reason, this woman sneered at me—"Now let's see you blow it up." (Why do I still cringe at the sting I felt?)

Adults also sometimes made critical statements to each other about peo-ple dear to me, on the assumption that I would not comprehend, but such statements often leave wounds that stay ragged. It was incomprehensible to me that others might criticize my family and relatives, even dislike them. Then again I became aware that all of my relatives were not necessarily in complete approval of one another. Slowly my idealism was becoming un-structured. I began to sense undercurrents beneath what had been to me smooth surfaces. Maybe, just maybe, everything was not as definable as I had imagined it to be.

I believe most of the little "scenes" between my father and mother were about money, but of course they could have concerned grades. I have noted that we were brought up in an atmosphere of little praise for expected excel-lence in behavior and scholastic achievement and even less patience with a poor showing in either. Such pressure was no problem for any of us children, as far as I know, and I set even higher standards for myself. If I wasn't at least among the highest in the class at all times, if not the absolute highest, I was convinced that this situation was owing to some fault of the teacher.

I knew better, however, than to impart this opinion to my parents; no teacher of ours was *ever* at fault, and no complaints about them were even tolerated. I was compelled to accept this state of affairs, but I didn't feel it was a fair one, and I still don't. It isn't possible that teachers are never remiss in unhappy teacher-child relationships. Teachers are human, and they are sometimes wrong. Personalities clash, and no one of any age should be made to feel that justice is out of reach, just as no one should be given a blank check to treat another human being unfairly, no matter the age or vulnerability of the victim.

It could be that I drove myself to reach a level of academic performance which my parents came to expect and take for granted, but it also got to the point where I would have given anything for an accolade. And I actually did carry on a "silent" (even occasional open) feud with one or two of my teach-ers, usually those for whom, with the brutal accuracy of the young, we stu-dents (or those going before us) had concocted apt or unkind nicknames. These antagonisms were not permitted by me to reach a point where they interfered with my grades.

The truth is I may have exaggerated in my own mind the degree of severity of any parental reaction that would have followed a personal letdown of scholarly accomplishment. I have no memory of being punished very often for anything as a child. I usually conformed to the house rules, and this cooperation meant that few "scenes" were called for. Their very rarity was probably one reason I shrank from those that involved my brother, although I seem to have resented them more than he.

I remember receiving only that one spanking from my mother and that, unfairly enough, the result of a reaction to the fall I suffered when I misjudged my timing while playing on the bag swing in my cousins' yard. The punishment struck me as a harsh instance of double jeopardy.

⇒◦⇐

As children, we were assigned several chores around the house for which we received compensation; so much for each dandelion removed from its habitat, so much for pulling sprouts from the potatoes kept in the bin in the basement. During the interludes when we were without domestic help, we were expected to help with the dishes, and even earlier, set the table in the dining room, where the Home sewing machine occupied a corner next to a jardiniere holding the fern that was an inevitable accessory of most Sumner homes.

Setting the table involved a strenuous preliminary procedure for little people with short arms. First the small helper had to strain to reach the 20-inch-tall, half-a-ton, cut-glass vase (no doubt a prized wedding gift from the past), lift it off the linen doily edged with handmade lace, grasp the doily in the middle and drop it into the vase, and finally transfer the vase to the sideboard. This procedure gradually evolved into a ritual.

All furniture (sold by the local store under the proprietorship of the undertaker) was of golden oak, and the woodwork was golden oak, too, all varnished to an enduring gleam that assaulted the eyeballs without pity. Golden oak was ugly and contributed to the nadir which interior design (and architecture) admittedly reached in the 20's. Rooms blighted by it were made even more inhospitable by muddy oil paintings sometimes barely relieved by ornate plaster of paris gilt frames.

The upright piano in the living room, that sometimes left room for little else, was likely to be the only item not afflicted with "golden oak disease" but was probably constructed of a dismal mahogany, as were the cabinet Victrolas boasted by some families (my aunt once hid a birthday cake in hers). We had a Graphophone, ourselves, and whether our parents' musical taste was their own or was determined by what was available is a moot question. In any case, Edison's industry and ingenuity made it possible for us to enjoy "The Pirates of Penzance" and the "William Tell Overture," and it was

422   *The Book Of Ruth*

necessary to have an honest desire to hear them, because these machines had to be wound up by hand, and then wound up again, and very likely again and again.

Some friends of mine owned a player piano that required even more effort to operate. My legs were almost too short to pump the pedals, and it was imperative for me to grasp this instrument under the keyboard in order to brace myself. But it was worth it to watch the nimble keys move up and down as the perforated paper unwound. The world needed to become even more aware that electricity could play a greater role than merely lighting up a room.

Our living room also contained what was called a Morris Chair, a leather monstrosity supposedly tailored to the male physique. Other upholstered chairs and divans came inexorably in sets and were made of singularly unattractive mohair or some such scratchy material. Antimacassars erupted on the arms and backs of these pieces, as if they could ever show wear. An assortment of crocheted and tatted doilies testifying to the dedication of the homemaker, sectional bookcases, a library table, white glass curtains, and just possibly a fringed piano scarf, did little to enhance the decor. And there it was— your 1920's Home Sweet Home.

Every dresser and table cried out for a cover, and the plea was answered with a vengeance. On the rare occasions when I had an urge to do something "ladylike," I bent my head over the latest "dresser scarf" my mother had purchased for me (at my unexplainable request) at Woolworth's in Waterloo or some other "dime store." The transfer design on these scarves or hand towels invariably involved six-petal daisies, and the colorful embroidery floss was one of the few cheerful ingredients of early 20th-century handiwork. It was a painstaking task to separate the six strands into two's or three's. After I managed to thread the needle and adjust the hoop, I was ready to show off my skill at anchoring the petals and manufacturing french knots (one of my specialties). If I ever finished one of these hem-stitched testimonies to my struggling-to-surface domesticity, I have no recollection of it, and, after all, some of them had *three* pieces! I'm sure my mother couldn't have been happier about my indifference. I heard little pertaining to "starting things you don't intend to finish."

Once a month or so, we went to the local barber shop for our Buster Brown haircuts. Often I had to wait in the row of chairs that were flanked by spittoons, while the barbers leisurely shaved members of Sumner's male population or visitors staying at Sumner's one hotel. At the close of this ritual of steamy towels, razors duly stropped on a wide leather strap, and shaving suds generously lathered on and carefully scraped off, one of the many bottles of perfumed shaving lotion (never called cologne) was chosen and a dash or two gently slapped on the customer's cheek.

Finally, it was my turn. Such snipping and clipping, such care expended! I felt that my haircut was terribly important to this gentle man with little to say, that it had to be just so. Then the apron was removed and given a shake, my neck was brushed with a flourish or two, and I was handed a mirror to judge the results. I always approved, handed the barber the 25 cents that had been tightly clutched in my sweaty palm, and left the shop to the men who could afford to be shaved professionally. For some reason, I seldom encountered another little girl Saturday mornings at the barber shop.

I remember two deaths in the homes on our block. When you died, in those days before funeral parlors and when the undertaker owned the furniture store, they hung a spray of flowers on the front door and "laid you out" in the living room. Neighbors and friends filed in to stare at your chalky face and commiserate with your loved ones. All around you, in the other rooms, your family went on living, either avoiding you or drawn to your side by a horrible fascination.

My mother's skill as a seamstress was well-known to her friends, and once or twice she made shrouds for the dear departed. I assume she was able to do this without the fittings to which I had to submit when she was sewing for me.

Many illnesses were fatal before antibiotics were discovered. A classmate of my sister's lay at the point of death several days before she died from peritonitis. The Lutheran church bells tolled her tender age. It all seemed unreal, and the day after the funeral, which I avoided, I rode by her home on my bicycle. Her mother and sister were shelling peas in the backyard. I hoped they hadn't seen my spying on them. I felt awful for being alive.

But the happy times outnumbered the sad times. Special days were anticipated and sometimes took much preparation. One of these was May Day, a date that has since taken on an ominous aspect in another part of the world, but that involved only feelings of goodwill and friendship when we celebrated it. No longer was there much interest in dancing around the maypole to herald the arrival of spring, but for weeks ahead of time, we gathered at the homes of friends to make May baskets from match boxes and cardboard cones obtained from merchants. We decorated these containers with construction paper and tissue paper fringe. At the last minute we walked along the railroad tracks to pick cowslips and add them to the candy and popcorn we had already put into the "baskets." (The cowslip is a dainty yellow flower that grows in moist places where cows could lose their footing. It deserved a better name.)

Very likely, only girls made these baskets, but as soon as the sun went down on the 1st of May, we began to deliver them to friends and favorite teachers. Ringing the bell and calling out, "May basket for Betty" (or whomever the recipient might be), we ran to hide behind a bush or a tree and wait to be chased and caught.

Do children still play hopscotch? It was a favorite recess or before-school pastime for grade-school girls at that time. We sat on the fire escape with relentless eyes fixed to catch any misstep or stone touching a line. No slightest infraction won our mercy. Today I seldom see a hopscotch court drawn on a sidewalk or driveway.

Some customs perished for a good reason, and the charivari was one of the discarded ones that will not be missed. It permitted a crowd of misguided well-wishers to descend on a bride and groom on the wedding night, beating on tin pans, making remarks not in the best of taste, raucously calling for the groom to appear and offer some kind of refreshment. Good riddance, "shivaree!"

<hr/>

Fun times could also be quiet times. In spite of ongoing efforts to establish one, Sumner had no public library in the 20's, but people had reading material of their own, and books were popular gifts. I read and re-read Grimms' and Andersen's *Fairy Tales*, the Bobbsey Twins (Nan and Bert, Flossie and Freddie), *Anne of Green Gables*, the *Five Little Peppers*, *Little Women*, and *The Girl of the Limberlost*. Other books were little more than religious tracts containing stories of good girls who temporarily lost their way. Jo's adventures as a "little woman" elicited tears, but it does little for my reputation as a discriminating reader to admit that for a time my favorite book concerned the tribulations of Elsie Dinsmore, a child whose stern father demanded instant obedience on her part, even of his sometimes apparently senseless commands. This brute inflicted harsh punishment for any hesitancy exhibited by Elsie, but all of his tyranny was justified when unquestioning cooperation on one occasion saved her from a rattlesnake. (It was not wise of Elsie to reason why.) At other times, Elnora's ill-fated moth collection and bad treatment at the hands of her mother drew me to the Limberlost.

The Elsie book belonged to my grandmother on my mother's side, and often I would walk to her house for the express purpose of reading it. First I ran to the place where the pie plant grew (later I learned this was "rhubarb" to some people). I broke off the tenderest, greenest stalks, and peeled them. Grabbing a shaker of coarse salt, I removed Elsie from the bookcase in the hall and flew upstairs to jump onto one of the featherbeds, where I disappeared from sight in a cocoon of my own. It was all "paradise enou," even with no companion to share my sadistic book, and with a salt shaker a fine substitute for the wine which solaced the poet.

Salt shakers were indispensable, for green apples, raw potatoes, lemon halves, and pie plant, but that was before salt was bad for you. We needed it for popcorn, too. Only popcorn *addicts* were willing to go through the ordeal of preparing it, although others would "have some, if you are going to make it." It spite of the difficulties, I was a popcorn addict, and on Sunday afternoons I set out to satisfy my craving.

"Baby rice" was the name of the product. It didn't come in a box or a plastic bag, but on short, fat cobs, to which it was attached in a way that only nature can attach something. It was necessary to rub these cobs together with enough intensity of purpose to dislodge the kernels. Then one must blow away the chaff, and finally shake the kernels over the burner in an iron skillet that might as well have been made of lead—all of this with little confidence that any great amount would pop.

Just about the time I had laboriously managed to create a sufficient supply for myself and all those who were all too eager to sponge off my efforts, Sunday guests might drop in, and the process had to begin all over again. Often someone decided to make fudge, in spite of past trials when much softball testing had seldom assured anything but runny or sugary disasters that could be eaten only with a spoon.

The cost of groceries was even then viewed with such despair that Mr. Gallagher and Mr. Sheen had it on their mind that "it was cheaper now to die" than to live with prices like five cents for soda pop and 30 cents for the blue plate at the only restaurant in town.

Restaurant charges hardly concerned us. We ate at home, the place where we did most of our living. All that living meant that a thorough housecleaning had to be undertaken twice a year. Although we were one of the earliest houses to have a central vacuum cleaner system powered by electricity, somehow it was necessary to drape all rugs over the clothesline semi-annually and pound them with a rug beater, while the areas of bare floor were duly washed, recoated with Johnson's paste wax, and polished on the hands and knees with a wool rag. Every Iowa housewife worthy of the title performed these "housecleaning" chores, as well as many others as exhausting. Maybe coal burning furnaces made it all imperative, but the phrase "spring housecleaning" created an understandable dread in the minds and hearts of the women of my mother's generation.

One of the largest and most impressive homes in Sumner boasted a ballroom on the third floor, but ballroom dancing did not come under the heading of sin-free behavior for the Sumner citizens I knew. The Campfire Girls met there a few times. We wore gray sateen shift-like dresses and headbands and earned merit badges in the shape of "feathers" cut of varied-colored material and sewed along the hems of our "uniforms."

With all the organizations available to the young and old of Sumner, no one felt a need for more entertainment, and few sensed that it would be provided by the new medium of radio. Our first set was of a make that assured us at least clean entertainment—it was antiseptically called a Radiodyne. Some people owned Atwater Kents. To put on the earphones and listen to a static-cursed KDKA in Pittsburgh was an activity that joined several others for whose performance there seemed to be no explanation. Too many wonders were occurring at once. The age of Edison and Ford was bearing fruit. I was not much interested in radio sets or radio waves either one, but my father was excited about both, and it wasn't long before we owned a Stromberg-Carlson cabinet model.

All of us Hurmence children were quite naturally more interested in telephones than in any new means of transmitting the human voice over the air. My brother Howard was particularly taken with stringing makeshift telephone lines from house to house in town or from stall to stall in a North Dakota barn. One such arrangement created by him and a cousin between our two houses had to be removed because it hung too low over one of Sumner's streets, but not until we had "broadcast" over it for several weeks. This was the same brother who attended one of the evangelist services at the United Brethren church only to find himself saved, a condition which gradually subsided into agnosticism.

In 1928 the Hurmence Telephone Company was absorbed into the Iowa State Telephone Company. My father became manager of the exchange at Newton, Iowa, and we moved there while I was in the eighth grade. It was time to say goodbye to my childhood and to cut the ties to Sumner more or less drastically at the same time.

I'm sure that if any of my siblings had written of their lives in Sumner, they would have recorded somewhat different memories, but I believe those memories would also have been happy ones, as mine were. As a small midwestern town, Sumner probably was not unique. But it has remained for me the childhood haven, the suspended interval when for many years everything was close to being right with the world.

To Sumner

Our roots are ever with us.
Nostalgia? No, more.
Our childhood coursing through the blood
Forever is our core
Of being. No, our very self,
And as we go our ways
To meet the winding down of years,
Come back! the Golden Days.

Index

Other books published by the Freedom From Religion Foundation

Women Without Superstition: "No Gods – No Masters"
THE COLLECTED WRITINGS OF WOMEN FREETHINKERS
OF THE NINETEENTH & TWENTIETH CENTURIES
edited by Annie Laurie Gaylor

Woe To The Women: The Bible Tells Me So
by Annie Laurie Gaylor

Losing Faith In Faith: From Preacher To Atheist
by Dan Barker

American Infidel: Robert G. Ingersoll
by Orvin Larson

One Woman's Fight
by Vashti McCollum

The World Famous Atheist Cookbook
compiled by Anne Nicol Gaylor

Just Pretend: A Freethought Book For Children
by Dan Barker

FFRF, Inc.
PO Box 750
Madison WI 53701
(608) 256-8900

www.ffrf.org